ZATCH BELL!

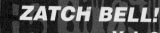

ZATCH BELL!
Vol. 6

STORY AND ART BY
MAKOTO RAIKU

English Adaptation/Fred Burke
Translation/David Ury
Touch-up Art & Lettering/Melanie Lewis
Design/Izumi Hirayama
Special Thanks/Jessica Villat, Miki Macaluso, Mitsuko Kitajima, and Akane Matsuo
Editor/Kit Fox

Editor in Chief, Books/Alvin Lu
Editor in Chief, Magazines/Marc Weidenbaum
VP of Publishing Licensing/Rika Inouye
VP of Sales/Gonzalo Ferreyra
Sr. VP of Marketing/Liza Coppola
Publisher/Hyoe Narita

Printed in the U.S.A.

Published by VIZ Media, LLC
P.O. Box 77010
San Francisco, CA 94107

10 9 8 7 6 5 4 3 2
First printing, April 2006
Second printing, November 2007

RATED T FOR TEEN

PARENTAL ADVISORY
ZATCH BELL! is rated T for Teen and is recommended for ages 13 and up. This volume contains realistic and fantasy violence.

ratings.viz.com

www.viz.com
store.viz.com

ZATCH BELL!

STORY AND ART BY

MAKOTO RAIKU

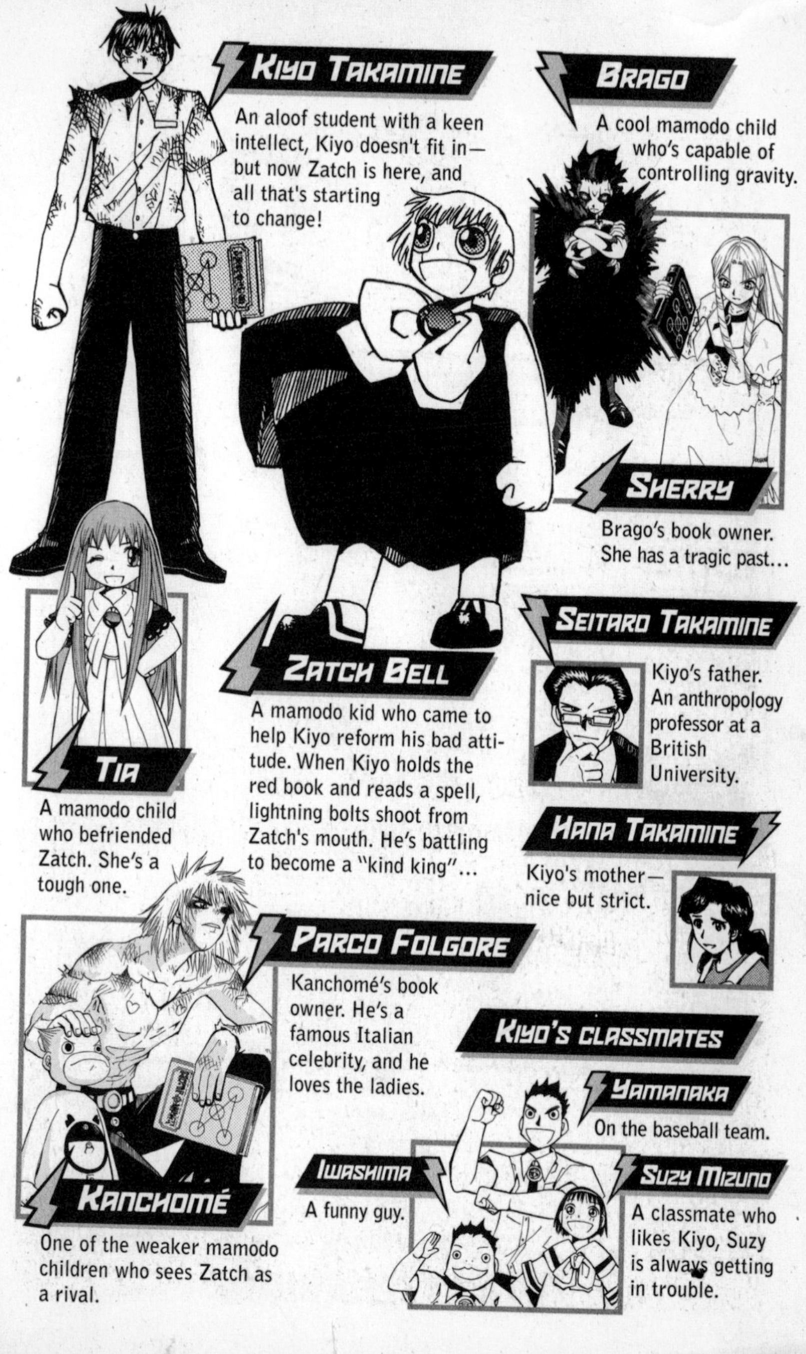
KIYO TAKAMINE
An aloof student with a keen intellect, Kiyo doesn't fit in—but now Zatch is here, and all that's starting to change!
BRAGO
A cool mamodo child who's capable of controlling gravity.
ZATCH BELL
A mamodo kid who came to help Kiyo reform his bad attitude. When Kiyo holds the red book and reads a spell, lightning bolts shoot from Zatch's mouth. He's battling to become a "kind king"...
SHERRY
Brago's book owner. She has a tragic past...
TIA
A mamodo child who befriended Zatch. She's a tough one.
SEITARO TAKAMINE
Kiyo's father. An anthropology professor at a British University.
HANA TAKAMINE
Kiyo's mother—nice but strict.
PARCO FOLGORE
Kanchomé's book owner. He's a famous Italian celebrity, and he loves the ladies.
KANCHOMÉ
One of the weaker mamodo children who sees Zatch as a rival.
KIYO'S CLASSMATES
YAMANAKA
On the baseball team.
IWASHIMA
A funny guy.
SUZY MIZUNO
A classmate who likes Kiyo, Suzy is always getting in trouble.

ZATCH'S PAST OPPONENTS

KOLULU

SUGINO

GOFURE

BRAGO

REYCOM

MARUSS

ROBNOS

KANCHOMÉ

ESHROS

FEIN

BALTRO

THE STORY THUS FAR

Kiyo is a junior high student who's so intelligent that he's bored by life and doesn't even go to school. But Kiyo's life changes when his father sends him an amazing child named Zatch as a birthday present. When Kiyo holds Zatch's red book (which only Kiyo can read) and utters a spell, Zatch displays awesome powers.

Soon the duo finds out that Zatch is one of 100 mamodo children chosen to fight in a battle that will determine who is king of the mamodo world for the next 1,000 years. The bond between Zatch and Kiyo deepens as they're forced to fight for survival.

Meanwhile, Zatch and Kiyo visit England where Zatch's look-alike has been spotted. As soon as they arrive, they find out that Kiyo's father has been kidnapped, but after a valiant battle, they manage to save his life. Later, Kiyo and Zatch visit the forest where Zatch used to live, and Zatch regains part of his lost memory...

ZATCHBELL! 6

CONTENTS

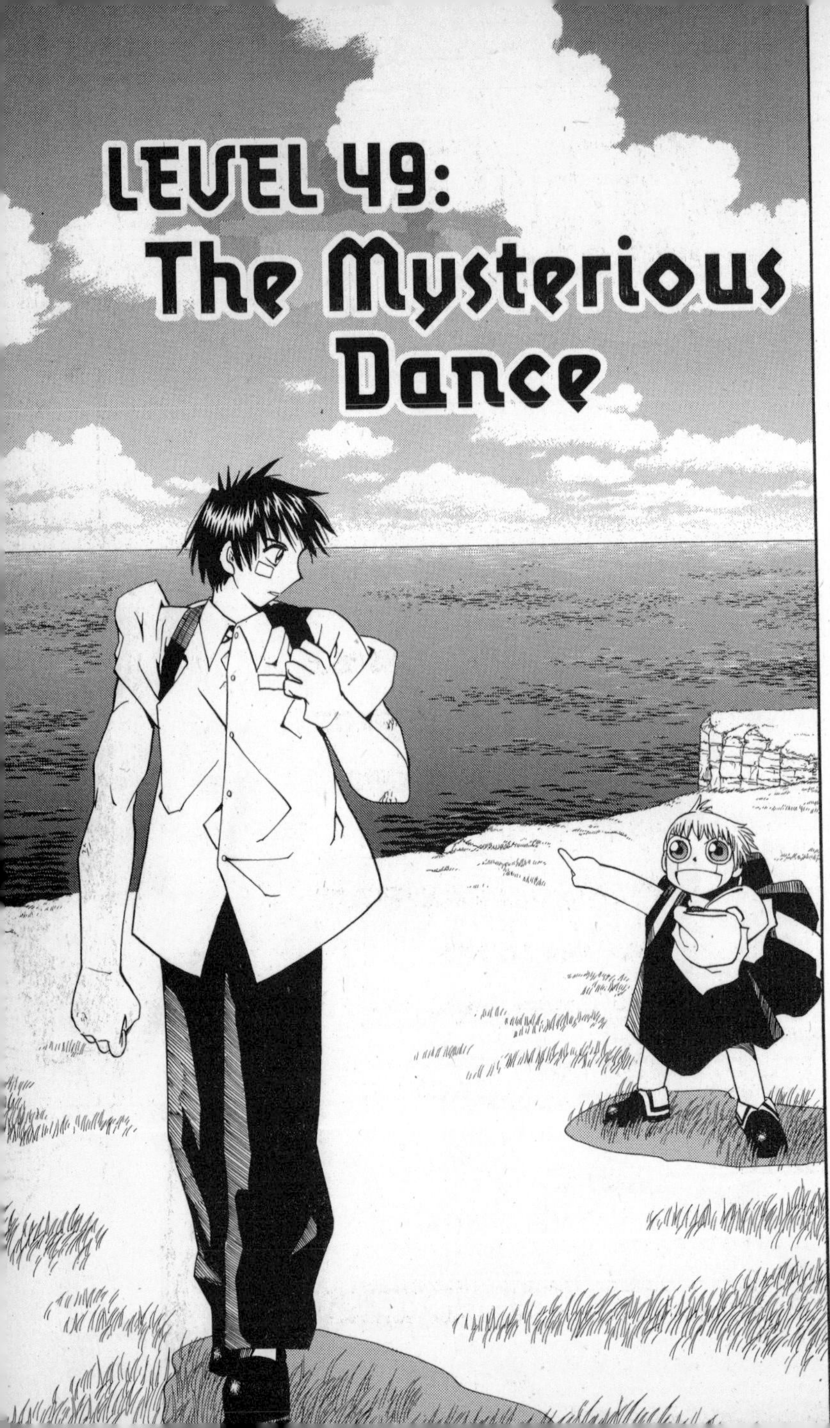
LEVEL 49:
The Mysterious
Dance

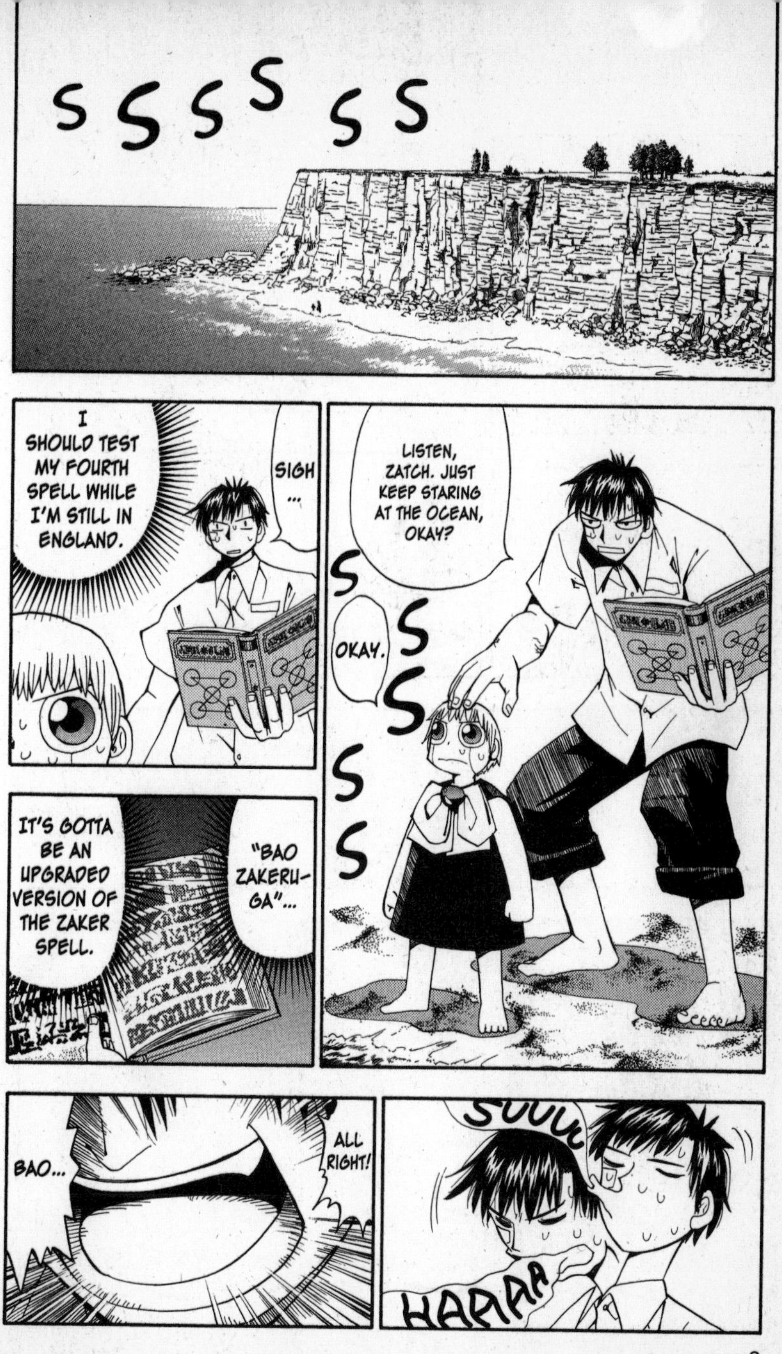
S S S S S S
LISTEN, ZATCH. JUST KEEP STARING AT THE OCEAN, OKAY?
OKAY.
S S S S S
SIGH...
I SHOULD TEST MY FOURTH SPELL WHILE I'M STILL IN ENGLAND.
"BAO ZAKERUGA"...
IT'S GOTTA BE AN UPGRADED VERSION OF THE ZAKER SPELL.
SUUU
HAAAA
ALL RIGHT!
BAO...

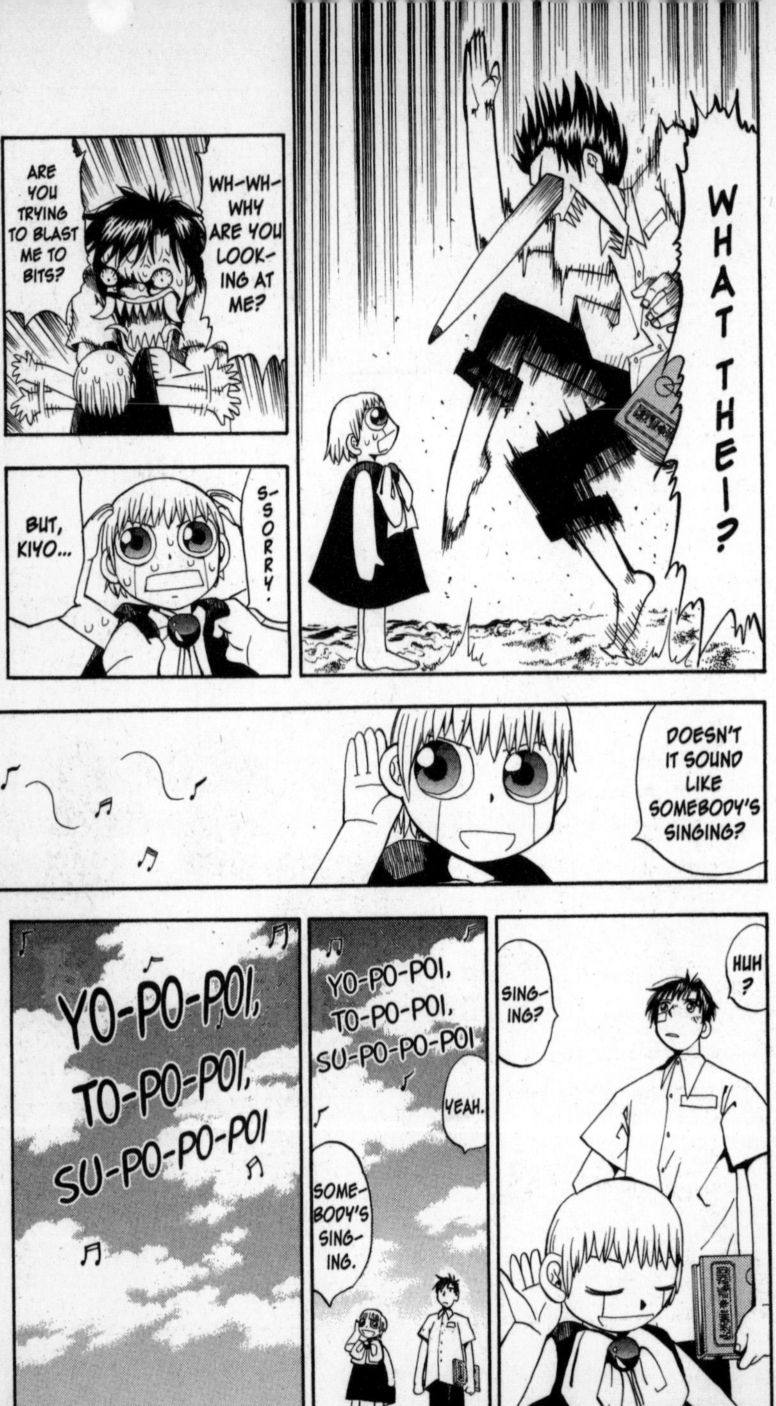
WHAT THE!?
WH-WH-WHY ARE YOU LOOKING AT ME?
ARE YOU TRYING TO BLAST ME TO BITS?
S-SORRY.
BUT, KIYO...
DOESN'T IT SOUND LIKE SOMEBODY'S SINGING?
HUH?
SING-ING?
YO-PO-POI, TO-PO-POI, SU-PO-PO-POI
YEAH.
SOME-BODY'S SING-ING.
YO-PO-POI, TO-PO-POI, SU-PO-PO-POI

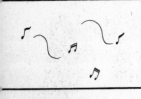

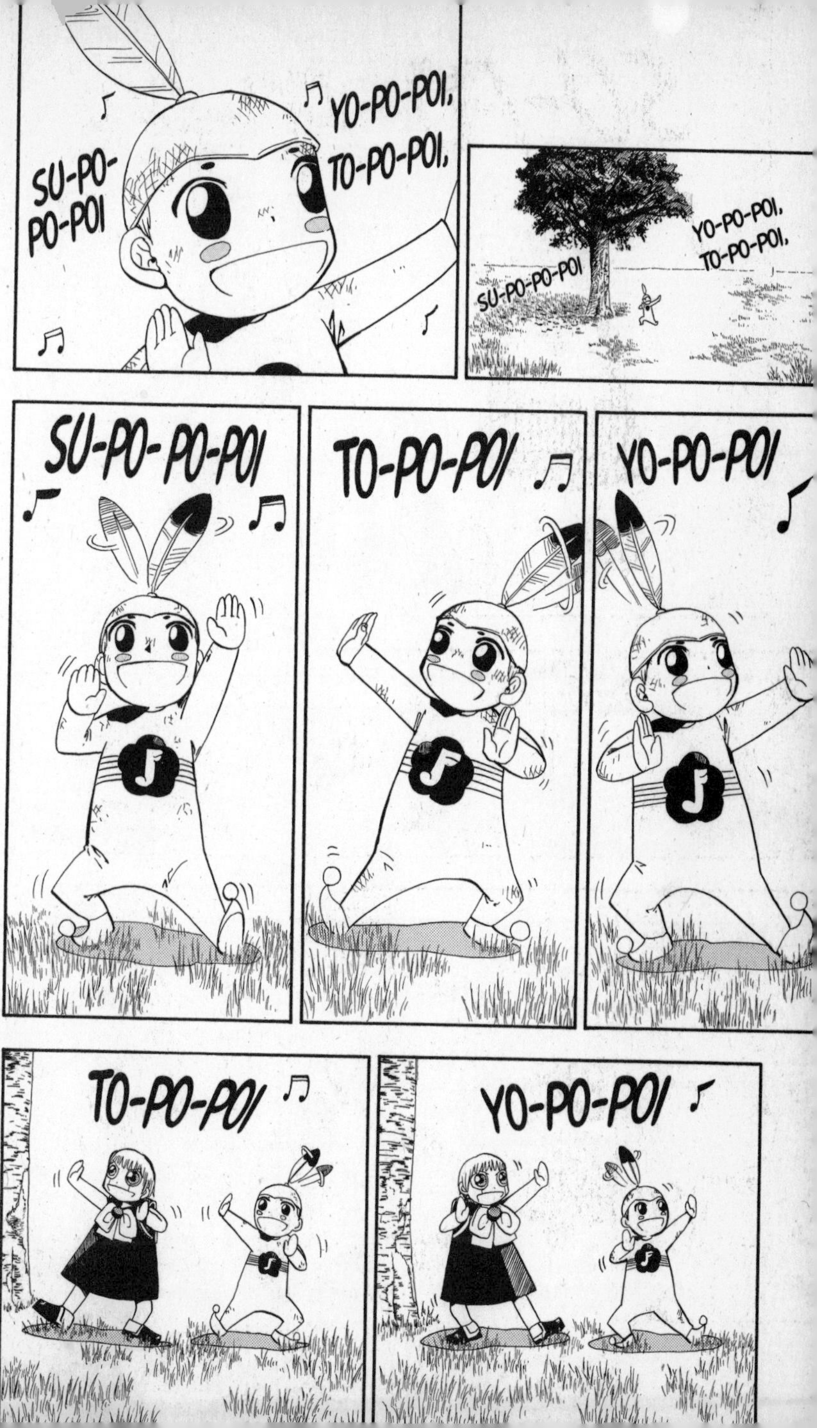
YO-PO-POI, TO-PO-POI,
SU-PO-PO-POI
YO-PO-POI, TO-PO-POI,
SU-PO-PO-POI
YO-PO-POI
TO-PO-POI
SU-PO-PO-POI
YO-PO-POI
TO-PO-POI

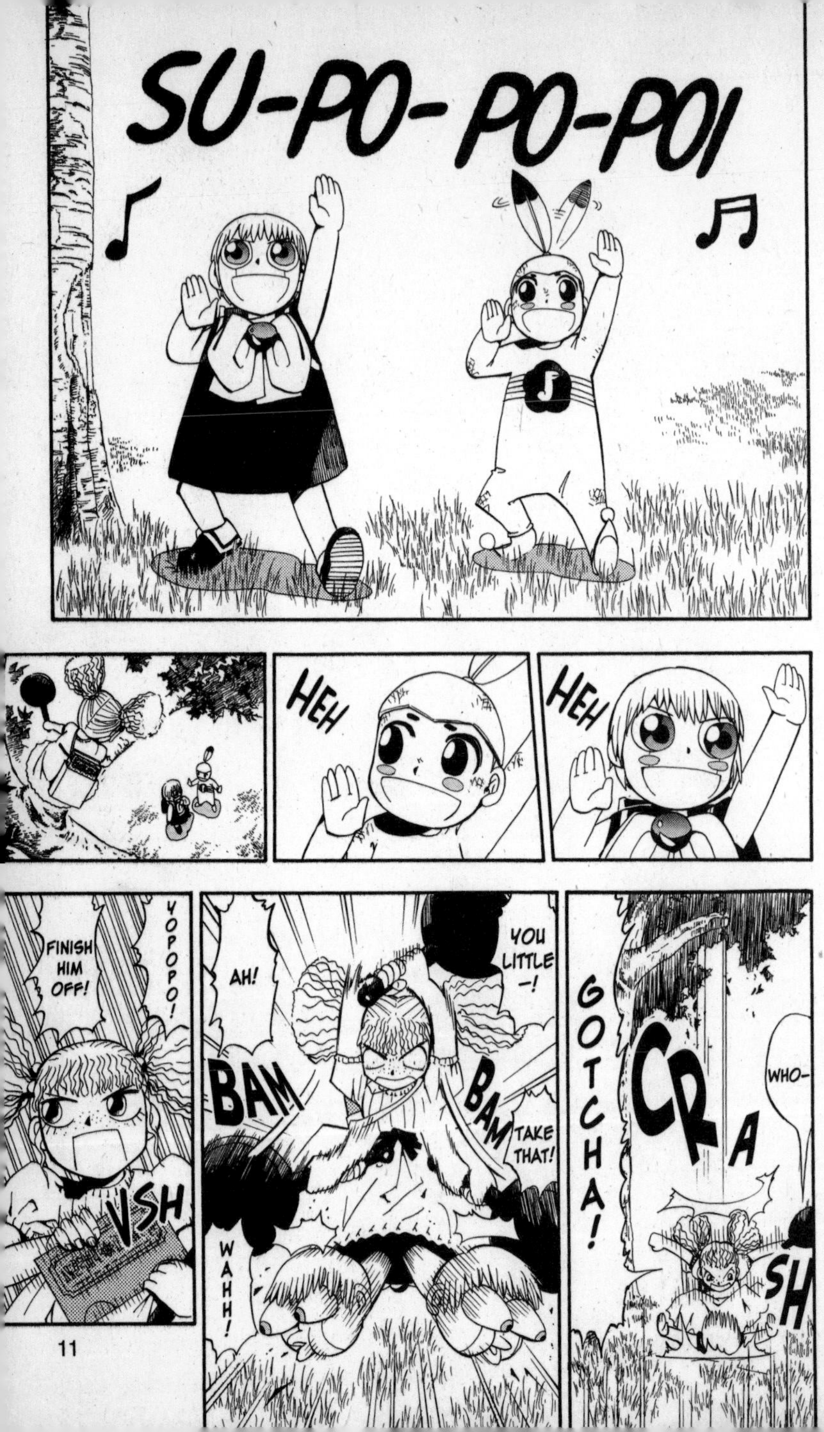
SU-PO-PO-POI
HEH
HEH
WHO-
CRA
GOTCHA!
SH
YOU LITTLE—!
AH!
BAM
BAM
TAKE THAT!
WAHH!
YOPOPO!
FINISH HIM OFF!
VSH

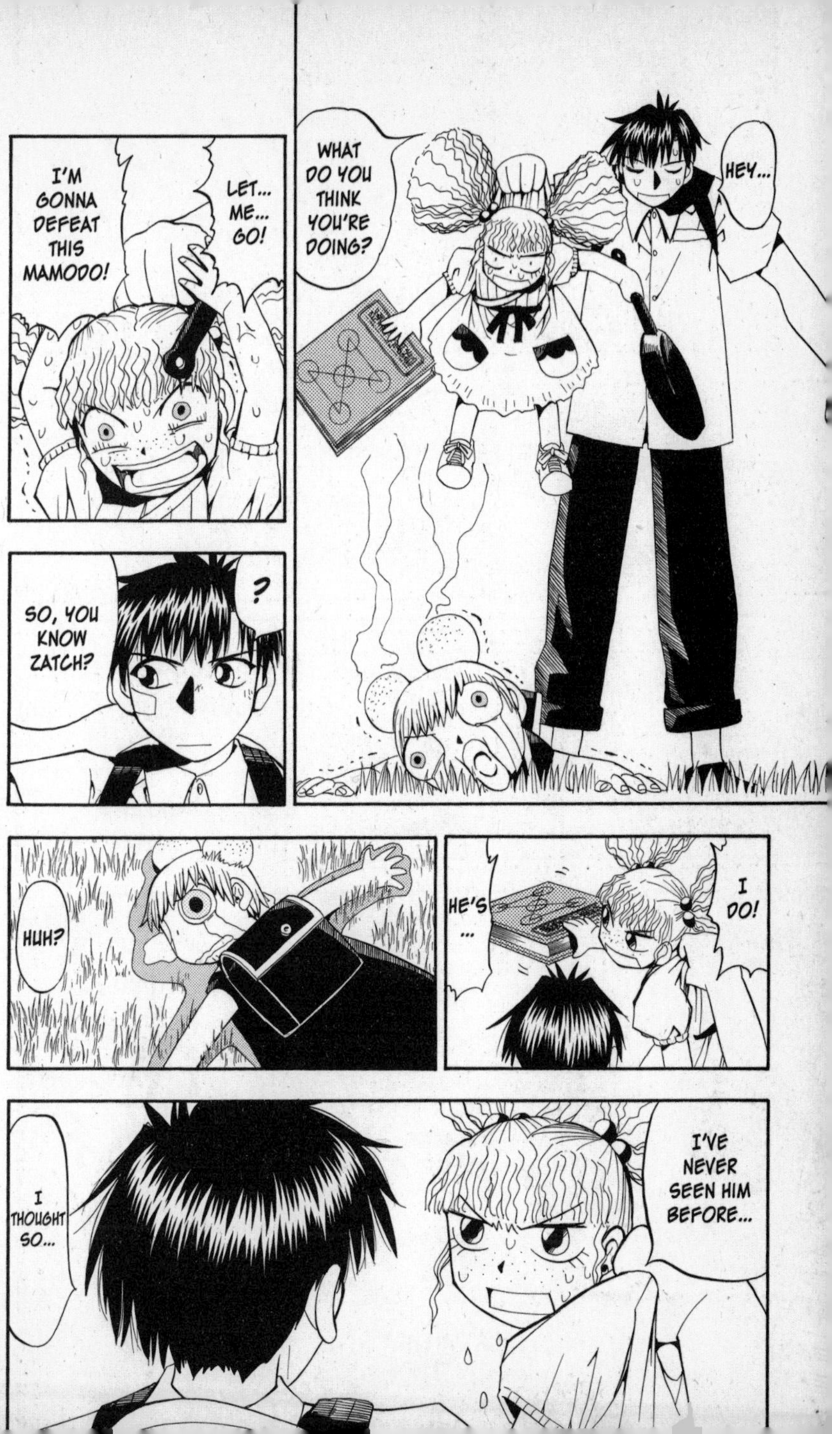
HEY...
WHAT DO YOU THINK YOU'RE DOING?
LET... ME... GO!
I'M GONNA DEFEAT THIS MAMODO!
?
SO, YOU KNOW ZATCH?
I DO!
HE'S ...
HUH?
I'VE NEVER SEEN HIM BEFORE...
I THOUGHT SO...

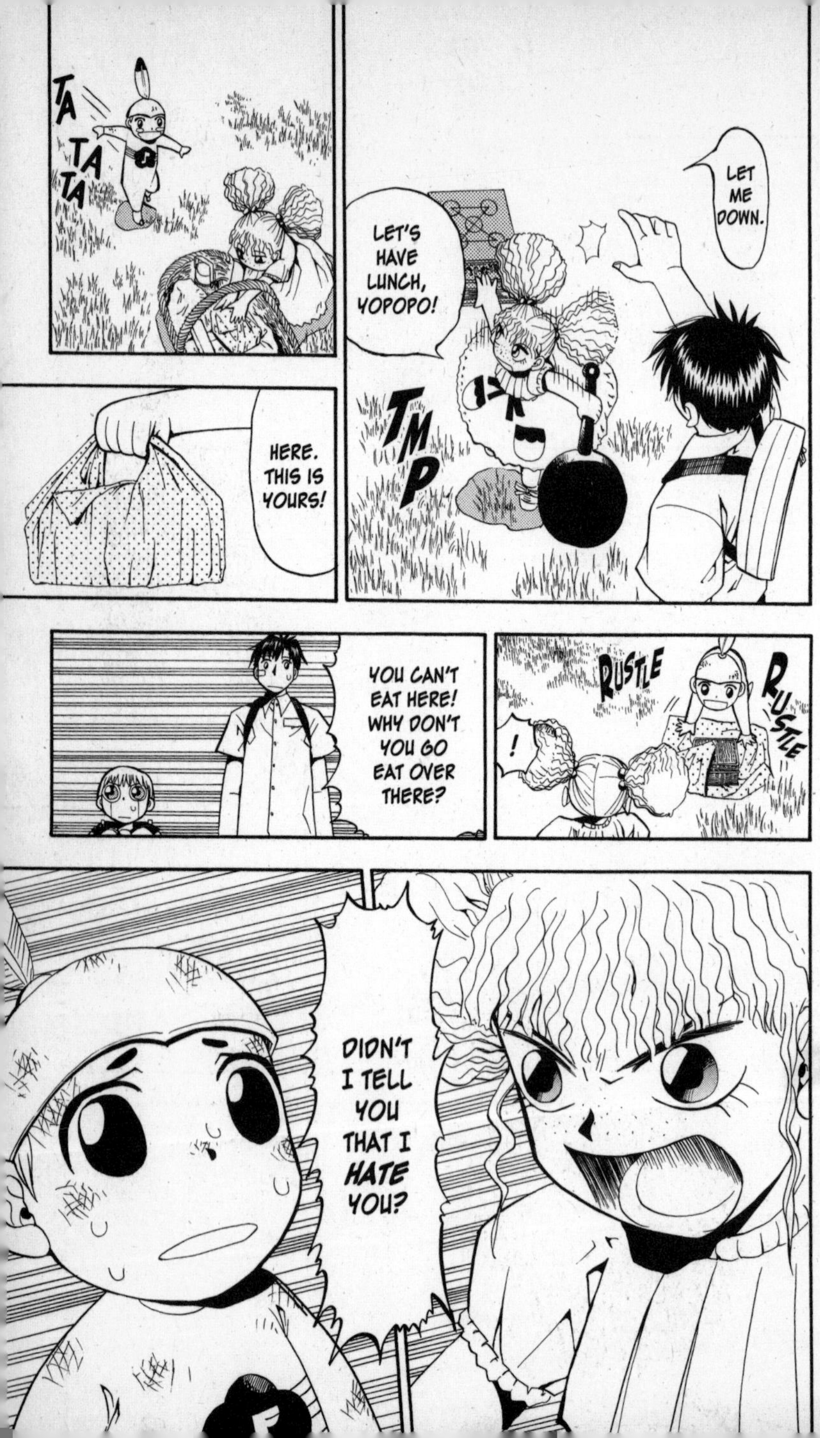
LET ME DOWN.
LET'S HAVE LUNCH, YOPOPO!
TMP
TA TA TA
HERE. THIS IS YOURS!
RUSTLE
RUSTLE
!
YOU CAN'T EAT HERE! WHY DON'T YOU GO EAT OVER THERE?
DIDN'T I TELL YOU THAT I HATE YOU?

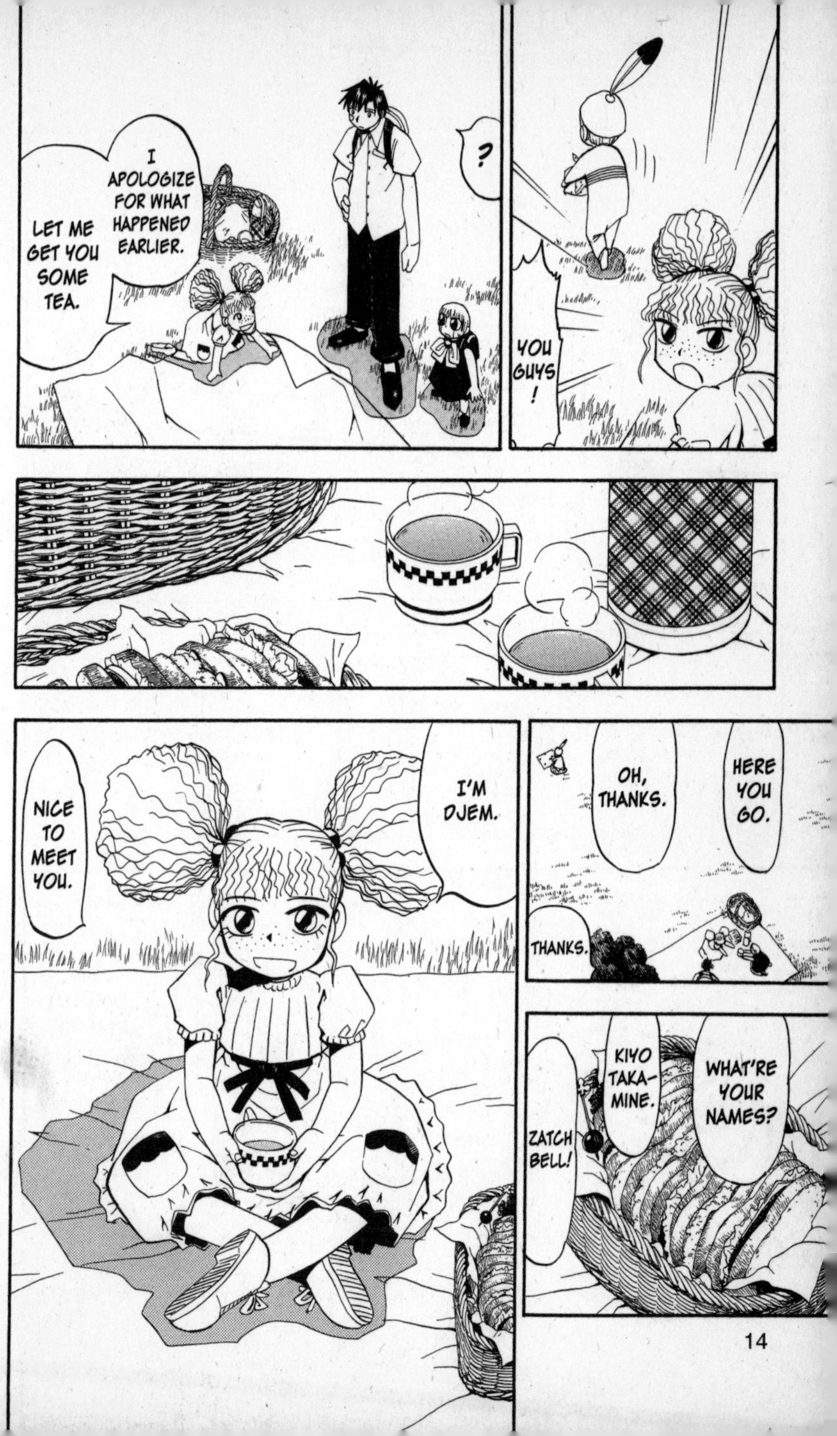
YOU GUYS!
?
I APOLOGIZE FOR WHAT HAPPENED EARLIER.
LET ME GET YOU SOME TEA.
HERE YOU GO.
OH, THANKS.
THANKS.
WHAT'RE YOUR NAMES?
KIYO TAKAMINE.
ZATCH BELL!
I'M DJEM.
NICE TO MEET YOU.

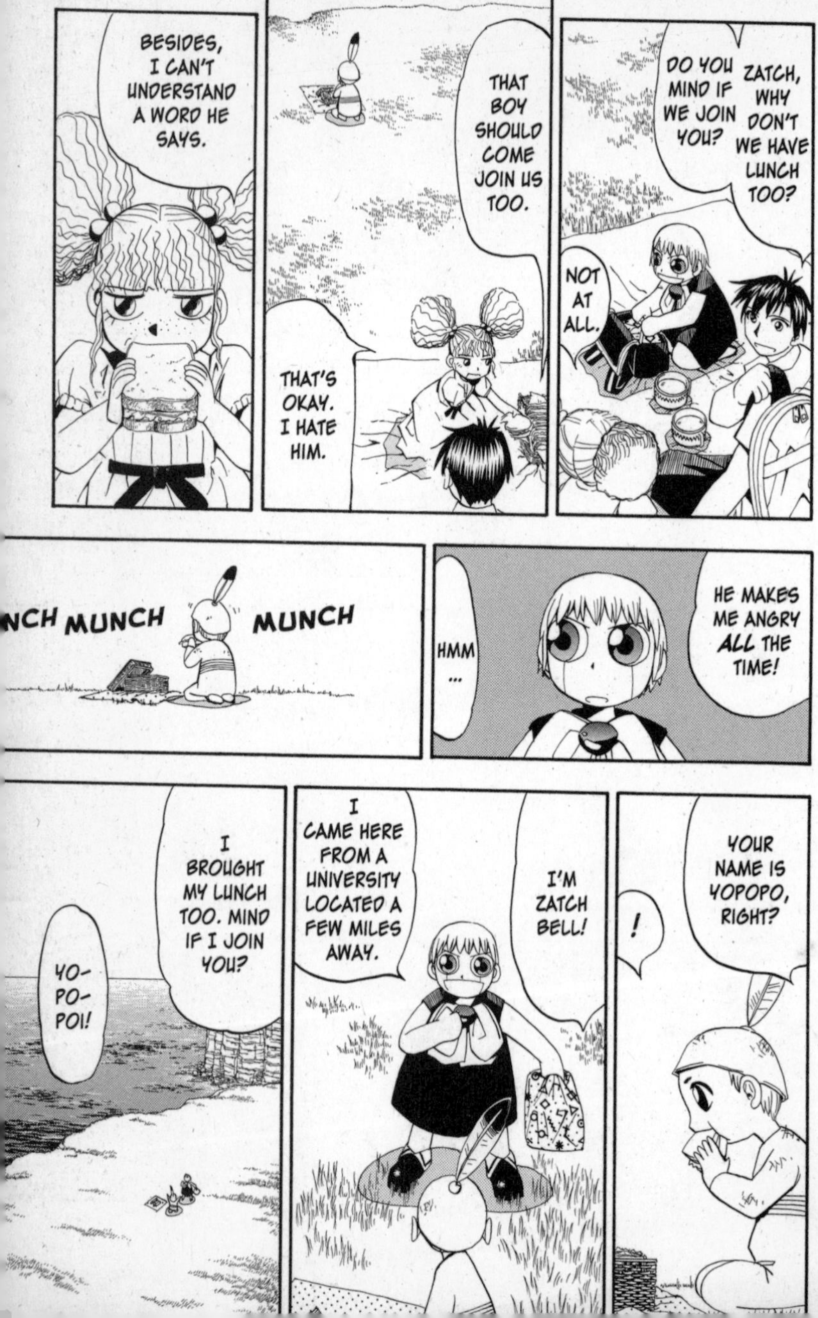
ZATCH, WHY DON'T WE HAVE LUNCH TOO?
DO YOU MIND IF WE JOIN YOU?
NOT AT ALL.
THAT BOY SHOULD COME JOIN US TOO.
THAT'S OKAY. I HATE HIM.
BESIDES, I CAN'T UNDERSTAND A WORD HE SAYS.
HE MAKES ME ANGRY ALL THE TIME!
HMM...
MUNCH
MUNCH
NCH
YOUR NAME IS YOPOPO, RIGHT?
!
I'M ZATCH BELL!
I CAME HERE FROM A UNIVERSITY LOCATED A FEW MILES AWAY.
I BROUGHT MY LUNCH TOO. MIND IF I JOIN YOU?
YO-PO-POI!

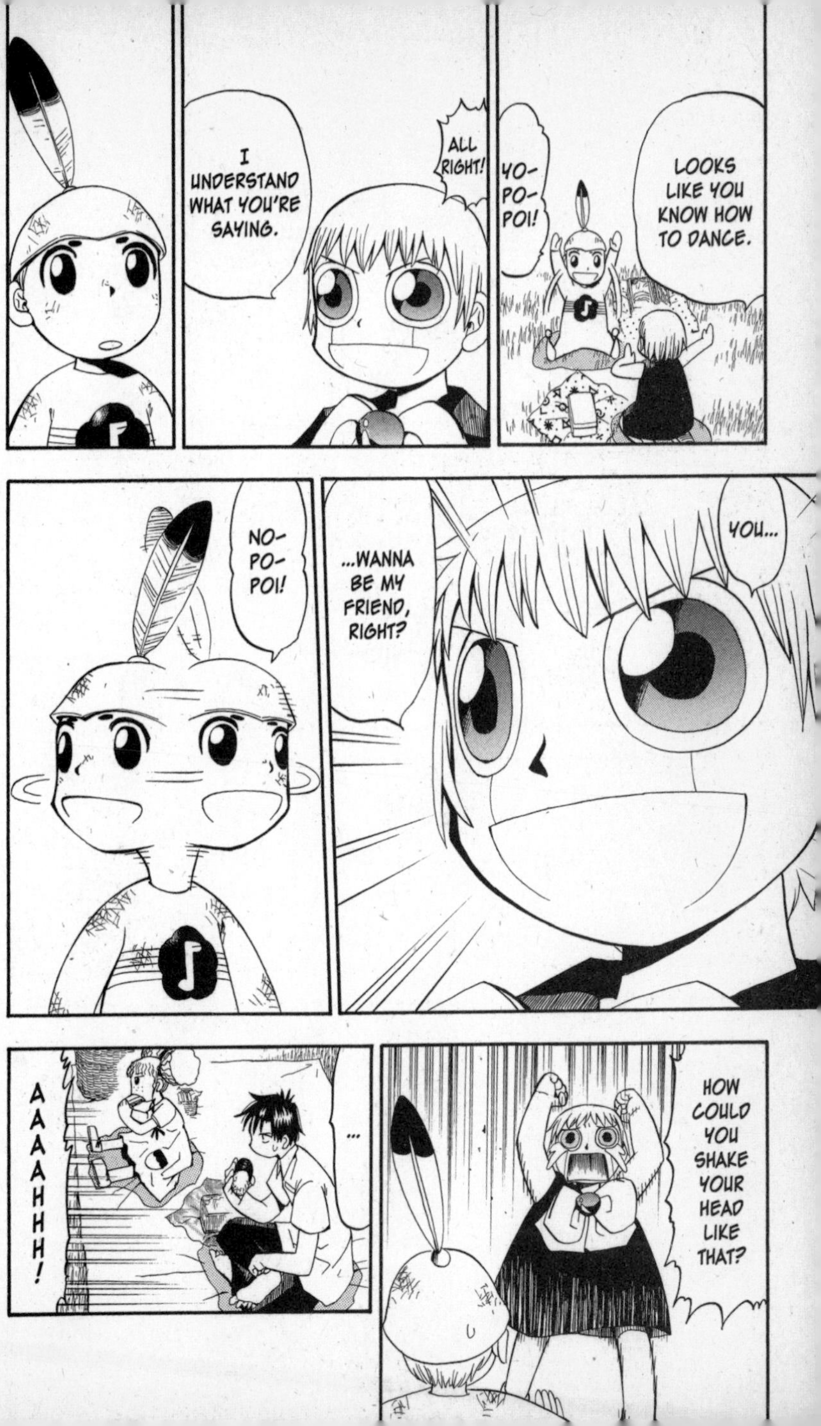
LOOKS LIKE YOU KNOW HOW TO DANCE.
YO-PO-POI!
ALL RIGHT!
I UNDERSTAND WHAT YOU'RE SAYING.
YOU...
...WANNA BE MY FRIEND, RIGHT?
NO-PO-POI!
HOW COULD YOU SHAKE YOUR HEAD LIKE THAT?
...
AAAAAHHHH!

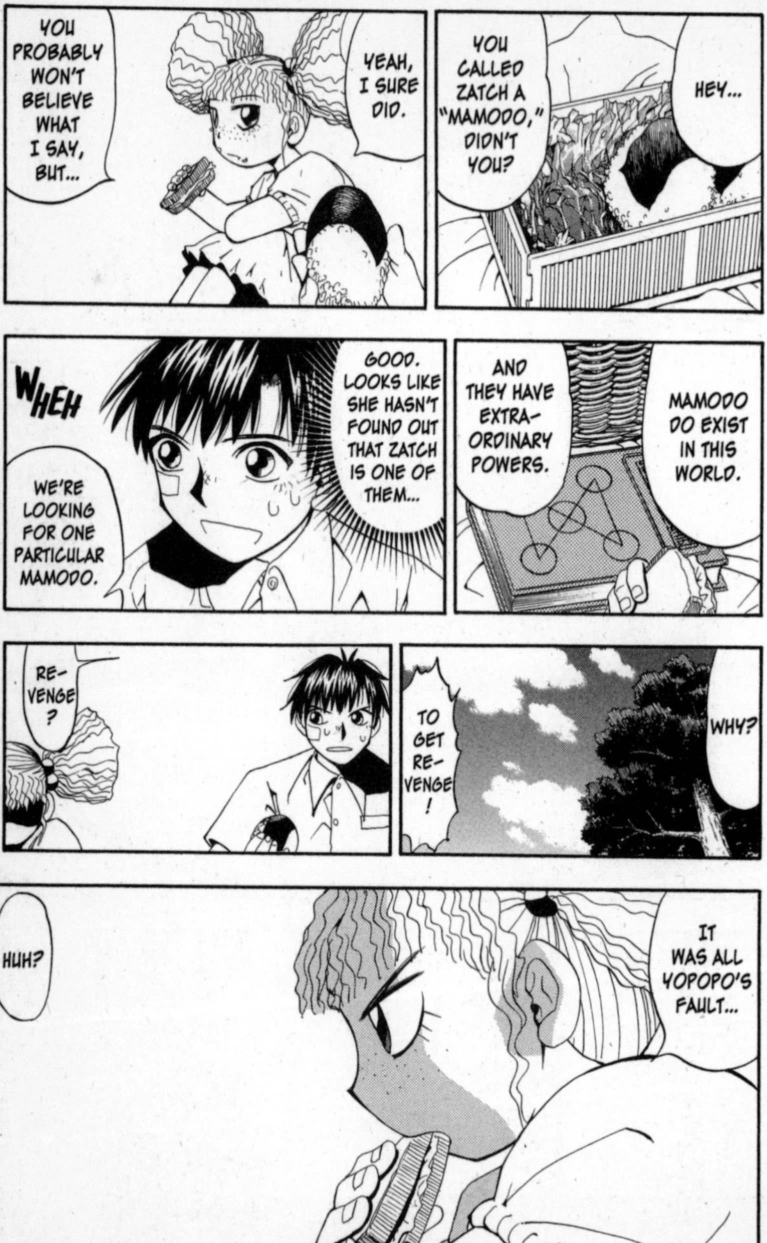
HEY...
YOU CALLED ZATCH A "MAMODO," DIDN'T YOU?
YEAH, I SURE DID.
YOU PROBABLY WON'T BELIEVE WHAT I SAY, BUT...
MAMODO DO EXIST IN THIS WORLD.
AND THEY HAVE EXTRA-ORDINARY POWERS.
GOOD. LOOKS LIKE SHE HASN'T FOUND OUT THAT ZATCH IS ONE OF THEM...
WHEH
WE'RE LOOKING FOR ONE PARTICULAR MAMODO.
WHY?
TO GET RE-VENGE!
RE-VENGE?
IT WAS ALL YOPOPO'S FAULT...
HUH?

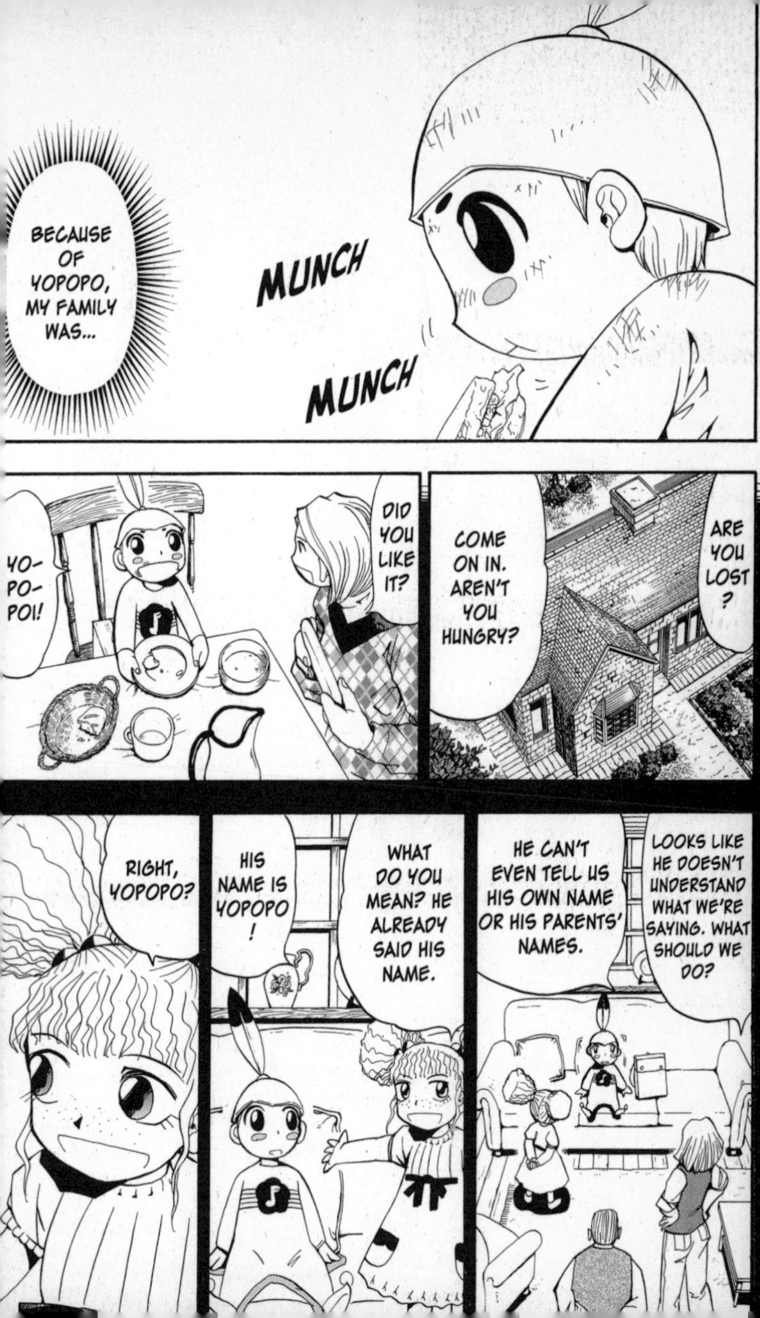
BECAUSE OF YOPOPO, MY FAMILY WAS...
MUNCH
MUNCH
ARE YOU LOST?
COME ON IN. AREN'T YOU HUNGRY?
DID YOU LIKE IT?
YO-PO-POI!
LOOKS LIKE HE DOESN'T UNDERSTAND WHAT WE'RE SAYING. WHAT SHOULD WE DO?
HE CAN'T EVEN TELL US HIS OWN NAME OR HIS PARENTS' NAMES.
WHAT DO YOU MEAN? HE ALREADY SAID HIS NAME.
HIS NAME IS YOPOPO!
RIGHT, YOPOPO?

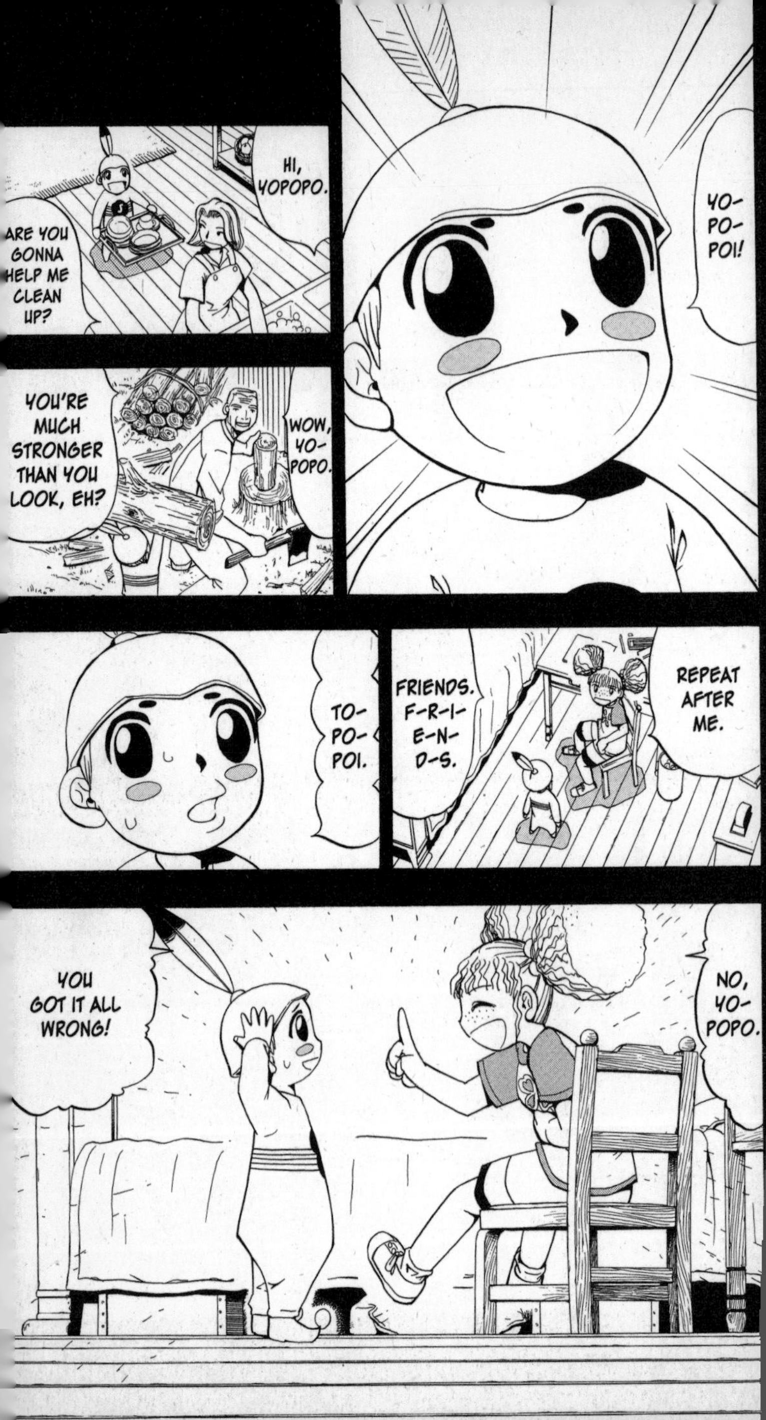
YO-PO-POI!
HI, YOPOPO.
ARE YOU GONNA HELP ME CLEAN UP?
WOW, YO-POPO.
YOU'RE MUCH STRONGER THAN YOU LOOK, EH?
REPEAT AFTER ME.
FRIENDS. F-R-I-E-N-D-S.
TO-PO-POI.
NO, YO-POPO.
YOU GOT IT ALL WRONG!

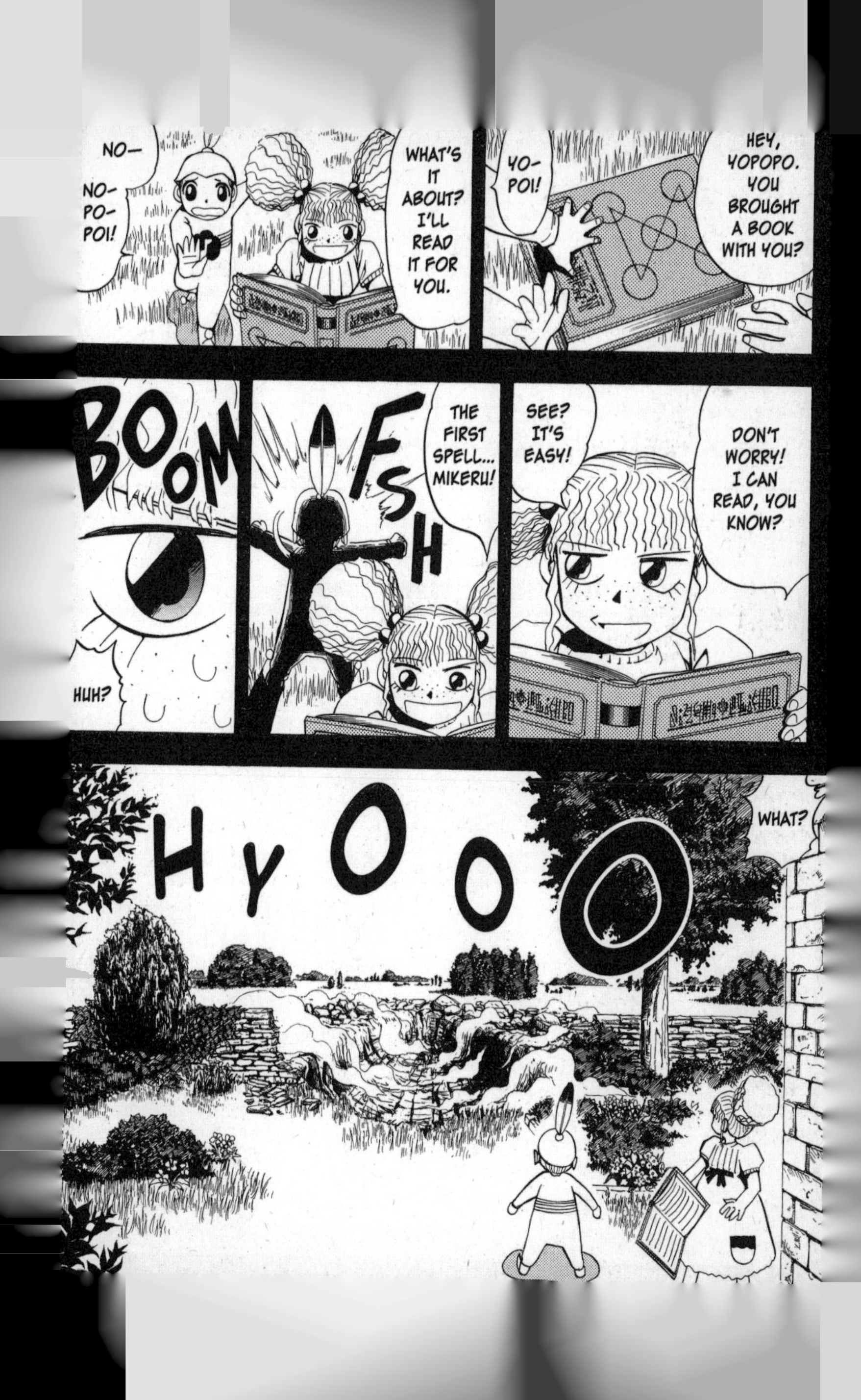
HEY, YOPOPO. YOU BROUGHT A BOOK WITH YOU?
YO-POI!
WHAT'S IT ABOUT? I'LL READ IT FOR YOU.
NO—
NO-PO-POI!
DON'T WORRY! I CAN READ, YOU KNOW?
SEE? IT'S EASY!
THE FIRST SPELL... MIKERU!
FSH
BOOM
HUH?
WHAT?
HYOOOO

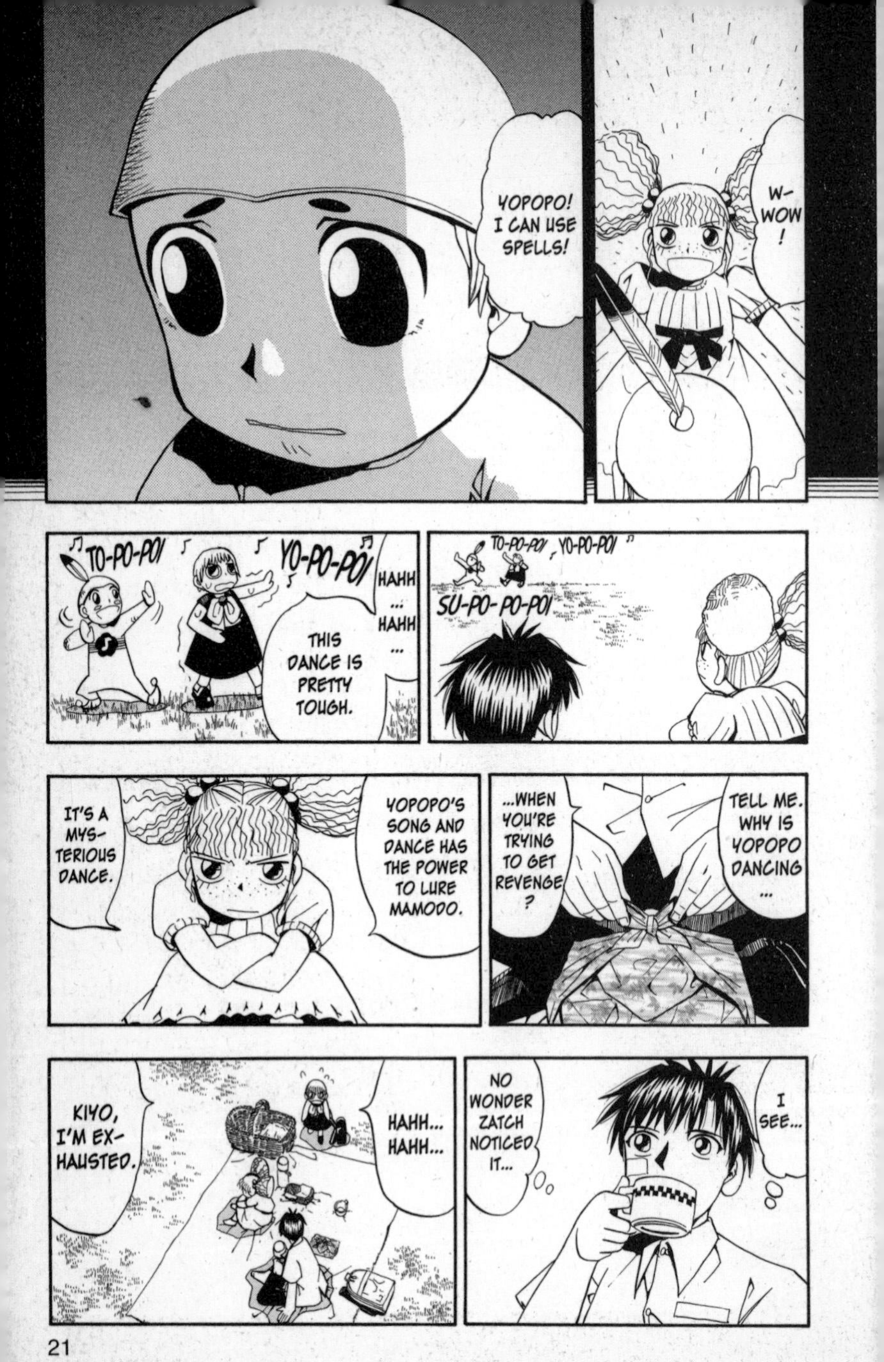
W-WOW!
YOPOPO! I CAN USE SPELLS!
YO-PO-POI
TO-PO-POI
SU-PO-PO-POI
HAHH... HAHH...
YO-PO-POI
TO-PO-POI
THIS DANCE IS PRETTY TOUGH.
TELL ME. WHY IS YOPOPO DANCING...
...WHEN YOU'RE TRYING TO GET REVENGE?
YOPOPO'S SONG AND DANCE HAS THE POWER TO LURE MAMODO.
IT'S A MYSTERIOUS DANCE.
I SEE...
NO WONDER ZATCH NOTICED IT...
HAHH... HAHH...
KIYO, I'M EXHAUSTED.

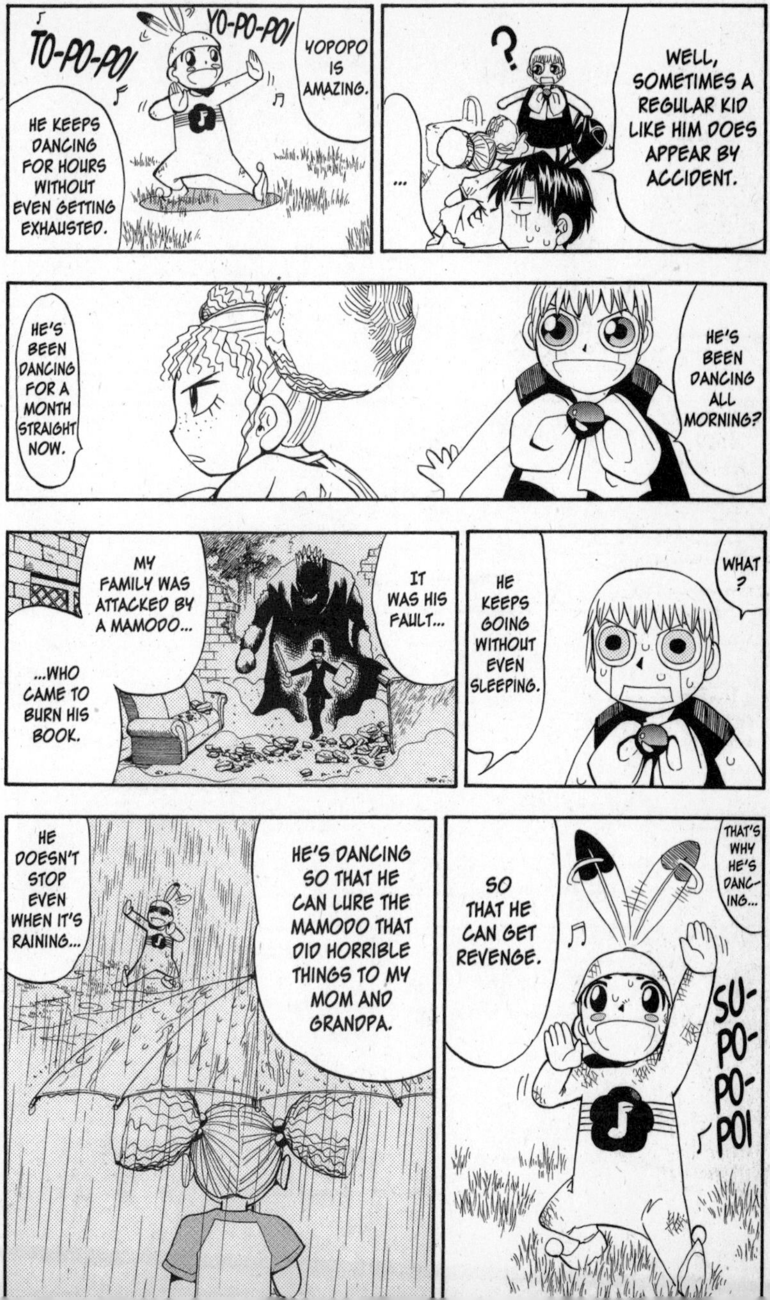
?
WELL, SOMETIMES A REGULAR KID LIKE HIM DOES APPEAR BY ACCIDENT.
...
YOPOPO IS AMAZING.
YO-PO-POI
TO-PO-POI
HE KEEPS DANCING FOR HOURS WITHOUT EVEN GETTING EXHAUSTED.
HE'S BEEN DANCING ALL MORNING?
HE'S BEEN DANCING FOR A MONTH STRAIGHT NOW.
WHAT?
HE KEEPS GOING WITHOUT EVEN SLEEPING.
IT WAS HIS FAULT...
MY FAMILY WAS ATTACKED BY A MAMODO...
...WHO CAME TO BURN HIS BOOK.
THAT'S WHY HE'S DANC-ING...
SO THAT HE CAN GET REVENGE.
SU-PO-PO-POI
HE'S DANCING SO THAT HE CAN LURE THE MAMODO THAT DID HORRIBLE THINGS TO MY MOM AND GRANDPA.
HE DOESN'T STOP EVEN WHEN IT'S RAINING...

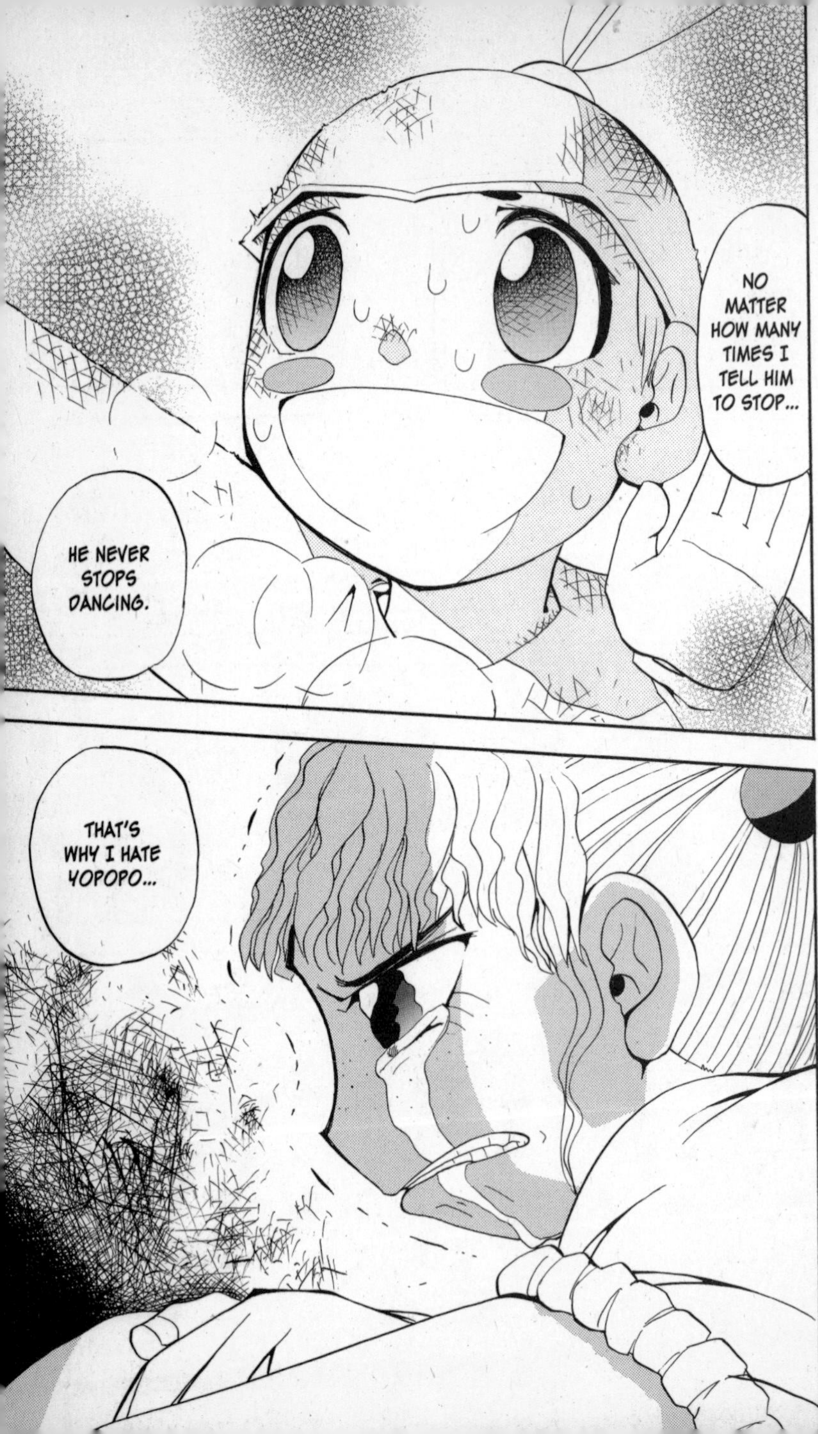
NO MATTER HOW MANY TIMES I TELL HIM TO STOP...
HE NEVER STOPS DANCING.
THAT'S WHY I HATE YOPOPO...

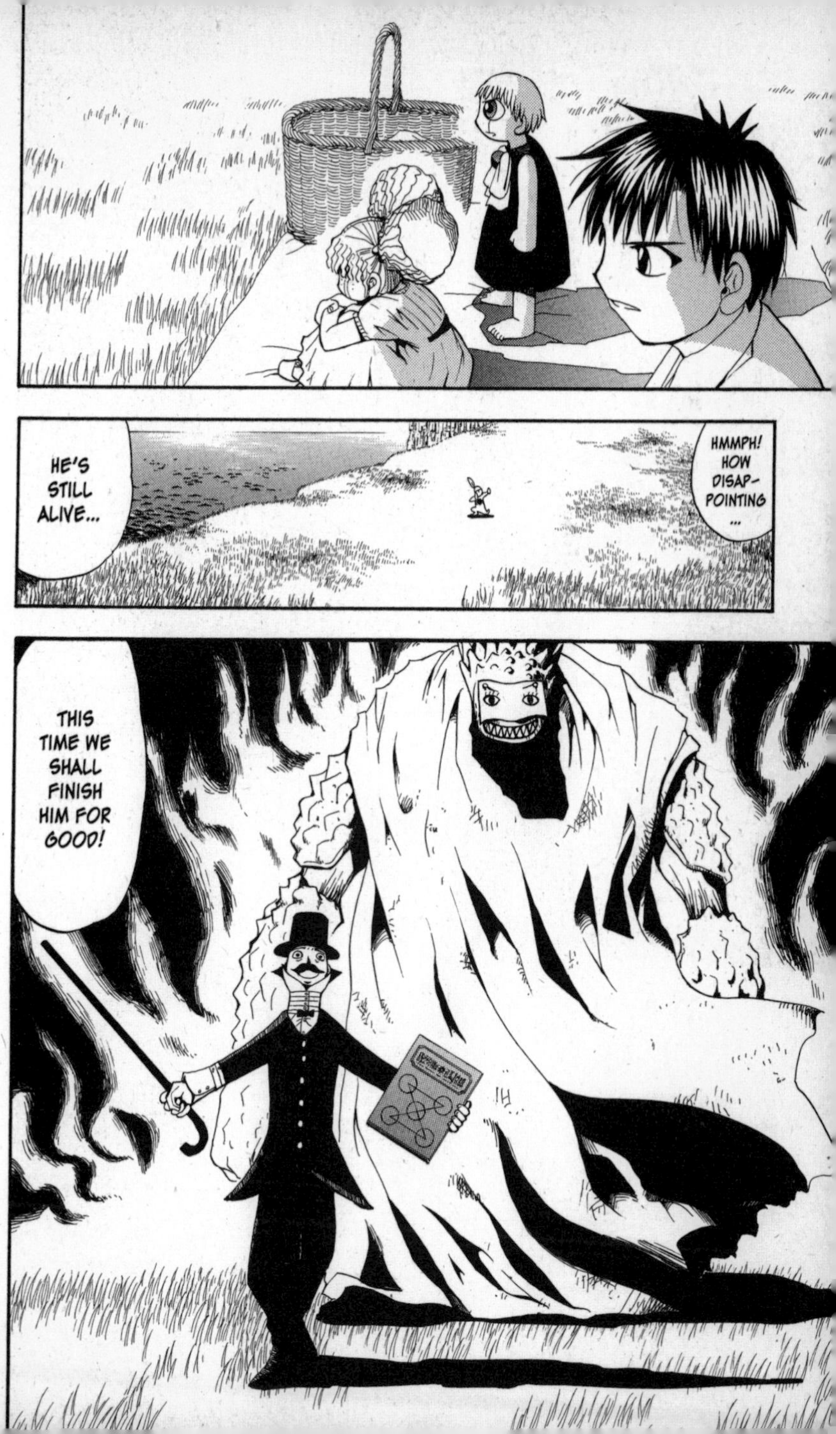
HMMPH! HOW DISAP-POINTING...
HE'S STILL ALIVE...
THIS TIME WE SHALL FINISH HIM FOR GOOD!

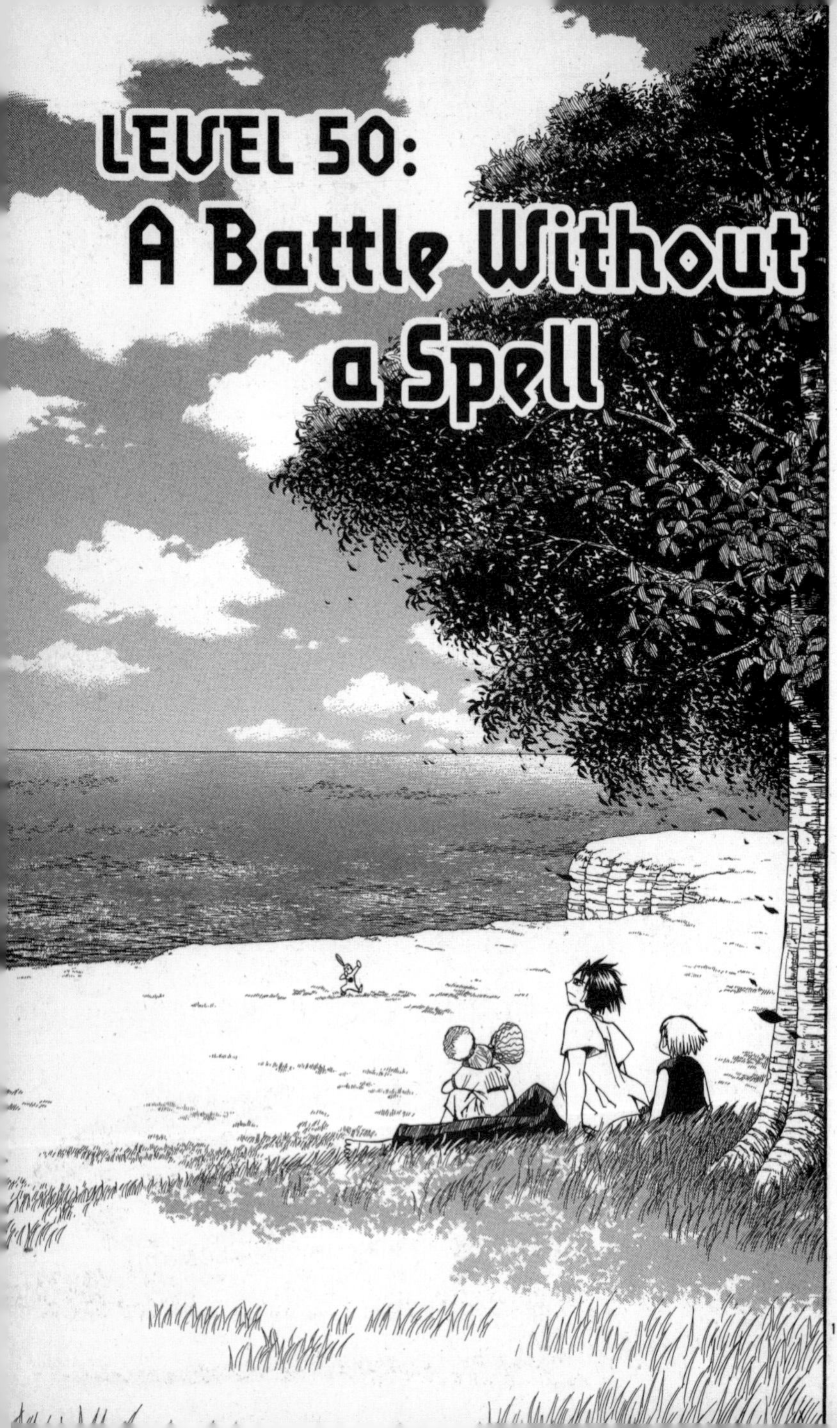
LEVEL 50:
A Battle Without a Spell

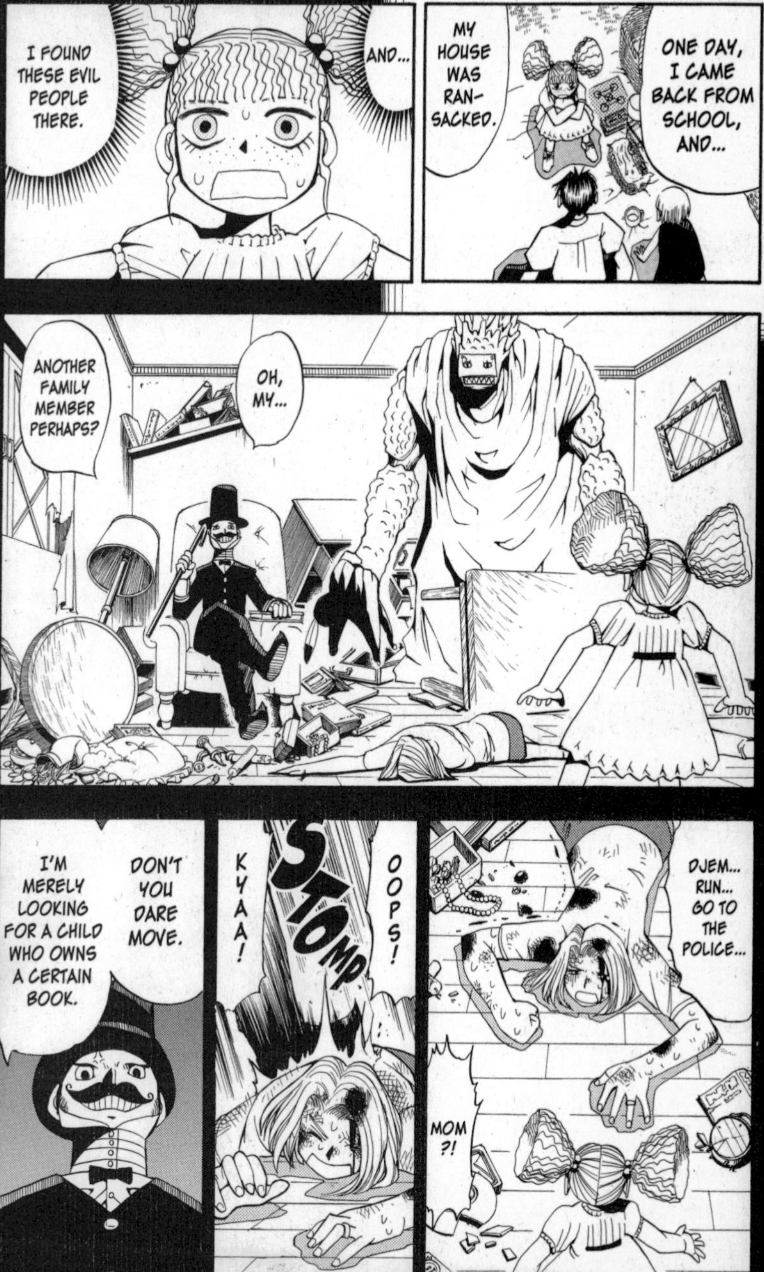
ONE DAY, I CAME BACK FROM SCHOOL, AND...
MY HOUSE WAS RAN-SACKED.
AND...
I FOUND THESE EVIL PEOPLE THERE.
OH, MY...
ANOTHER FAMILY MEMBER PERHAPS?
DJEM... RUN... GO TO THE POLICE...
MOM?!
OOPS!
STOMP
KYAA!
DON'T YOU DARE MOVE.
I'M MERELY LOOKING FOR A CHILD WHO OWNS A CERTAIN BOOK.

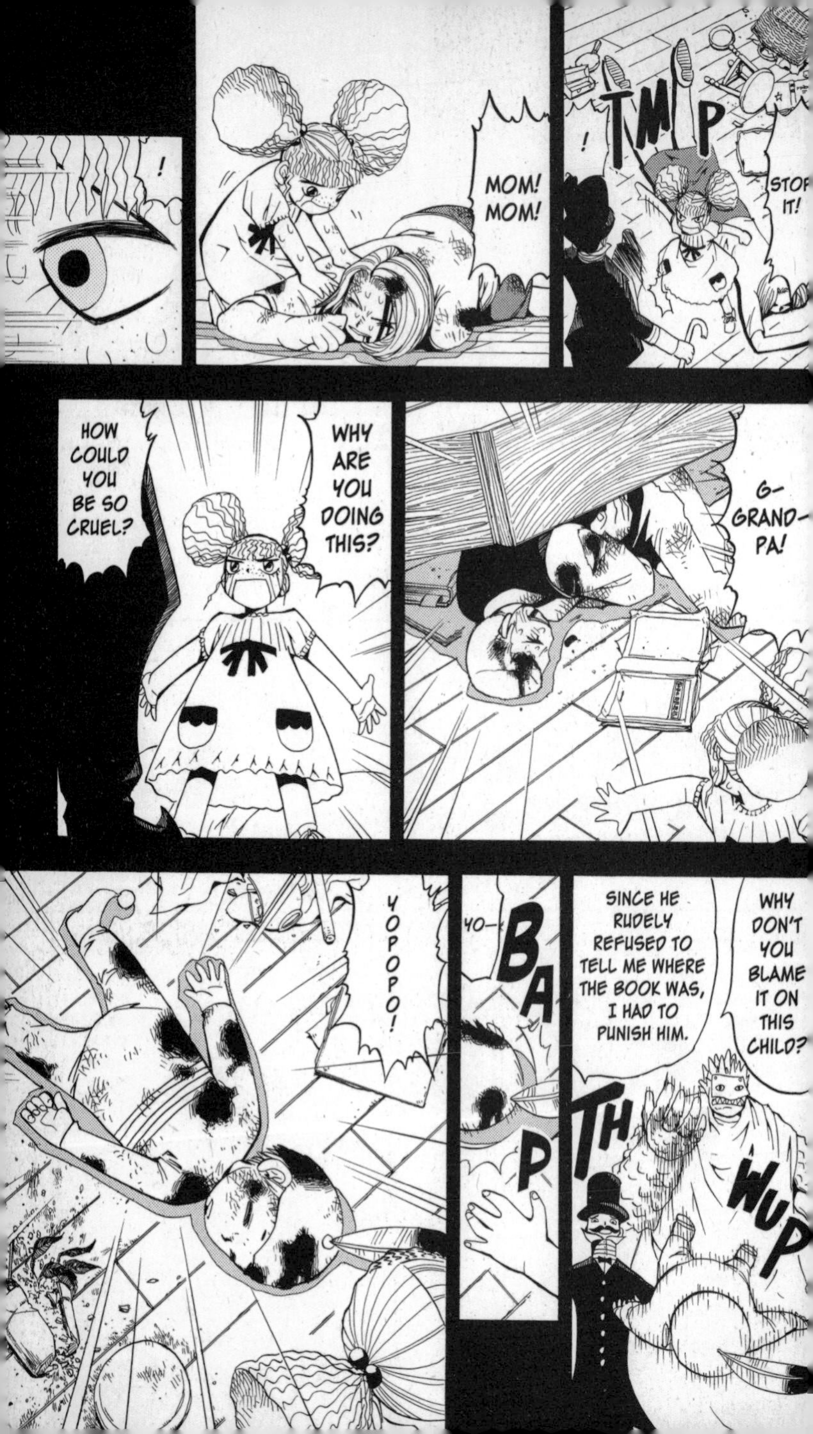
TMP
STOP IT!
!
MOM! MOM!
!
G-GRANDPA!
WHY ARE YOU DOING THIS?
HOW COULD YOU BE SO CRUEL?
WHY DON'T YOU BLAME IT ON THIS CHILD?
SINCE HE RUDELY REFUSED TO TELL ME WHERE THE BOOK WAS, I HAD TO PUNISH HIM.
THWUP
YO-
BAP
YOPOPO!

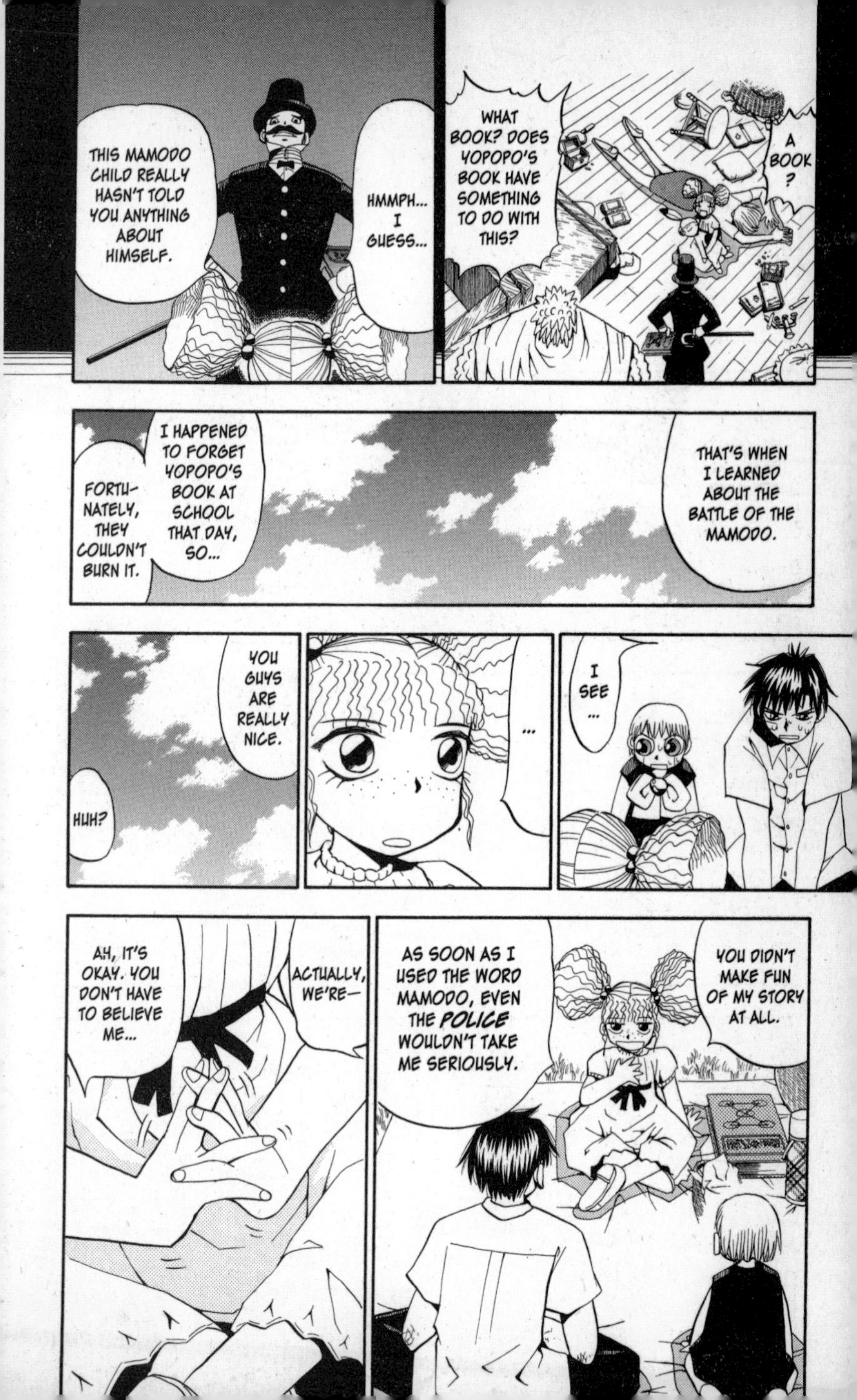
A BOOK?
WHAT BOOK? DOES YOPOPO'S BOOK HAVE SOMETHING TO DO WITH THIS?
HMMPH... I GUESS...
THIS MAMODO CHILD REALLY HASN'T TOLD YOU ANYTHING ABOUT HIMSELF.
THAT'S WHEN I LEARNED ABOUT THE BATTLE OF THE MAMODO.
I HAPPENED TO FORGET YOPOPO'S BOOK AT SCHOOL THAT DAY, SO...
FORTU-NATELY, THEY COULDN'T BURN IT.
I SEE ...
...
YOU GUYS ARE REALLY NICE.
HUH?
YOU DIDN'T MAKE FUN OF MY STORY AT ALL.
AS SOON AS I USED THE WORD MAMODO, EVEN THE *POLICE* WOULDN'T TAKE ME SERIOUSLY.
ACTUALLY, WE'RE—
AH, IT'S OKAY. YOU DON'T HAVE TO BELIEVE ME...

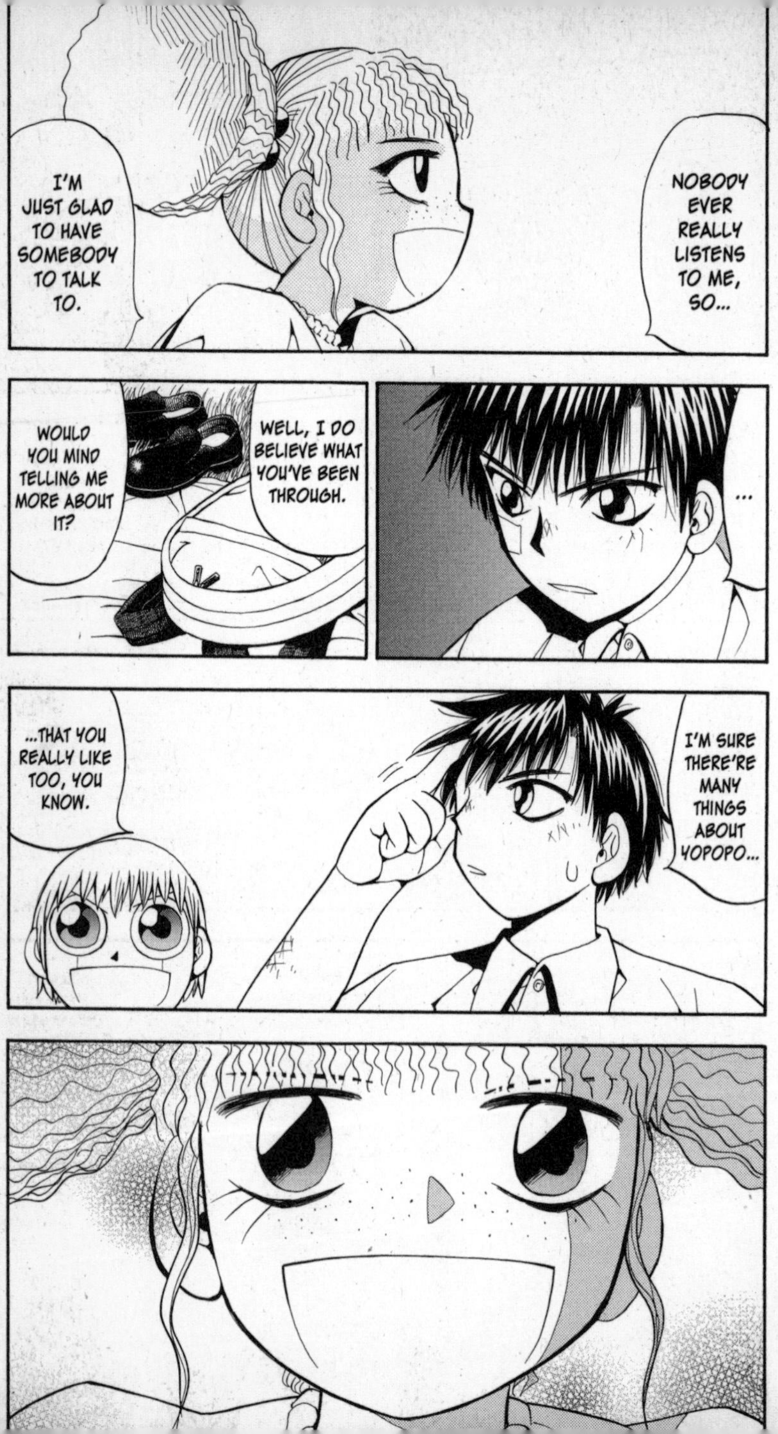
NOBODY EVER REALLY LISTENS TO ME, SO...
I'M JUST GLAD TO HAVE SOMEBODY TO TALK TO.
...
WELL, I DO BELIEVE WHAT YOU'VE BEEN THROUGH.
WOULD YOU MIND TELLING ME MORE ABOUT IT?
I'M SURE THERE'RE MANY THINGS ABOUT YOPOPO...
...THAT YOU REALLY LIKE TOO, YOU KNOW.

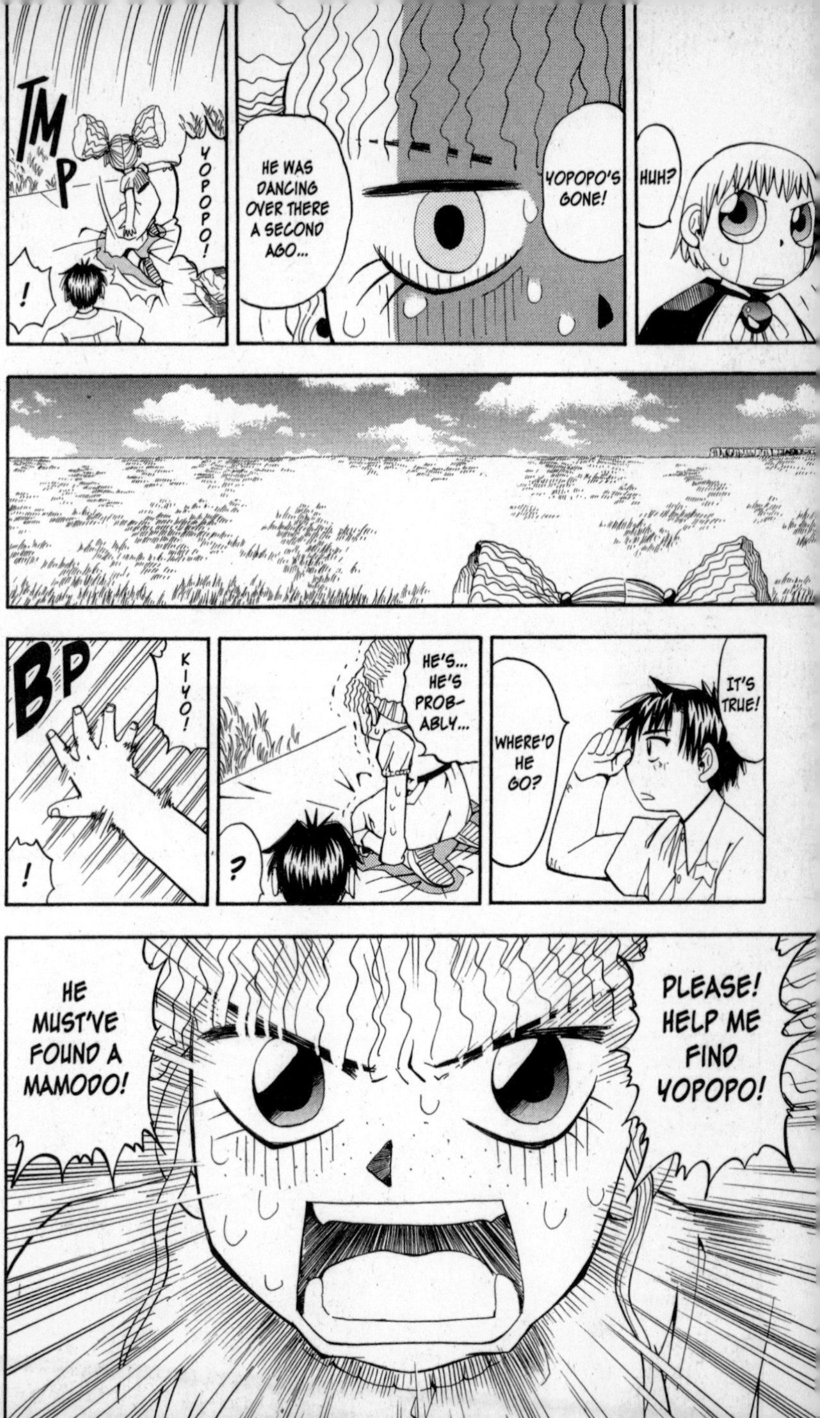
HUH?
YOPOPO'S GONE!
HE WAS DANCING OVER THERE A SECOND AGO...
YOPOPO!
TMP
!
IT'S TRUE!
WHERE'D HE GO?
HE'S... HE'S PROBABLY...
?
KIYO!
BP
!
PLEASE! HELP ME FIND YOPOPO!
HE MUST'VE FOUND A MAMODO!

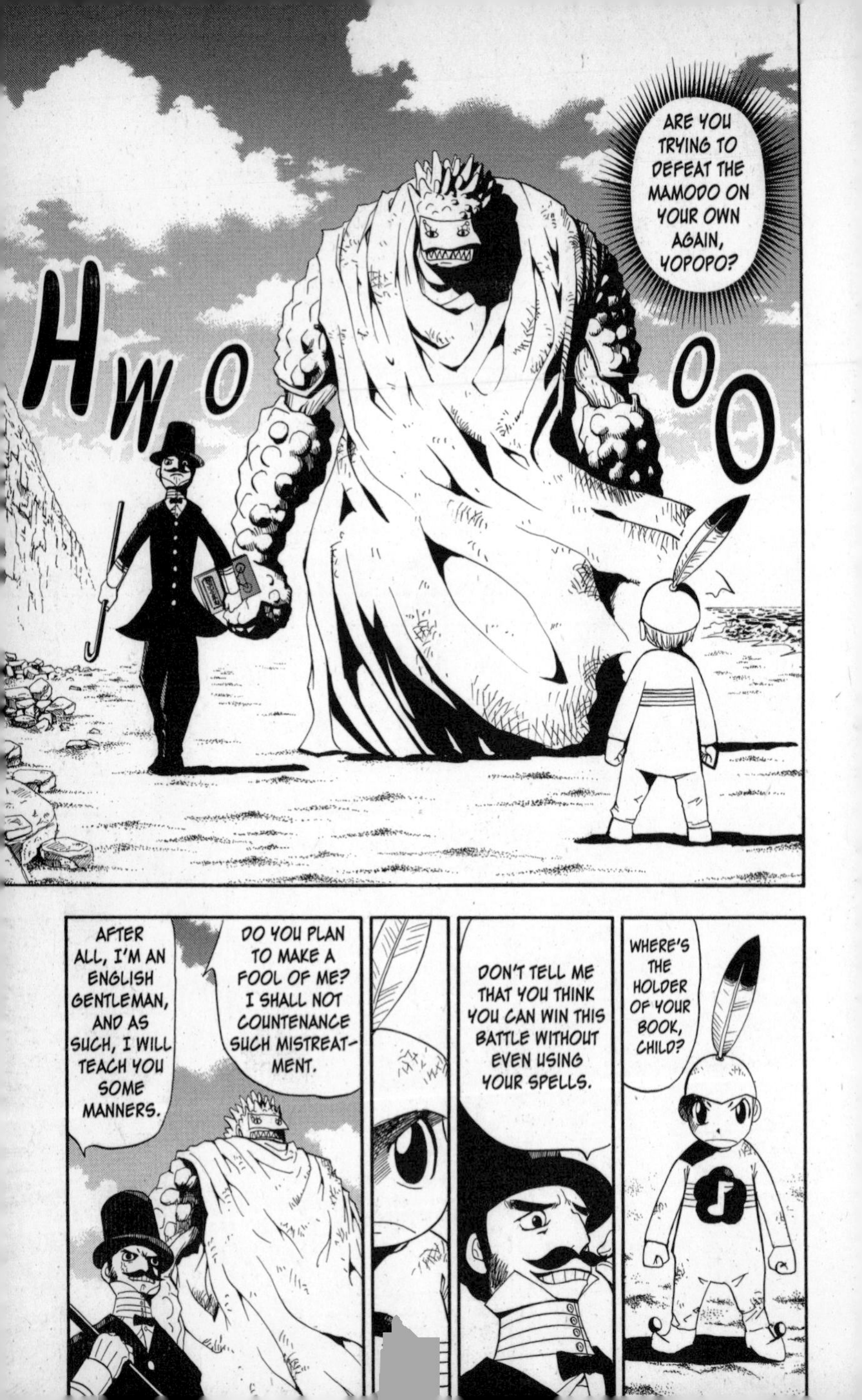
ARE YOU TRYING TO DEFEAT THE MAMODO ON YOUR OWN AGAIN, YOPOPO?
HWOOO
WHERE'S THE HOLDER OF YOUR BOOK, CHILD?
DON'T TELL ME THAT YOU THINK YOU CAN WIN THIS BATTLE WITHOUT EVEN USING YOUR SPELLS.
DO YOU PLAN TO MAKE A FOOL OF ME? I SHALL NOT COUNTENANCE SUCH MISTREAT-MENT.
AFTER ALL, I'M AN ENGLISH GENTLEMAN, AND AS SUCH, I WILL TEACH YOU SOME MANNERS.

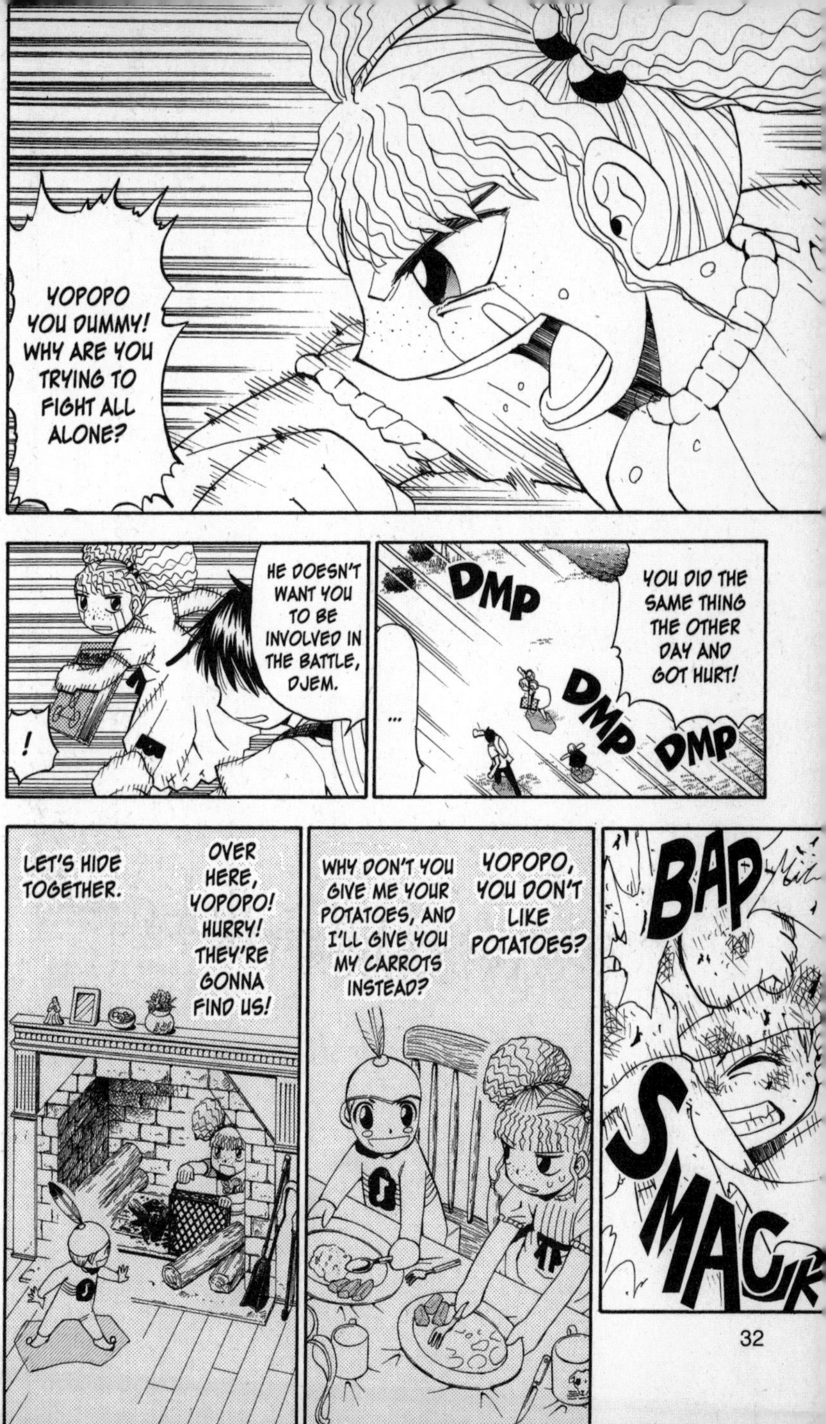
YOPOPO YOU DUMMY! WHY ARE YOU TRYING TO FIGHT ALL ALONE?
YOU DID THE SAME THING THE OTHER DAY AND GOT HURT!
DMP
DMP
DMP
...
HE DOESN'T WANT YOU TO BE INVOLVED IN THE BATTLE, DJEM.
!
BAP
SMACK
YOPOPO, YOU DON'T LIKE POTATOES?
WHY DON'T YOU GIVE ME YOUR POTATOES, AND I'LL GIVE YOU MY CARROTS INSTEAD?
OVER HERE, YOPOPO! HURRY! THEY'RE GONNA FIND US!
LET'S HIDE TOGETHER.

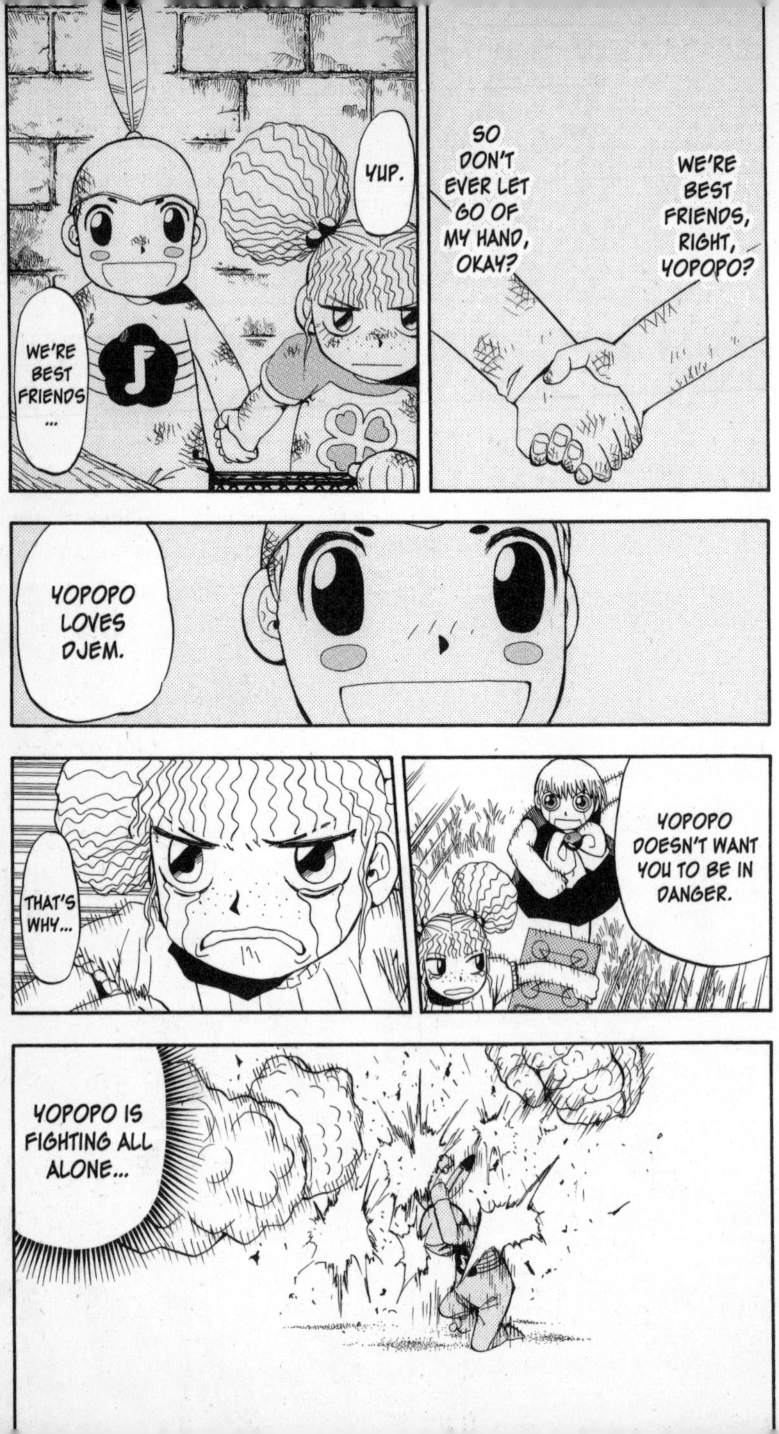
WE'RE BEST FRIENDS, RIGHT, YOPOPO?
SO DON'T EVER LET GO OF MY HAND, OKAY?
YUP.
WE'RE BEST FRIENDS ...
YOPOPO LOVES DJEM.
YOPOPO DOESN'T WANT YOU TO BE IN DANGER.
THAT'S WHY...
YOPOPO IS FIGHTING ALL ALONE...

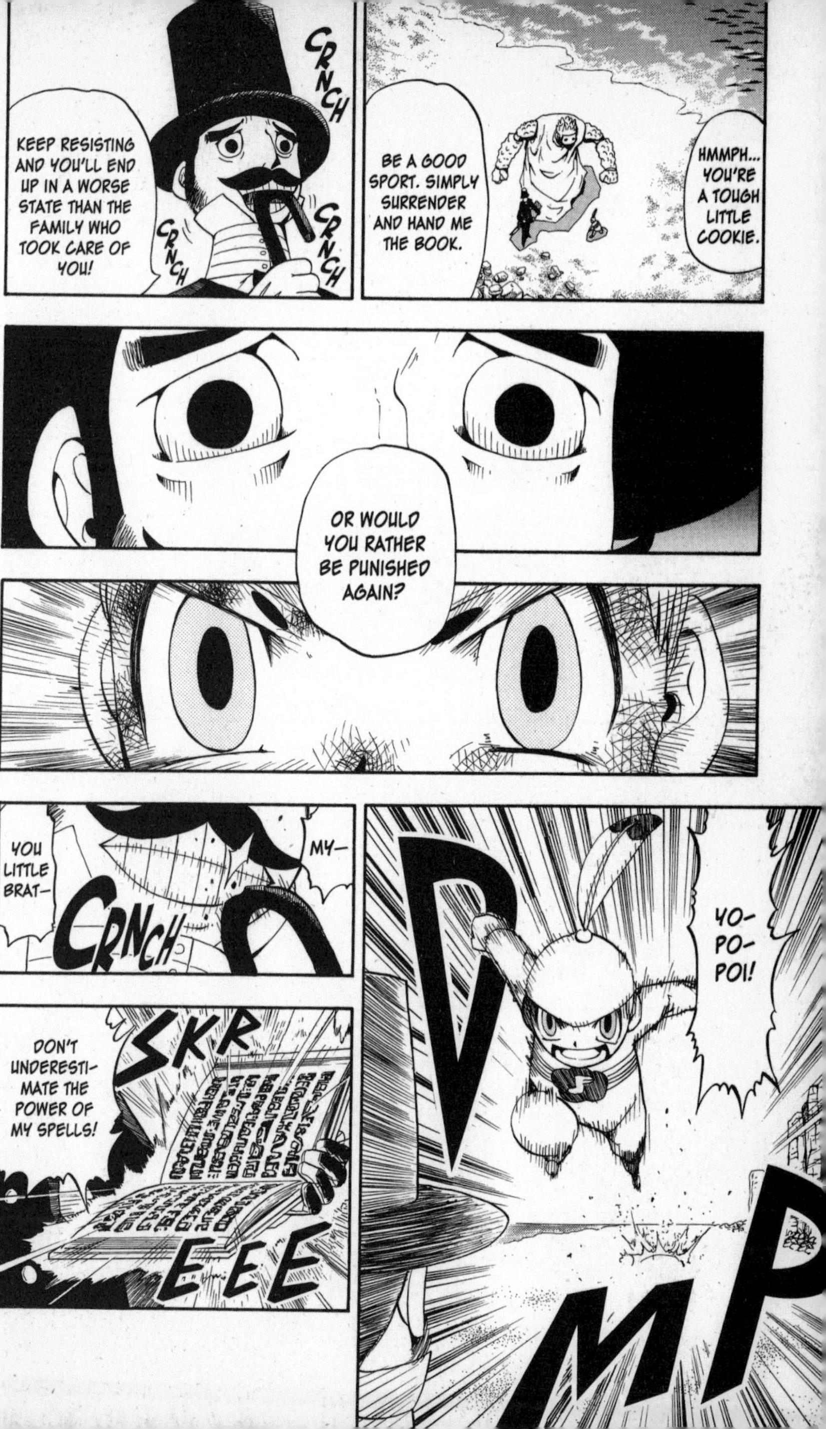
HMMPH... YOU'RE A TOUGH LITTLE COOKIE.
BE A GOOD SPORT. SIMPLY SURRENDER AND HAND ME THE BOOK.
CRNCH
KEEP RESISTING AND YOU'LL END UP IN A WORSE STATE THAN THE FAMILY WHO TOOK CARE OF YOU!
CRNCH
CRNCH
OR WOULD YOU RATHER BE PUNISHED AGAIN?
YO-PO-POI!
DMP
MY—
YOU LITTLE BRAT—
CRNCH
SKR
DON'T UNDERESTI-MATE THE POWER OF MY SPELLS!
EEE

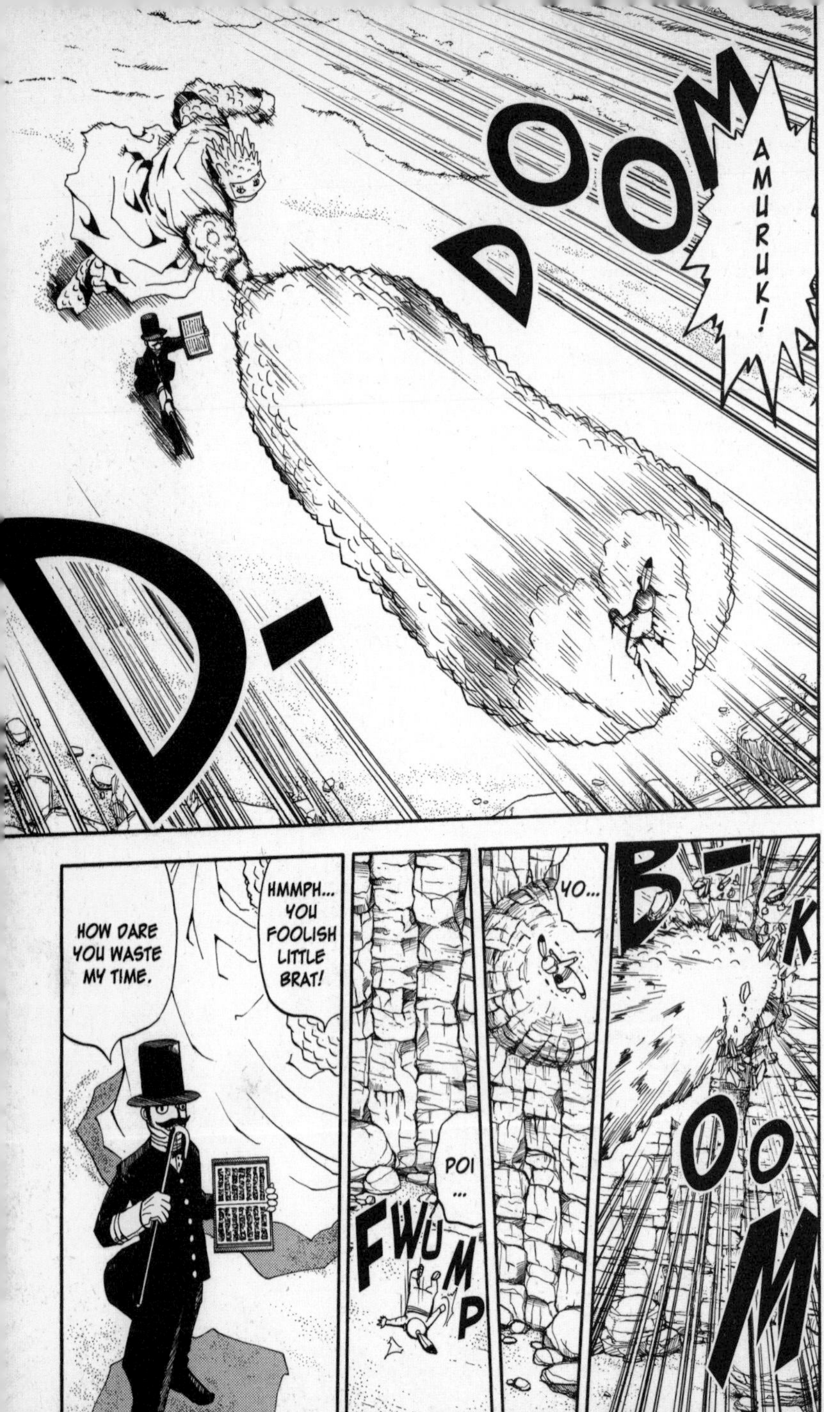
AMURUK!
D-DOOM
B-
K
OOM
YO...
POI
...
FWUMP
HMMPH... YOU FOOLISH LITTLE BRAT!
HOW DARE YOU WASTE MY TIME.

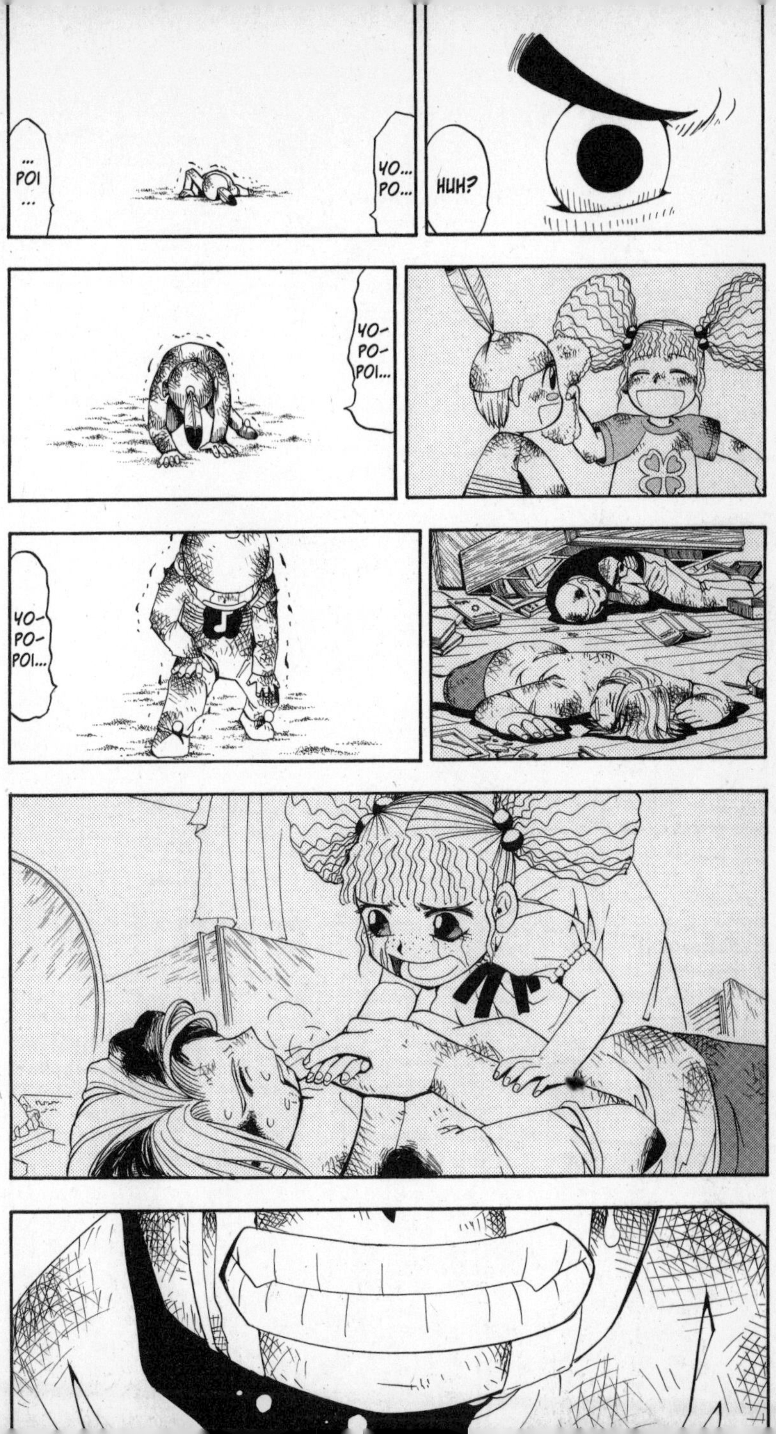
HUH?
YO... PO...
... POI ...
YO-PO-POI...
YO-PO-POI...

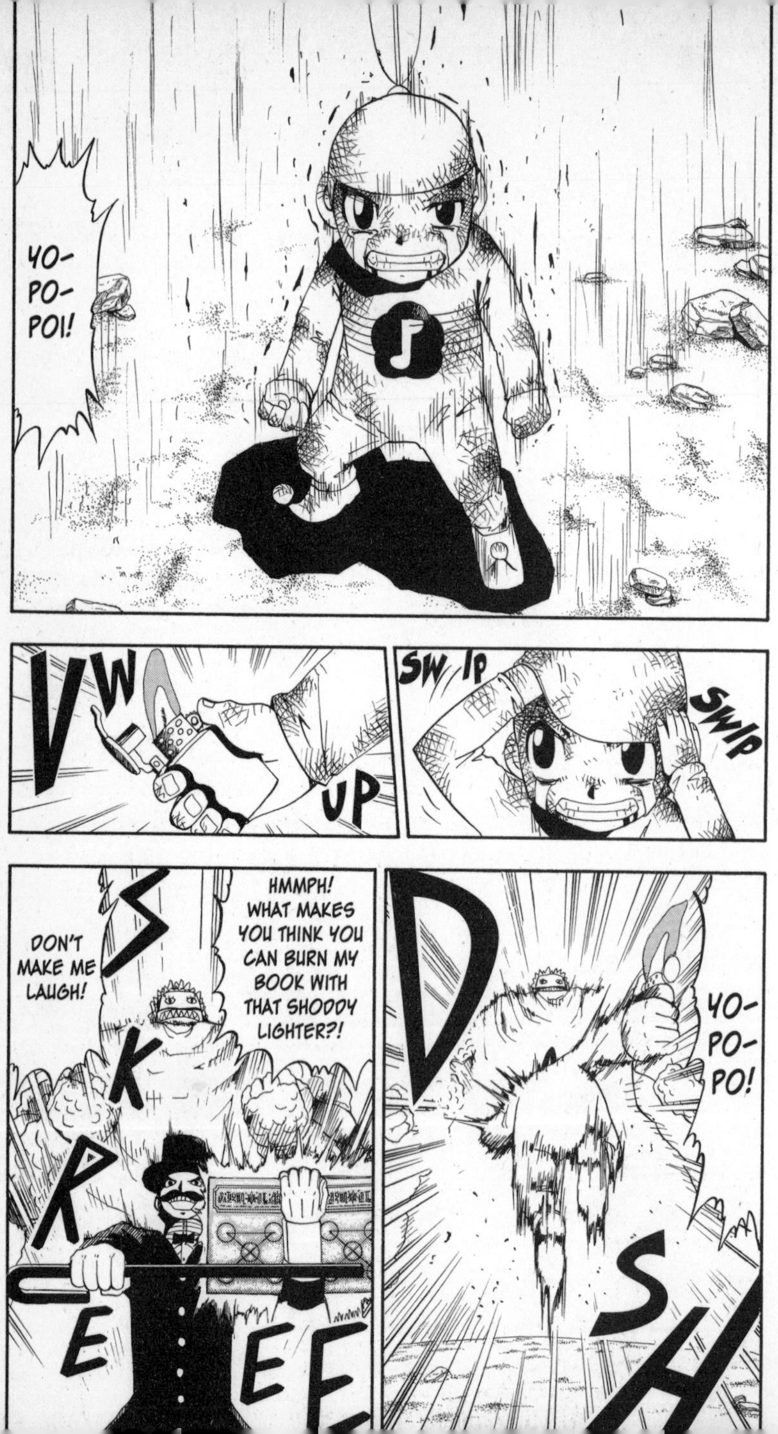
YO-PO-POI!
SWIP
SWIP
VWUP
YO-PO-PO!
DSH
HMMPH! WHAT MAKES YOU THINK YOU CAN BURN MY BOOK WITH THAT SHODDY LIGHTER?!
DON'T MAKE ME LAUGH!
SKREEE

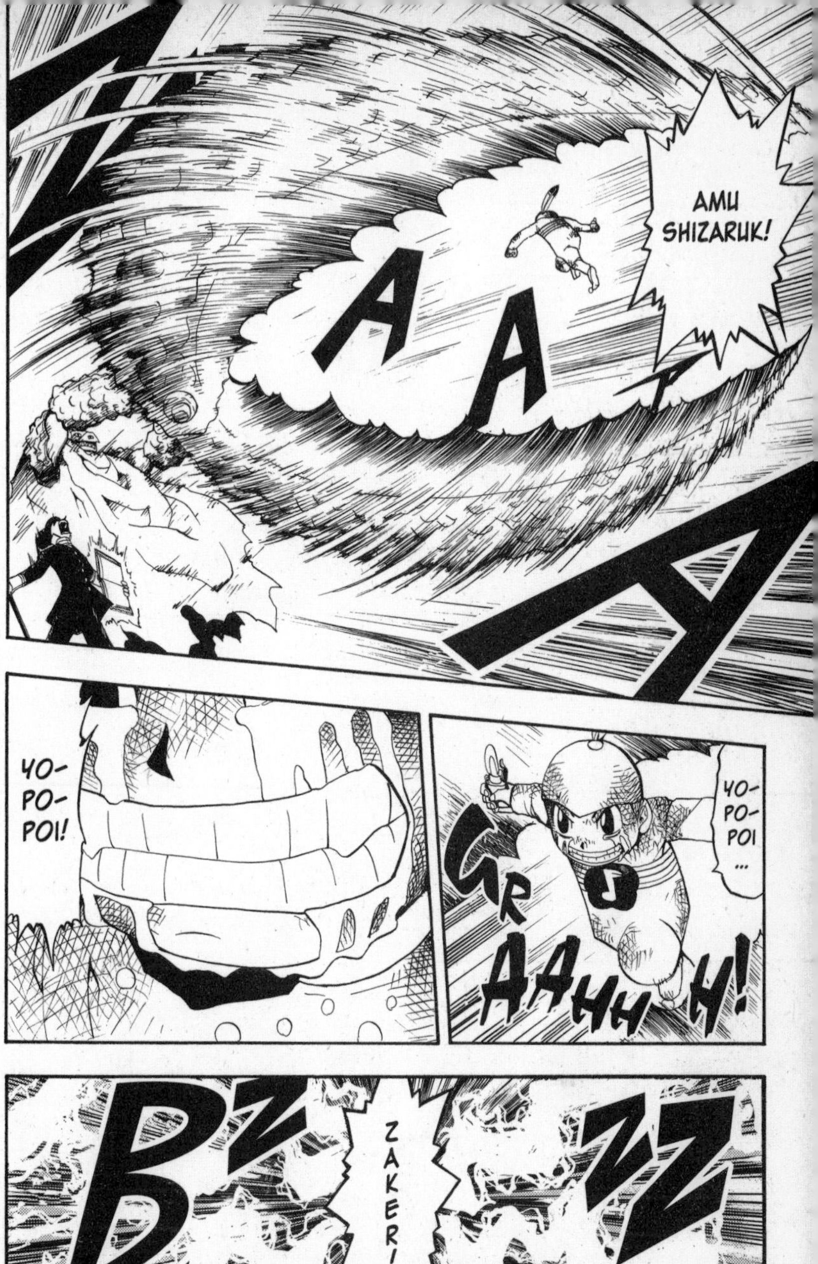
AMU SHIZARUK!
AAA
YO-PO-POI...
GRAAHHH!
YO-PO-POI!
BZZZ
ZAKER!

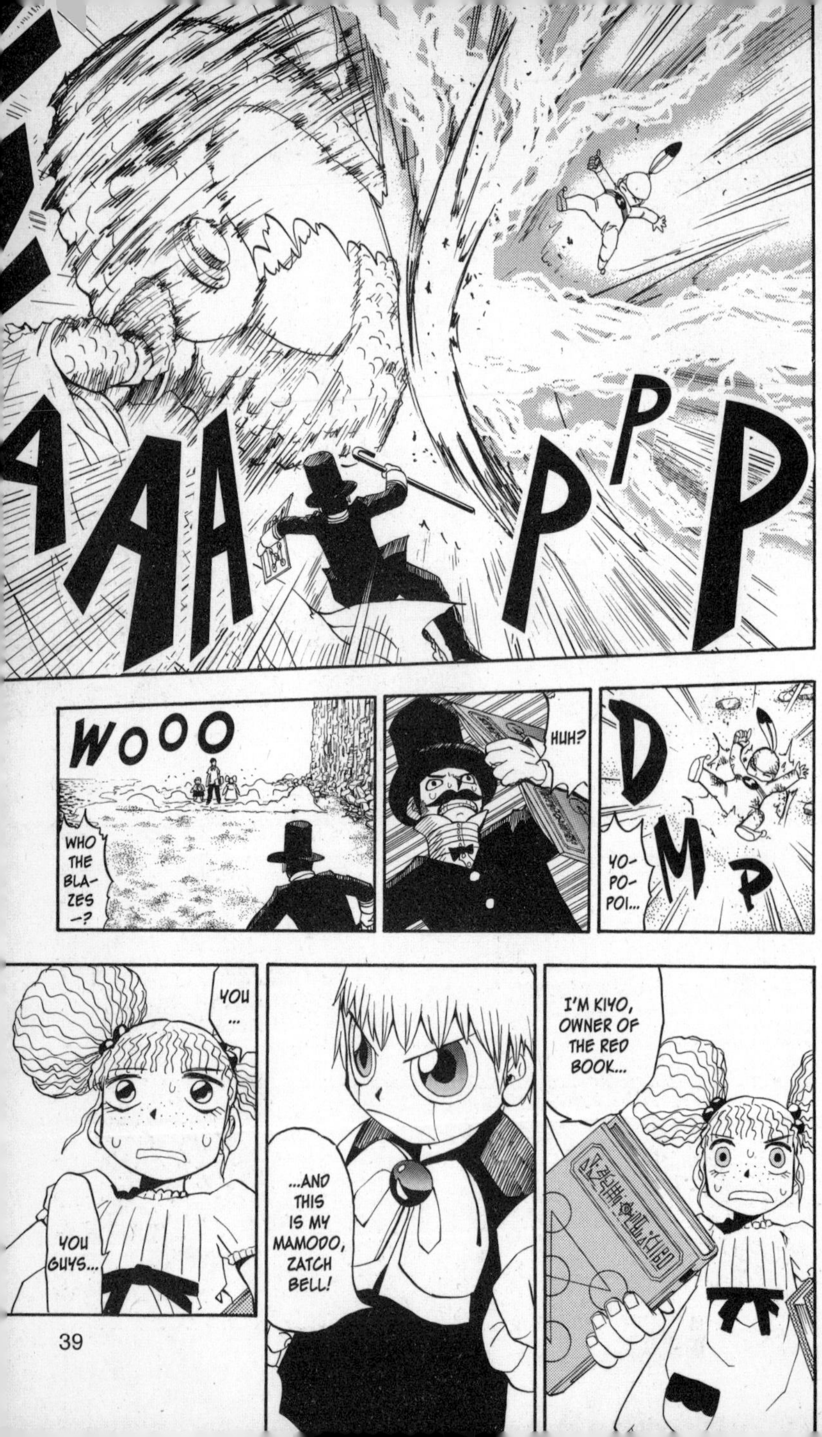
AAAPPPP
YO-PO-POI...
DMP
HUH?
WOOO
WHO THE BLAZES—?
I'M KIYO, OWNER OF THE RED BOOK...
...AND THIS IS MY MAMODO, ZATCH BELL!
YOU...
YOU GUYS...

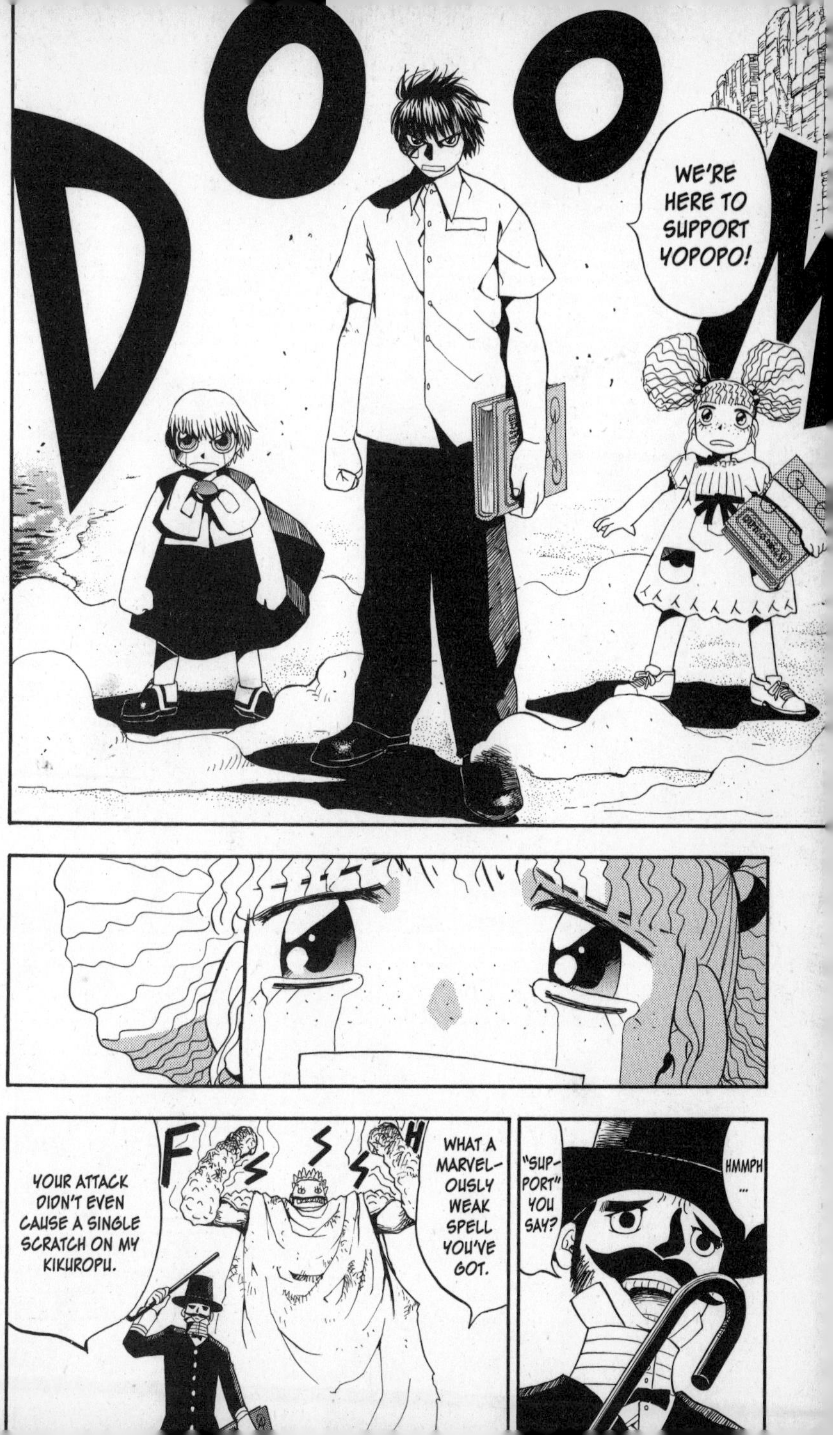
DOOM
WE'RE HERE TO SUPPORT YOPOPO!
HMMPH ...
"SUP-PORT" YOU SAY?
FSSSH
WHAT A MARVEL-OUSLY WEAK SPELL YOU'VE GOT.
YOUR ATTACK DIDN'T EVEN CAUSE A SINGLE SCRATCH ON MY KIKUROPU.

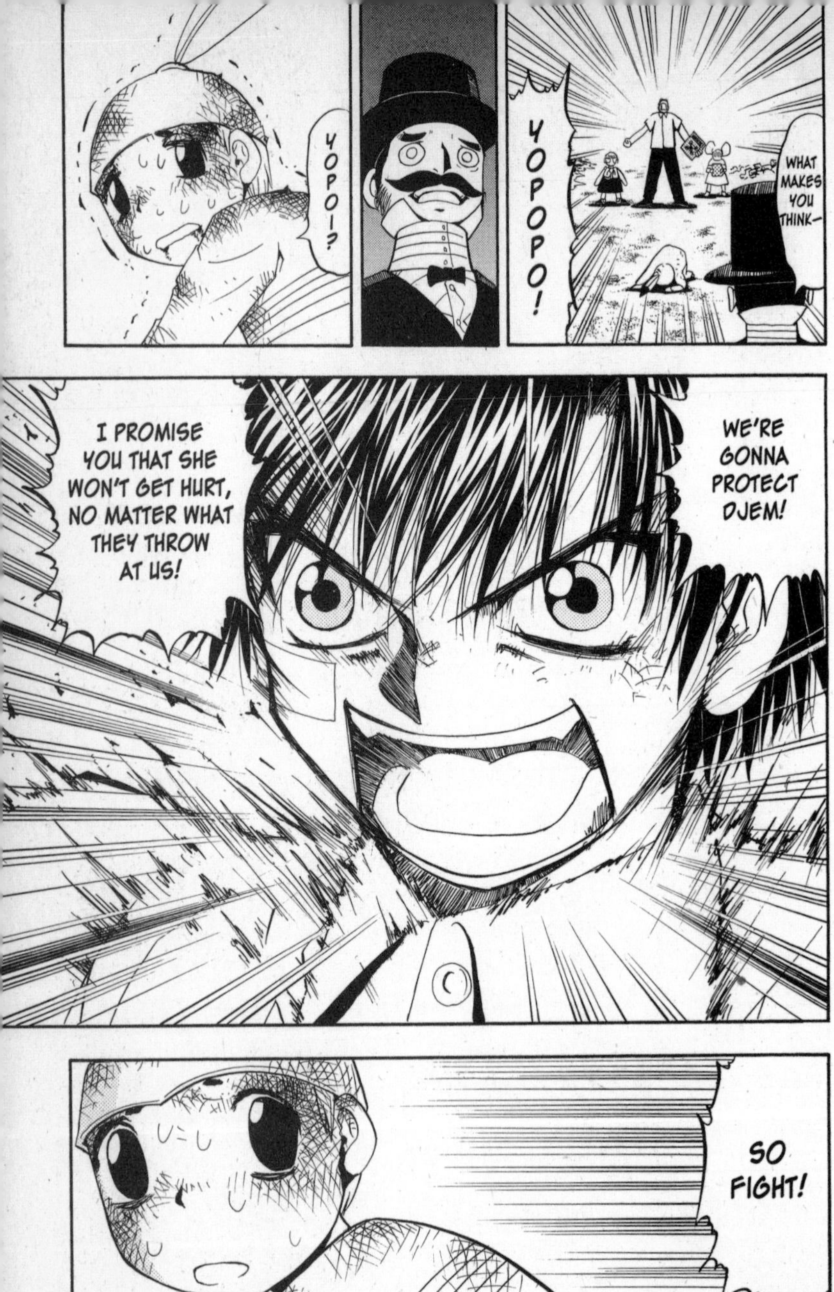
WHAT MAKES YOU THINK—
YOPOPO!
YOPOI?
WE'RE GONNA PROTECT DJEM!
I PROMISE YOU THAT SHE WON'T GET HURT, NO MATTER WHAT THEY THROW AT US!
SO FIGHT!

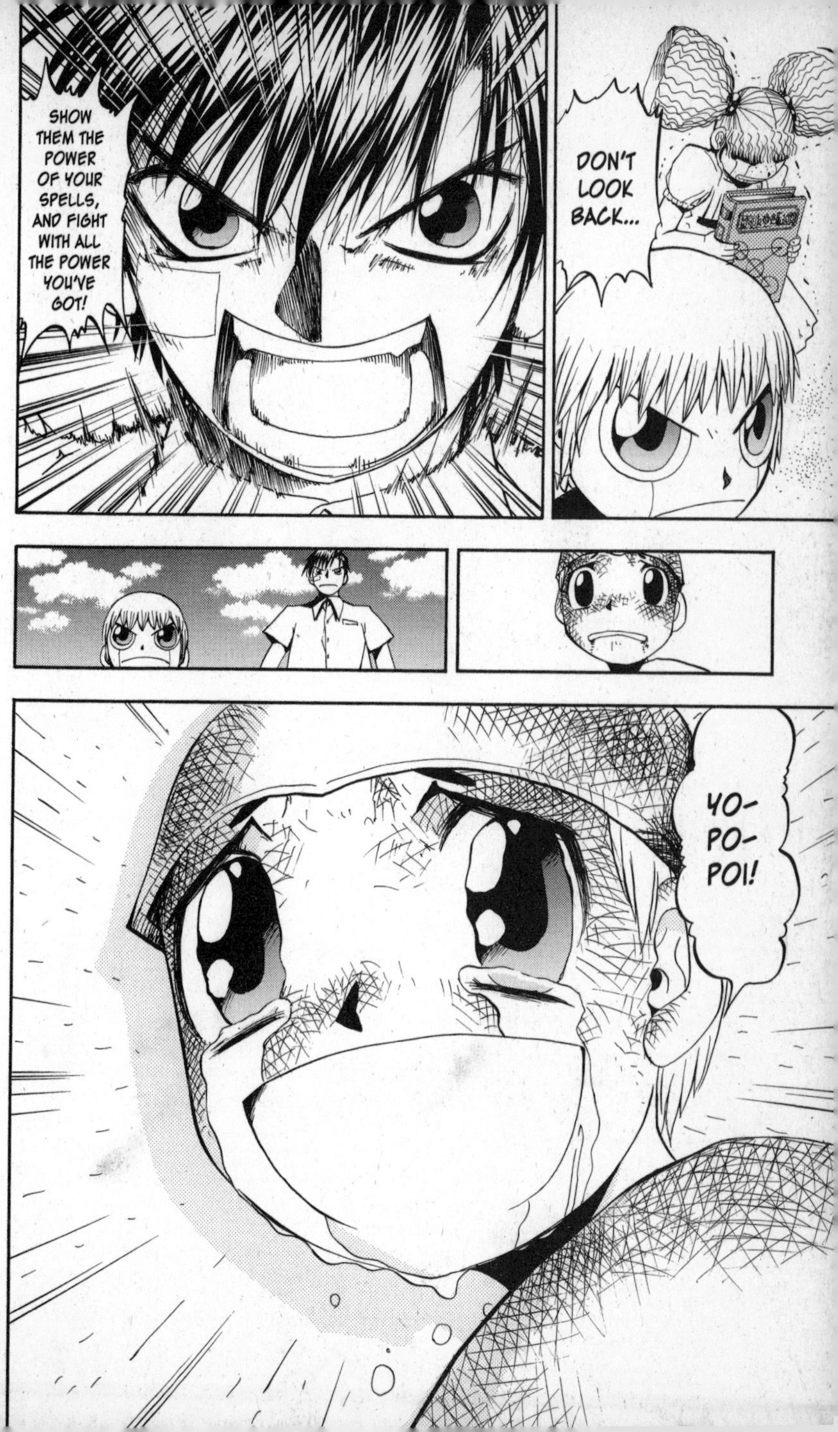
DON'T LOOK BACK...
SHOW THEM THE POWER OF YOUR SPELLS, AND FIGHT WITH ALL THE POWER YOU'VE GOT!
YO-PO-POI!

LEVEL 51: A Warrior's Commitment

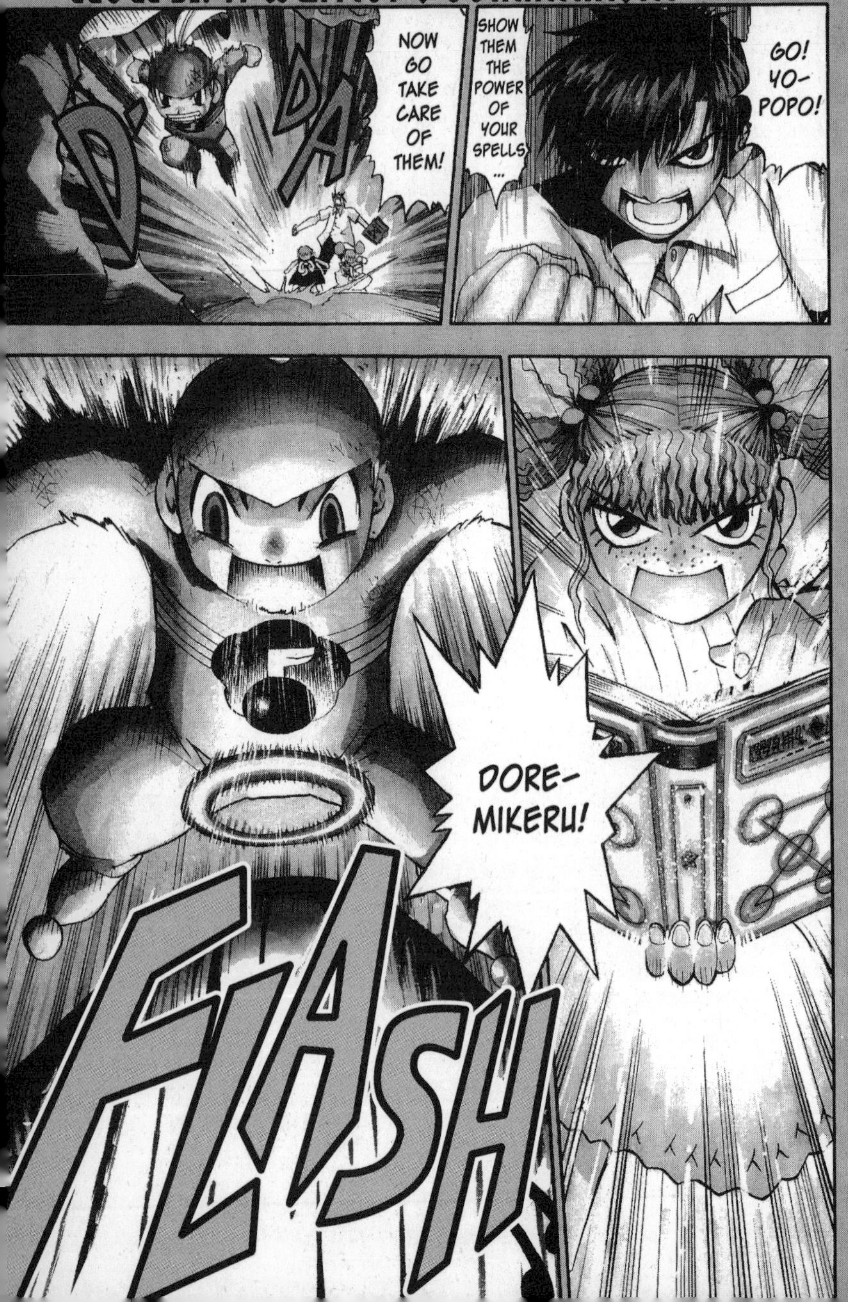
GO! YO-POPO!
SHOW THEM THE POWER OF YOUR SPELLS...
NOW GO TAKE CARE OF THEM!
DA
DORE-MIKERU!
FLASH

LEVEL 51: A Warrior's Commitment

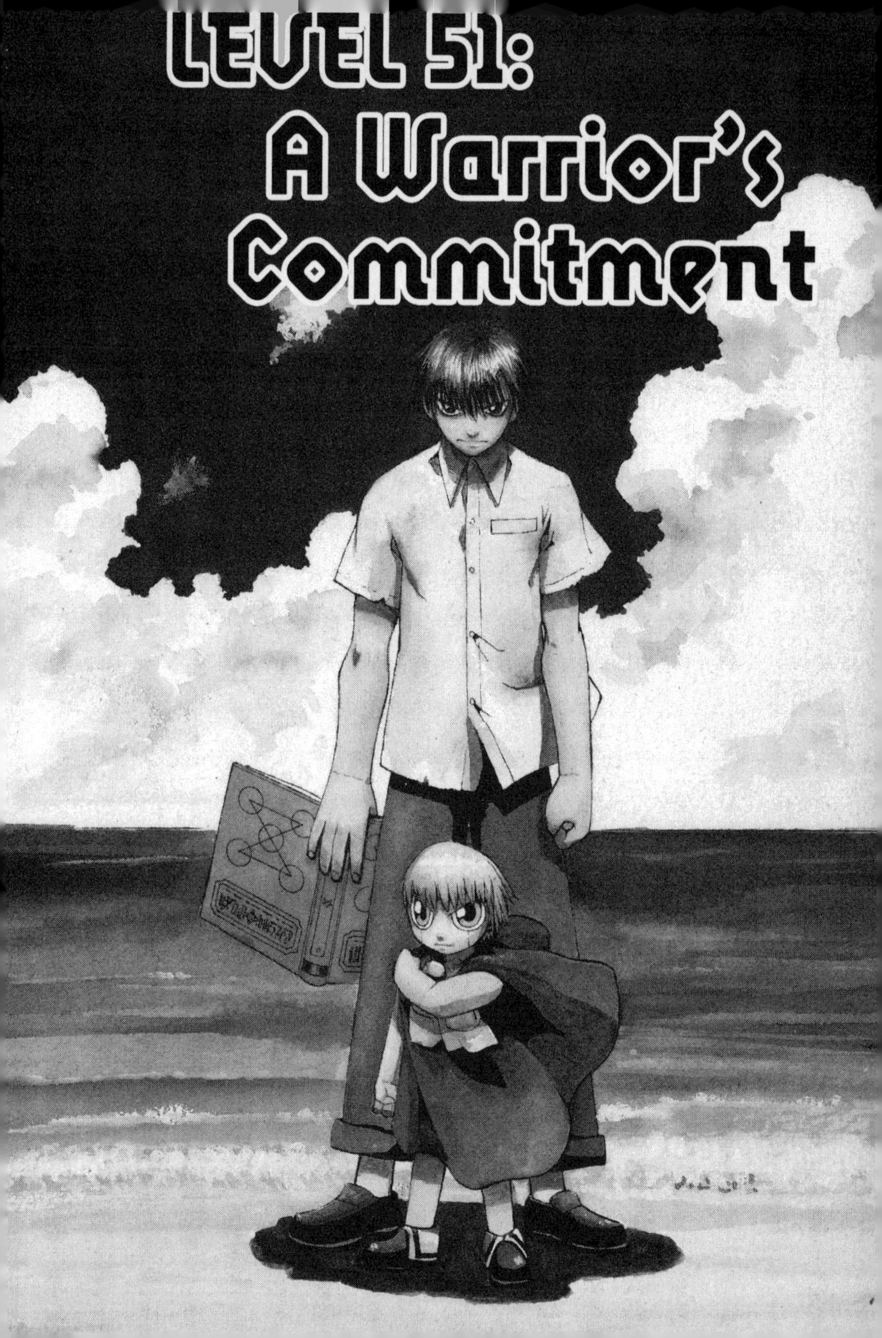

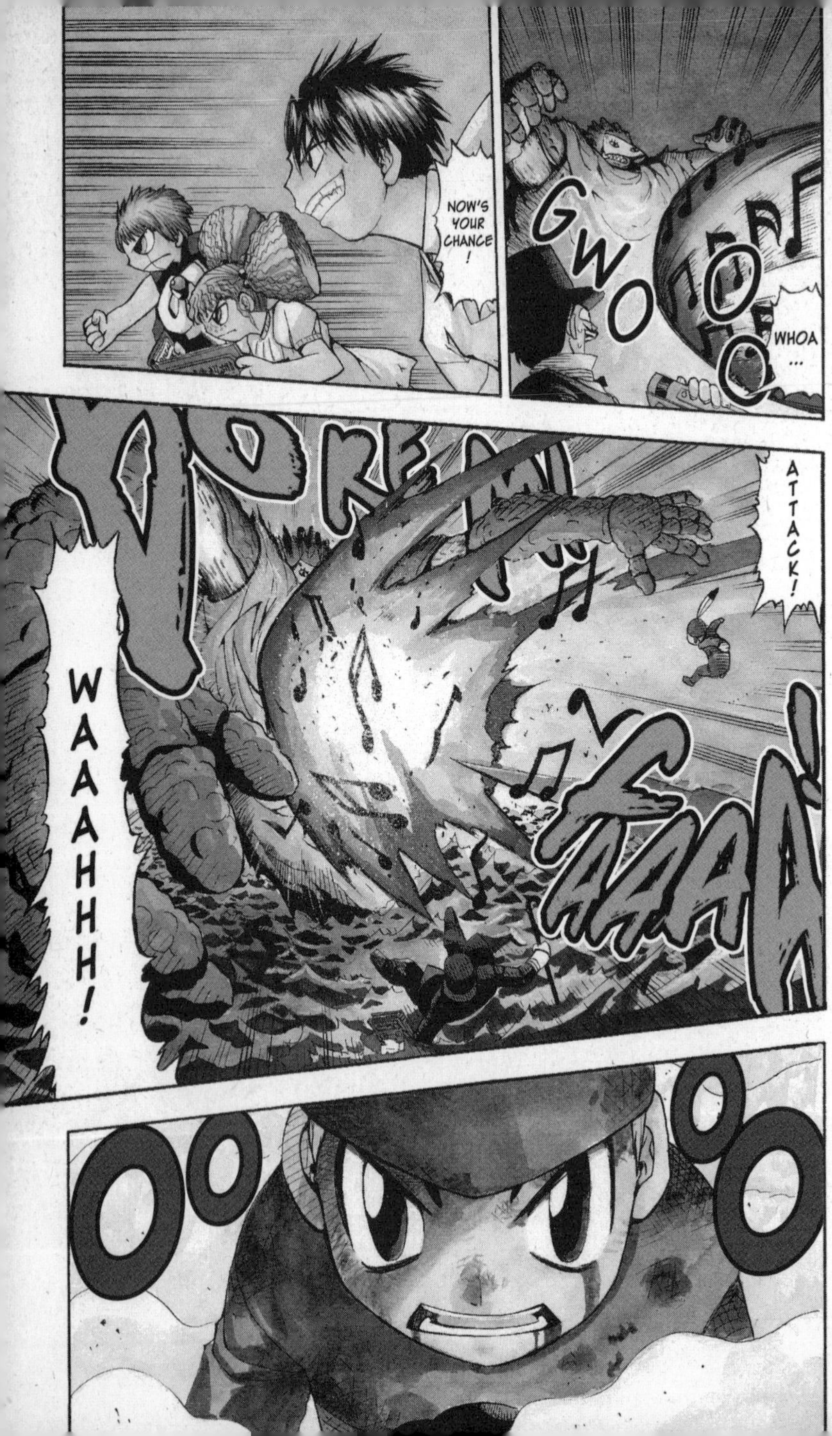
WHOA ...
NOW'S YOUR CHANCE!
ATTACK!
WAAAAHHH!

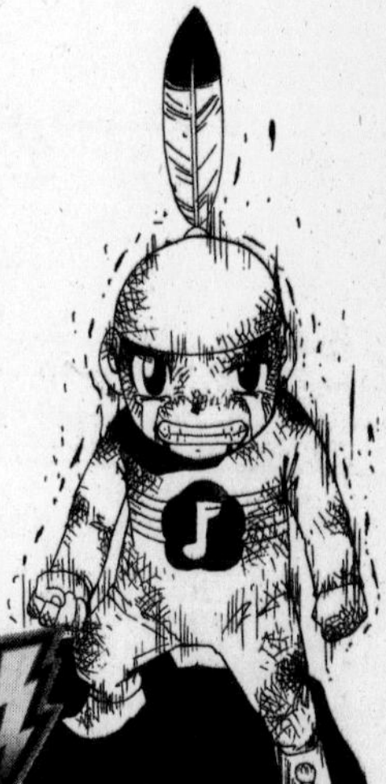

ZATCH BELL!

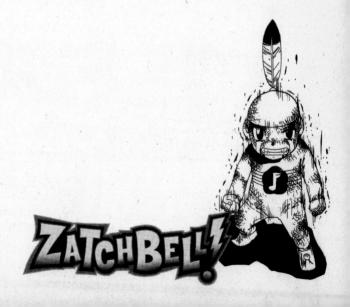

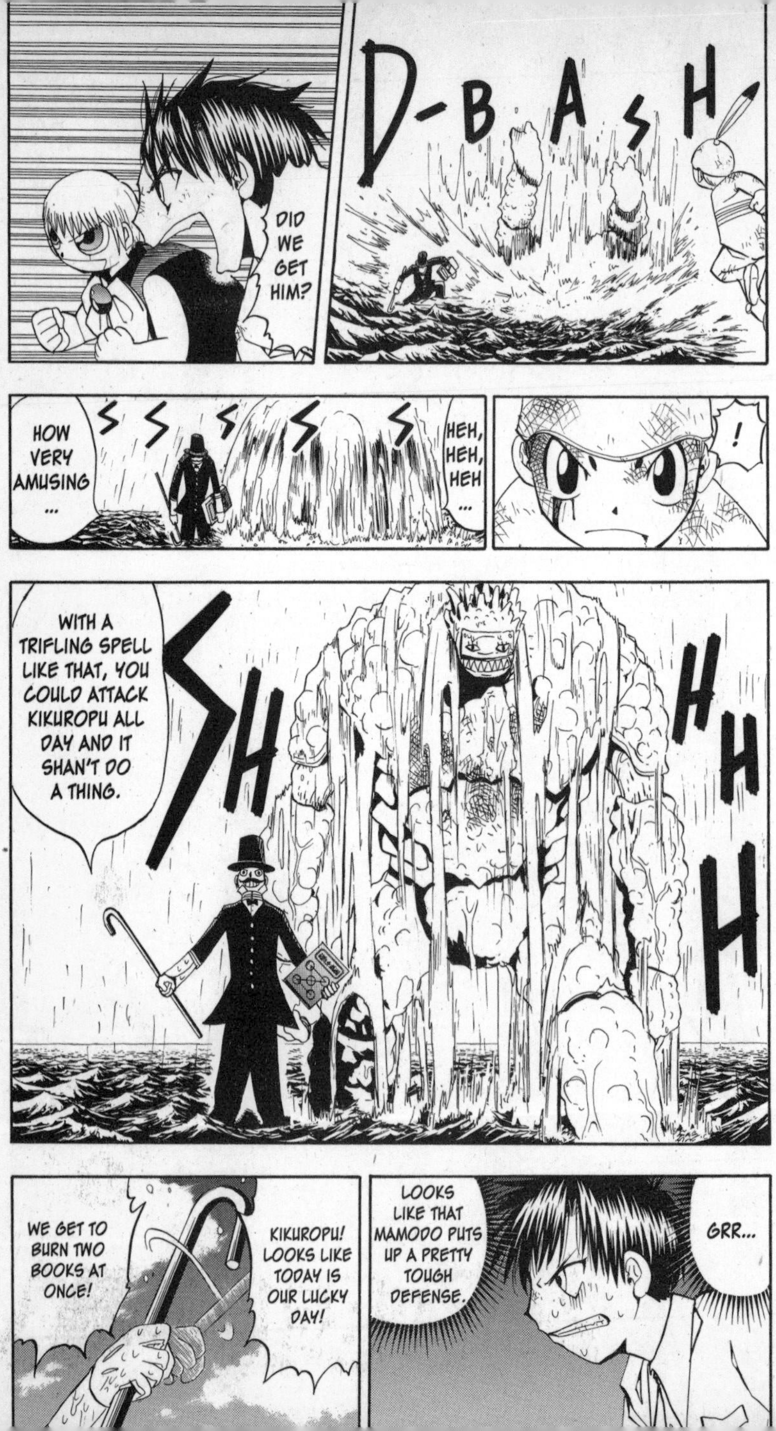
D-BASH
DID WE GET HIM?
!
HEH, HEH, HEH ...
SSSSS
HOW VERY AMUSING ...
SHHHH
WITH A TRIFLING SPELL LIKE THAT, YOU COULD ATTACK KIKUROPU ALL DAY AND IT SHAN'T DO A THING.
GRR...
LOOKS LIKE THAT MAMODO PUTS UP A PRETTY TOUGH DEFENSE.
KIKUROPU! LOOKS LIKE TODAY IS OUR LUCKY DAY!
WE GET TO BURN TWO BOOKS AT ONCE!

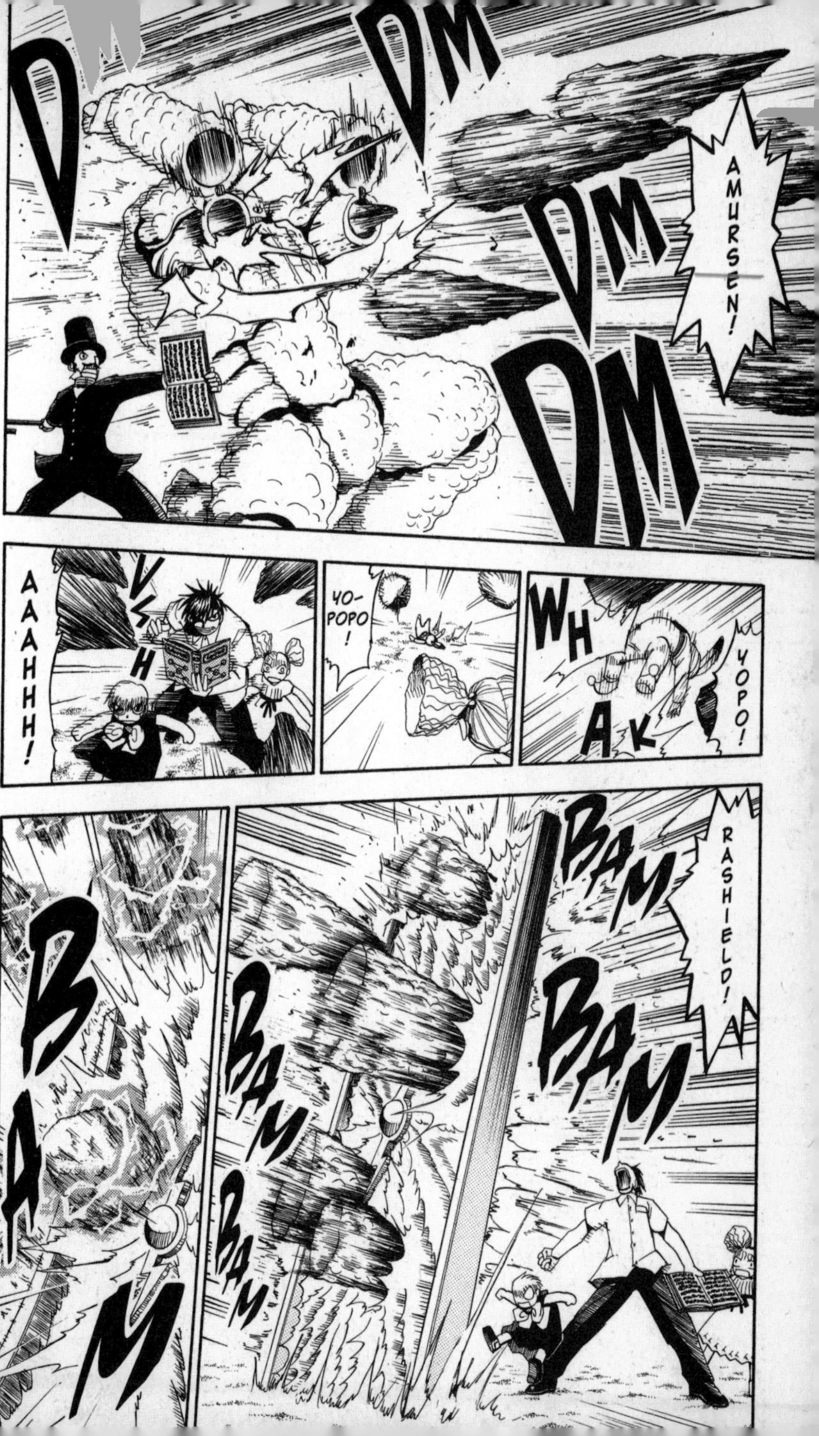
AMURSEN!
DM
DM
DM
DM
D
YOPO!
WHAK
YO-POPO!
VSH
AAAAHHHH!
RASHIELD!
BAM
BAM
BAM
BAM
BAM
BAAM

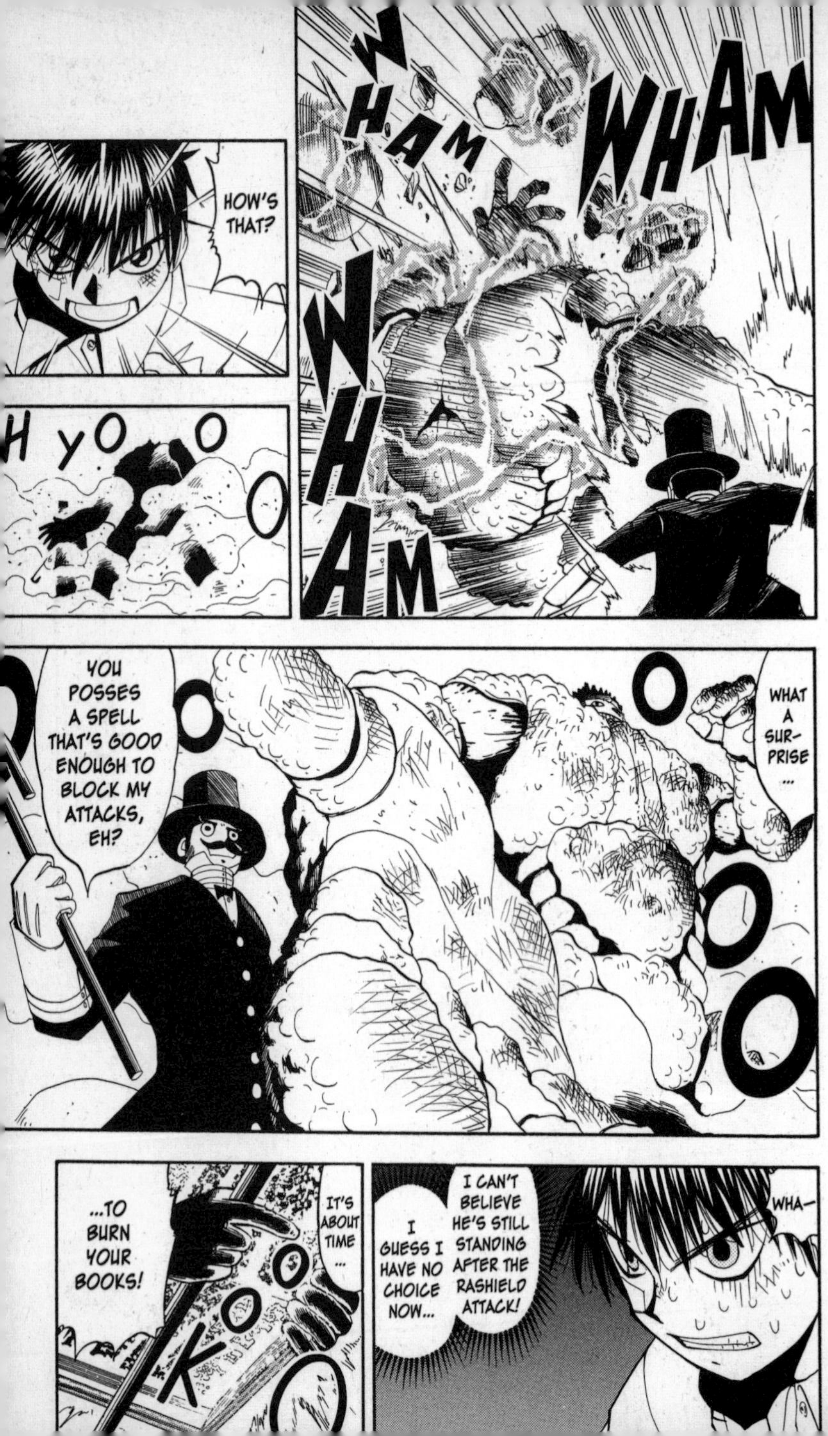
WHAM
WHAM
WHAM
HOW'S THAT?
HYOOO
WHAT A SURPRISE...
YOU POSSES A SPELL THAT'S GOOD ENOUGH TO BLOCK MY ATTACKS, EH?
WHA-
I CAN'T BELIEVE HE'S STILL STANDING AFTER THE RASHIELD ATTACK!
I GUESS I HAVE NO CHOICE NOW...
IT'S ABOUT TIME...
...TO BURN YOUR BOOKS!
K

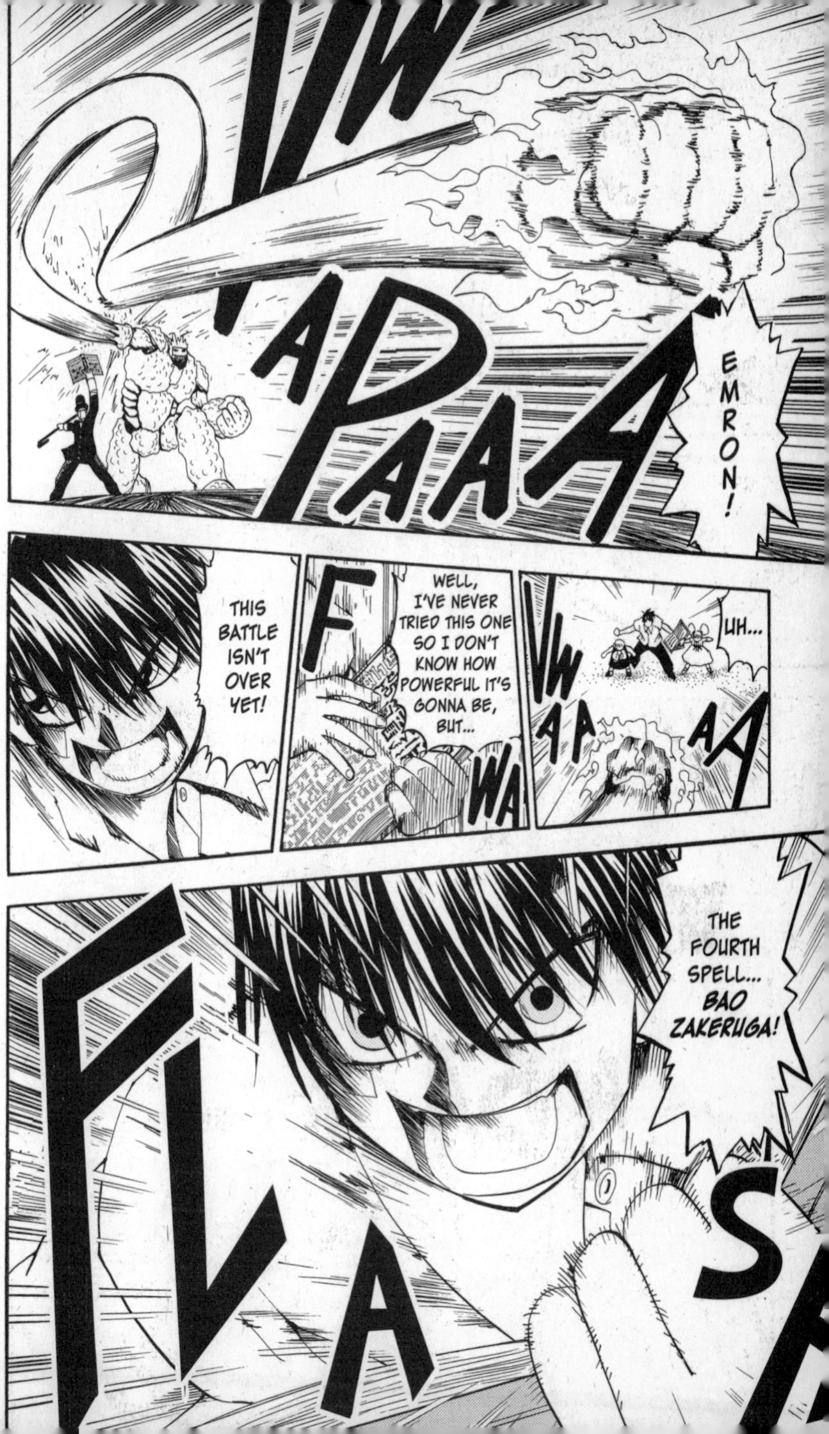
EMRON!
UH...
WELL, I'VE NEVER TRIED THIS ONE SO I DON'T KNOW HOW POWERFUL IT'S GONNA BE, BUT...
THIS BATTLE ISN'T OVER YET!
THE FOURTH SPELL... BAO ZAKERUGA!

WHA
-?

VW

DJEM!

GRR...

WHY?
WHY
ISN'T IT
WORKING
?

N-NO
WAY!

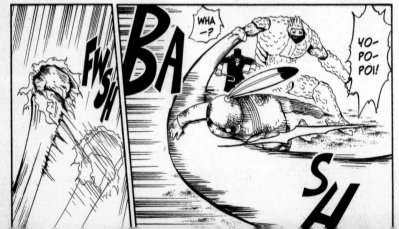

FWSH

BA

WHA
-?

YO-
PO-
POI!

SH

AH!

B-BooM

KYAAAA!

WAHHH!

DMP

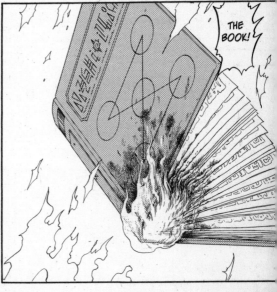

THE BOOK!

YOPOPO'S GONNA DISAPPEAR!

AHH, YOPOPO...

OUCH!

FAP

NO!

NO!

WHA

52

YOPOPO!

I'M SORRY, YOPOPO!

WHAT?

YO-PO-PO!

HEE

...SMI-LING...?

HE'S...

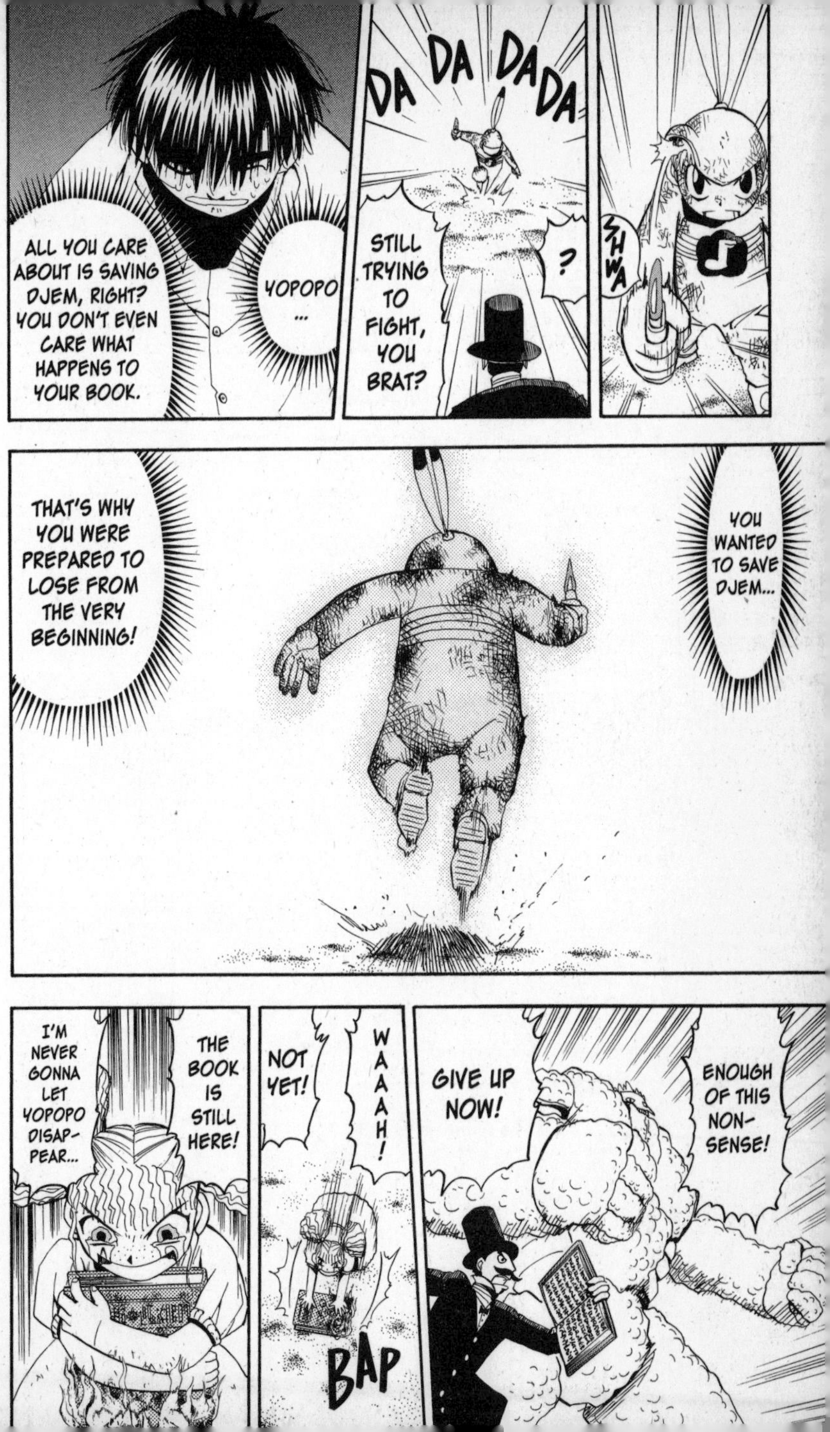

SHWA
DA DA DA DA DA
?
STILL TRYING TO FIGHT, YOU BRAT?
YOPOPO...
ALL YOU CARE ABOUT IS SAVING DJEM, RIGHT? YOU DON'T EVEN CARE WHAT HAPPENS TO YOUR BOOK.
YOU WANTED TO SAVE DJEM...
THAT'S WHY YOU WERE PREPARED TO LOSE FROM THE VERY BEGINNING!
ENOUGH OF THIS NON-SENSE!
GIVE UP NOW!
WAAAAH!
NOT YET!
BAP
THE BOOK IS STILL HERE!
I'M NEVER GONNA LET YOPOPO DISAP-PEAR...

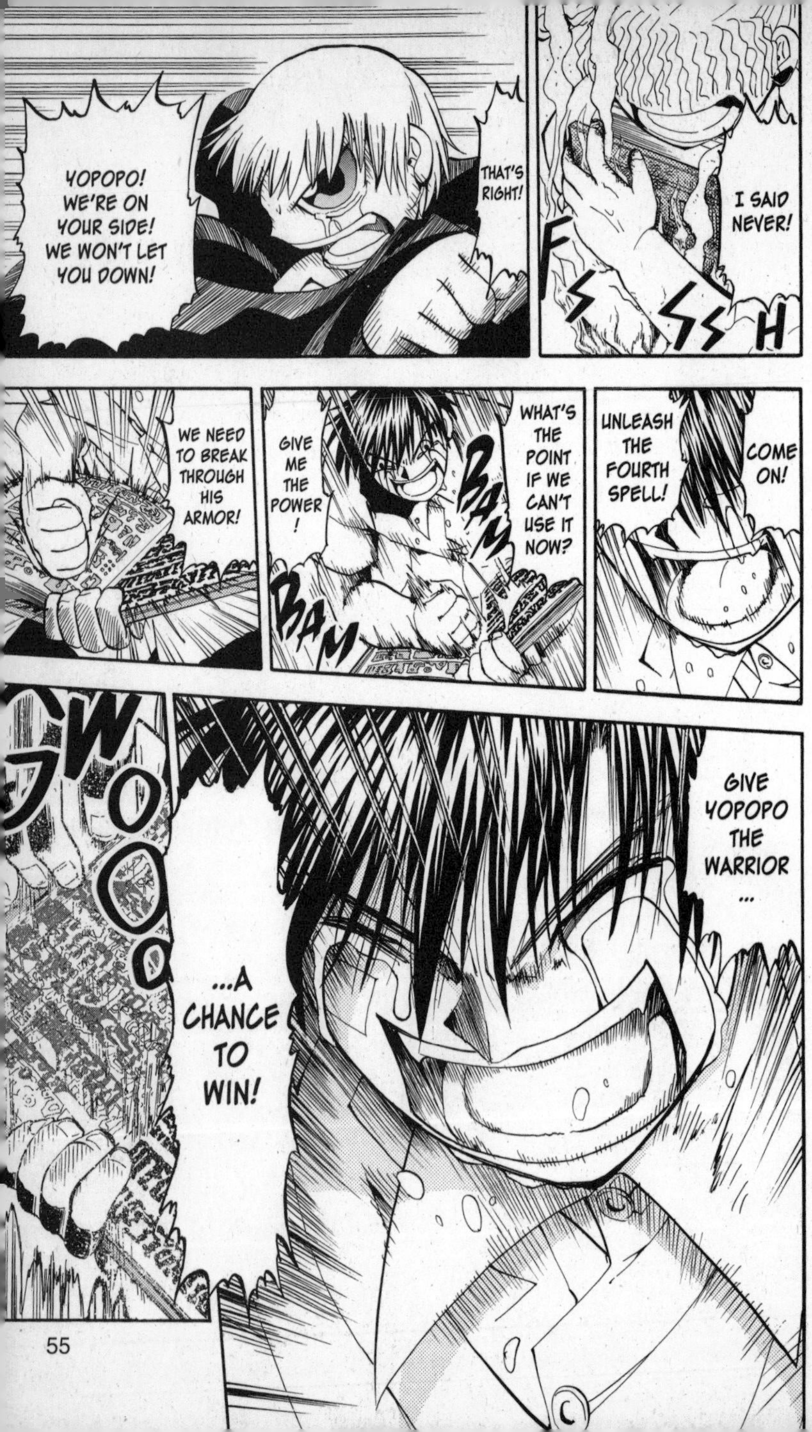
I SAID NEVER!
FSSSH
THAT'S RIGHT!
YOPOPO! WE'RE ON YOUR SIDE! WE WON'T LET YOU DOWN!
COME ON!
UNLEASH THE FOURTH SPELL!
WHAT'S THE POINT IF WE CAN'T USE IT NOW?
BAM
GIVE ME THE POWER!
BAM
WE NEED TO BREAK THROUGH HIS ARMOR!
GIVE YOPOPO THE WARRIOR...
GWOOOO
...A CHANCE TO WIN!

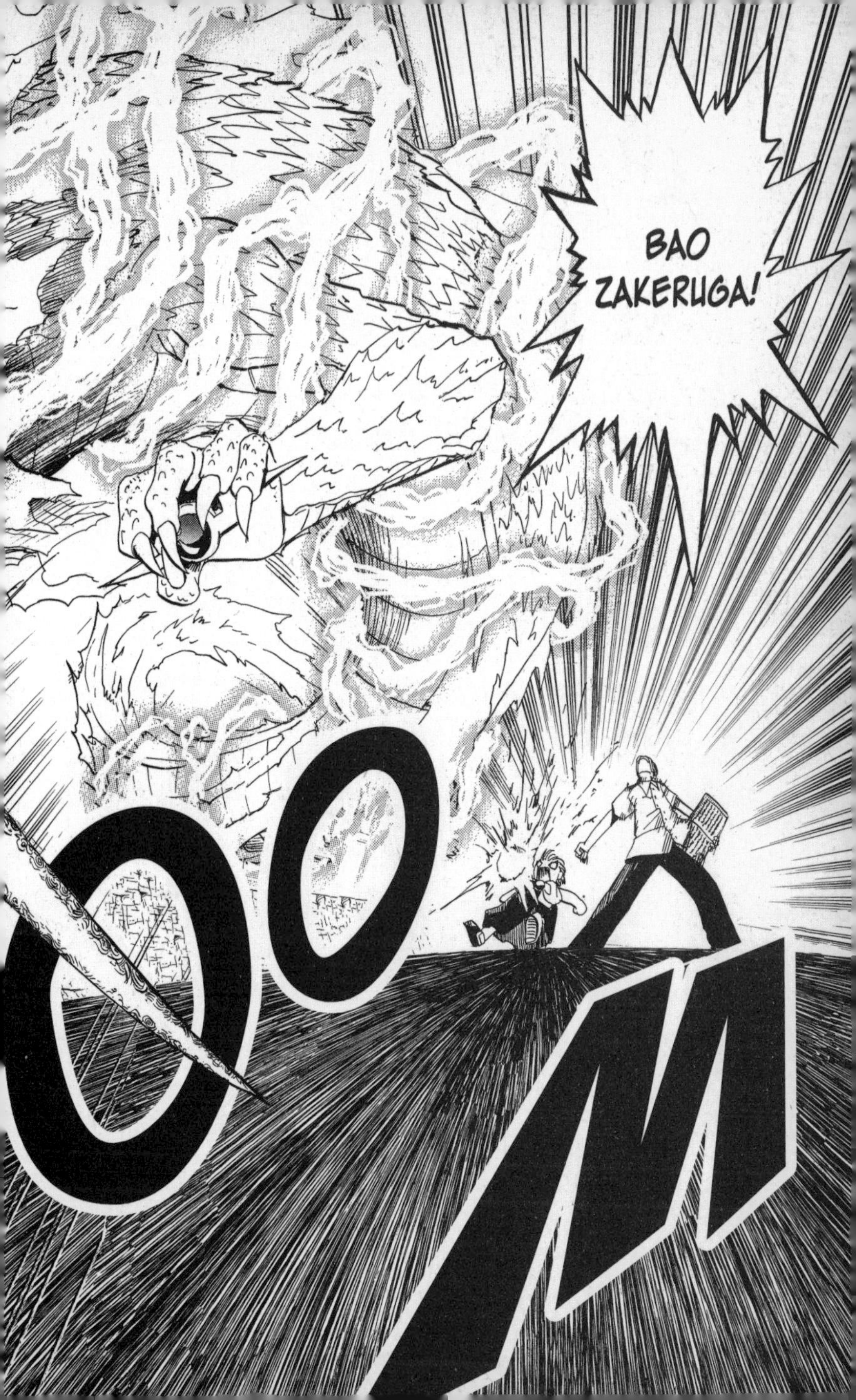
BAO ZAKERUGA!
OOM

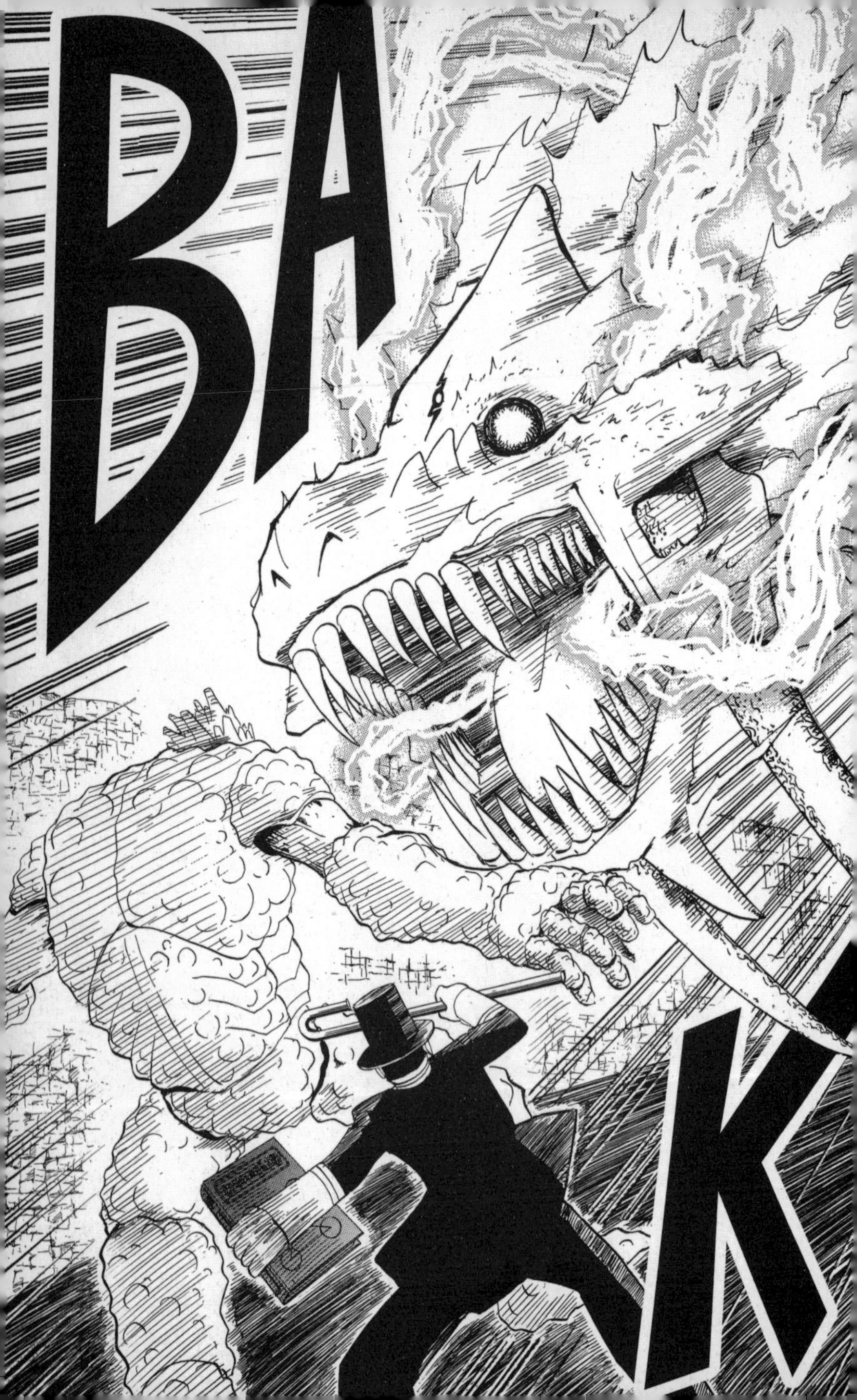
BA
K

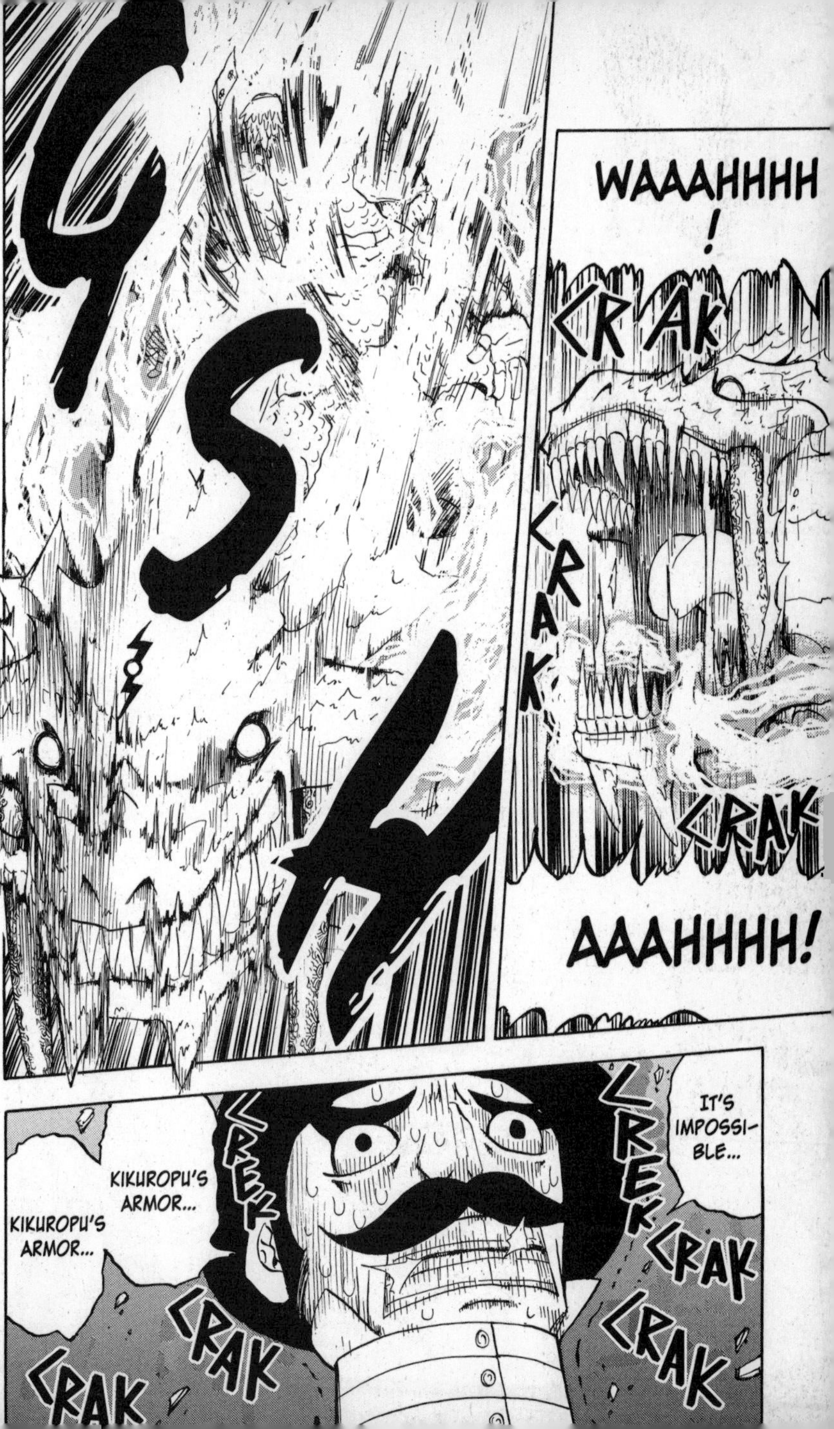
WAAAHHHH
!
CRAK
CRAK
CRAK
AAAHHHH!
IT'S IMPOSSI-BLE...
CREK
CRAK
CRAK
KIKUROPU'S ARMOR...
KIKUROPU'S ARMOR...
CREK
CRAK
CRAK

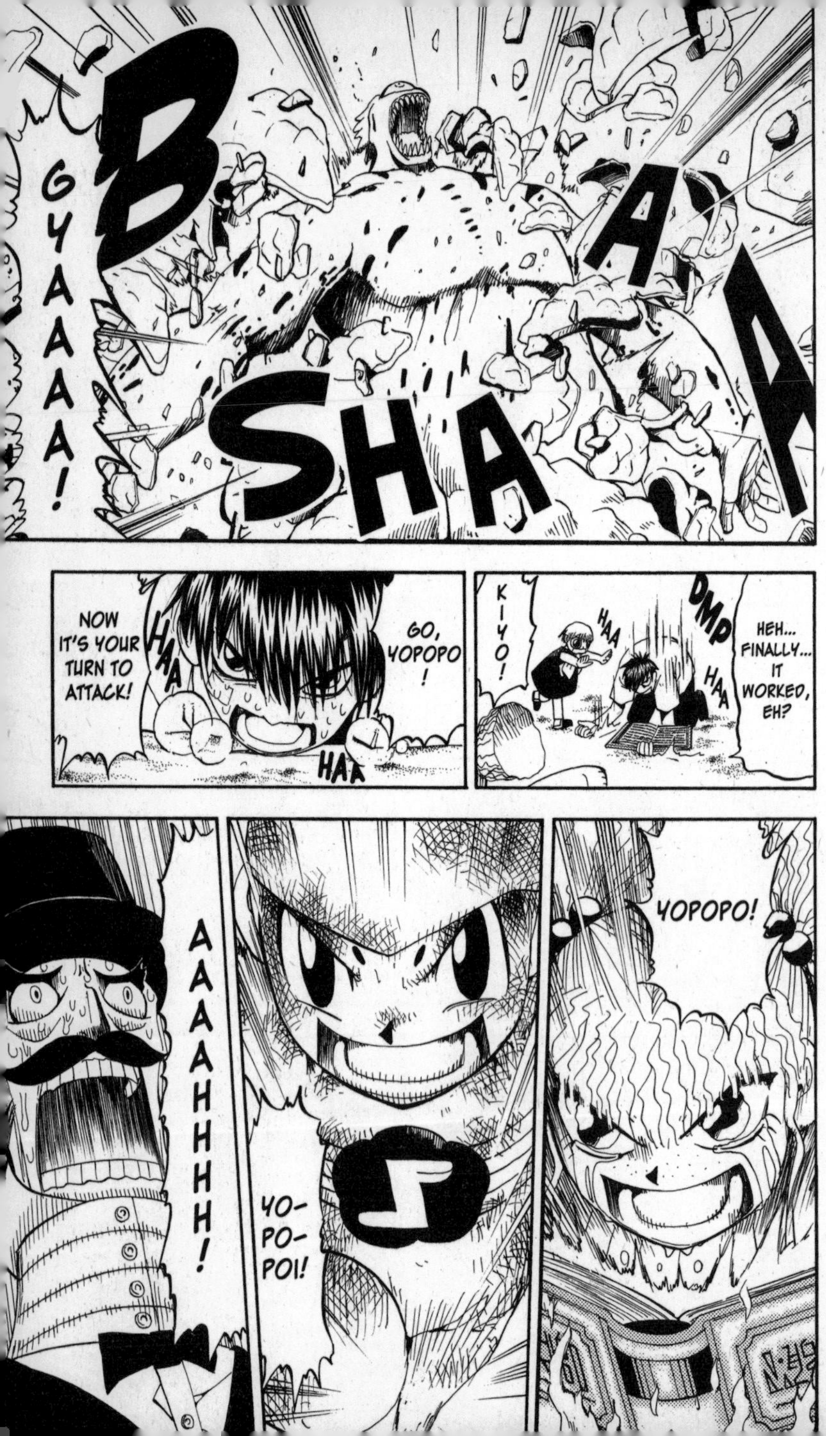
B
AA
SHA
GYAAAAA!
HEH... FINALLY... IT WORKED, EH?
HAA
DMP
HAA
KIYO!
GO, YOPOPO!
NOW IT'S YOUR TURN TO ATTACK!
HAA
HAA
YOPOPO!
YO-PO-POI!
AAAAHHHH!

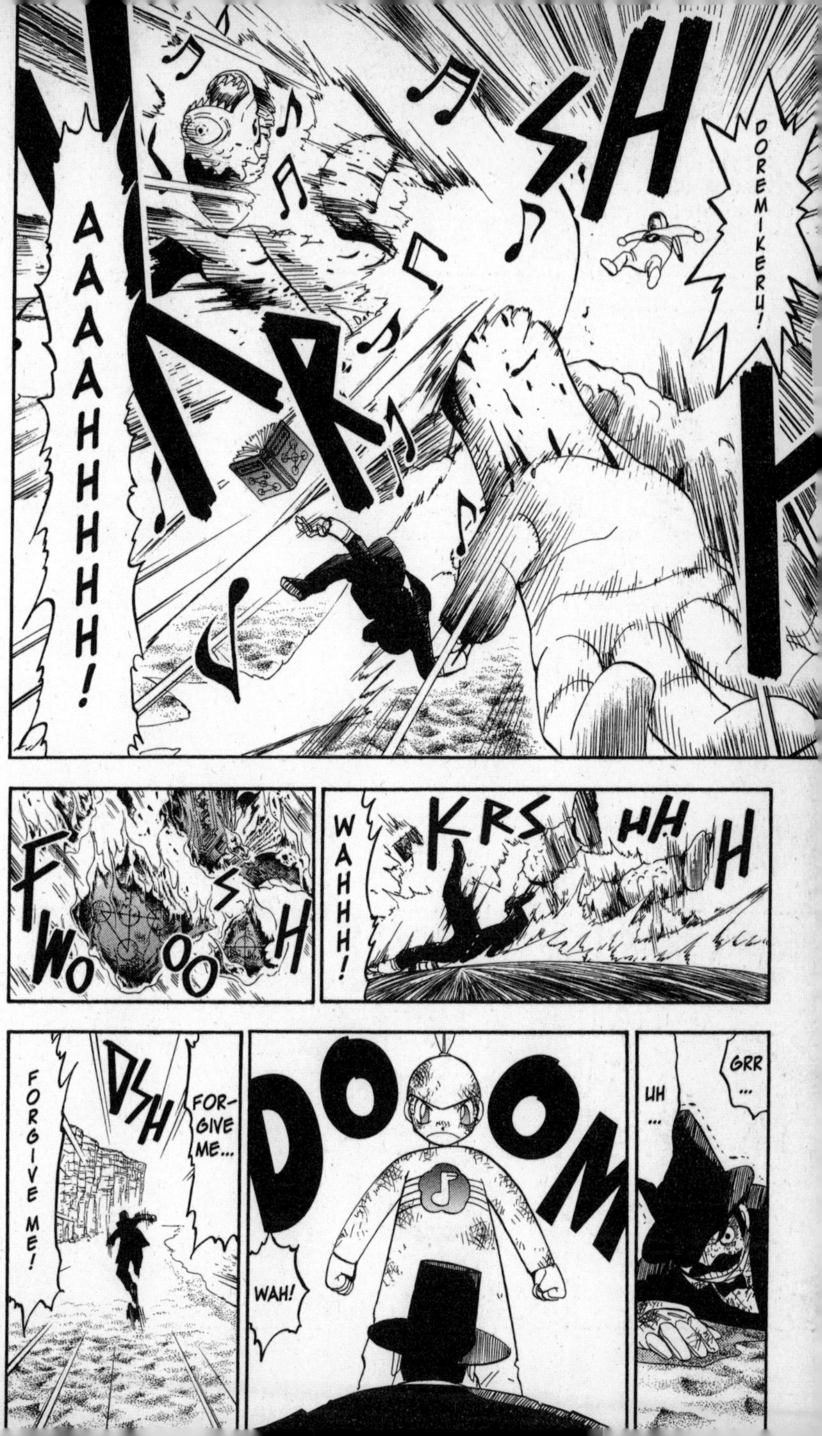
DOREMIKERU!
SH
KR
AAAAHHHHHH!
KRS HH H
WAHHHH!
FWOOOSH
GRR...
UH...
DOOOM
WAH!
FOR-GIVE ME...
FORGIVE ME!
DSH

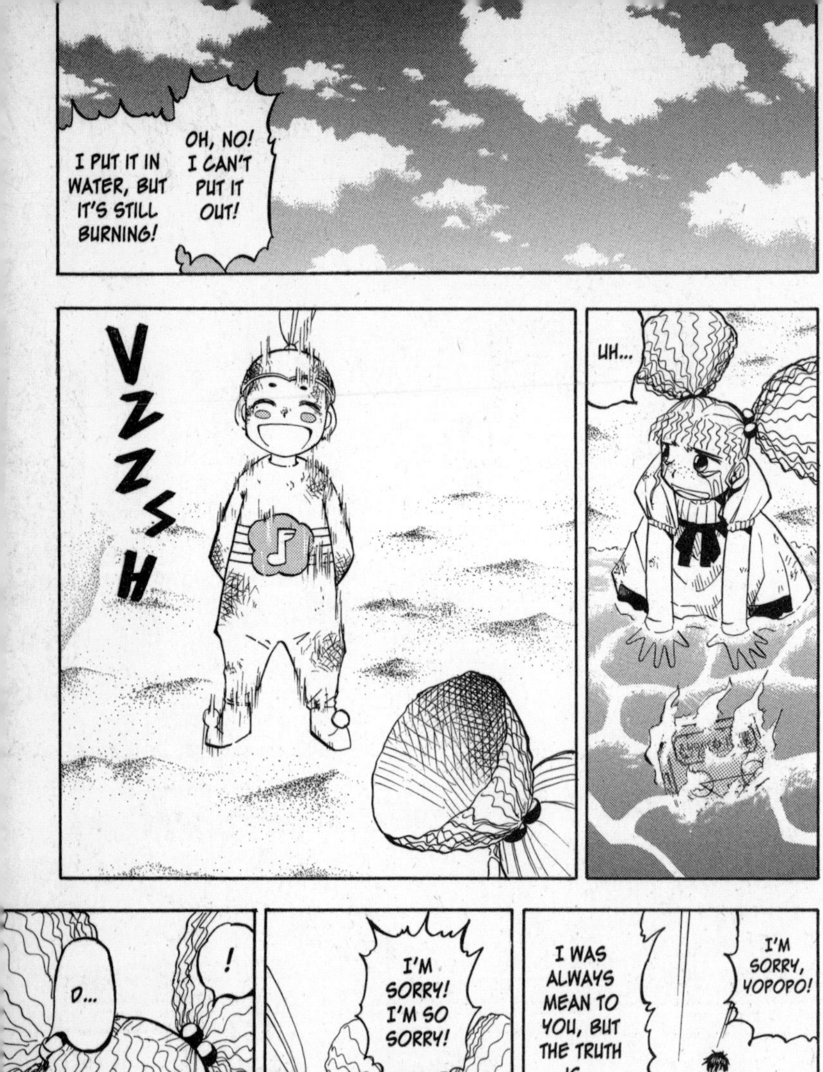
OH, NO! I CAN'T PUT IT OUT!
I PUT IT IN WATER, BUT IT'S STILL BURNING!
UH...
VZZSH
I'M SORRY, YOPOPO!
I WAS ALWAYS MEAN TO YOU, BUT THE TRUTH IS...
I'M SORRY! I'M SO SORRY!
TAP
!
O...

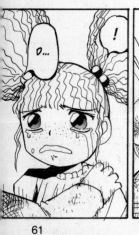

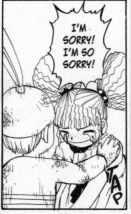

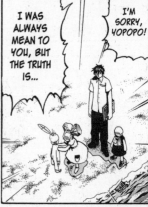

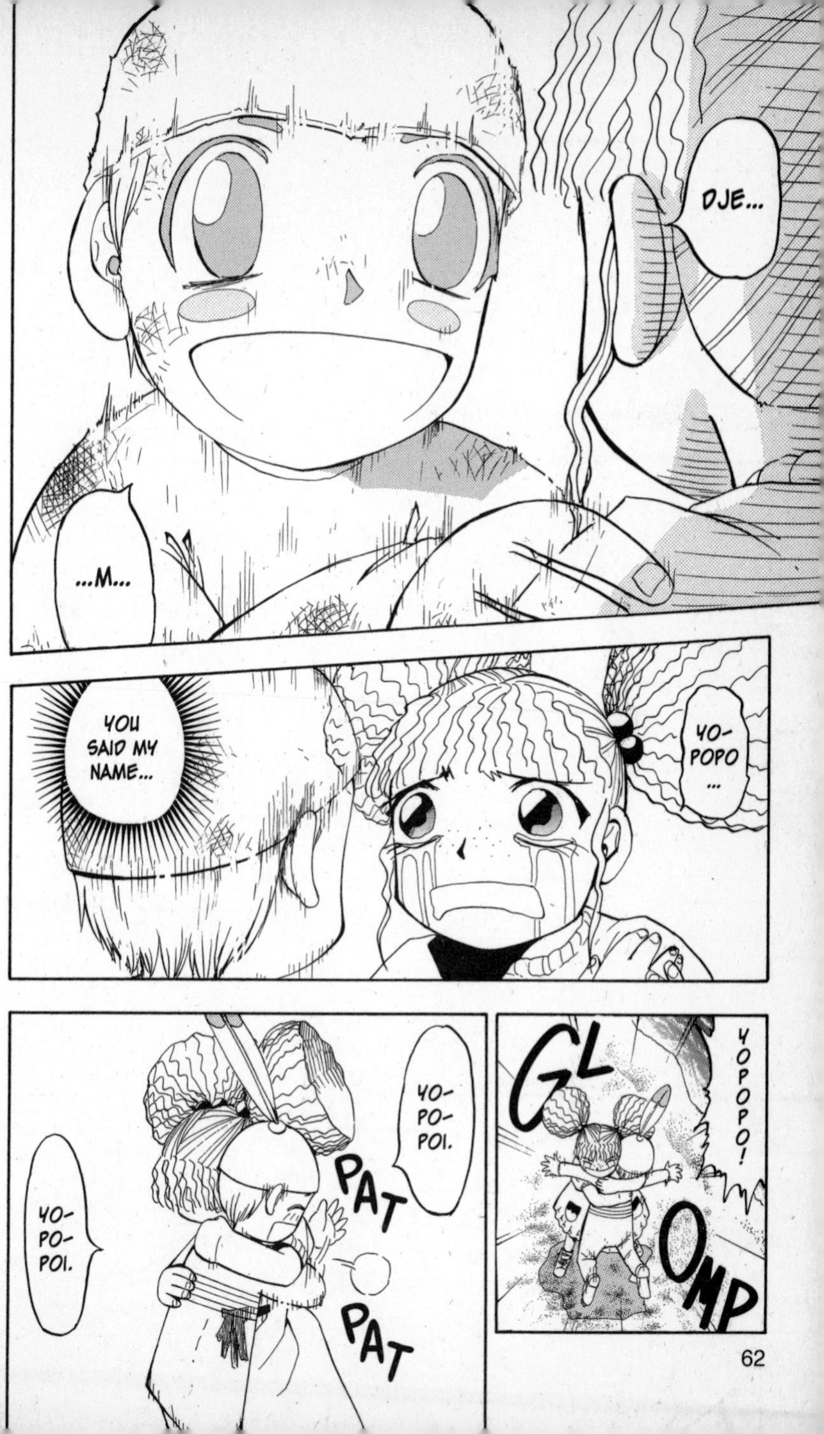
DJE...
...M...
YO-POPO ...
YOU SAID MY NAME...
GL OMP
YOPOPO!
YO-PO-POI.
PAT PAT
YO-PO-POI.

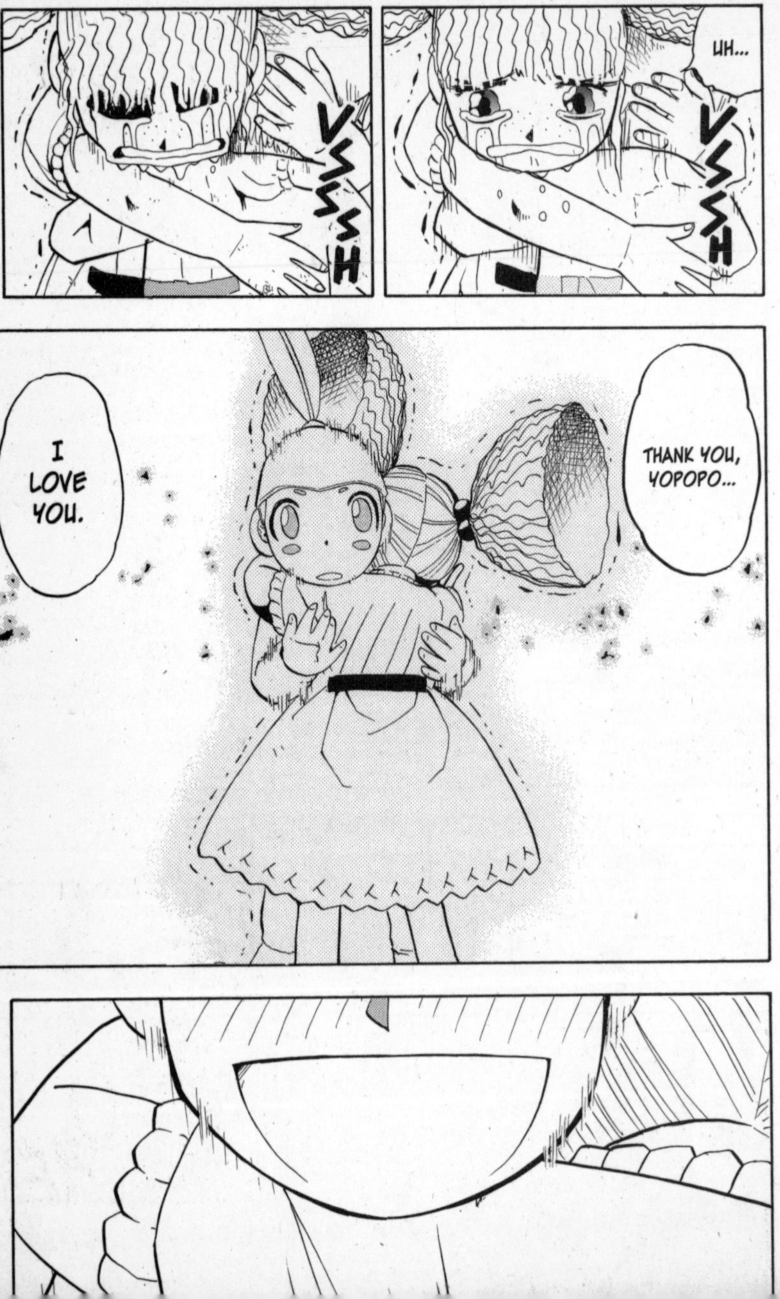
UH...
VSSSH
VSSSH
THANK YOU, YOPOPO...
I LOVE YOU.

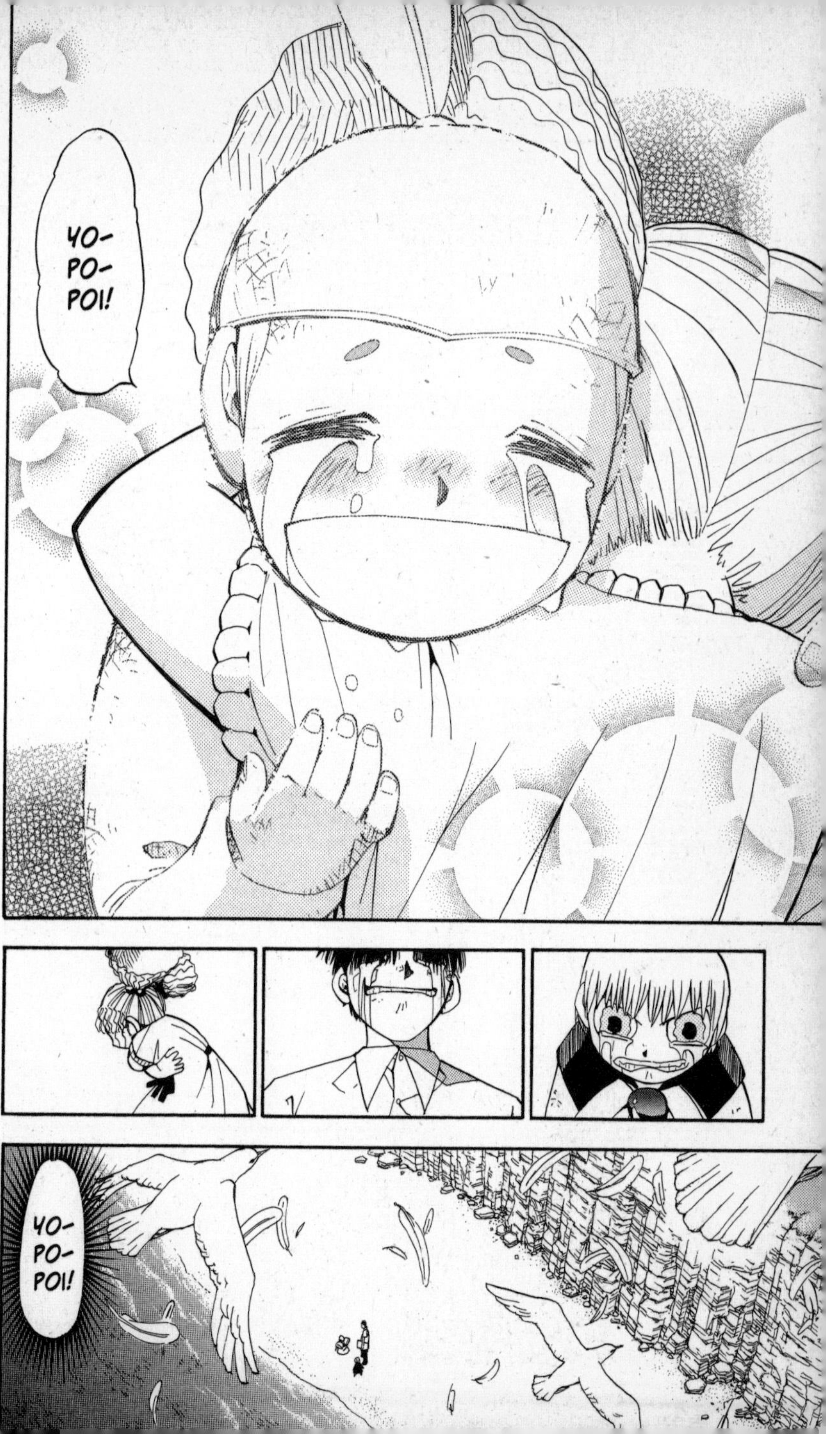
YO-PO-POI!
YO-PO-POI!

LEVEL 52: The Unwanted Reunion

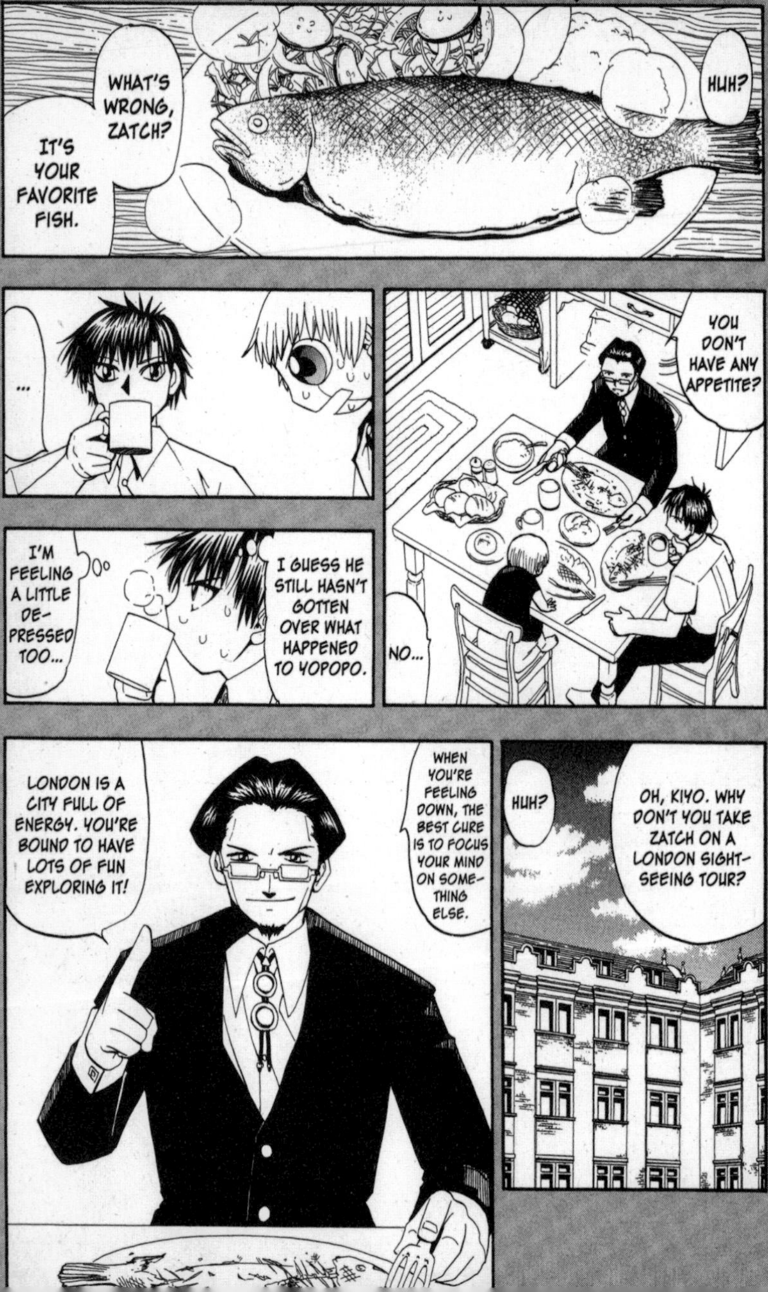
WHAT'S WRONG, ZATCH?
IT'S YOUR FAVORITE FISH.
HUH?
YOU DON'T HAVE ANY APPETITE?
NO...
...
I GUESS HE STILL HASN'T GOTTEN OVER WHAT HAPPENED TO YOPOPO.
I'M FEELING A LITTLE DE-PRESSED TOO...
OH, KIYO. WHY DON'T YOU TAKE ZATCH ON A LONDON SIGHT-SEEING TOUR?
HUH?
WHEN YOU'RE FEELING DOWN, THE BEST CURE IS TO FOCUS YOUR MIND ON SOME-THING ELSE.
LONDON IS A CITY FULL OF ENERGY. YOU'RE BOUND TO HAVE LOTS OF FUN EXPLORING IT!

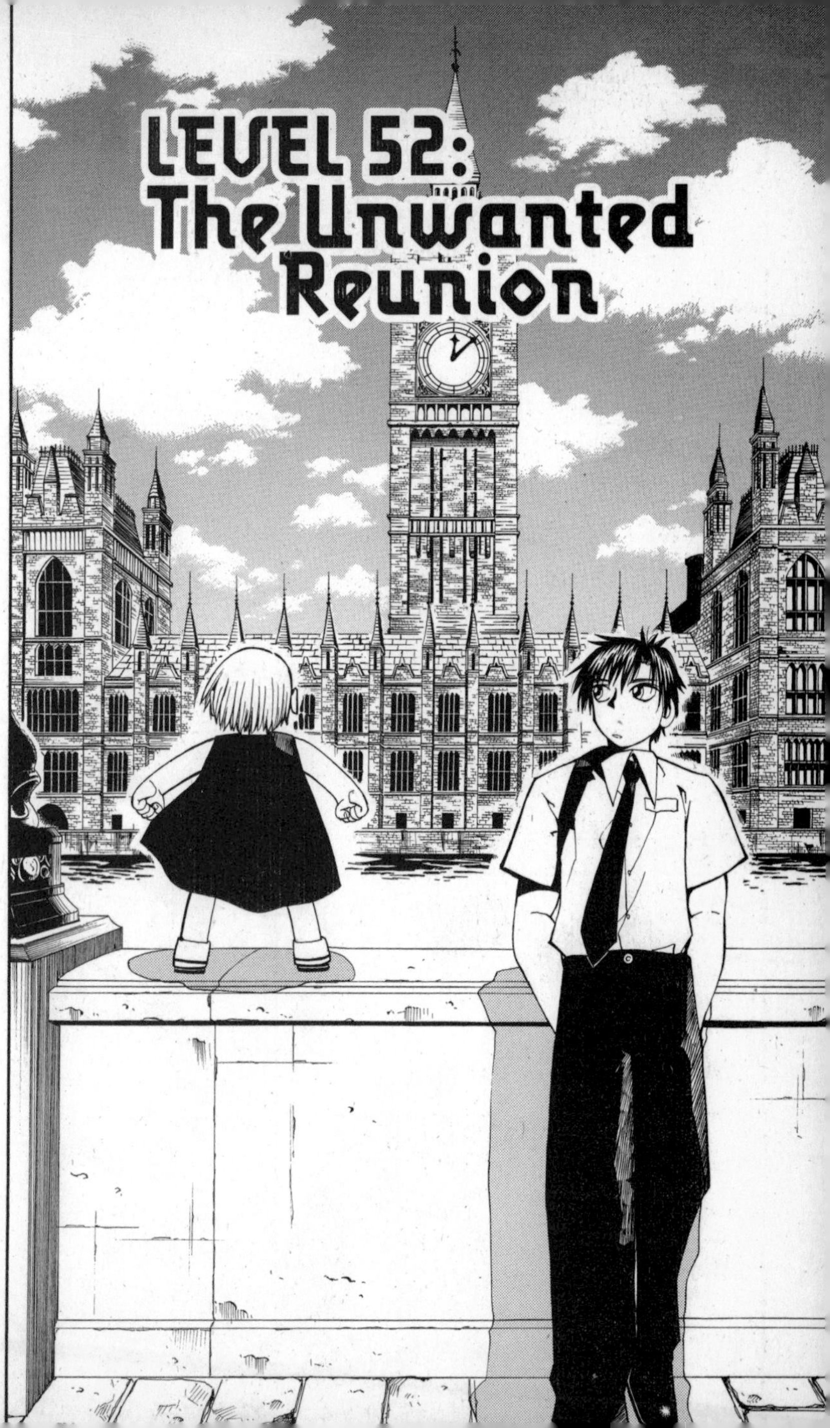
LEVEL 52:
The Unwanted Reunion

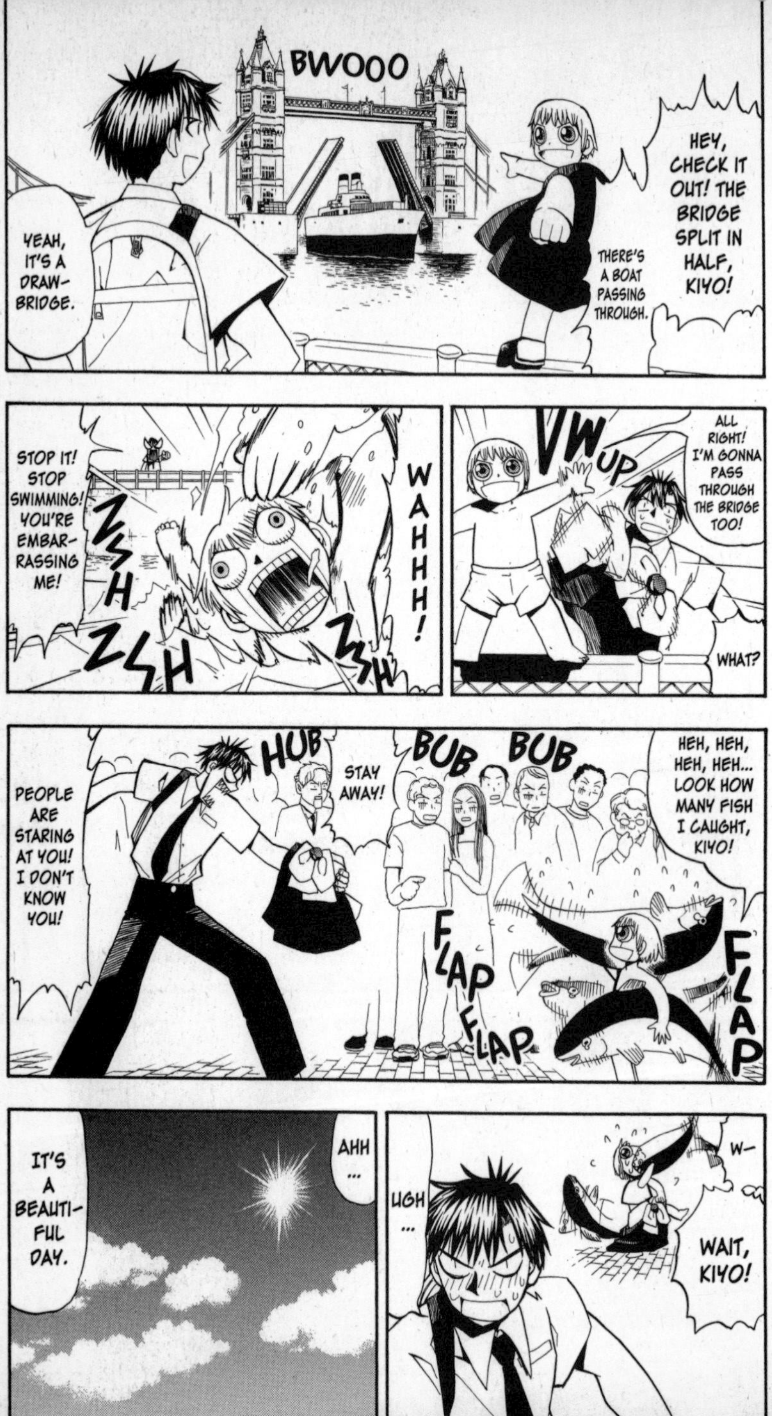
HEY, CHECK IT OUT! THE BRIDGE SPLIT IN HALF, KIYO!
THERE'S A BOAT PASSING THROUGH.
BWOOO
YEAH, IT'S A DRAW-BRIDGE.
ALL RIGHT! I'M GONNA PASS THROUGH THE BRIDGE TOO!
VWUP
WHAT?
WAHHHH!
ZSH
STOP IT! STOP SWIMMING! YOU'RE EMBAR-RASSING ME!
ZSH
ZSH
HEH, HEH, HEH, HEH... LOOK HOW MANY FISH I CAUGHT, KIYO!
FLAP
BUB
BUB
FLAP
FLAP
STAY AWAY!
HUB
PEOPLE ARE STARING AT YOU! I DON'T KNOW YOU!
W-
WAIT, KIYO!
UGH...
AHH...
IT'S A BEAUTI-FUL DAY.

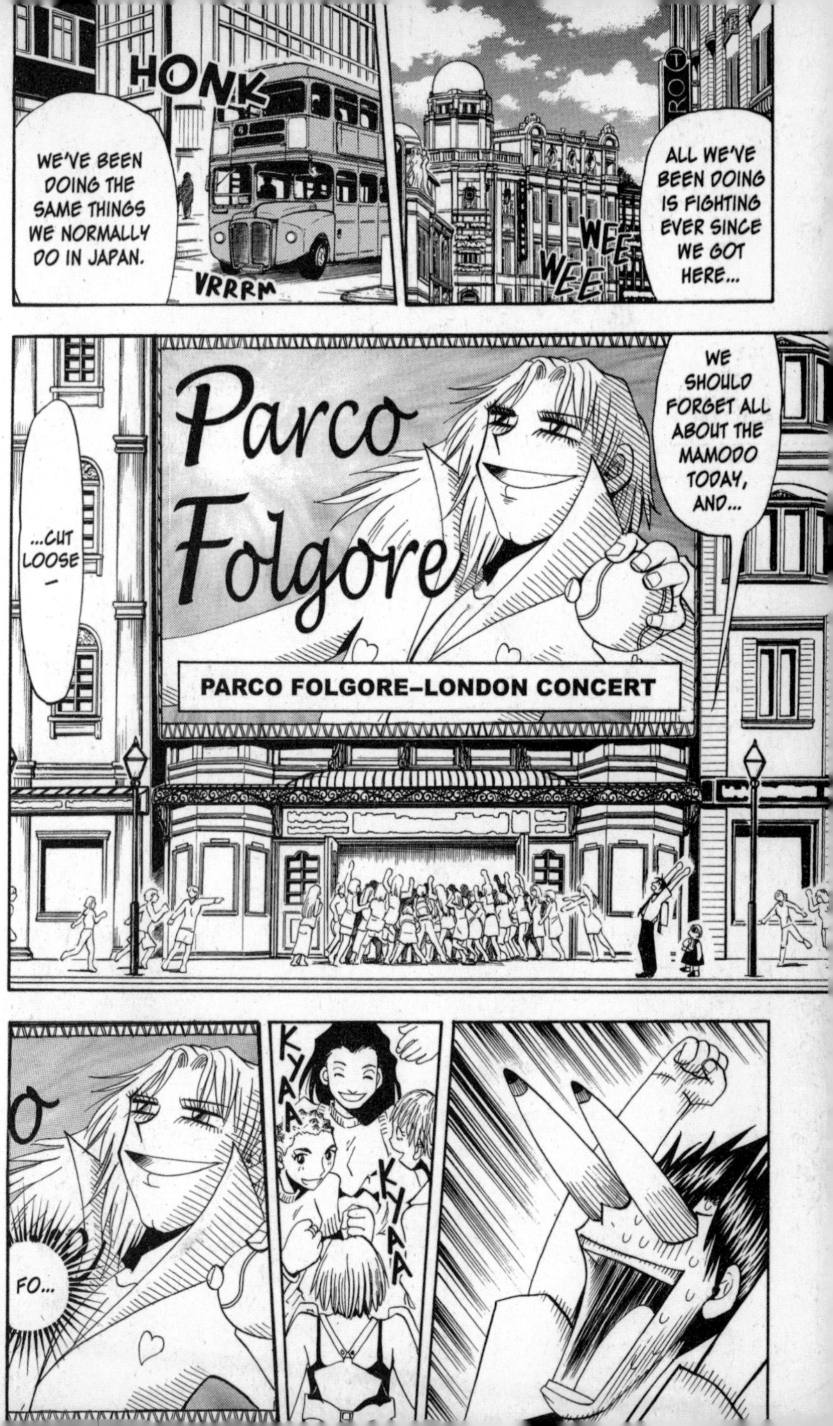
ALL WE'VE BEEN DOING IS FIGHTING EVER SINCE WE GOT HERE...
WEE WEE
HONK
WE'VE BEEN DOING THE SAME THINGS WE NORMALLY DO IN JAPAN.
VRRRM
WE SHOULD FORGET ALL ABOUT THE MAMODO TODAY, AND...
Parco Folgore
PARCO FOLGORE–LONDON CONCERT
...CUT LOOSE—
KYAA
KYAA
FO...

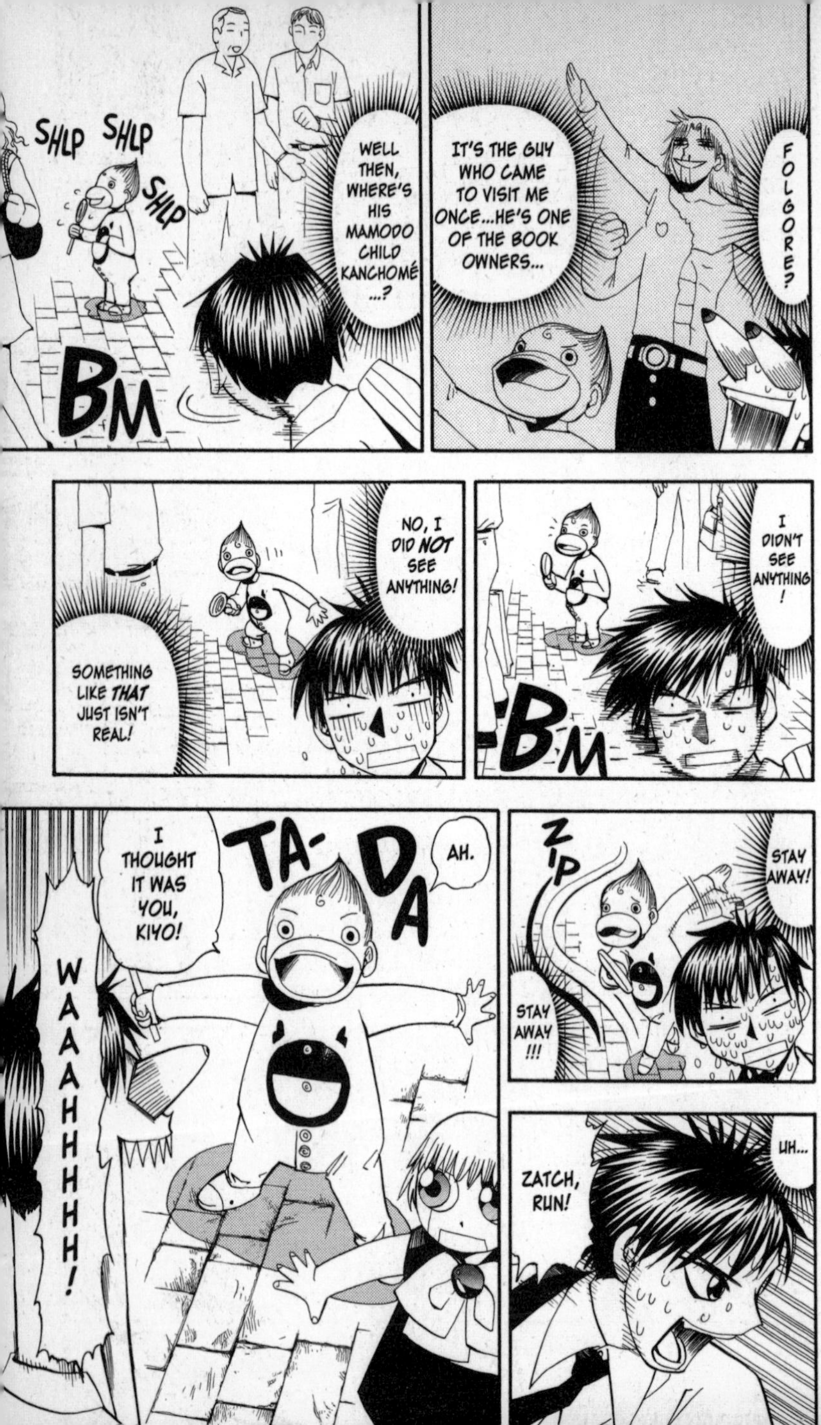
FOLGORE?
IT'S THE GUY WHO CAME TO VISIT ME ONCE...HE'S ONE OF THE BOOK OWNERS...
WELL THEN, WHERE'S HIS MAMODO CHILD KANCHOMÉ ...?
SHLP
SHLP
SHLP
BM
I DIDN'T SEE ANYTHING!
BM
NO, I DID NOT SEE ANYTHING!
SOMETHING LIKE THAT JUST ISN'T REAL!
STAY AWAY!
ZIP
STAY AWAY!!!
UH...
ZATCH, RUN!
AH.
TA-DA
I THOUGHT IT WAS YOU, KIYO!
WAAAHHHHHH!

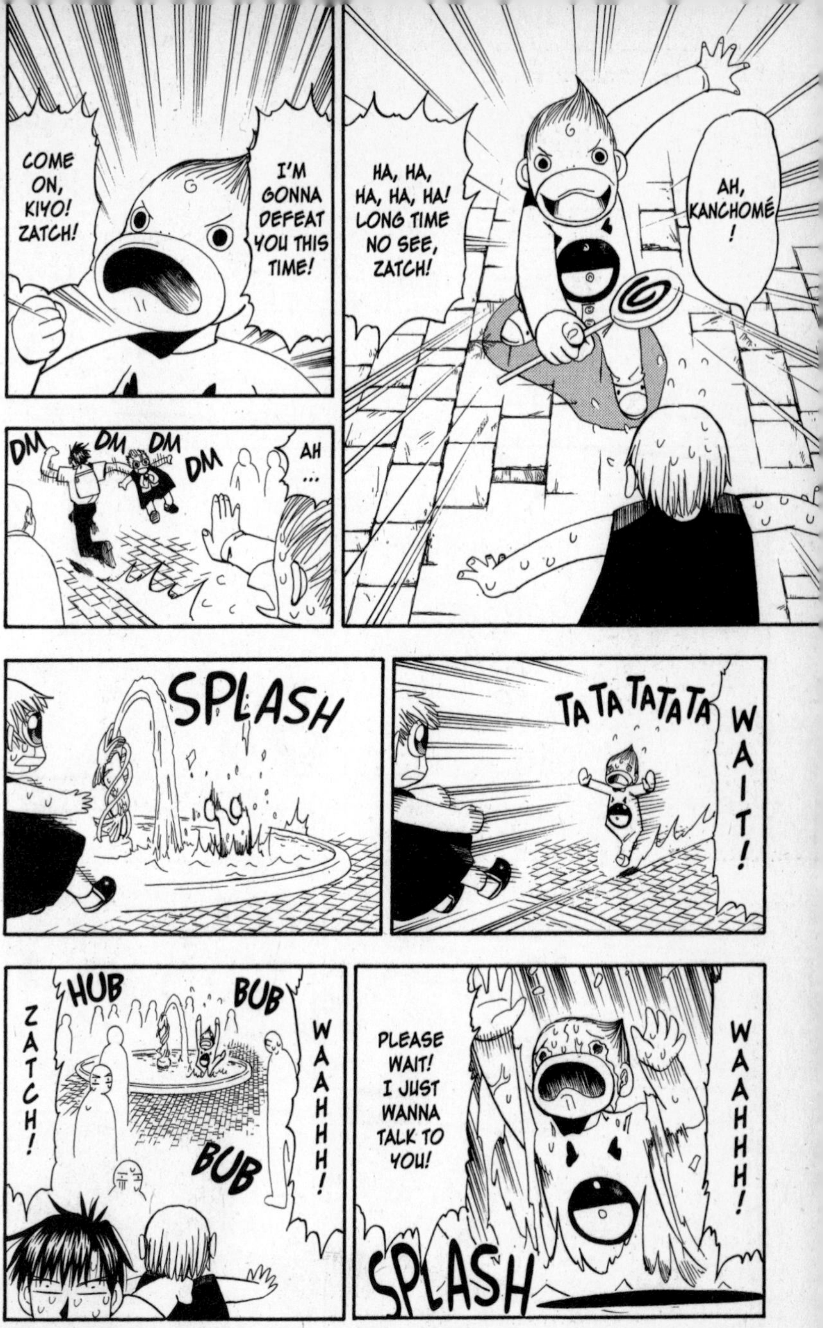
AH, KANCHOMÉ!
HA, HA, HA, HA, HA! LONG TIME NO SEE, ZATCH!
I'M GONNA DEFEAT YOU THIS TIME!
COME ON, KIYO! ZATCH!
AH ...
DM
DM
DM
DM
WAIT!
TA TA TATATA
SPLASH
WAAHHH!
PLEASE WAIT! I JUST WANNA TALK TO YOU!
SPLASH
WAAHHH!
BUB
HUB
BUB
ZATCH!

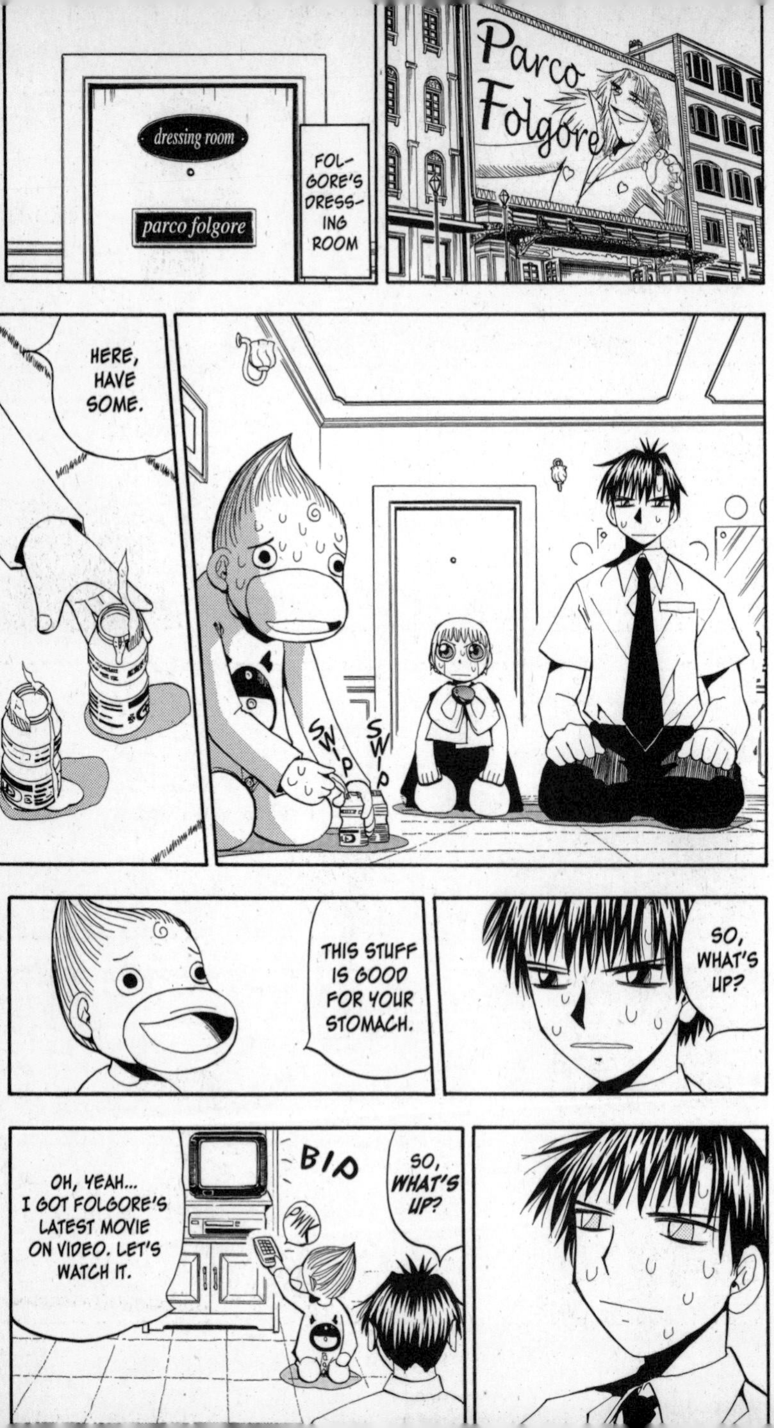

Parco Folgore
dressing room
parco folgore
FOLGORE'S DRESSING ROOM
SWIP
SWIP
HERE, HAVE SOME.
SO, WHAT'S UP?
THIS STUFF IS GOOD FOR YOUR STOMACH.
SO, WHAT'S UP?
BIP
PWIK
OH, YEAH... I GOT FOLGORE'S LATEST MOVIE ON VIDEO. LET'S WATCH IT.

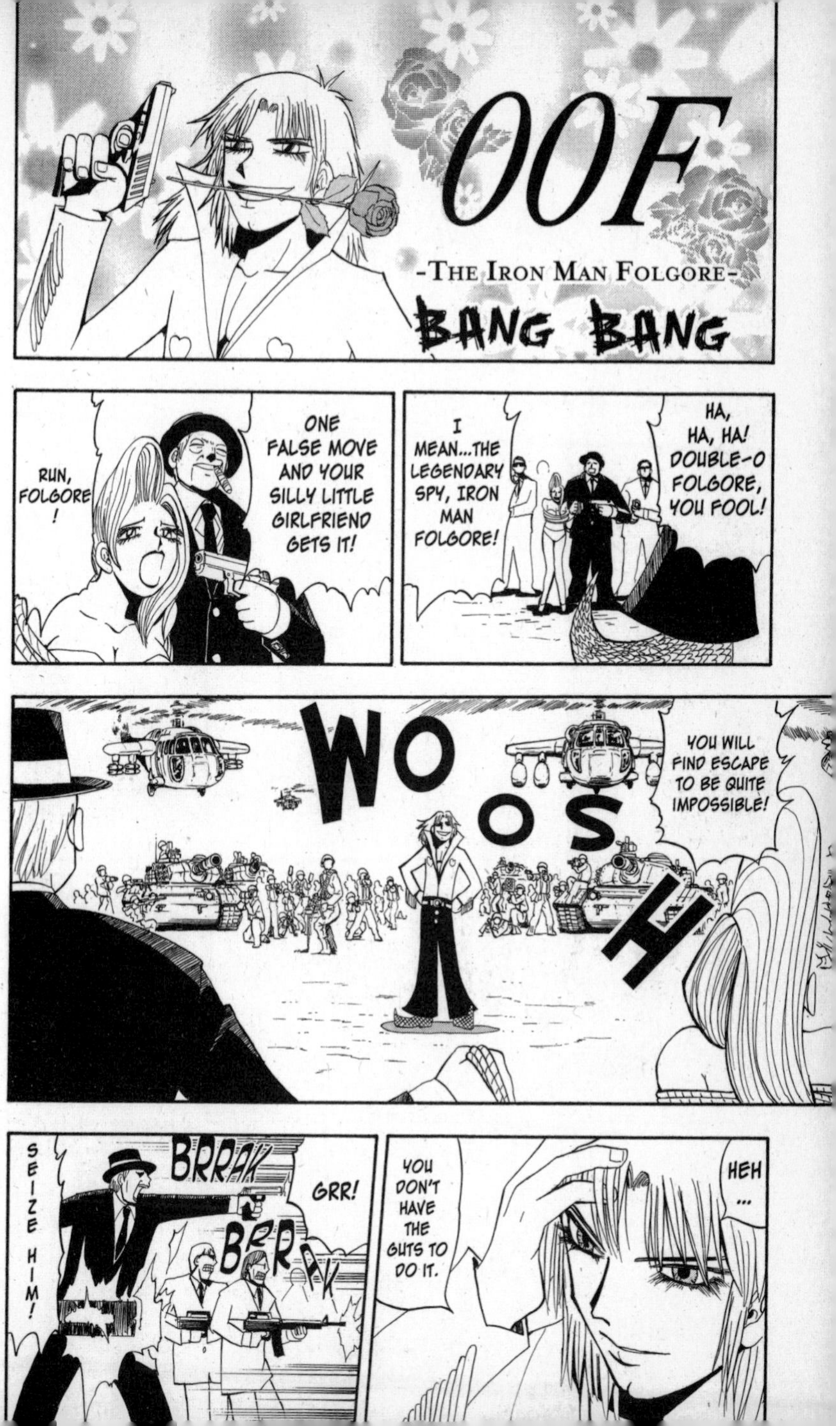
00F
-THE IRON MAN FOLGORE-
BANG BANG
HA, HA, HA! DOUBLE-O FOLGORE, YOU FOOL!
I MEAN...THE LEGENDARY SPY, IRON MAN FOLGORE!
ONE FALSE MOVE AND YOUR SILLY LITTLE GIRLFRIEND GETS IT!
RUN, FOLGORE!
YOU WILL FIND ESCAPE TO BE QUITE IMPOSSIBLE!
WOOSH
HEH...
YOU DON'T HAVE THE GUTS TO DO IT.
GRR!
BRRAK
BRRAK
SEIZE HIM!

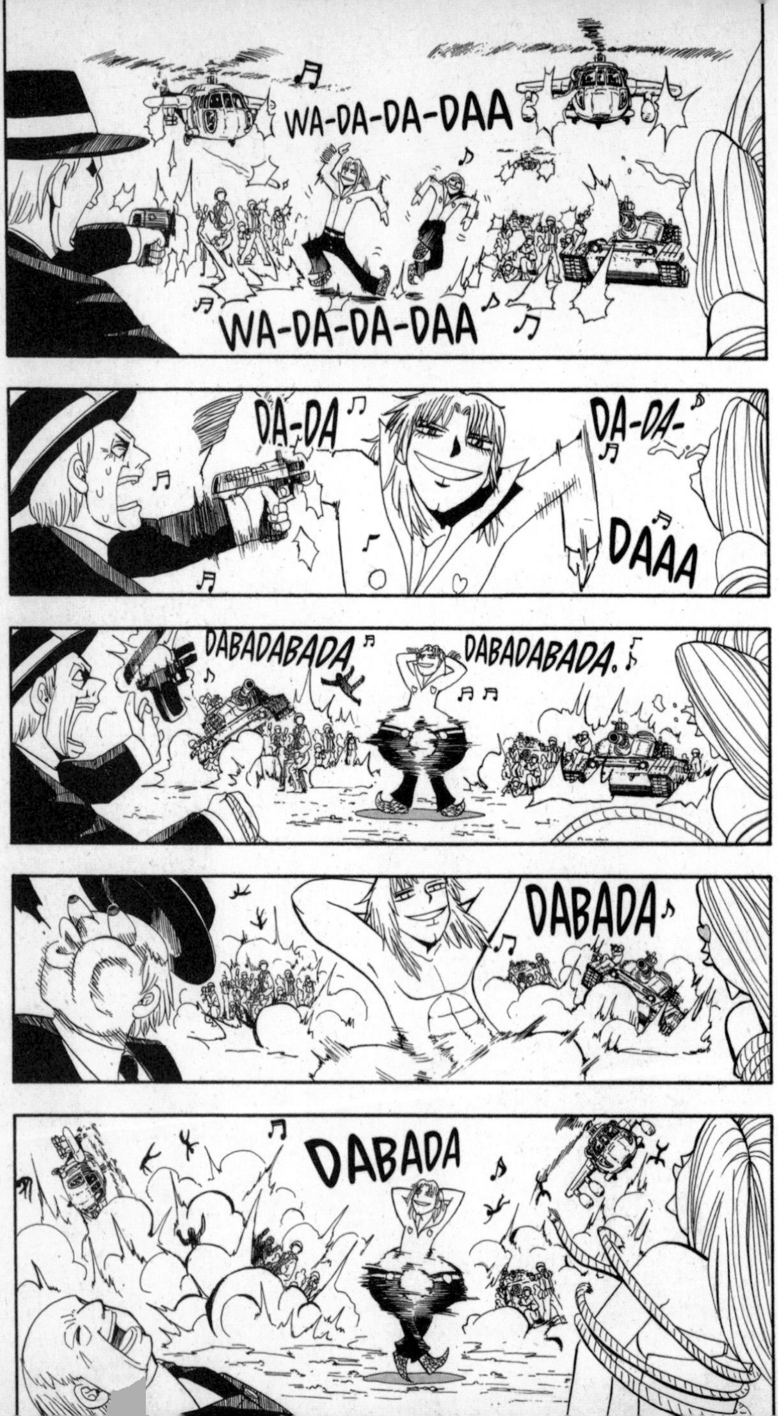
WA-DA-DA-DAA
WA-DA-DA-DAA
DA-DA-
DAAA
DA-DA
DABADABADA.
DABADABADA,
DABADA
DABADA

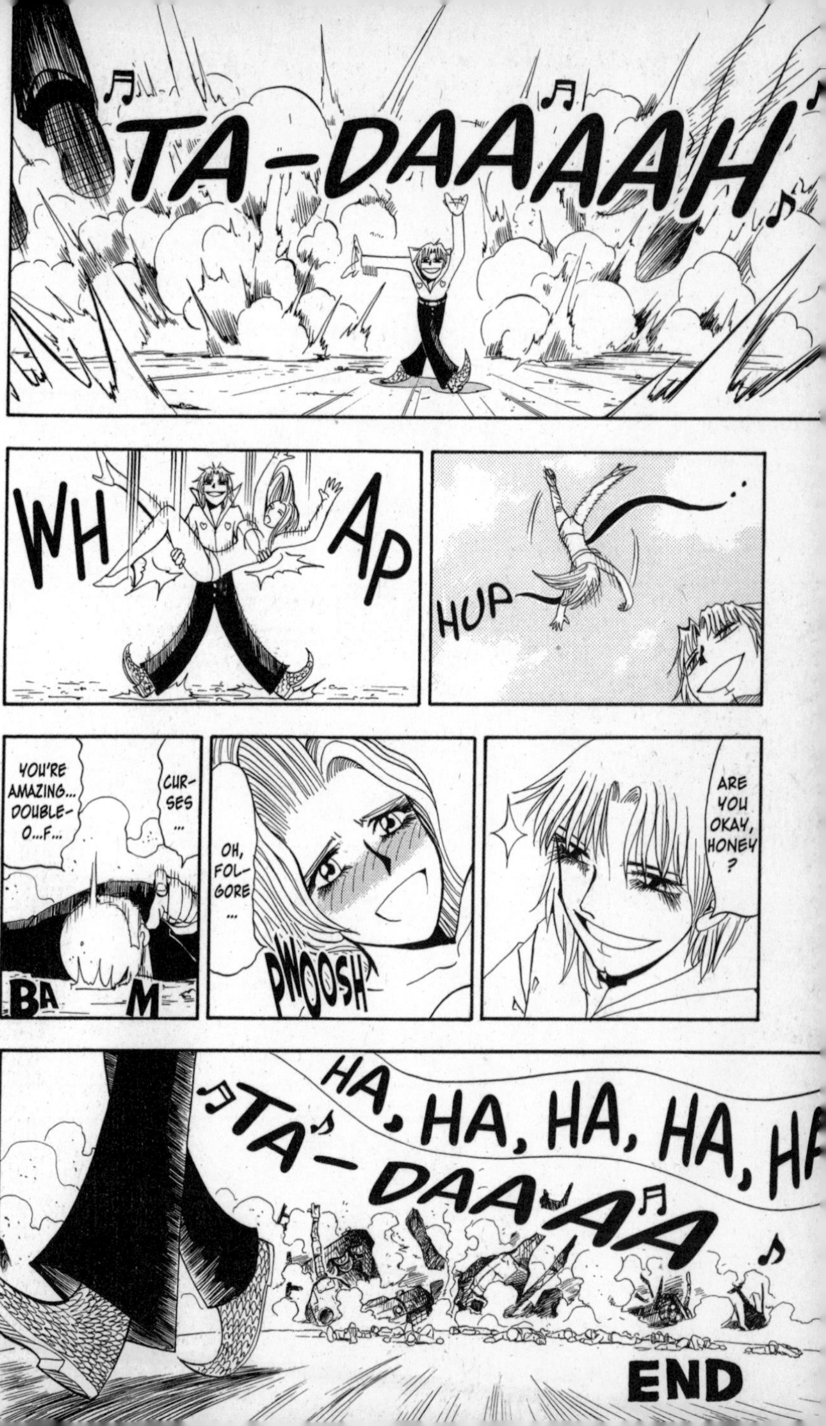
TA-DAAAAH
HUP~
WHAP
ARE YOU OKAY, HONEY?
OH, FOLGORE...
PWOOSH
CURSES...
YOU'RE AMAZING... DOUBLE-O...F...
BAM
HA, HA, HA, HA, HA
TA-DAAAAA
END

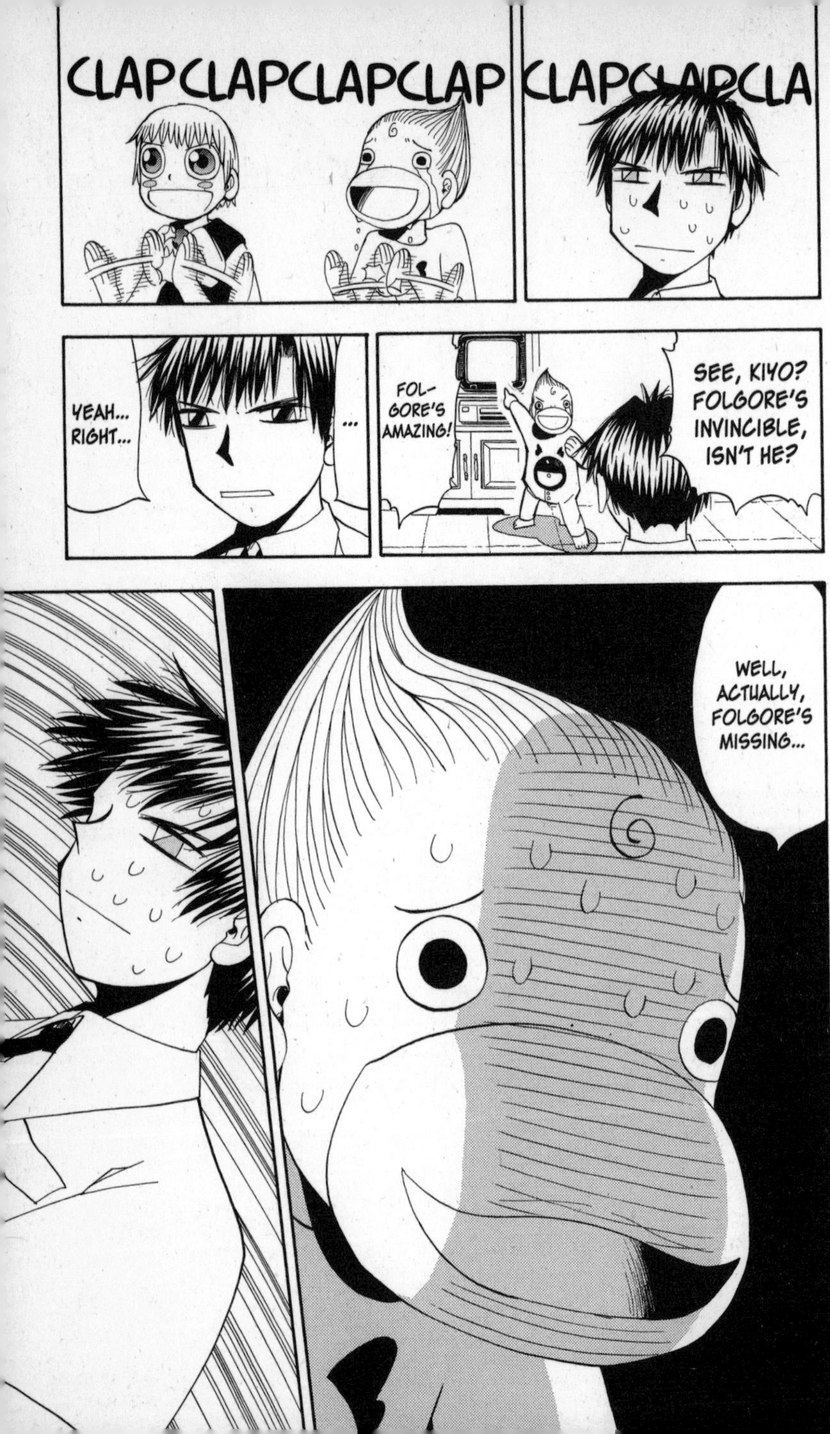
CLAPCLAPCLA
CLAPCLAPCLAPCLAP
SEE, KIYO? FOLGORE'S INVINCIBLE, ISN'T HE?
FOL-GORE'S AMAZING!
...
YEAH... RIGHT...
WELL, ACTUALLY, FOLGORE'S MISSING...

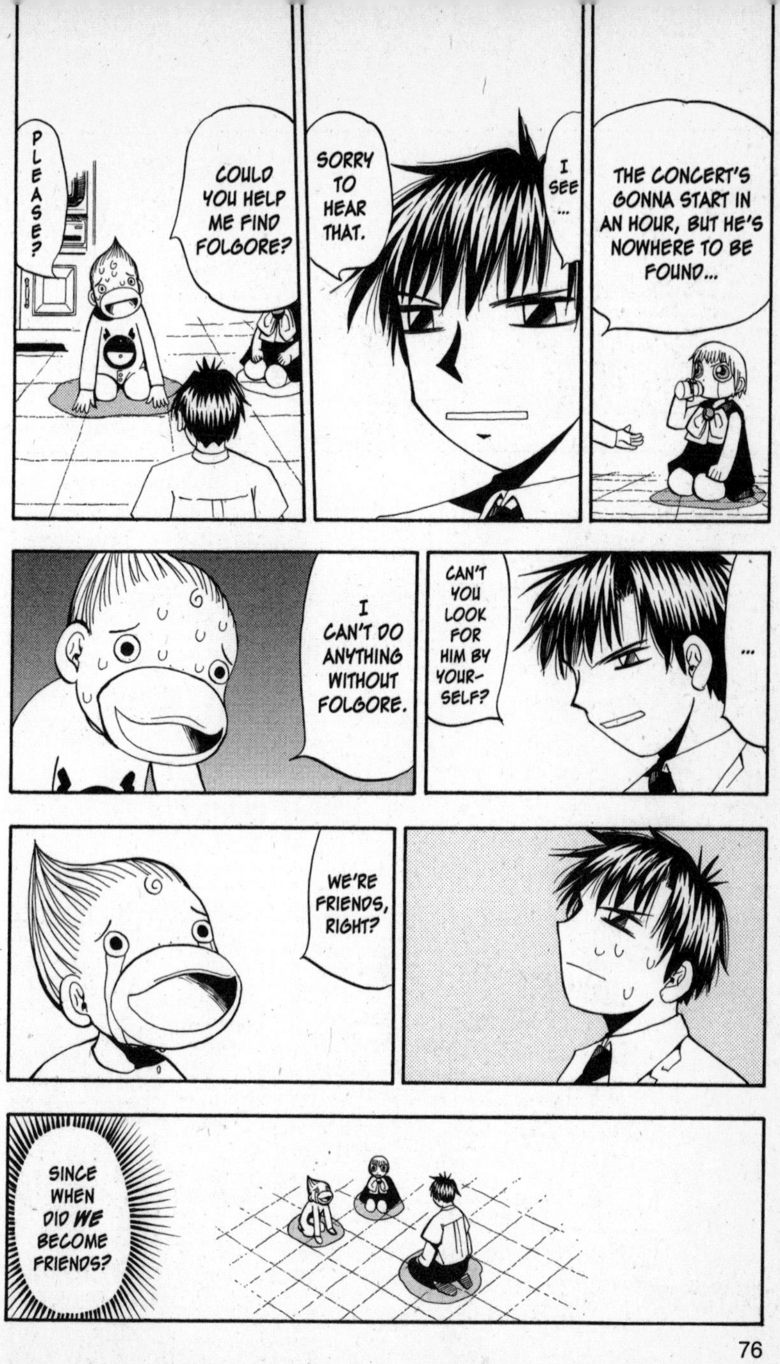
THE CONCERT'S GONNA START IN AN HOUR, BUT HE'S NOWHERE TO BE FOUND...
I SEE...
SORRY TO HEAR THAT.
COULD YOU HELP ME FIND FOLGORE?
PLEASE?
...
CAN'T YOU LOOK FOR HIM BY YOURSELF?
I CAN'T DO ANYTHING WITHOUT FOLGORE.
WE'RE FRIENDS, RIGHT?
SINCE WHEN DID *WE* BECOME FRIENDS?

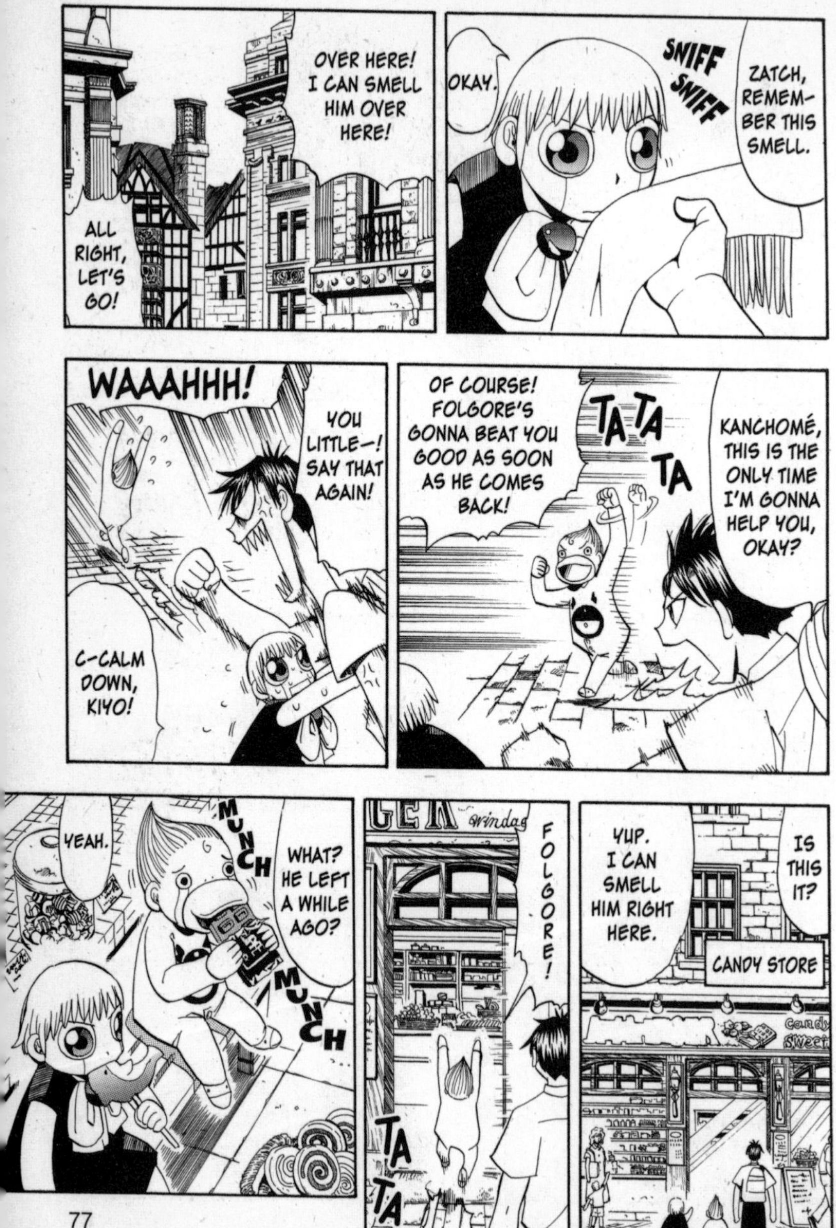
ZATCH, REMEMBER THIS SMELL.
SNIFF SNIFF
OKAY.
OVER HERE! I CAN SMELL HIM OVER HERE!
ALL RIGHT, LET'S GO!
KANCHOMÉ, THIS IS THE ONLY TIME I'M GONNA HELP YOU, OKAY?
TA TA TA TA
OF COURSE! FOLGORE'S GONNA BEAT YOU GOOD AS SOON AS HE COMES BACK!
WAAAHHH!
YOU LITTLE—! SAY THAT AGAIN!
C-CALM DOWN, KIYO!
IS THIS IT?
YUP. I CAN SMELL HIM RIGHT HERE.
CANDY STORE
FOLGORE!
TA TA TA
WHAT? HE LEFT A WHILE AGO?
MUNCH MUNCH
YEAH.

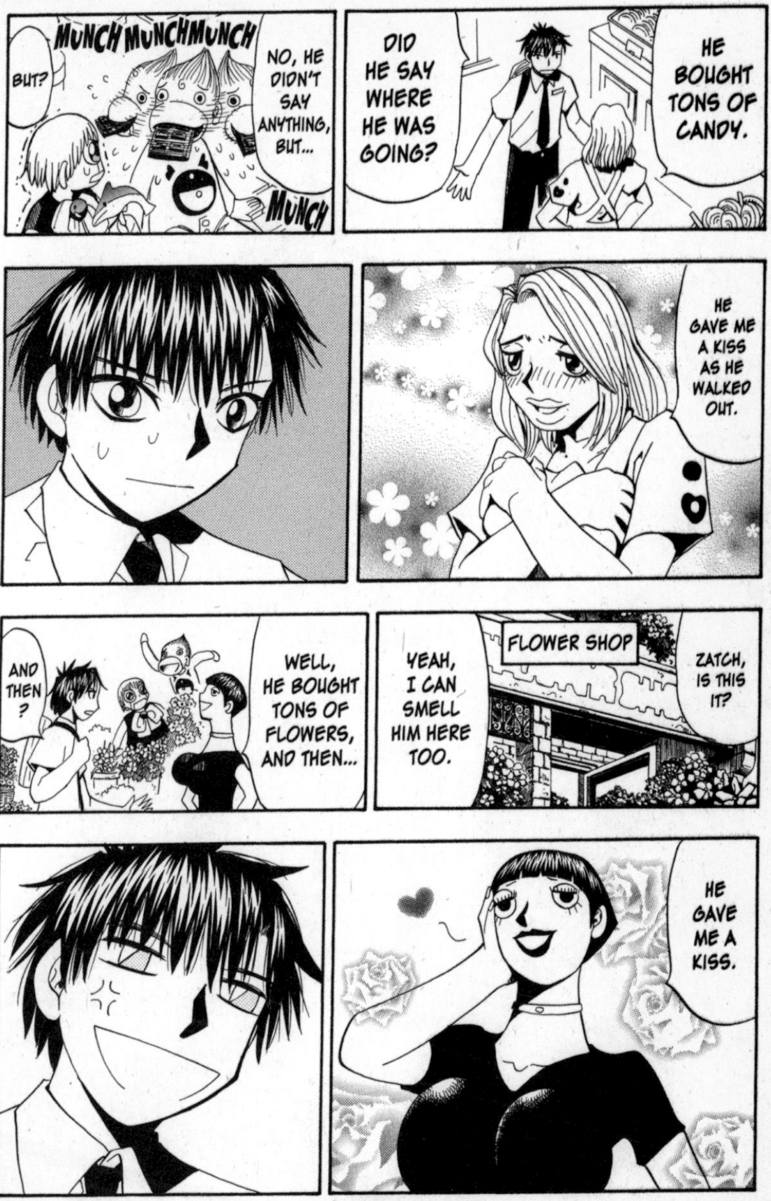
HE BOUGHT TONS OF CANDY.
DID HE SAY WHERE HE WAS GOING?
NO, HE DIDN'T SAY ANYTHING, BUT...
MUNCH MUNCHMUNCH
MUNCH
BUT?
HE GAVE ME A KISS AS HE WALKED OUT.
ZATCH, IS THIS IT?
FLOWER SHOP
YEAH, I CAN SMELL HIM HERE TOO.
WELL, HE BOUGHT TONS OF FLOWERS, AND THEN...
AND THEN ?
HE GAVE ME A KISS.

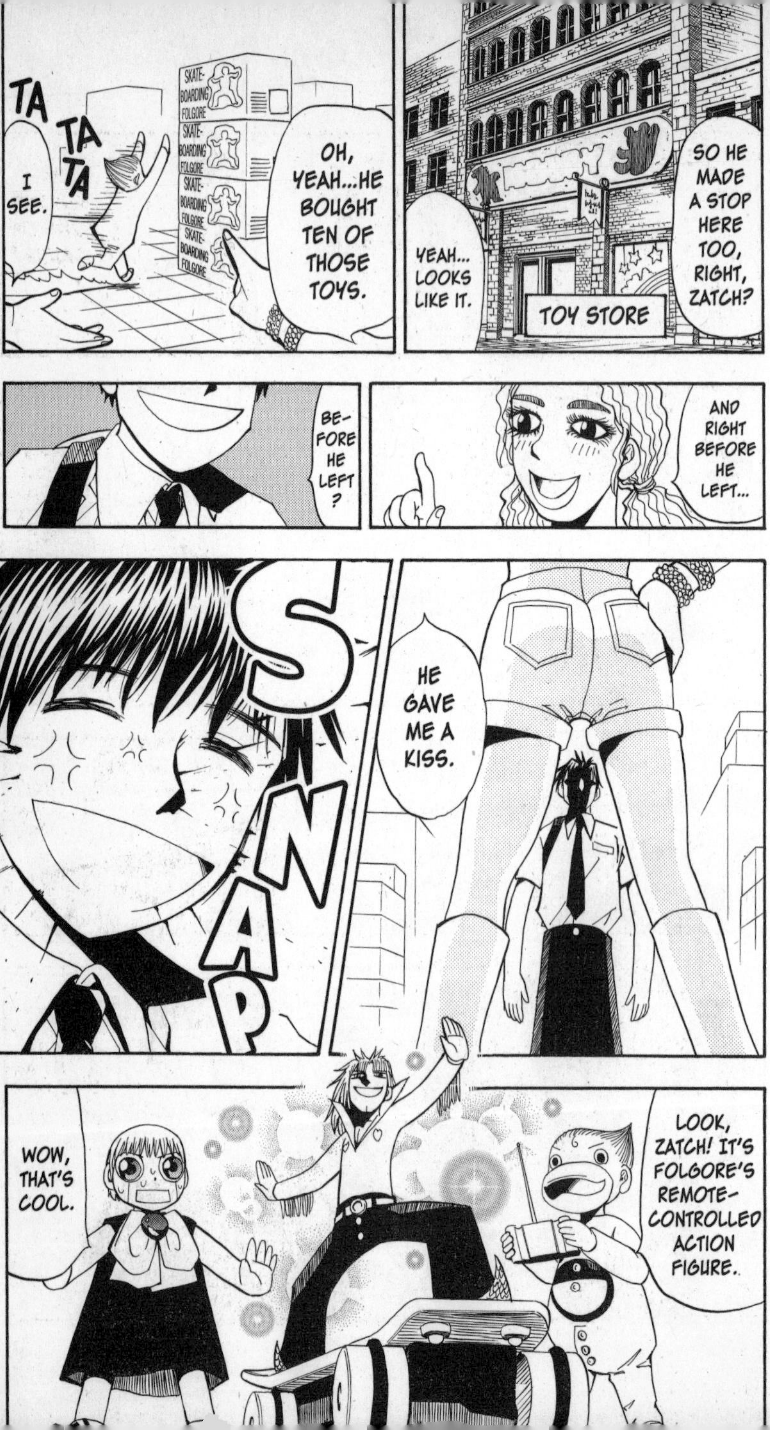
SO HE MADE A STOP HERE TOO, RIGHT, ZATCH?
TOY STORE
YEAH... LOOKS LIKE IT.
OH, YEAH...HE BOUGHT TEN OF THOSE TOYS.
SKATE-BOARDING FOLGORE
SKATE-BOARDING FOLGORE
SKATE-BOARDING FOLGORE
SKATE-BOARDING FOLGORE
TA TA TA
I SEE.
AND RIGHT BEFORE HE LEFT...
BE-FORE HE LEFT?
HE GAVE ME A KISS.
SNAP
LOOK, ZATCH! IT'S FOLGORE'S REMOTE-CONTROLLED ACTION FIGURE.
WOW, THAT'S COOL.

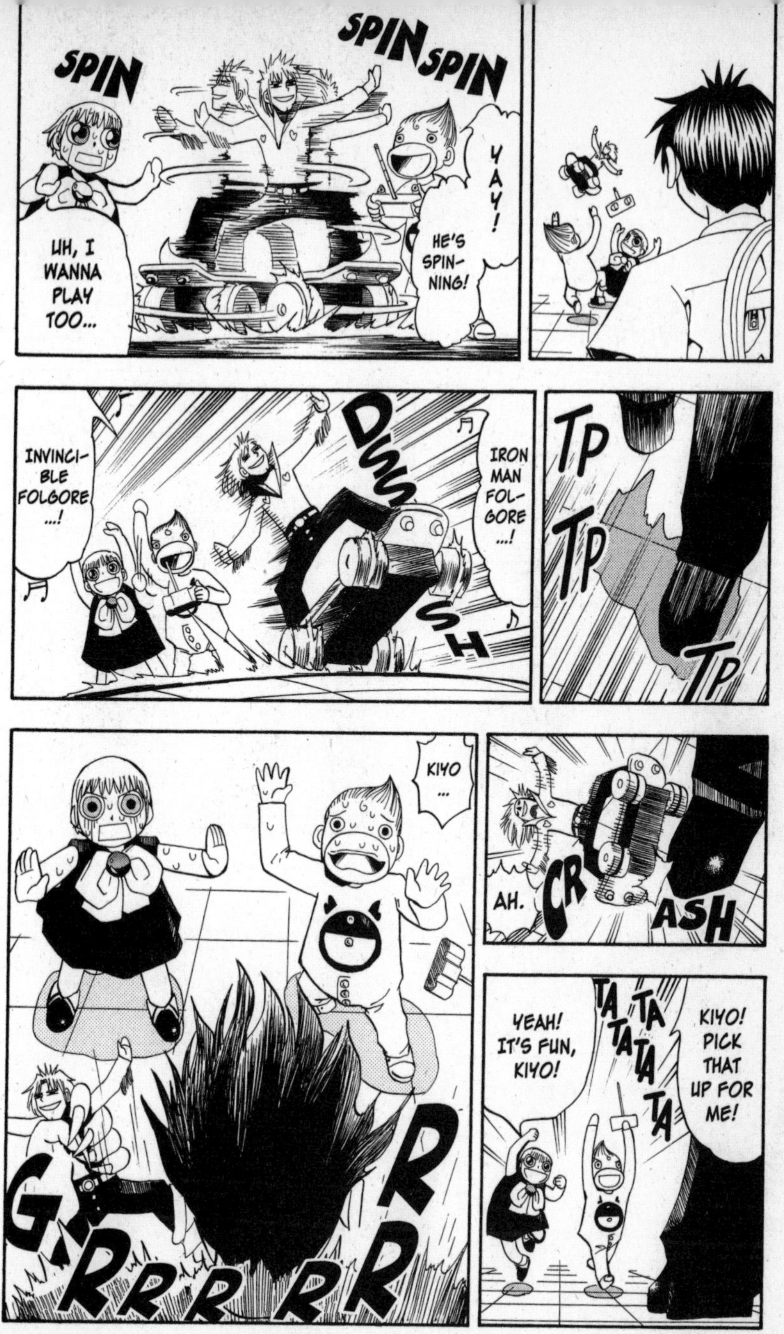
SPIN SPIN
YAY!
HE'S SPIN-NING!
SPIN
UH, I WANNA PLAY TOO...
TP TP TP
IRON MAN FOL-GORE ...!
DASH
INVINCI-BLE FOLGORE ...!
CRASH
AH.
KIYO! PICK THAT UP FOR ME!
TA TA TA TA TA TA
YEAH! IT'S FUN, KIYO!
KIYO ...
GRRRRRR

UH-HUH...

THERE'S ONE THING I SHOULD'VE ASKED YOU BEFORE...

YES?

KANCHOMÉ...

YEAH...

GRRRRRRR

DID FOLGORE MENTION ANYTHING TO YOU BEFORE HE LEFT?

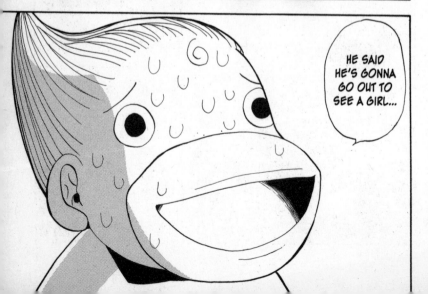

HE SAID HE'S GONNA GO OUT TO SEE A GIRL...

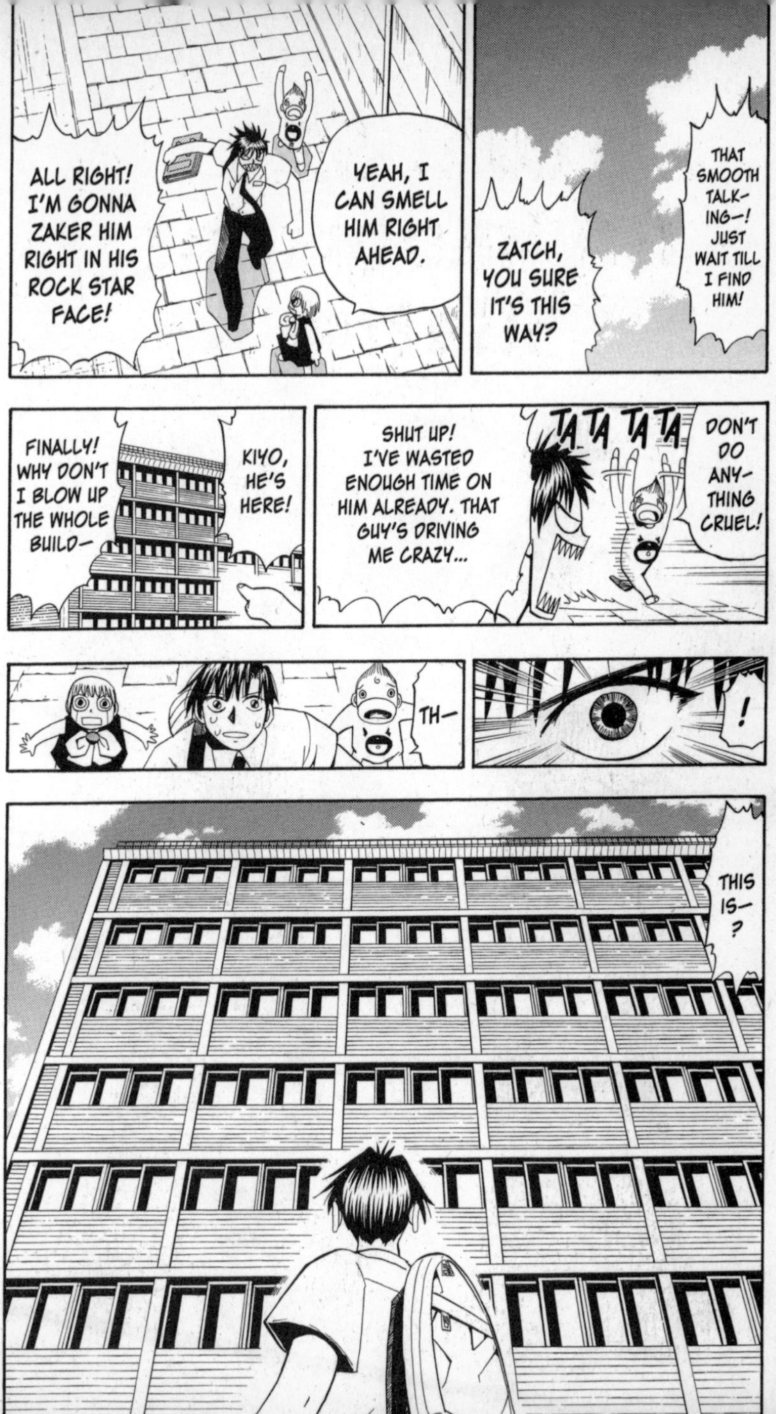
THAT SMOOTH TALKING—! JUST WAIT TILL I FIND HIM!
ZATCH, YOU SURE IT'S THIS WAY?
YEAH, I CAN SMELL HIM RIGHT AHEAD.
ALL RIGHT! I'M GONNA ZAKER HIM RIGHT IN HIS ROCK STAR FACE!
DON'T DO ANYTHING CRUEL!
TA TA TA TA
SHUT UP! I'VE WASTED ENOUGH TIME ON HIM ALREADY. THAT GUY'S DRIVING ME CRAZY...
KIYO, HE'S HERE!
FINALLY! WHY DON'T I BLOW UP THE WHOLE BUILD—
!
TH—
THIS IS—?

LEVEL 53: An Important Matter

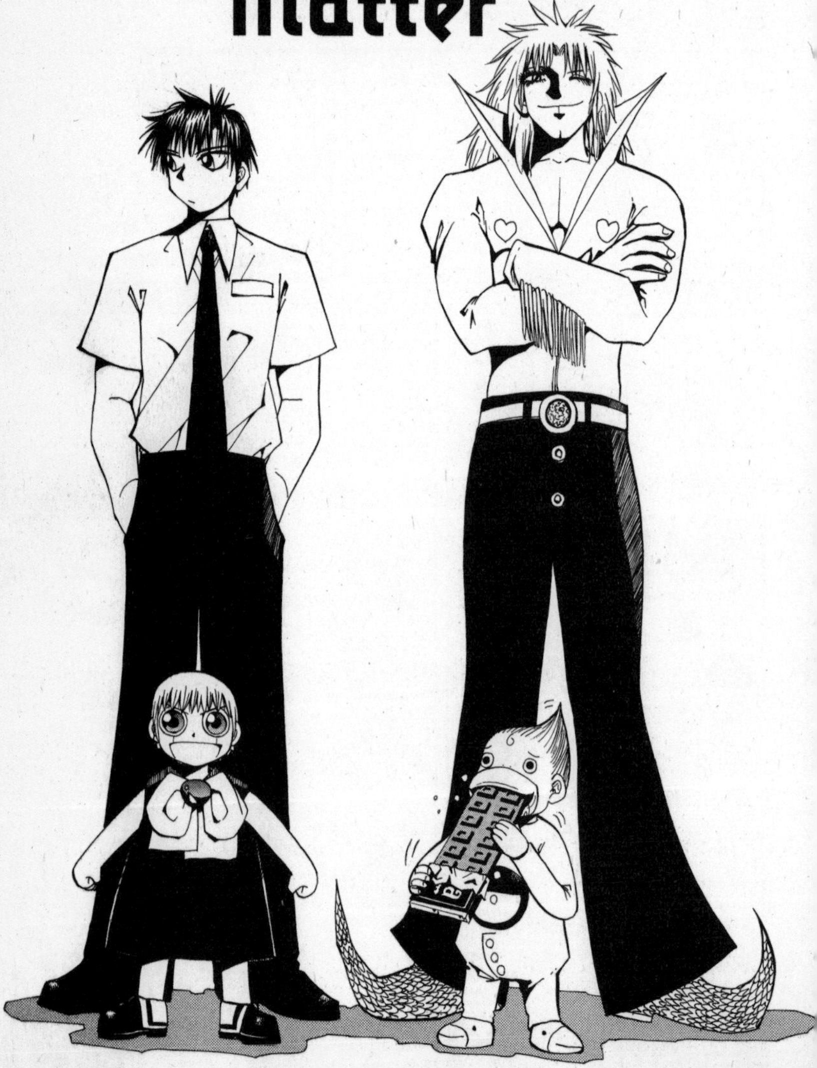

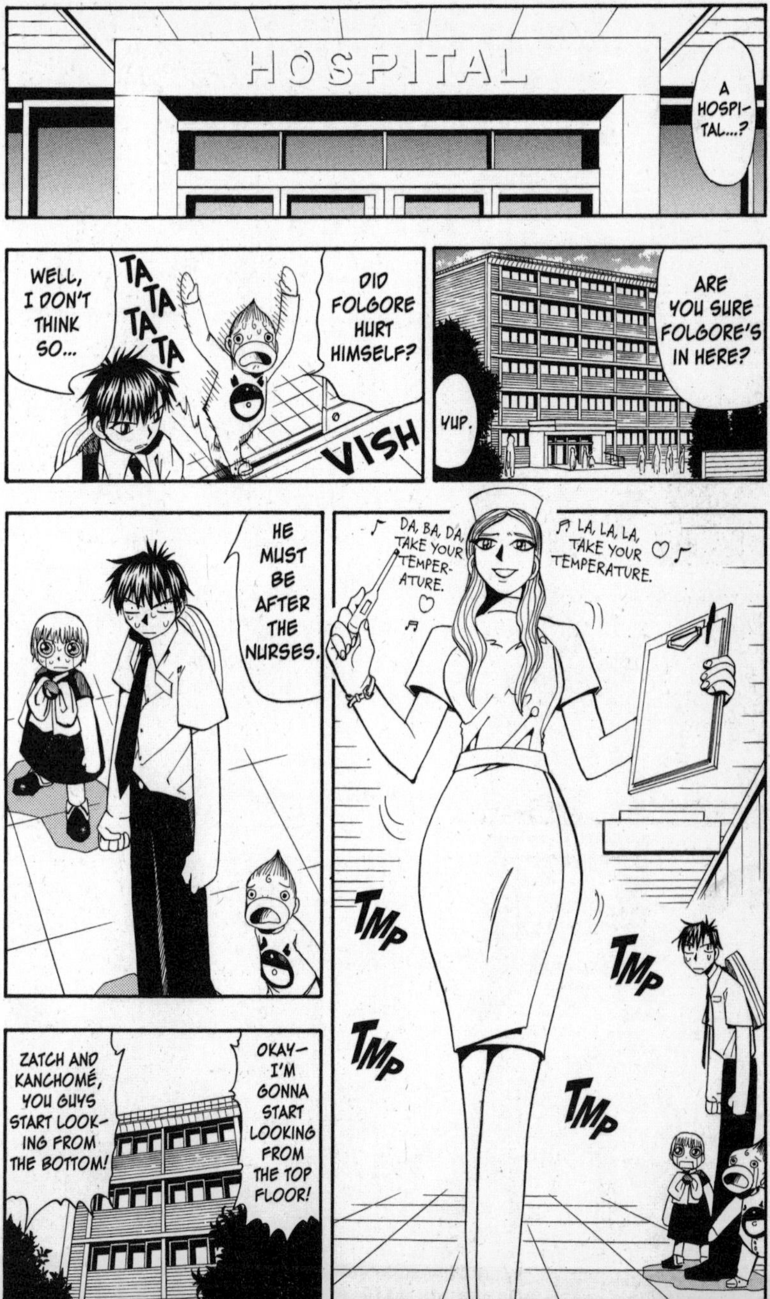
HOSPITAL
A HOSPITAL...?
ARE YOU SURE FOLGORE'S IN HERE?
YUP.
DID FOLGORE HURT HIMSELF?
TA TA TA TA
WELL, I DON'T THINK SO...
VISH
LA, LA, LA, TAKE YOUR TEMPERATURE.
DA, BA, DA, TAKE YOUR TEMPERATURE.
TMP
TMP
TMP
TMP
HE MUST BE AFTER THE NURSES.
OKAY— I'M GONNA START LOOKING FROM THE TOP FLOOR!
ZATCH AND KANCHOMÉ, YOU GUYS START LOOKING FROM THE BOTTOM!

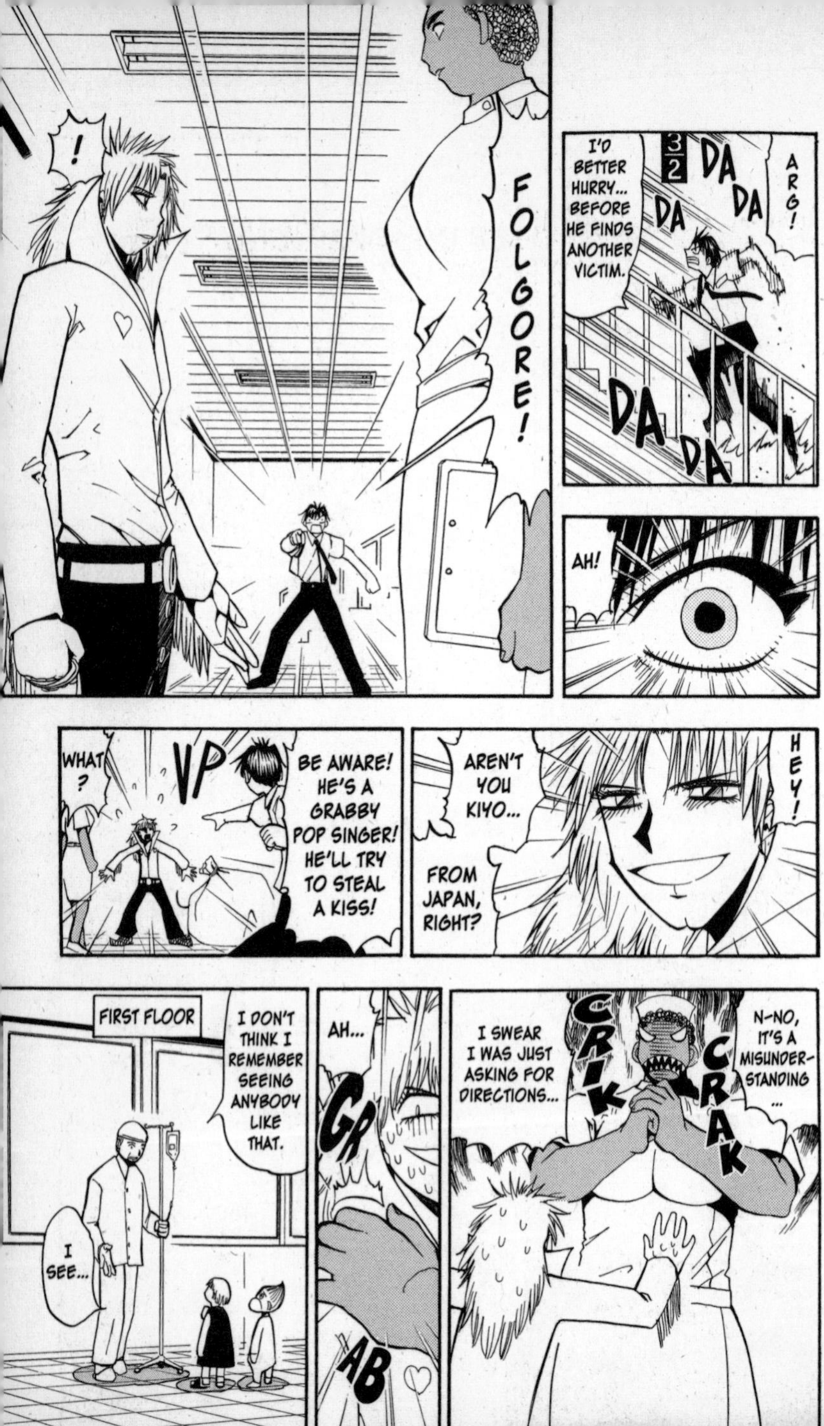

32
I'D BETTER HURRY... BEFORE HE FINDS ANOTHER VICTIM.
DA DA DA
ARG!
DA DA
AH!
FOLGORE!
!
HEY!
AREN'T YOU KIYO...
FROM JAPAN, RIGHT?
BE AWARE! HE'S A GRABBY POP SINGER! HE'LL TRY TO STEAL A KISS!
VP
WHAT?
N-NO, IT'S A MISUNDER-STANDING...
CRIK CRAK
I SWEAR I WAS JUST ASKING FOR DIRECTIONS...
AH...
GR
AB
FIRST FLOOR
I DON'T THINK I REMEMBER SEEING ANYBODY LIKE THAT.
I SEE...

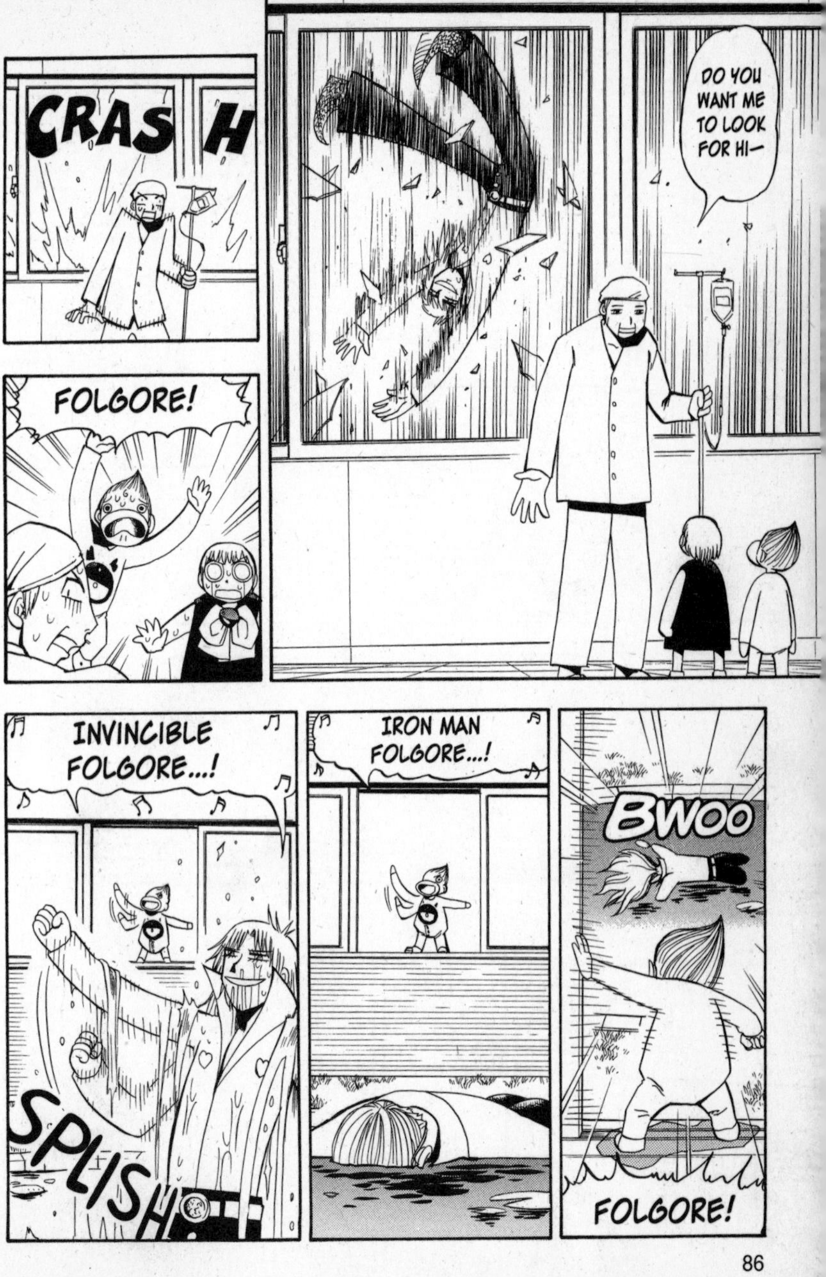
DO YOU WANT ME TO LOOK FOR HI—
CRAS H
FOLGORE!
BWOO
FOLGORE!
IRON MAN FOLGORE...!
INVINCIBLE FOLGORE...!
SPLISH

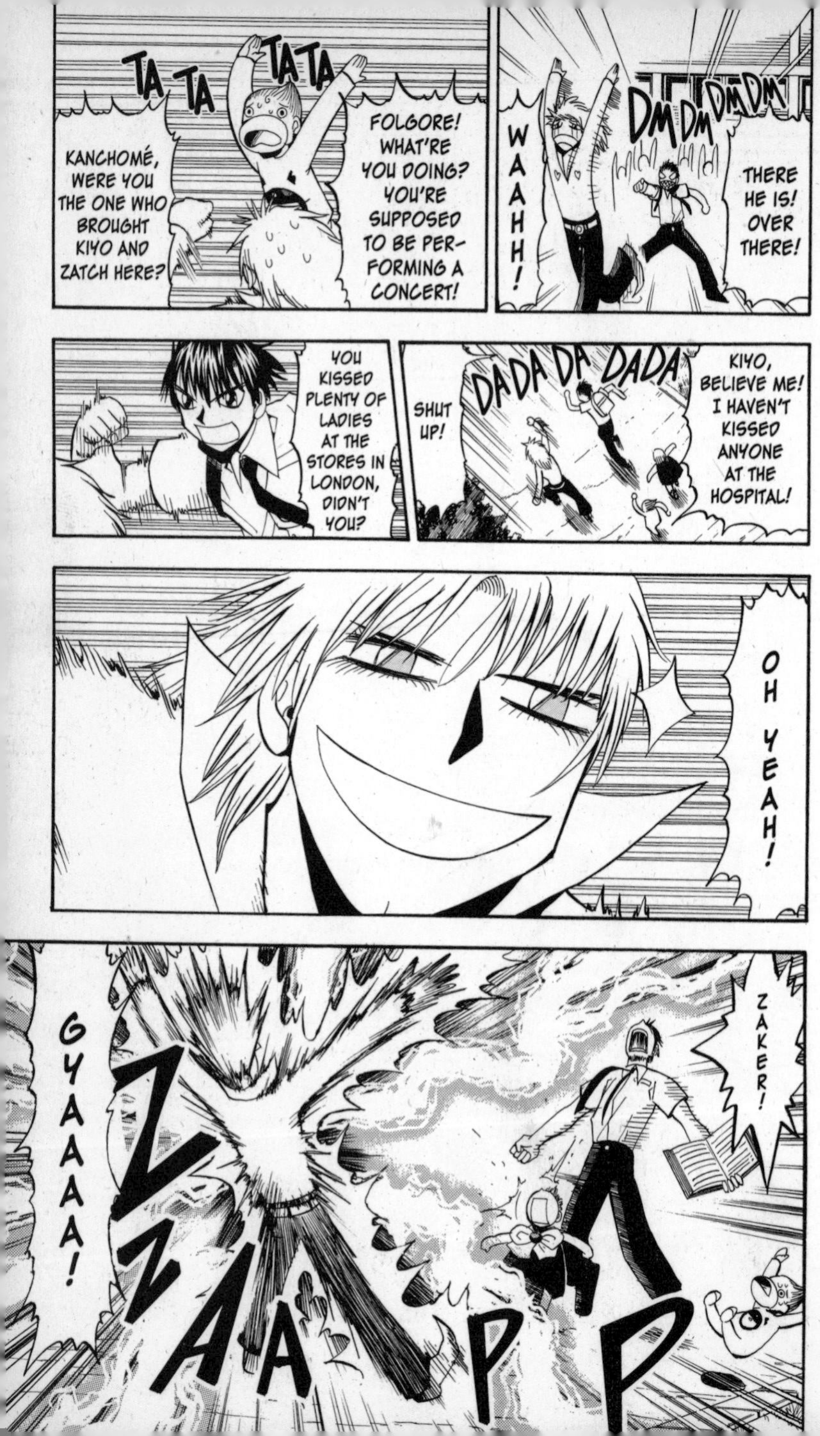
DMDM DMDM
THERE HE IS! OVER THERE!
WAAHH!
TATA
FOLGORE! WHAT'RE YOU DOING? YOU'RE SUPPOSED TO BE PER-FORMING A CONCERT!
TA TA
KANCHOMÉ, WERE YOU THE ONE WHO BROUGHT KIYO AND ZATCH HERE?
KIYO, BELIEVE ME! I HAVEN'T KISSED ANYONE AT THE HOSPITAL!
DADA DA DADA
SHUT UP!
YOU KISSED PLENTY OF LADIES AT THE STORES IN LONDON, DIDN'T YOU?
OH YEAH!
ZAKER!
GYAAAAA!
ZAAPP

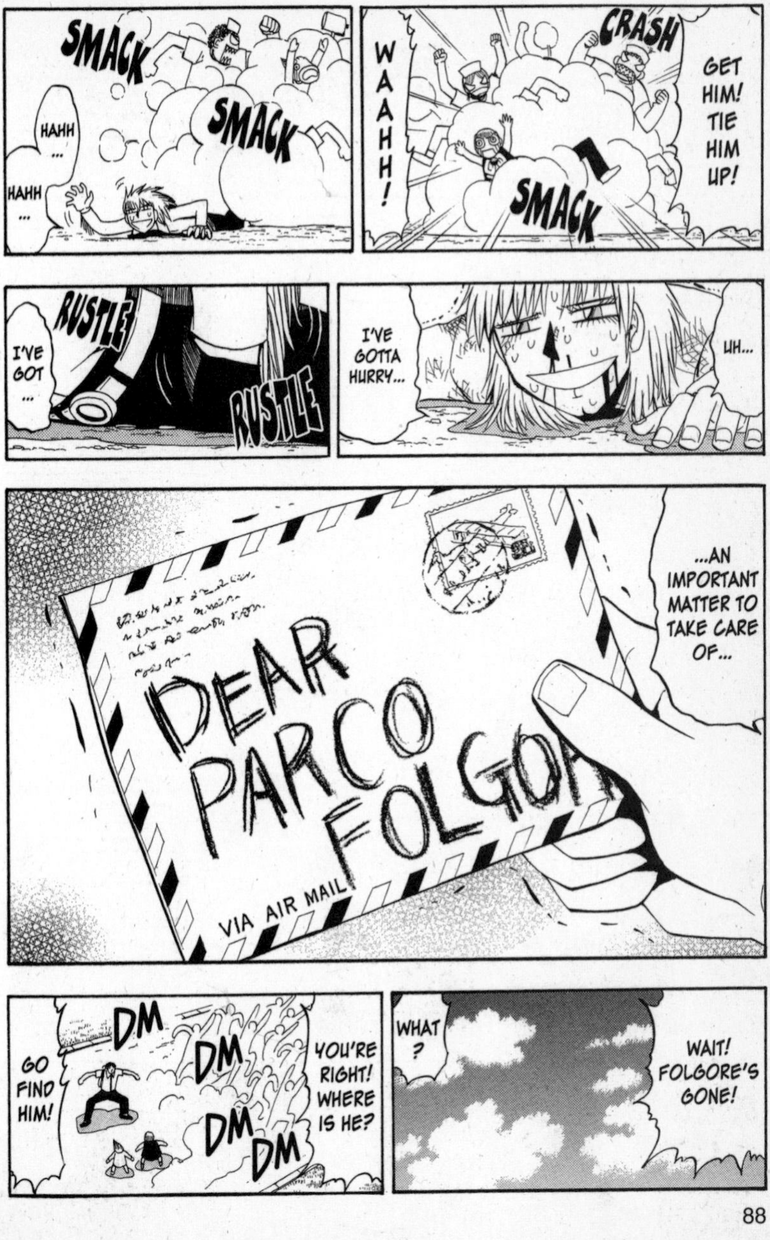
CRASH
GET HIM! TIE HIM UP!
WAAHH!
SMACK
SMACK
SMACK
HAHH ...
HAHH ...
UH...
I'VE GOTTA HURRY...
RUSTLE
I'VE GOT ...
RUSTLE
...AN IMPORTANT MATTER TO TAKE CARE OF...
DEAR PARCO FOLGOR
VIA AIR MAIL
WAIT! FOLGORE'S GONE!
WHAT ?
YOU'RE RIGHT! WHERE IS HE?
DM
DM
DM
DM
GO FIND HIM!

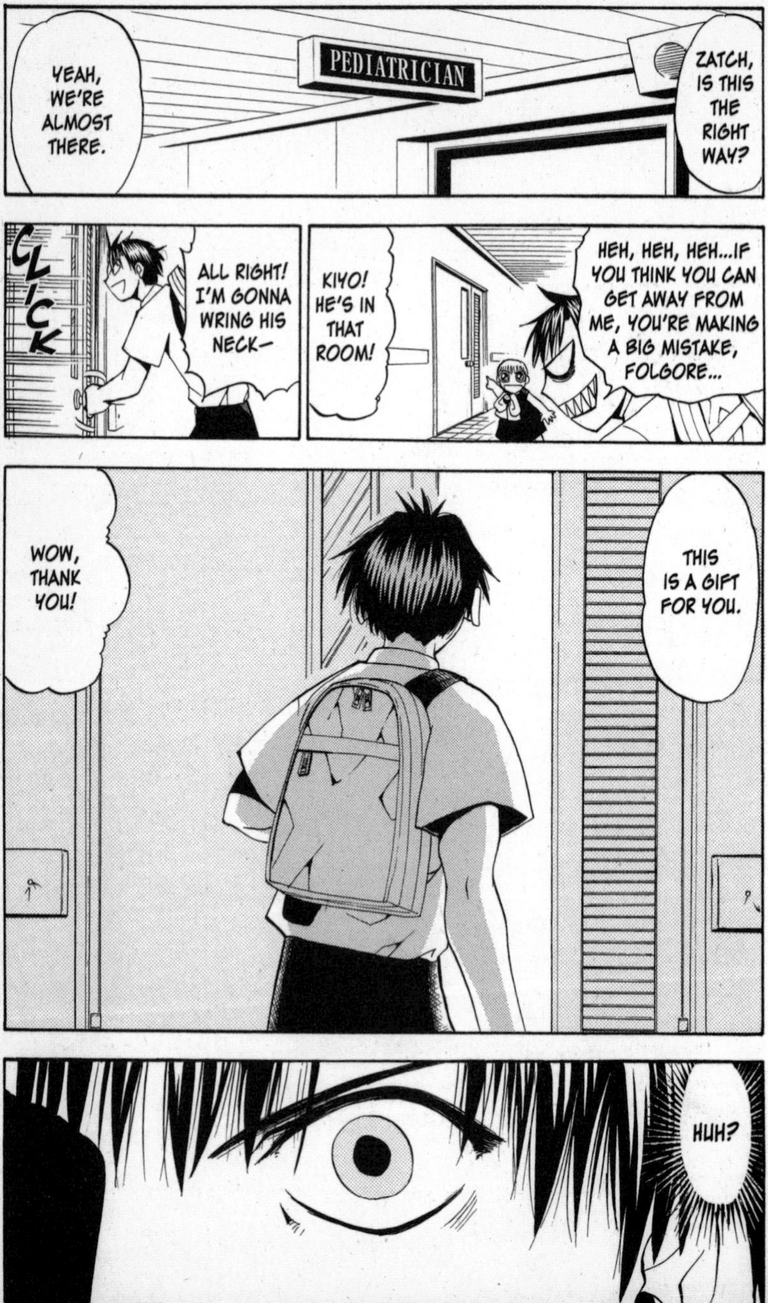
ZATCH, IS THIS THE RIGHT WAY?
PEDIATRICIAN
YEAH, WE'RE ALMOST THERE.
HEH, HEH, HEH...IF YOU THINK YOU CAN GET AWAY FROM ME, YOU'RE MAKING A BIG MISTAKE, FOLGORE...
KIYO! HE'S IN THAT ROOM!
ALL RIGHT! I'M GONNA WRING HIS NECK—
CLICK
THIS IS A GIFT FOR YOU.
WOW, THANK YOU!
HUH?

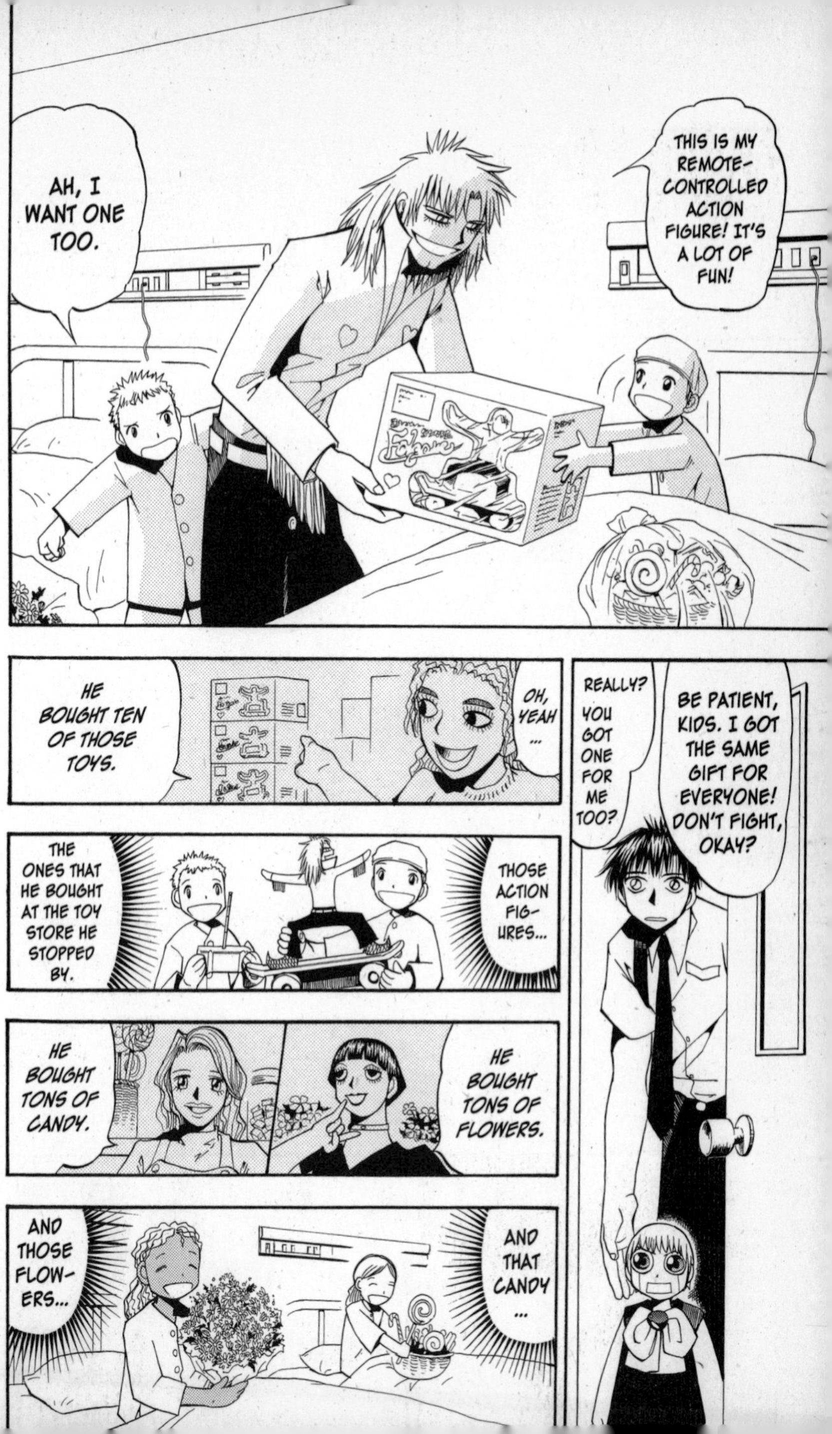
THIS IS MY REMOTE-CONTROLLED ACTION FIGURE! IT'S A LOT OF FUN!
AH, I WANT ONE TOO.
BE PATIENT, KIDS. I GOT THE SAME GIFT FOR EVERYONE! DON'T FIGHT, OKAY?
REALLY? YOU GOT ONE FOR ME TOO?
OH, YEAH...
HE BOUGHT TEN OF THOSE TOYS.
THOSE ACTION FIGURES...
THE ONES THAT HE BOUGHT AT THE TOY STORE HE STOPPED BY.
HE BOUGHT TONS OF FLOWERS.
HE BOUGHT TONS OF CANDY.
AND THAT CANDY...
AND THOSE FLOWERS...

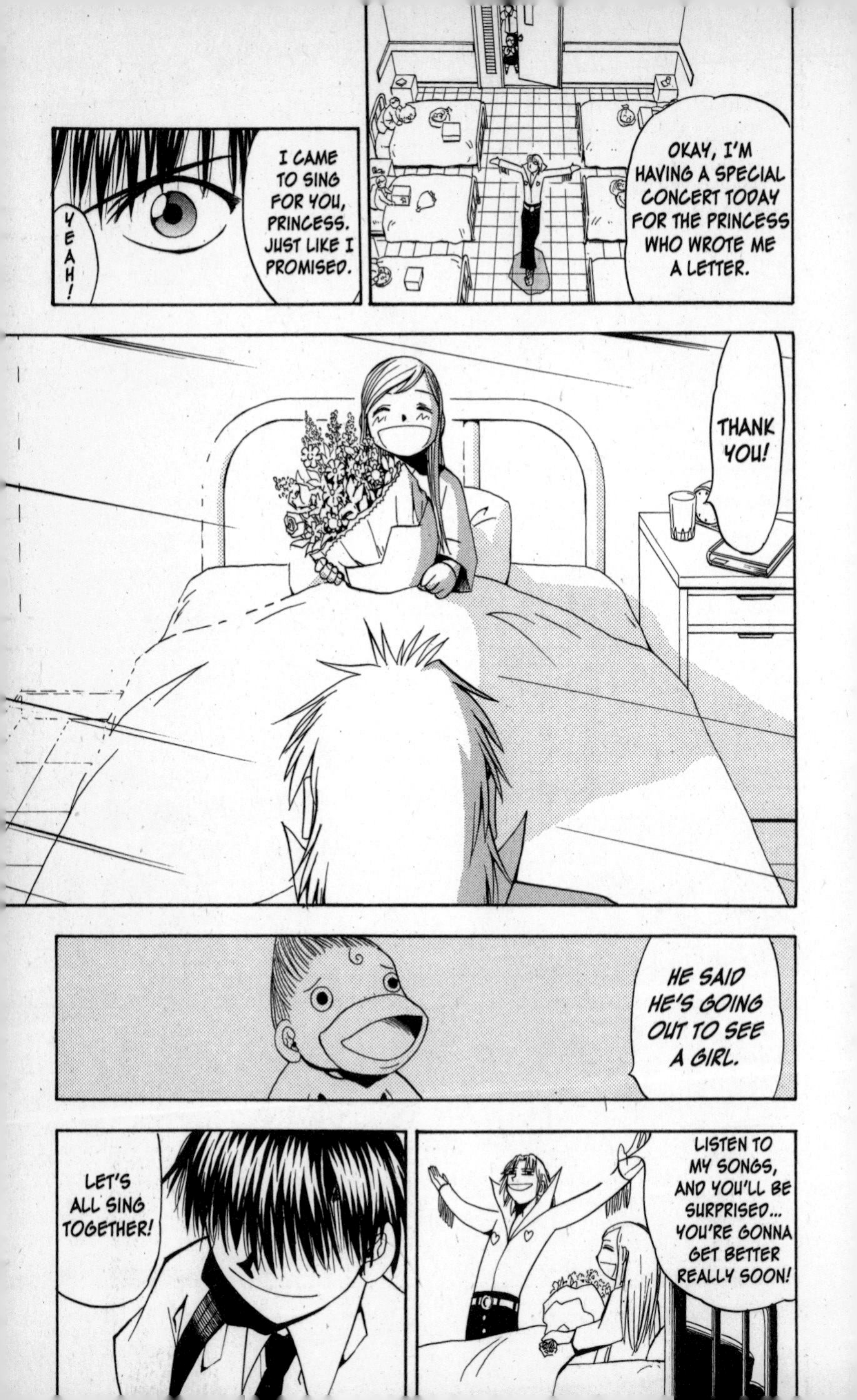
OKAY, I'M HAVING A SPECIAL CONCERT TODAY FOR THE PRINCESS WHO WROTE ME A LETTER.
I CAME TO SING FOR YOU, PRINCESS. JUST LIKE I PROMISED.
YEAH!
THANK YOU!
HE SAID HE'S GOING OUT TO SEE A GIRL.
LISTEN TO MY SONGS, AND YOU'LL BE SURPRISED... YOU'RE GONNA GET BETTER REALLY SOON!
LET'S ALL SING TOGETHER!

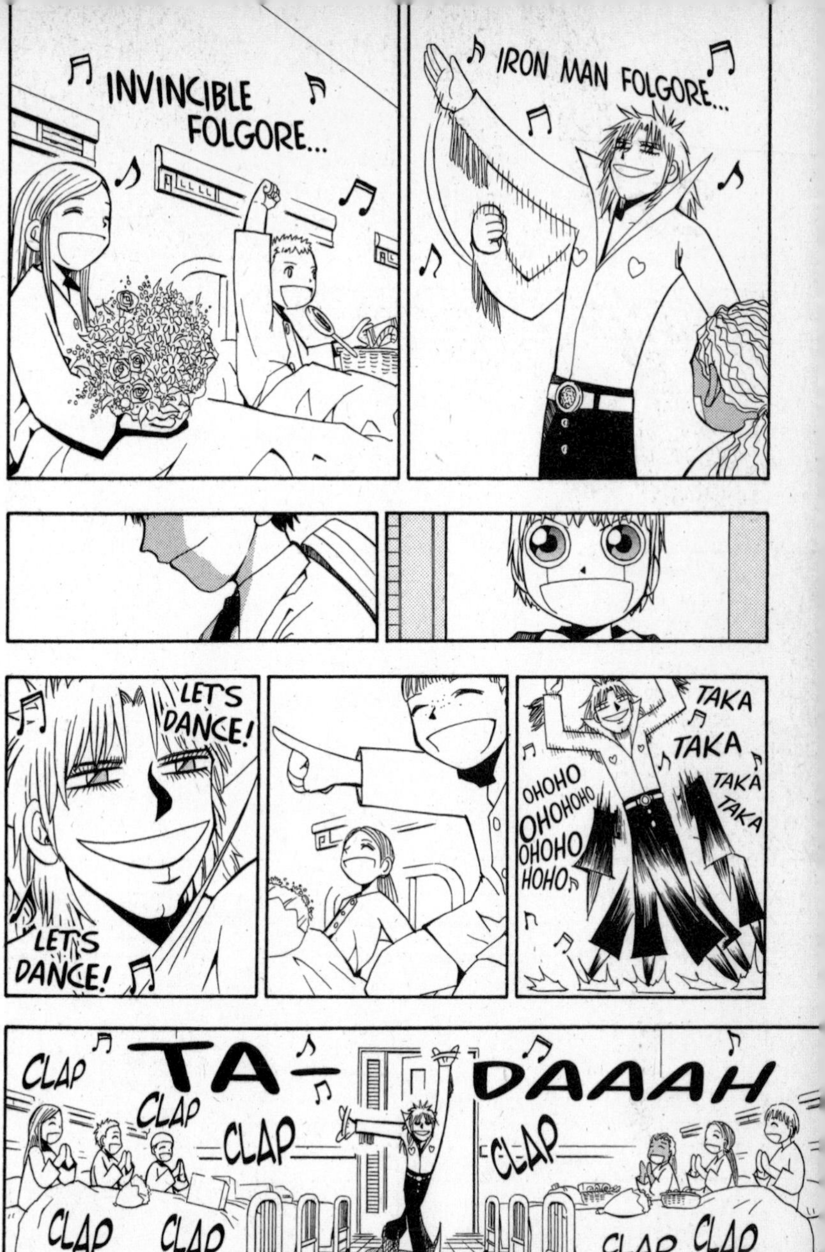
IRON MAN FOLGORE...
INVINCIBLE FOLGORE...
TAKA
TAKA
TAKA
TAKA
OHOHO
OHOHOHO
OHOHO
OHOHO
HOHO
LET'S DANCE!
LET'S DANCE!
TA-DAAAH
CLAP
CLAP
CLAP
CLAP
CLAP CLAP
CLAP
CLAP
CLAP

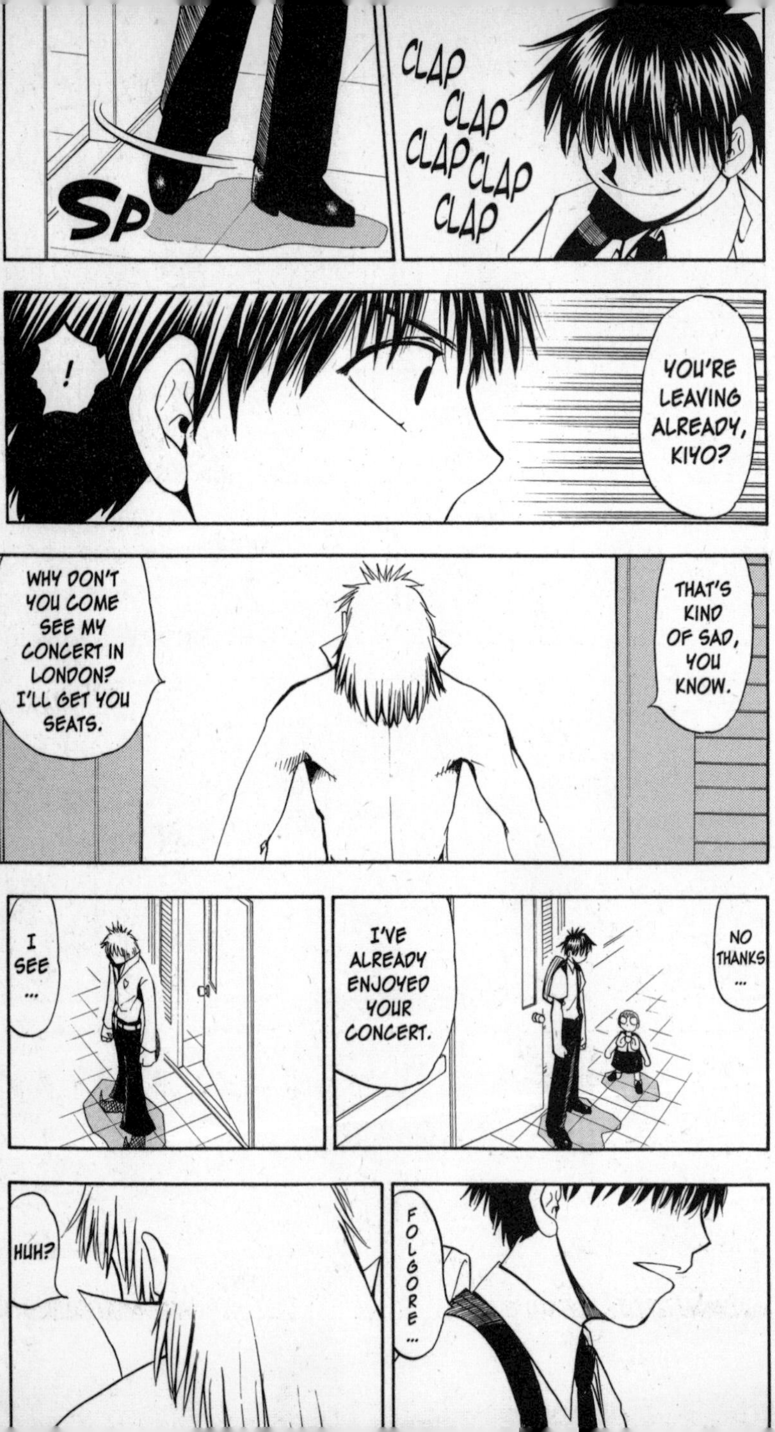
CLAP CLAP CLAP CLAP CLAP
SP
YOU'RE LEAVING ALREADY, KIYO?
!
THAT'S KIND OF SAD, YOU KNOW.
WHY DON'T YOU COME SEE MY CONCERT IN LONDON? I'LL GET YOU SEATS.
NO THANKS...
I'VE ALREADY ENJOYED YOUR CONCERT.
I SEE...
FOLGORE...
HUH?

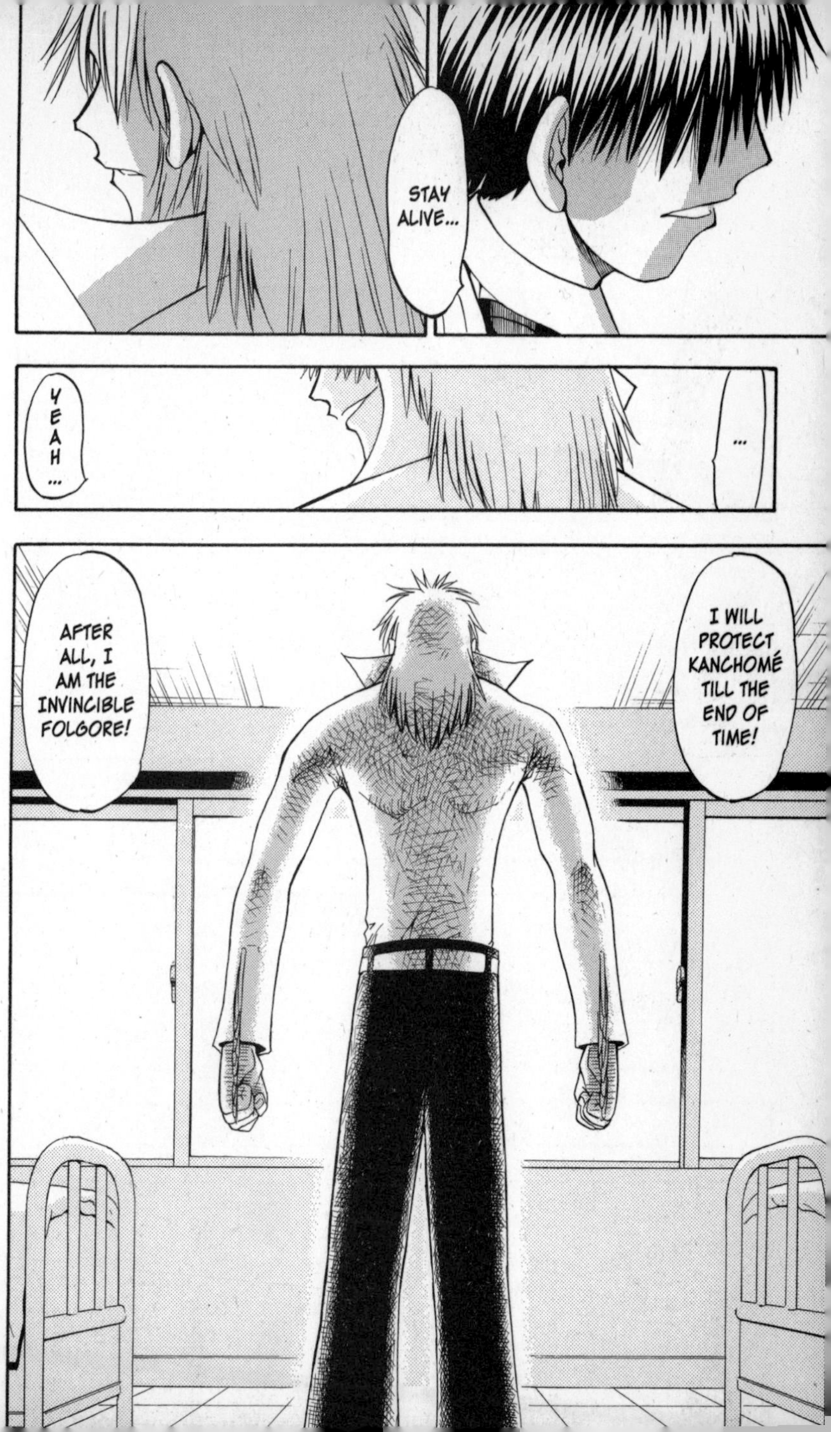
STAY ALIVE...
...
YEAH...
I WILL PROTECT KANCHOMÉ TILL THE END OF TIME!
AFTER ALL, I AM THE INVINCIBLE FOLGORE!

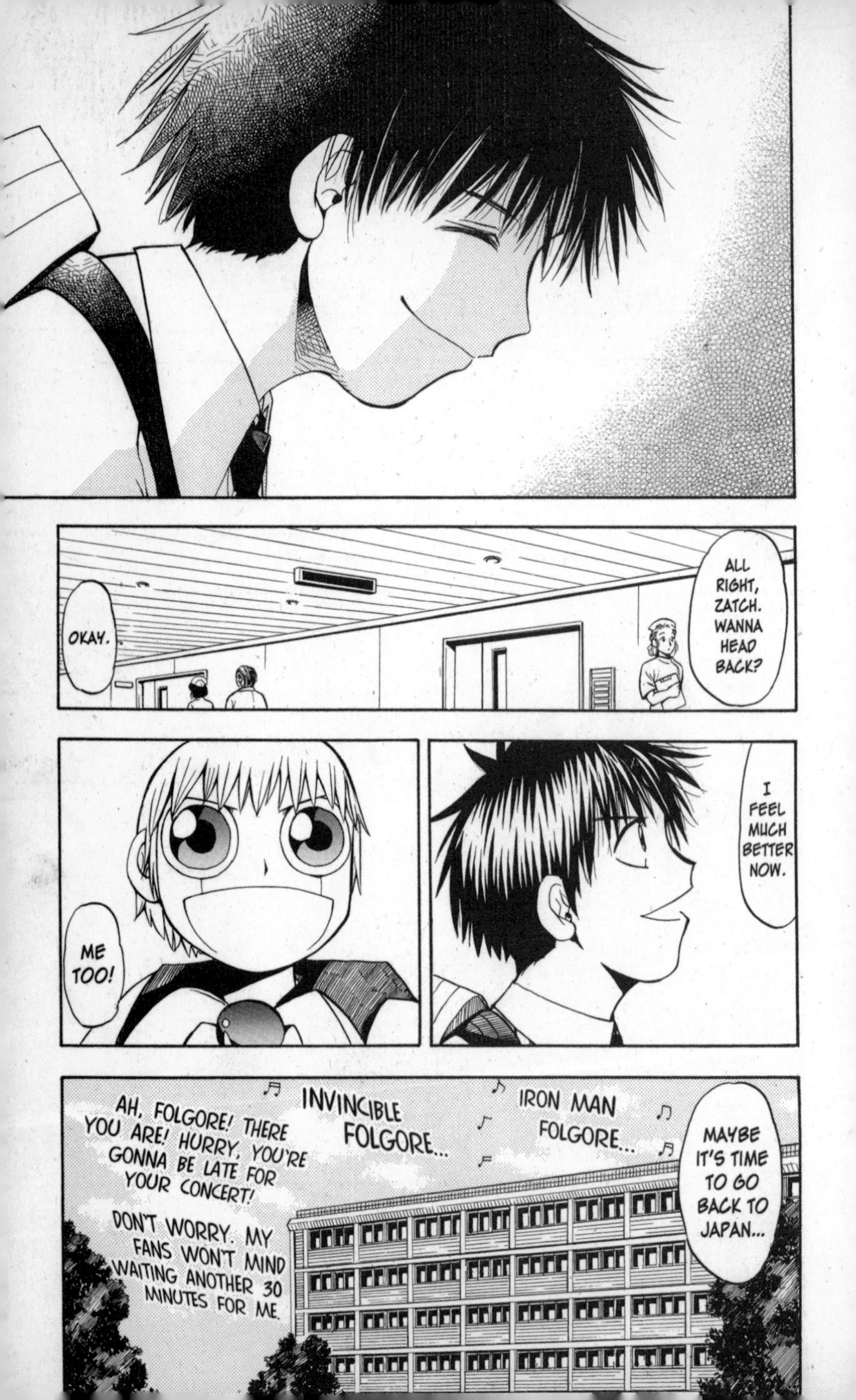
ALL RIGHT, ZATCH. WANNA HEAD BACK?
OKAY.
I FEEL MUCH BETTER NOW.
ME TOO!
MAYBE IT'S TIME TO GO BACK TO JAPAN...
IRON MAN FOLGORE...
INVINCIBLE FOLGORE...
AH, FOLGORE! THERE YOU ARE! HURRY, YOU'RE GONNA BE LATE FOR YOUR CONCERT!
DON'T WORRY. MY FANS WON'T MIND WAITING ANOTHER 30 MINUTES FOR ME.

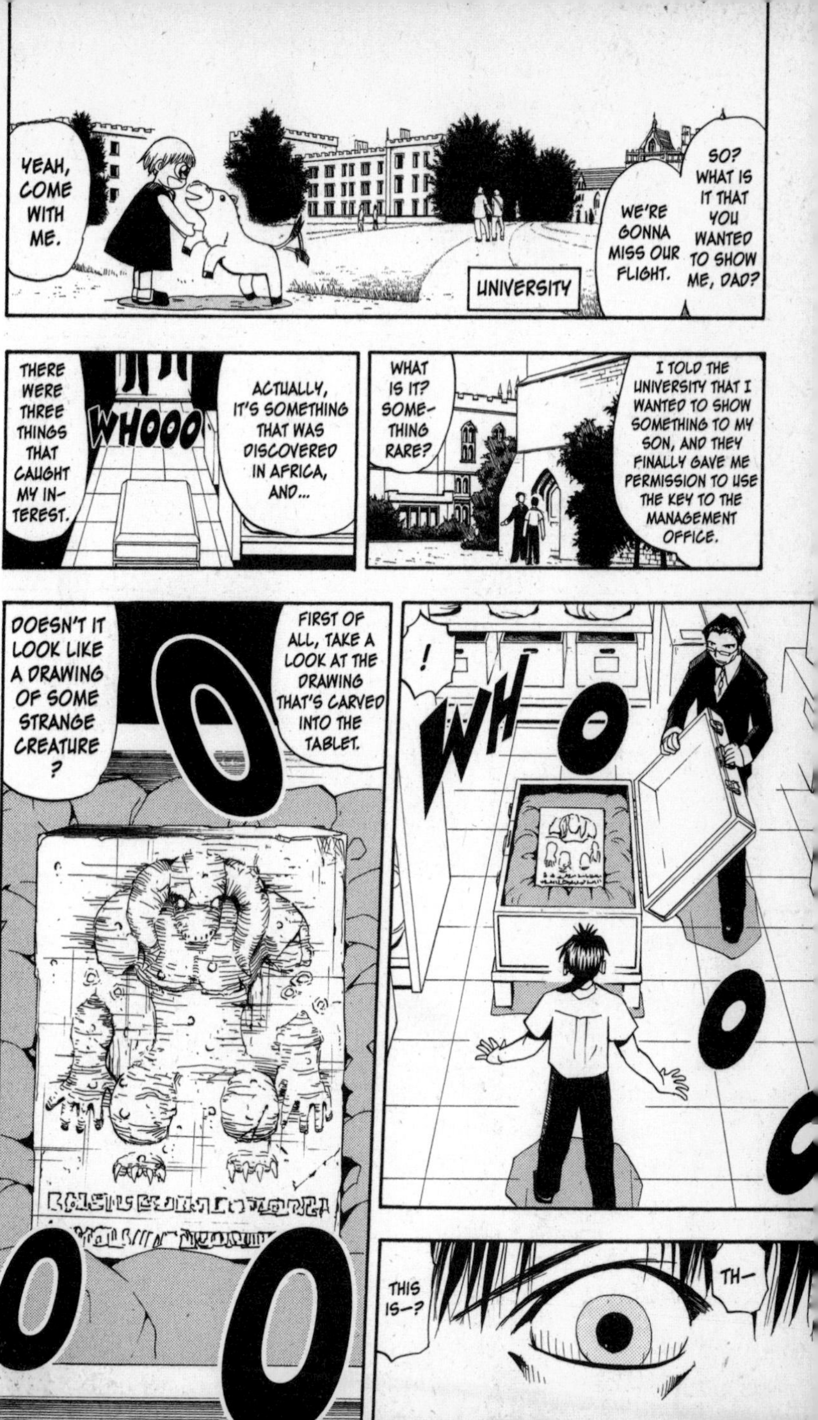
SO? WHAT IS IT THAT YOU WANTED TO SHOW ME, DAD?
WE'RE GONNA MISS OUR FLIGHT.
UNIVERSITY
YEAH, COME WITH ME.
I TOLD THE UNIVERSITY THAT I WANTED TO SHOW SOMETHING TO MY SON, AND THEY FINALLY GAVE ME PERMISSION TO USE THE KEY TO THE MANAGEMENT OFFICE.
WHAT IS IT? SOMETHING RARE?
ACTUALLY, IT'S SOMETHING THAT WAS DISCOVERED IN AFRICA, AND...
WHOOO
THERE WERE THREE THINGS THAT CAUGHT MY INTEREST.
!
WHOOO
TH—
THIS IS—?
FIRST OF ALL, TAKE A LOOK AT THE DRAWING THAT'S CARVED INTO THE TABLET.
DOESN'T IT LOOK LIKE A DRAWING OF SOME STRANGE CREATURE?
OOO

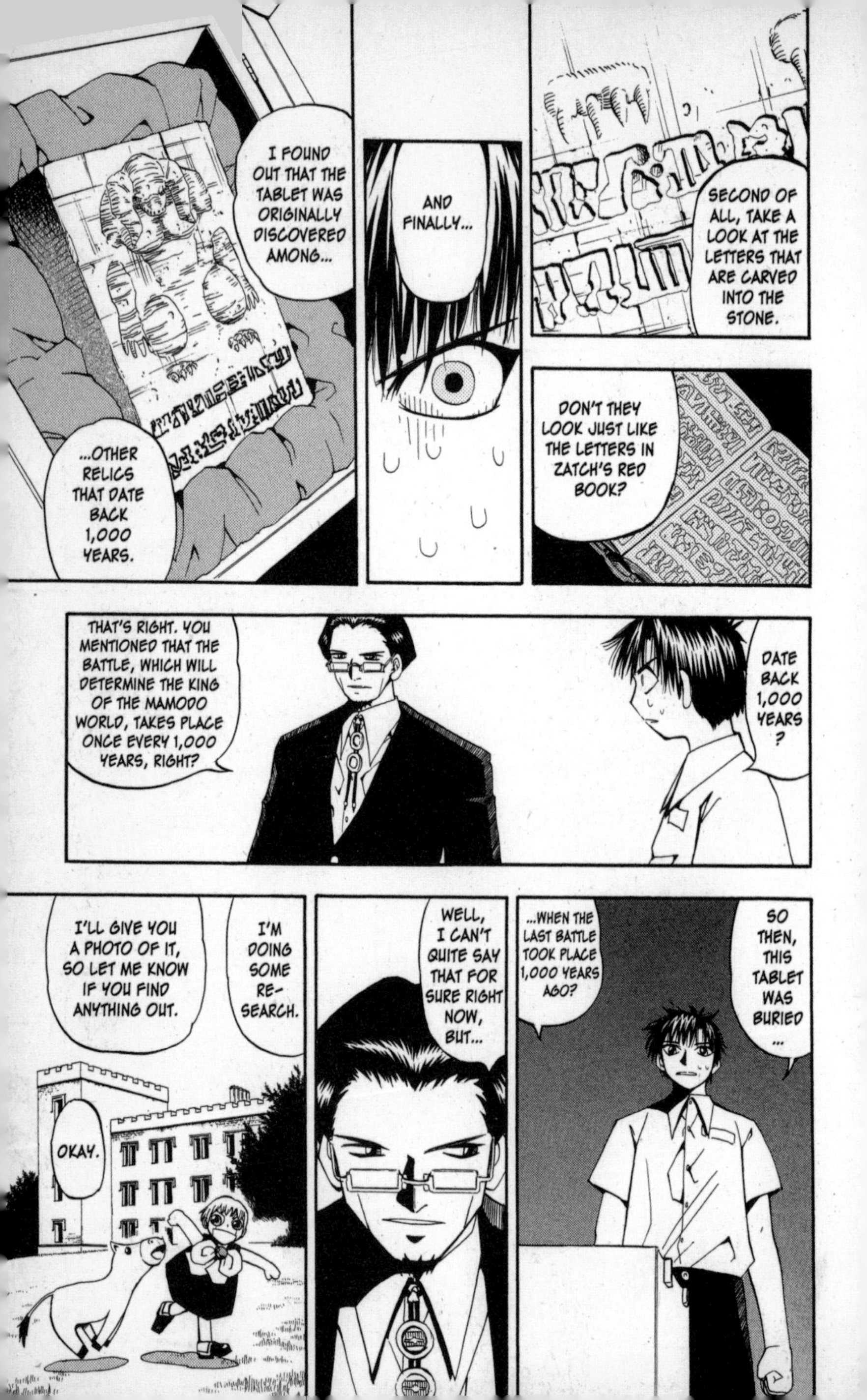
SECOND OF ALL, TAKE A LOOK AT THE LETTERS THAT ARE CARVED INTO THE STONE.
DON'T THEY LOOK JUST LIKE THE LETTERS IN ZATCH'S RED BOOK?
AND FINALLY...
I FOUND OUT THAT THE TABLET WAS ORIGINALLY DISCOVERED AMONG...
...OTHER RELICS THAT DATE BACK 1,000 YEARS.
DATE BACK 1,000 YEARS?
THAT'S RIGHT. YOU MENTIONED THAT THE BATTLE, WHICH WILL DETERMINE THE KING OF THE MAMODO WORLD, TAKES PLACE ONCE EVERY 1,000 YEARS, RIGHT?
SO THEN, THIS TABLET WAS BURIED...
...WHEN THE LAST BATTLE TOOK PLACE 1,000 YEARS AGO?
WELL, I CAN'T QUITE SAY THAT FOR SURE RIGHT NOW, BUT...
I'M DOING SOME RE-SEARCH.
I'LL GIVE YOU A PHOTO OF IT, SO LET ME KNOW IF YOU FIND ANYTHING OUT.
OKAY.

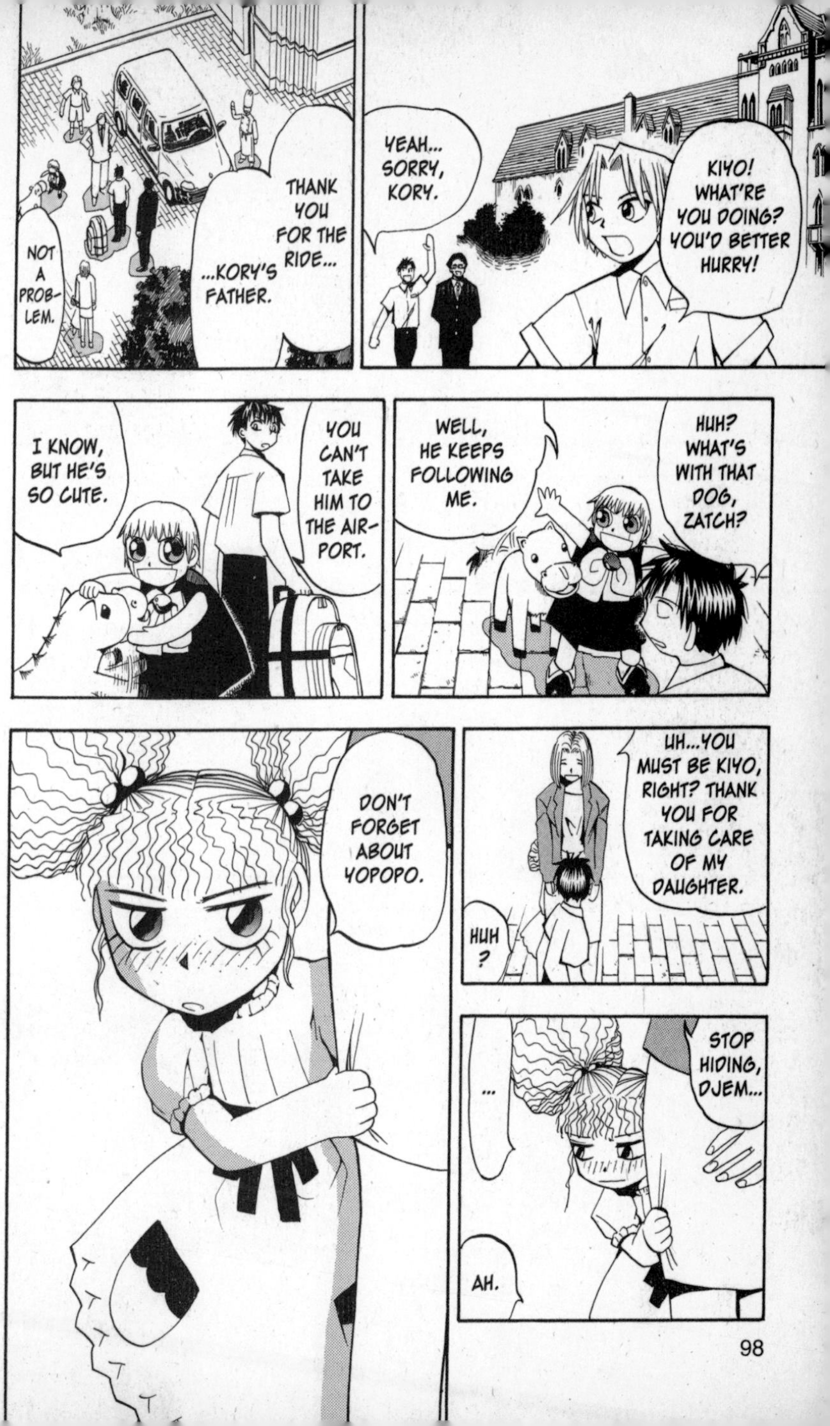
KIYO! WHAT'RE YOU DOING? YOU'D BETTER HURRY!
YEAH... SORRY, KORY.
THANK YOU FOR THE RIDE...
...KORY'S FATHER.
NOT A PROBLEM.
HUH? WHAT'S WITH THAT DOG, ZATCH?
WELL, HE KEEPS FOLLOWING ME.
YOU CAN'T TAKE HIM TO THE AIRPORT.
I KNOW, BUT HE'S SO CUTE.
UH...YOU MUST BE KIYO, RIGHT? THANK YOU FOR TAKING CARE OF MY DAUGHTER.
HUH?
STOP HIDING, DJEM...
...
AH.
DON'T FORGET ABOUT YOPOPO.

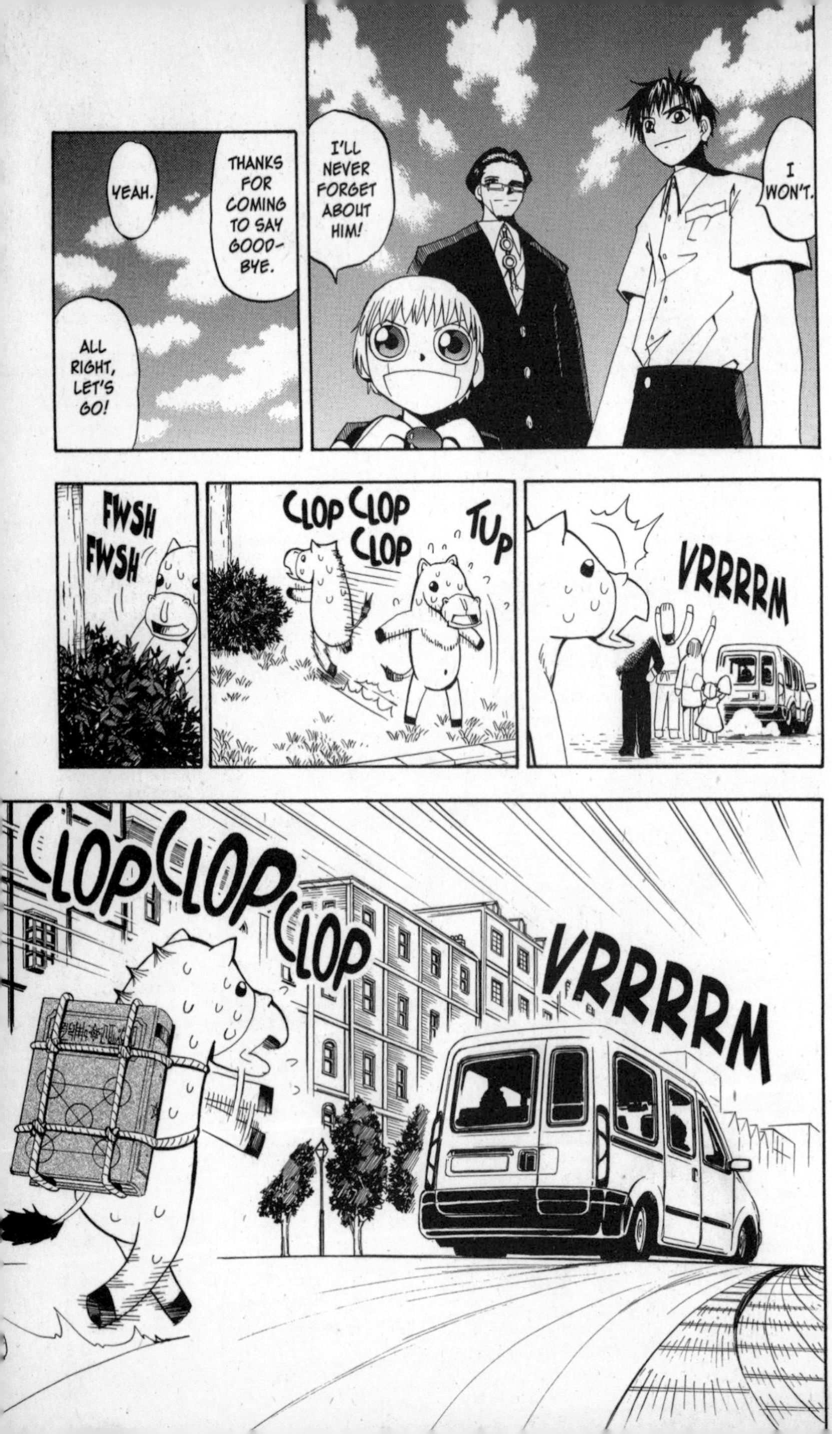
I WON'T.
I'LL NEVER FORGET ABOUT HIM!
THANKS FOR COMING TO SAY GOOD-BYE.
YEAH.
ALL RIGHT, LET'S GO!
VRRRRM
TUP
CLOP CLOP CLOP
FWSH FWSH
VRRRRM
CLOP CLOP CLOP

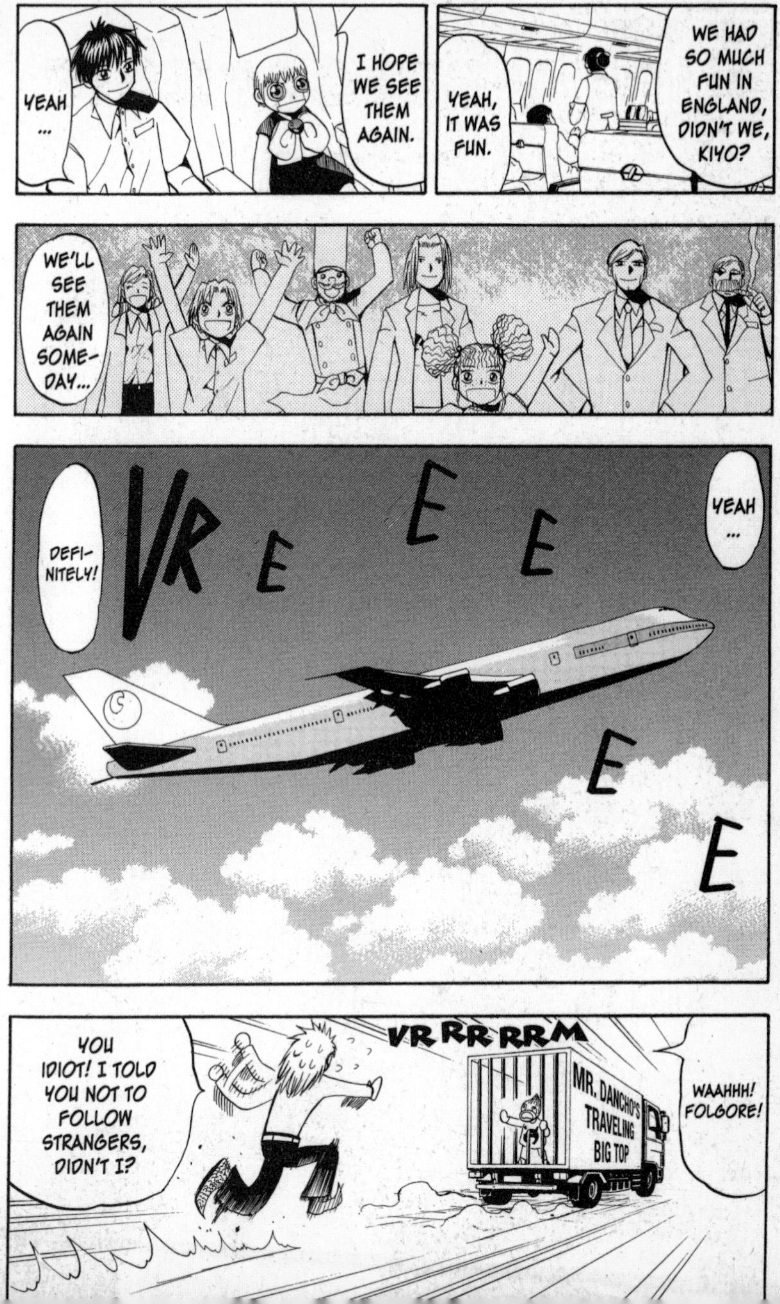
WE HAD SO MUCH FUN IN ENGLAND, DIDN'T WE, KIYO?
YEAH, IT WAS FUN.
I HOPE WE SEE THEM AGAIN.
YEAH ...
WE'LL SEE THEM AGAIN SOME-DAY...
YEAH ...
VREEEEEE
DEFI-NITELY!
WAAHHH! FOLGORE!
VRRRRRM
MR. DANCHO'S TRAVELING BIG TOP
YOU IDIOT! I TOLD YOU NOT TO FOLLOW STRANGERS, DIDN'T I?

LEVEL 54: An Irreplaceable Friend

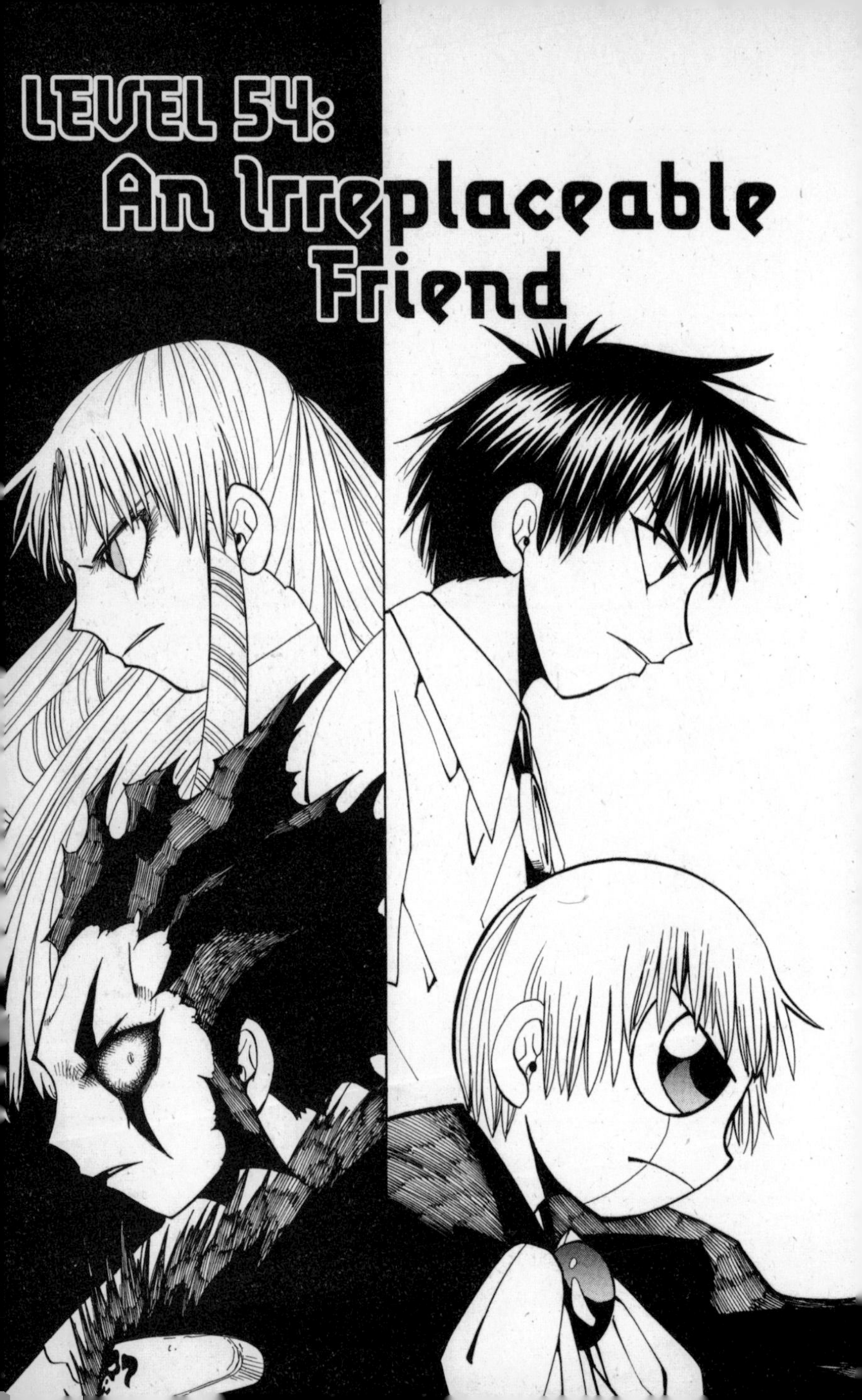

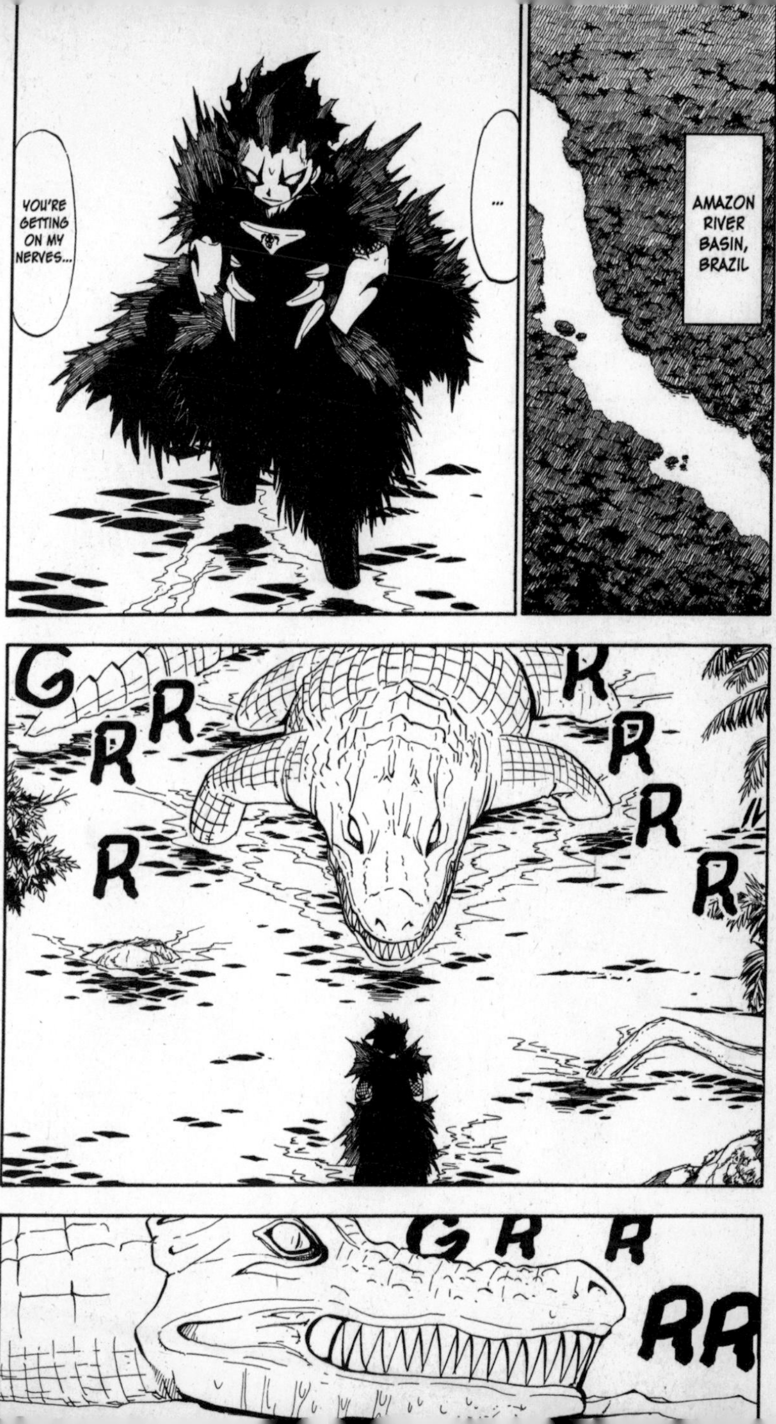
AMAZON RIVER BASIN, BRAZIL
...
YOU'RE GETTING ON MY NERVES...
GRRRRRRRR
GRRRRRRR
GRRRRRR

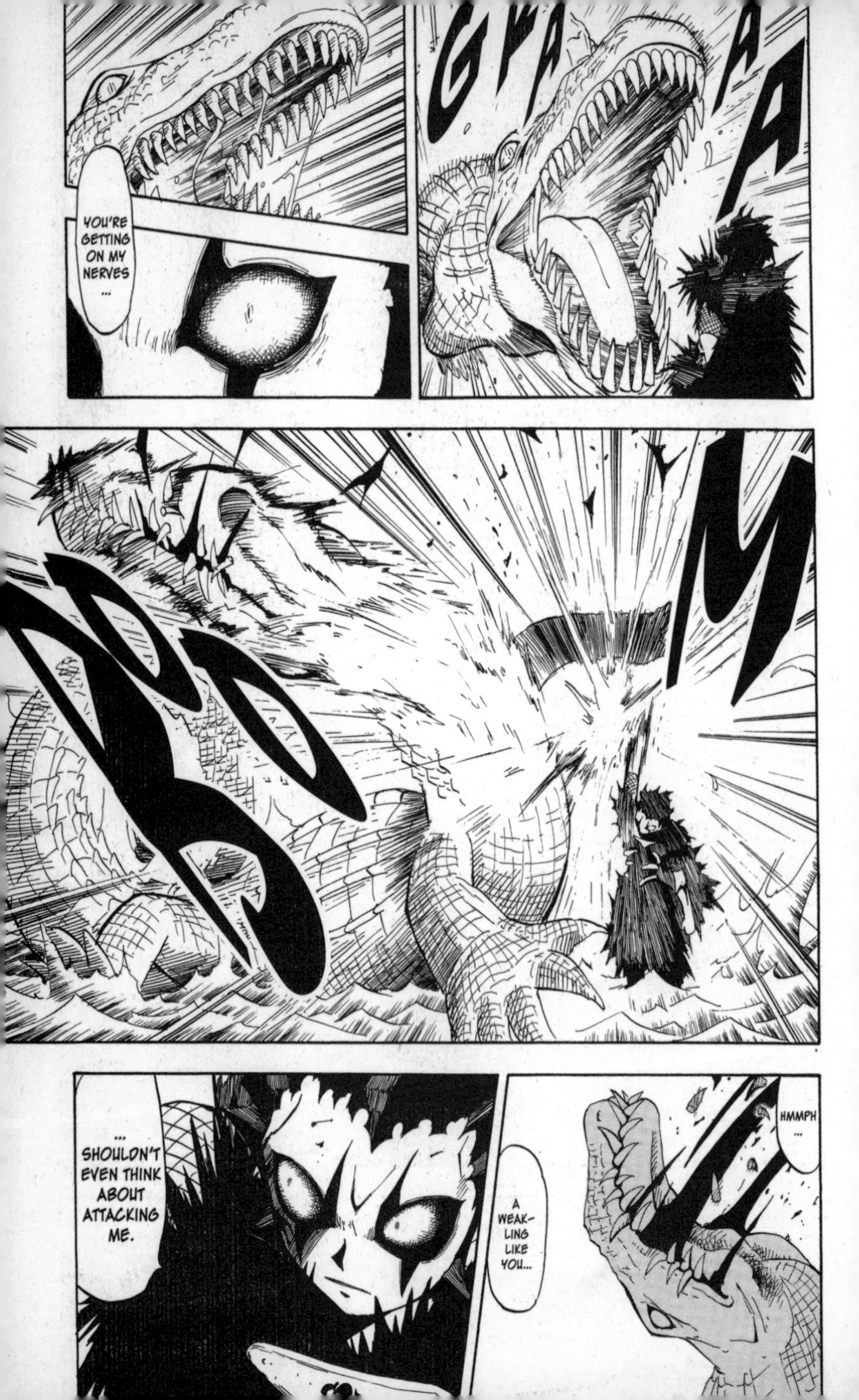
GYAAA
YOU'RE GETTING ON MY NERVES ...
HMMPH ...
A WEAK-LING LIKE YOU...
... SHOULDN'T EVEN THINK ABOUT ATTACKING ME.

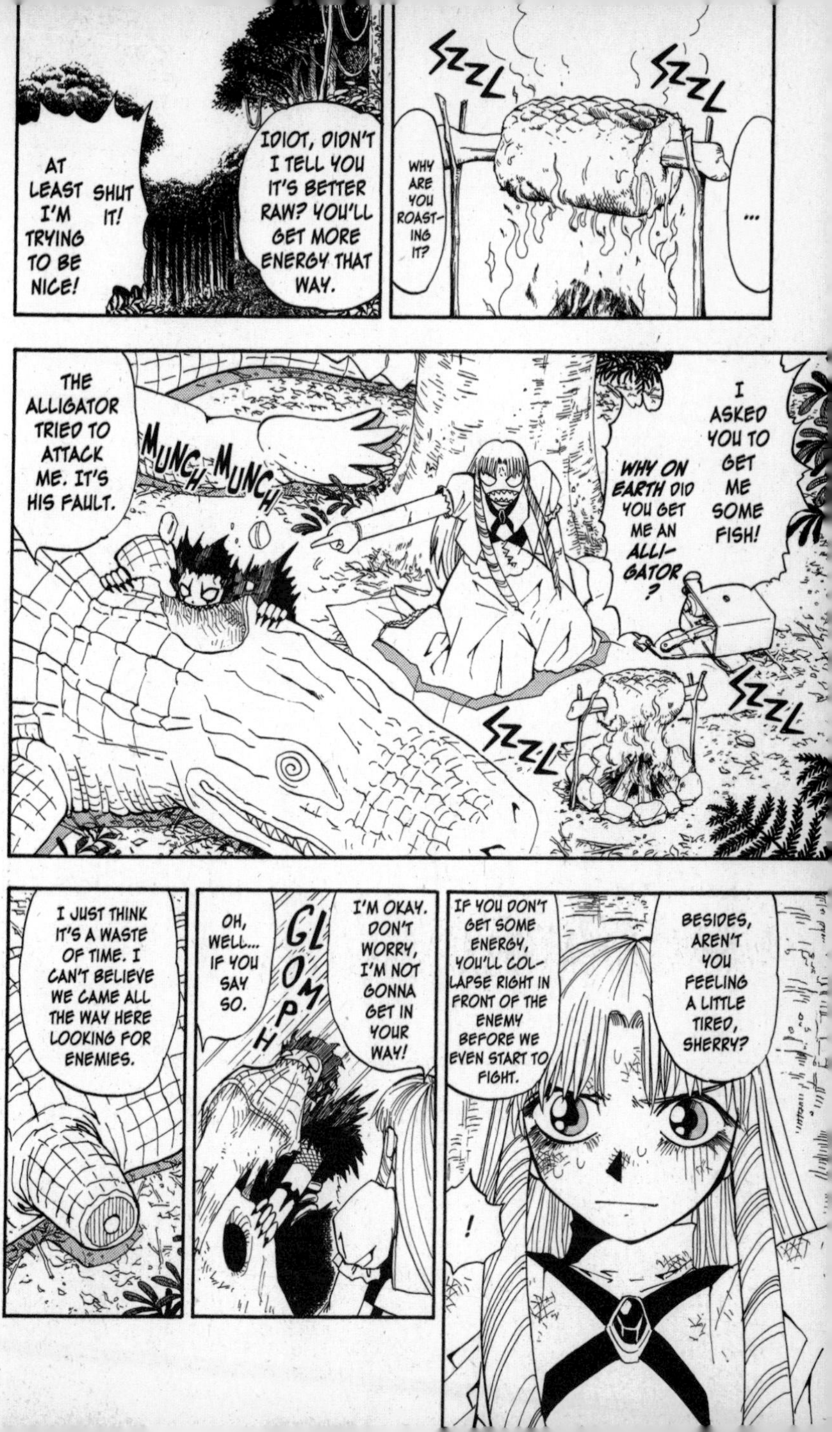
SZZL
SZZL
...
WHY ARE YOU ROASTING IT?
IDIOT, DIDN'T I TELL YOU IT'S BETTER RAW? YOU'LL GET MORE ENERGY THAT WAY.
SHUT IT!
AT LEAST I'M TRYING TO BE NICE!
I ASKED YOU TO GET ME SOME FISH!
WHY ON EARTH DID YOU GET ME AN ALLIGATOR?
MUNCH MUNCH
THE ALLIGATOR TRIED TO ATTACK ME. IT'S HIS FAULT.
SZZL
SZZL
BESIDES, AREN'T YOU FEELING A LITTLE TIRED, SHERRY?
IF YOU DON'T GET SOME ENERGY, YOU'LL COLLAPSE RIGHT IN FRONT OF THE ENEMY BEFORE WE EVEN START TO FIGHT.
!
I'M OKAY. DON'T WORRY, I'M NOT GONNA GET IN YOUR WAY!
GLOMPH
OH, WELL... IF YOU SAY SO.
I JUST THINK IT'S A WASTE OF TIME. I CAN'T BELIEVE WE CAME ALL THE WAY HERE LOOKING FOR ENEMIES.

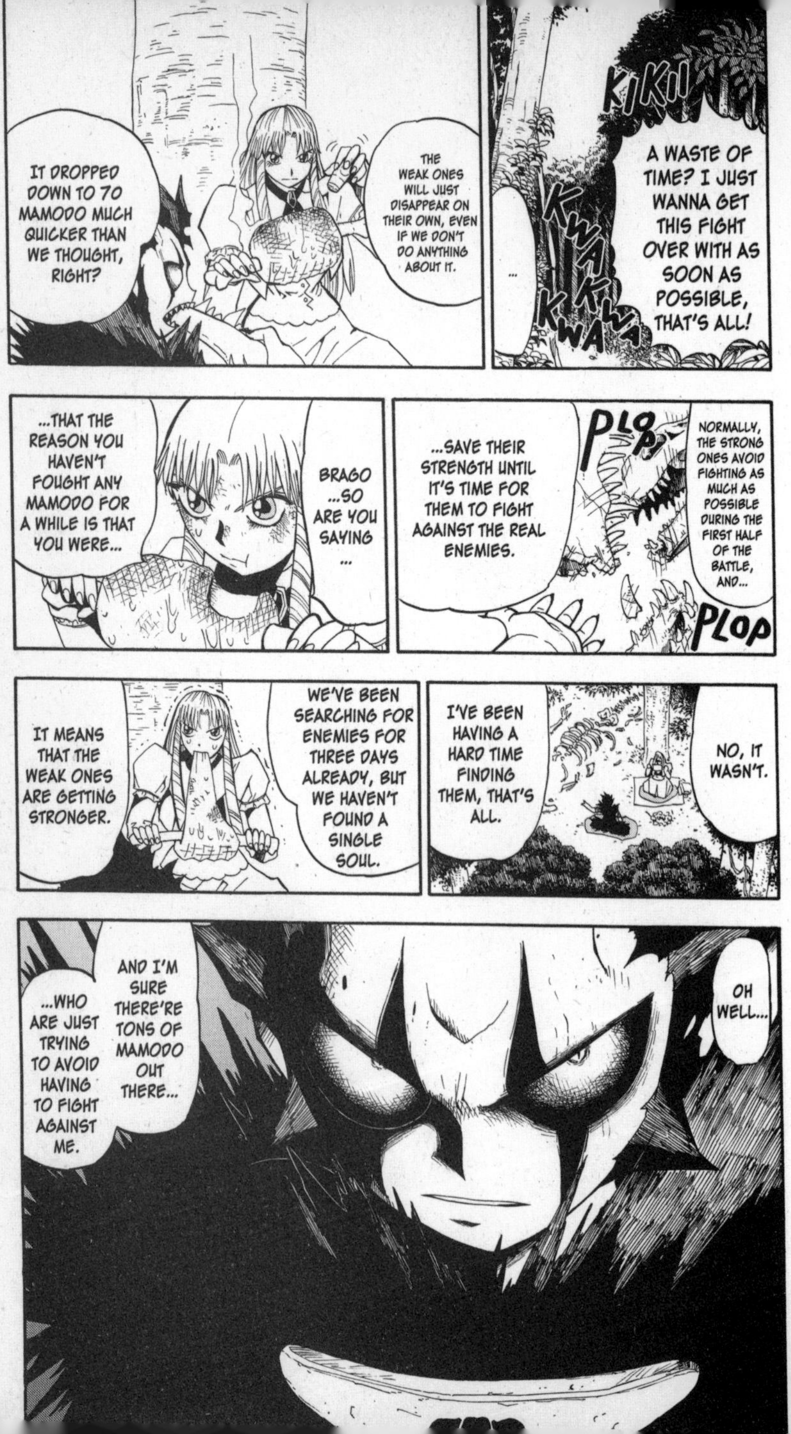
KIKII
A WASTE OF TIME? I JUST WANNA GET THIS FIGHT OVER WITH AS SOON AS POSSIBLE, THAT'S ALL!
KWA KWA KWA
...
THE WEAK ONES WILL JUST DISAPPEAR ON THEIR OWN, EVEN IF WE DON'T DO ANYTHING ABOUT IT.
IT DROPPED DOWN TO 70 MAMODO MUCH QUICKER THAN WE THOUGHT, RIGHT?
PLOP
NORMALLY, THE STRONG ONES AVOID FIGHTING AS MUCH AS POSSIBLE DURING THE FIRST HALF OF THE BATTLE, AND...
...SAVE THEIR STRENGTH UNTIL IT'S TIME FOR THEM TO FIGHT AGAINST THE REAL ENEMIES.
PLOP
BRAGO ...SO ARE YOU SAYING ...
...THAT THE REASON YOU HAVEN'T FOUGHT ANY MAMODO FOR A WHILE IS THAT YOU WERE...
NO, IT WASN'T.
I'VE BEEN HAVING A HARD TIME FINDING THEM, THAT'S ALL.
WE'VE BEEN SEARCHING FOR ENEMIES FOR THREE DAYS ALREADY, BUT WE HAVEN'T FOUND A SINGLE SOUL.
IT MEANS THAT THE WEAK ONES ARE GETTING STRONGER.
OH WELL...
AND I'M SURE THERE'RE TONS OF MAMODO OUT THERE...
...WHO ARE JUST TRYING TO AVOID HAVING TO FIGHT AGAINST ME.

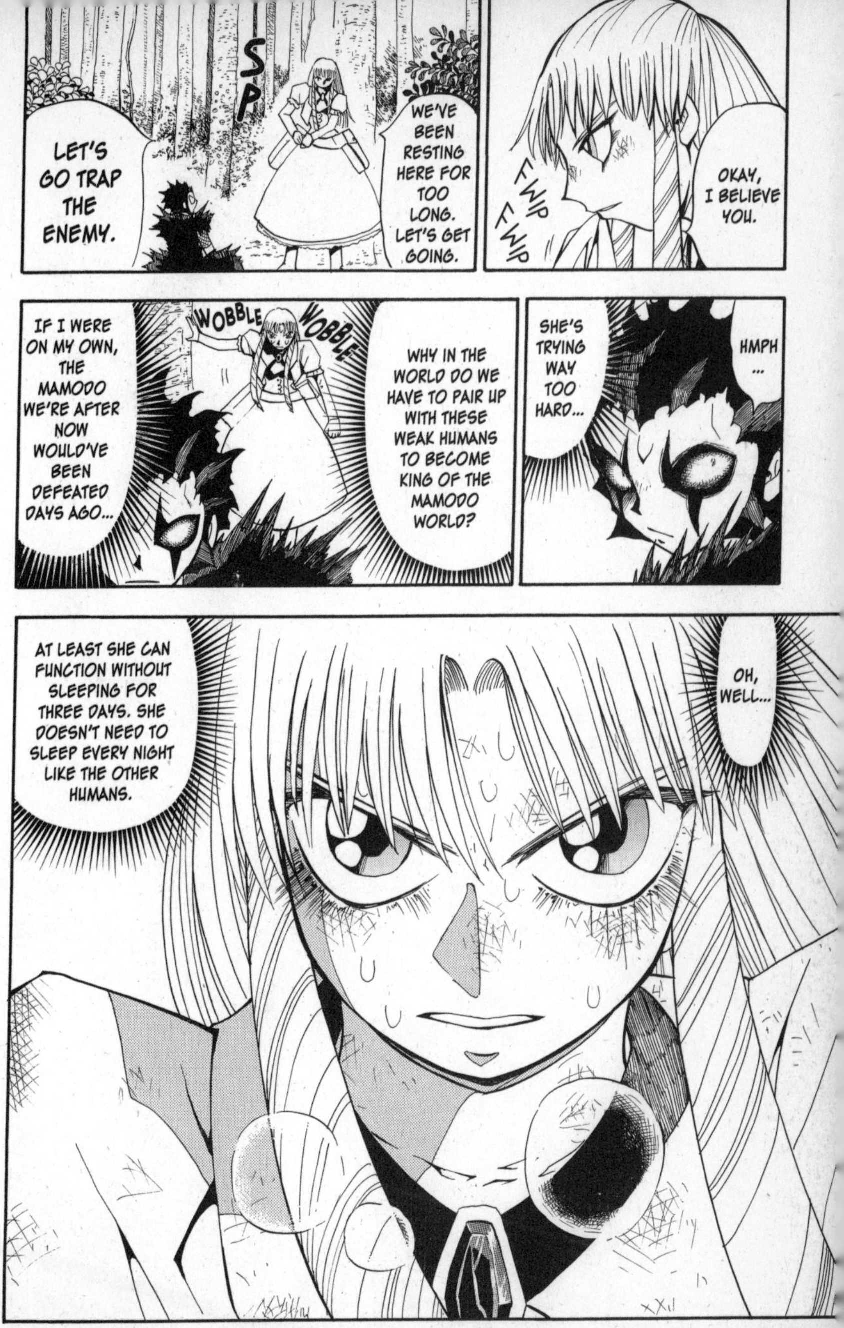

OKAY, I BELIEVE YOU.
FWIP FWIP
WE'VE BEEN RESTING HERE FOR TOO LONG. LET'S GET GOING.
SP
LET'S GO TRAP THE ENEMY.
HMPH...
SHE'S TRYING WAY TOO HARD...
WHY IN THE WORLD DO WE HAVE TO PAIR UP WITH THESE WEAK HUMANS TO BECOME KING OF THE MAMODO WORLD?
WOBBLE WOBBLE
IF I WERE ON MY OWN, THE MAMODO WE'RE AFTER NOW WOULD'VE BEEN DEFEATED DAYS AGO...
OH, WELL...
AT LEAST SHE CAN FUNCTION WITHOUT SLEEPING FOR THREE DAYS. SHE DOESN'T NEED TO SLEEP EVERY NIGHT LIKE THE OTHER HUMANS.

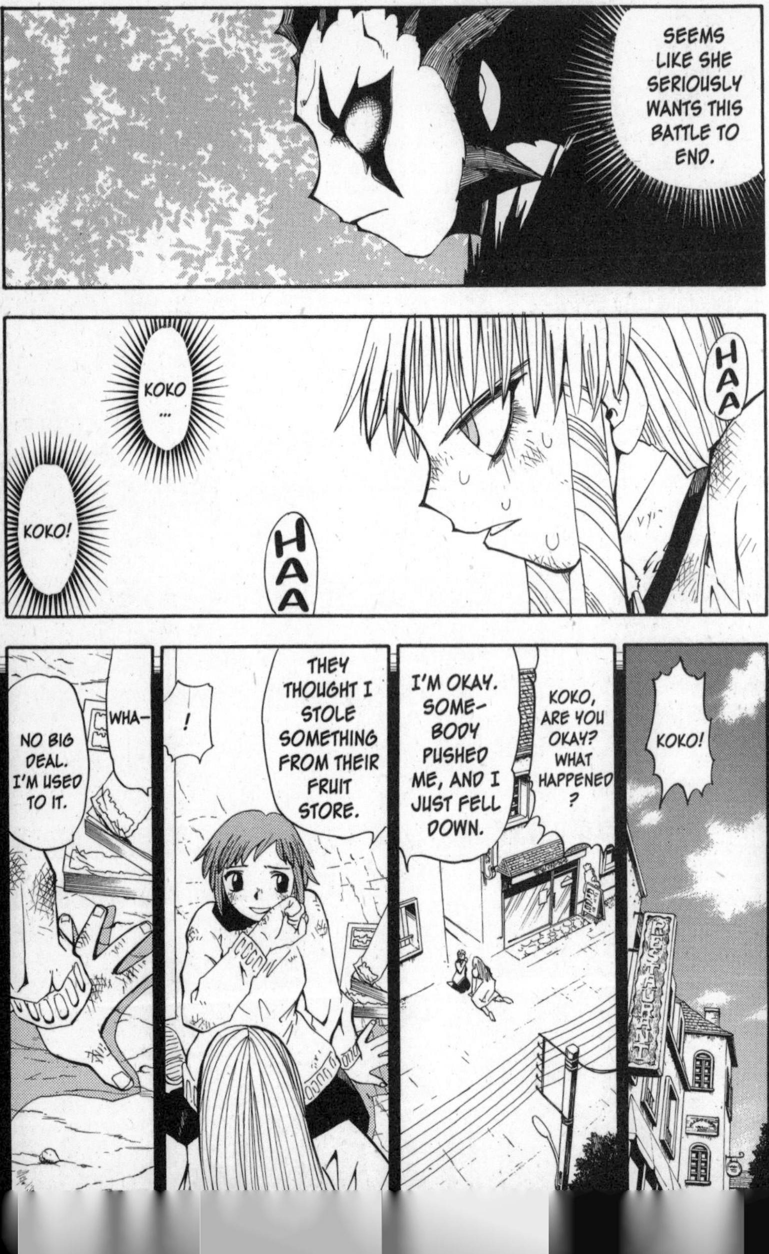
SEEMS LIKE SHE SERIOUSLY WANTS THIS BATTLE TO END.
HAA
KOKO...
HAA
KOKO!
KOKO!
KOKO, ARE YOU OKAY? WHAT HAPPENED?
I'M OKAY. SOME-BODY PUSHED ME, AND I JUST FELL DOWN.
THEY THOUGHT I STOLE SOMETHING FROM THEIR FRUIT STORE.
!
WHA-
NO BIG DEAL. I'M USED TO IT.
RESTAURANT

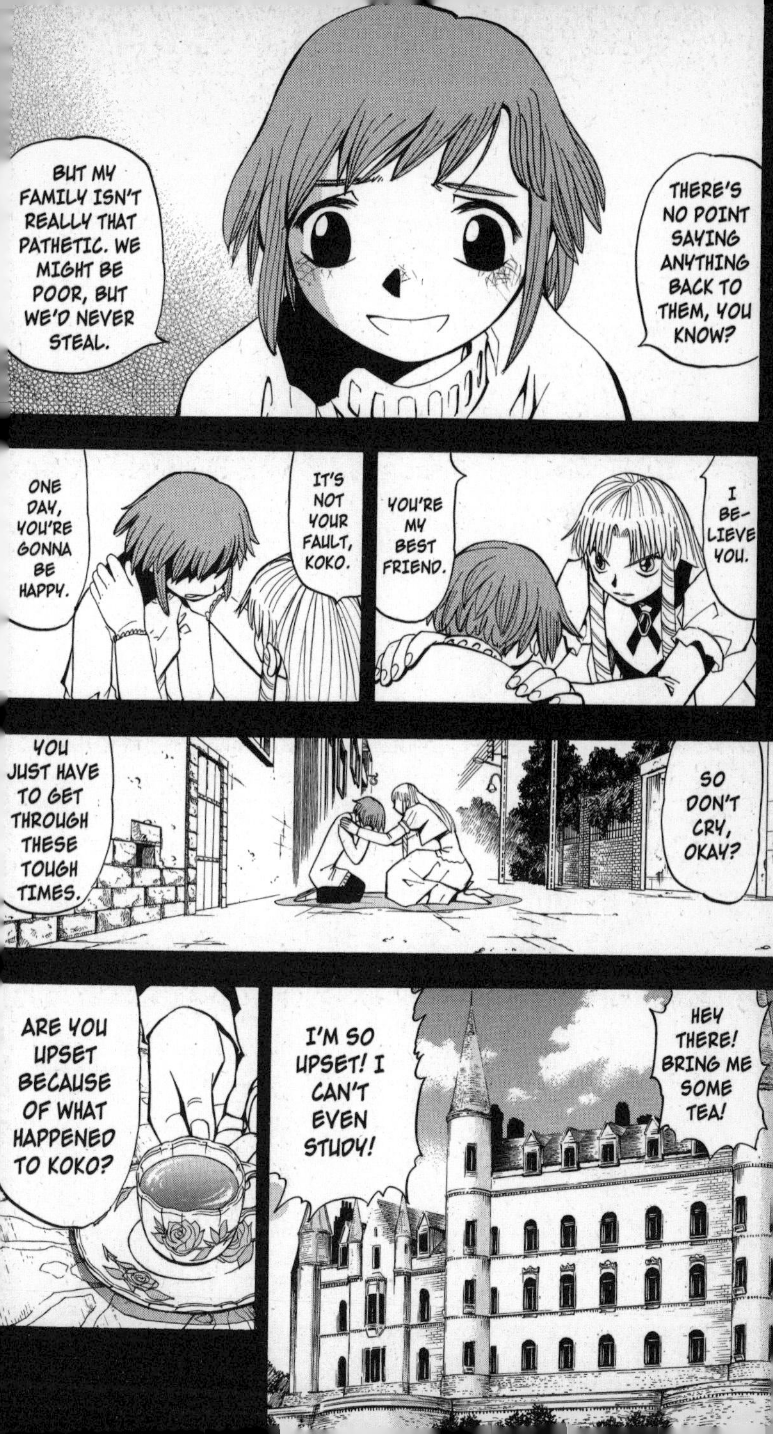
THERE'S NO POINT SAYING ANYTHING BACK TO THEM, YOU KNOW?
BUT MY FAMILY ISN'T REALLY THAT PATHETIC. WE MIGHT BE POOR, BUT WE'D NEVER STEAL.
I BE-LIEVE YOU.
YOU'RE MY BEST FRIEND.
IT'S NOT YOUR FAULT, KOKO.
ONE DAY, YOU'RE GONNA BE HAPPY.
SO DON'T CRY, OKAY?
YOU JUST HAVE TO GET THROUGH THESE TOUGH TIMES.
HEY THERE! BRING ME SOME TEA!
I'M SO UPSET! I CAN'T EVEN STUDY!
ARE YOU UPSET BECAUSE OF WHAT HAPPENED TO KOKO?

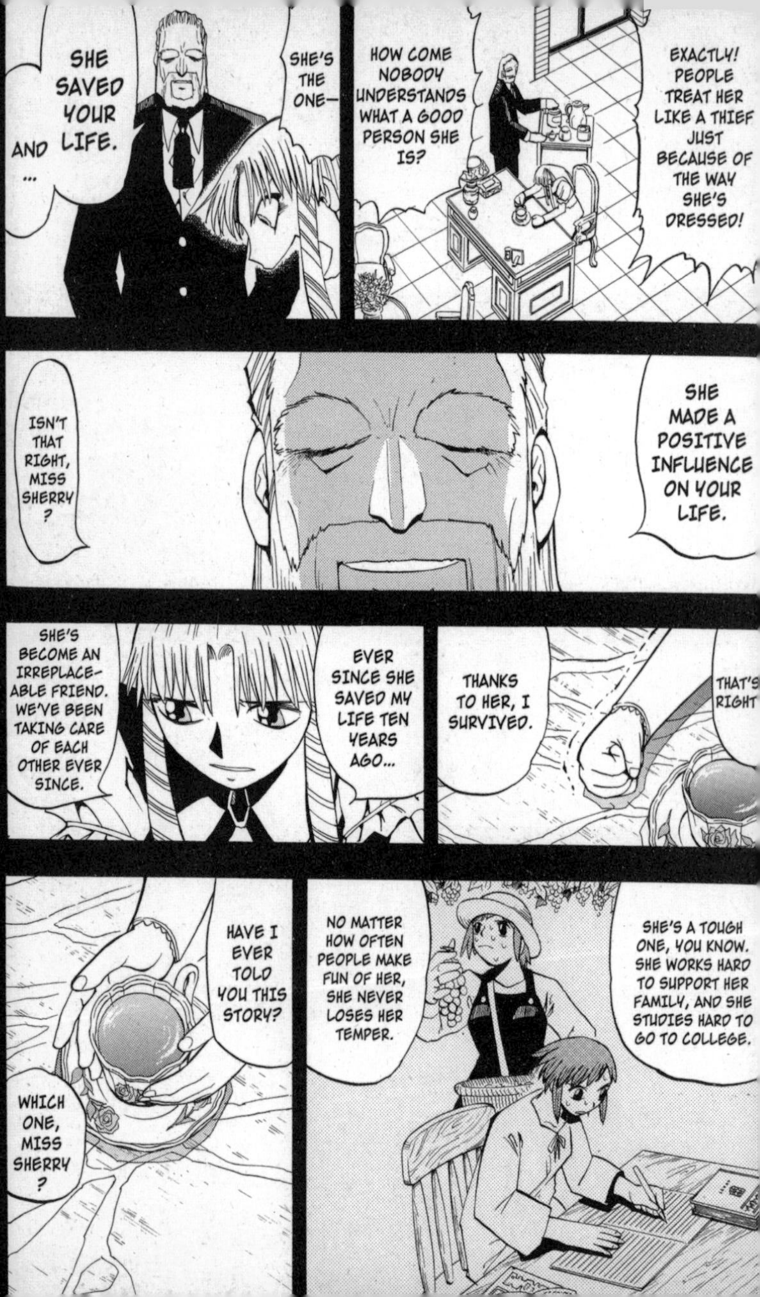
EXACTLY! PEOPLE TREAT HER LIKE A THIEF JUST BECAUSE OF THE WAY SHE'S DRESSED!
HOW COME NOBODY UNDERSTANDS WHAT A GOOD PERSON SHE IS?
SHE'S THE ONE—
SHE SAVED YOUR LIFE.
AND ...
SHE MADE A POSITIVE INFLUENCE ON YOUR LIFE.
ISN'T THAT RIGHT, MISS SHERRY?
THAT'S RIGHT
THANKS TO HER, I SURVIVED.
EVER SINCE SHE SAVED MY LIFE TEN YEARS AGO...
SHE'S BECOME AN IRREPLACE-ABLE FRIEND. WE'VE BEEN TAKING CARE OF EACH OTHER EVER SINCE.
SHE'S A TOUGH ONE, YOU KNOW. SHE WORKS HARD TO SUPPORT HER FAMILY, AND SHE STUDIES HARD TO GO TO COLLEGE.
NO MATTER HOW OFTEN PEOPLE MAKE FUN OF HER, SHE NEVER LOSES HER TEMPER.
HAVE I EVER TOLD YOU THIS STORY?
WHICH ONE, MISS SHERRY?

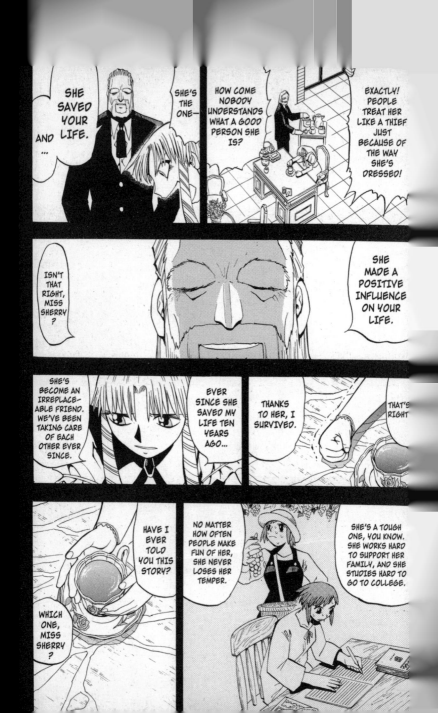

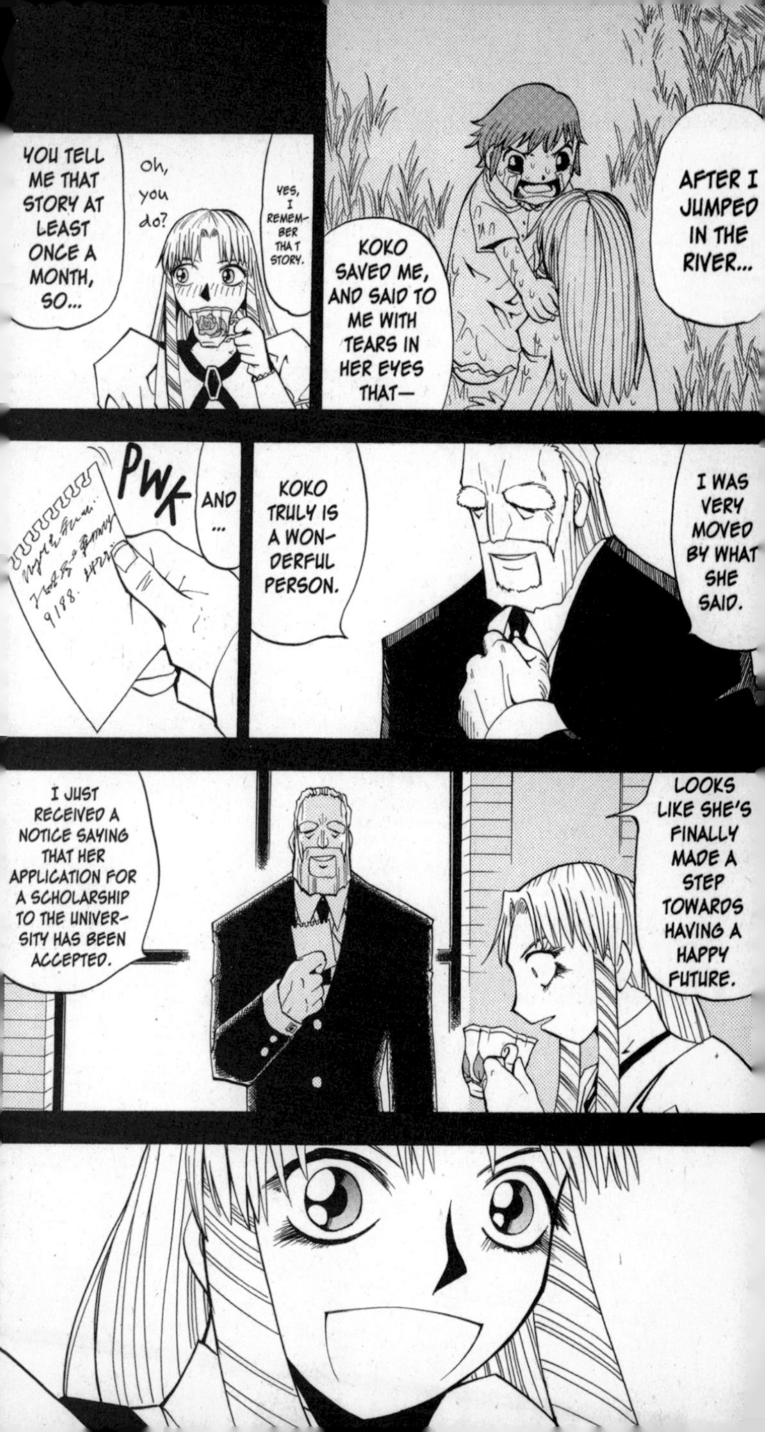
AFTER I JUMPED IN THE RIVER...
KOKO SAVED ME, AND SAID TO ME WITH TEARS IN HER EYES THAT—
YES, I REMEMBER THAT STORY.
Oh, you do?
YOU TELL ME THAT STORY AT LEAST ONCE A MONTH, SO...
I WAS VERY MOVED BY WHAT SHE SAID.
KOKO TRULY IS A WONDERFUL PERSON.
AND ...
PWK
LOOKS LIKE SHE'S FINALLY MADE A STEP TOWARDS HAVING A HAPPY FUTURE.
I JUST RECEIVED A NOTICE SAYING THAT HER APPLICATION FOR A SCHOLARSHIP TO THE UNIVERSITY HAS BEEN ACCEPTED.

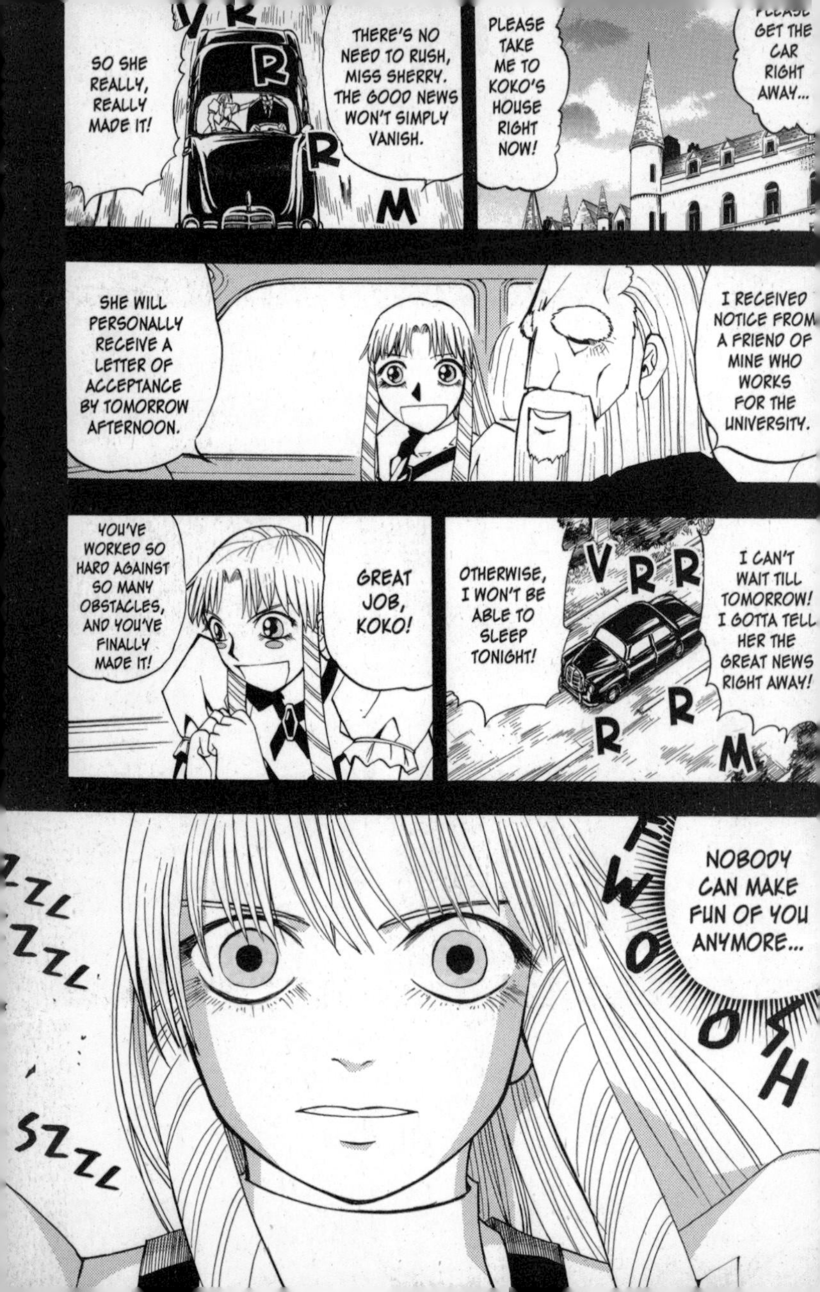
GET THE CAR RIGHT AWAY...
PLEASE TAKE ME TO KOKO'S HOUSE RIGHT NOW!
THERE'S NO NEED TO RUSH, MISS SHERRY. THE GOOD NEWS WON'T SIMPLY VANISH.
SO SHE REALLY, REALLY MADE IT!
I RECEIVED NOTICE FROM A FRIEND OF MINE WHO WORKS FOR THE UNIVERSITY.
SHE WILL PERSONALLY RECEIVE A LETTER OF ACCEPTANCE BY TOMORROW AFTERNOON.
I CAN'T WAIT TILL TOMORROW! I GOTTA TELL HER THE GREAT NEWS RIGHT AWAY!
OTHERWISE, I WON'T BE ABLE TO SLEEP TONIGHT!
VRRRRM
GREAT JOB, KOKO!
YOU'VE WORKED SO HARD AGAINST SO MANY OBSTACLES, AND YOU'VE FINALLY MADE IT!
NOBODY CAN MAKE FUN OF YOU ANYMORE...
WHOOSH
SZZZ

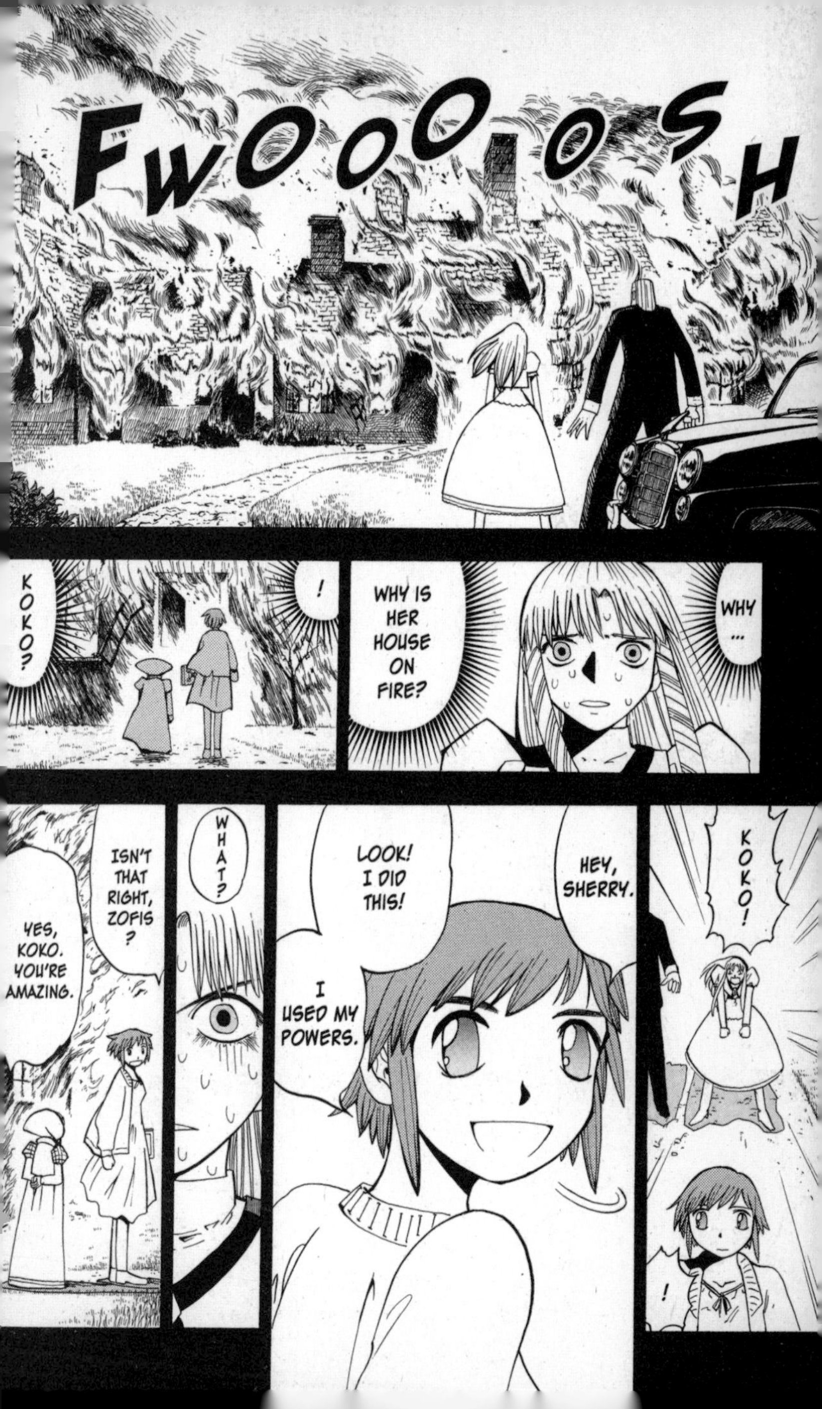
FWOOOOSH
WHY ...
WHY IS HER HOUSE ON FIRE?
!
KOKO?
KOKO!
!
HEY, SHERRY.
LOOK! I DID THIS!
I USED MY POWERS.
WHAT?
ISN'T THAT RIGHT, ZOFIS?
YES, KOKO. YOU'RE AMAZING.

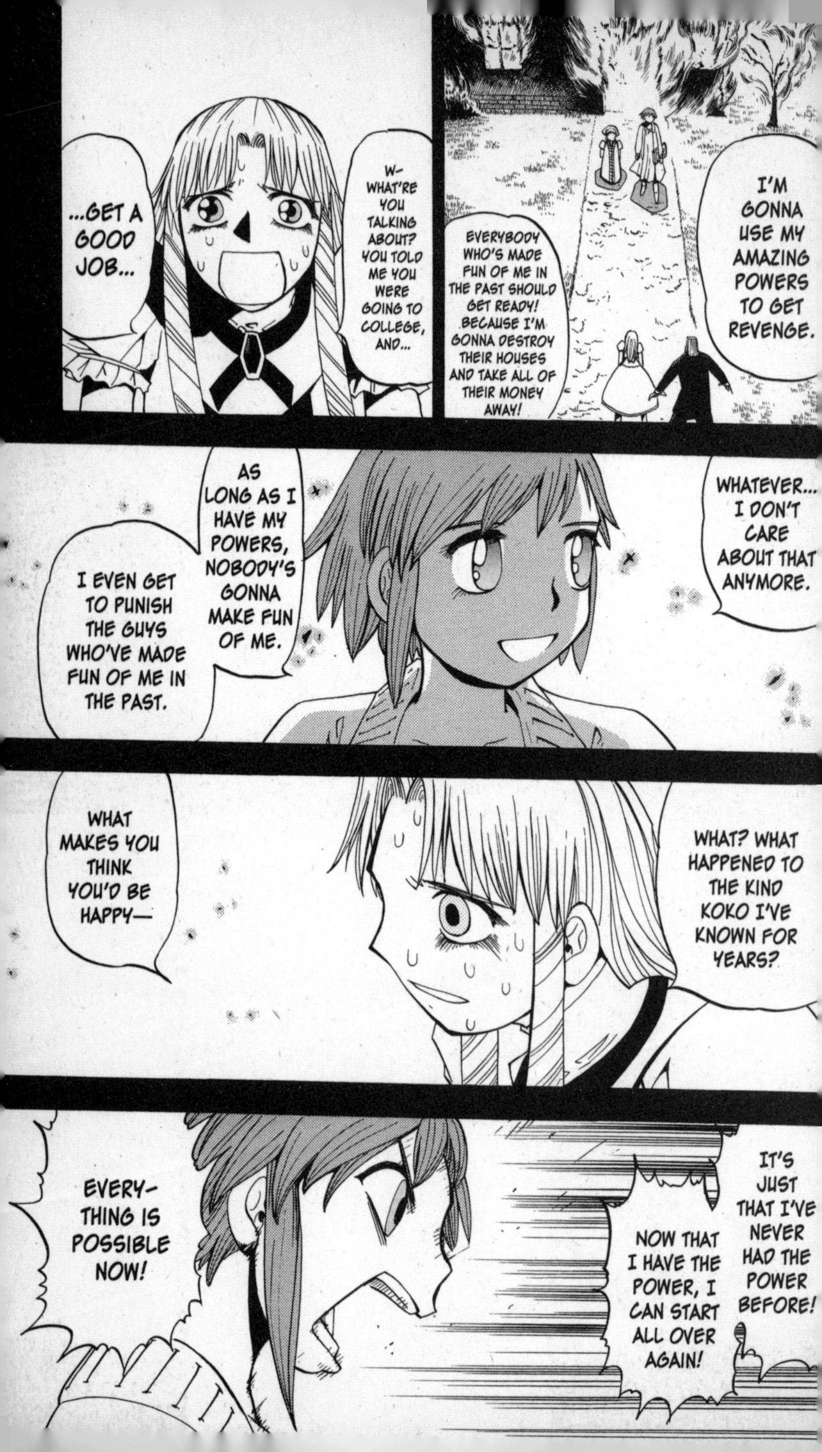
I'M GONNA USE MY AMAZING POWERS TO GET REVENGE.
EVERYBODY WHO'S MADE FUN OF ME IN THE PAST SHOULD GET READY! BECAUSE I'M GONNA DESTROY THEIR HOUSES AND TAKE ALL OF THEIR MONEY AWAY!
W- WHAT'RE YOU TALKING ABOUT? YOU TOLD ME YOU WERE GOING TO COLLEGE, AND...
...GET A GOOD JOB...
WHATEVER... I DON'T CARE ABOUT THAT ANYMORE.
AS LONG AS I HAVE MY POWERS, NOBODY'S GONNA MAKE FUN OF ME.
I EVEN GET TO PUNISH THE GUYS WHO'VE MADE FUN OF ME IN THE PAST.
WHAT? WHAT HAPPENED TO THE KIND KOKO I'VE KNOWN FOR YEARS?
WHAT MAKES YOU THINK YOU'D BE HAPPY—
IT'S JUST THAT I'VE NEVER HAD THE POWER BEFORE!
NOW THAT I HAVE THE POWER, I CAN START ALL OVER AGAIN!
EVERY-THING IS POSSIBLE NOW!

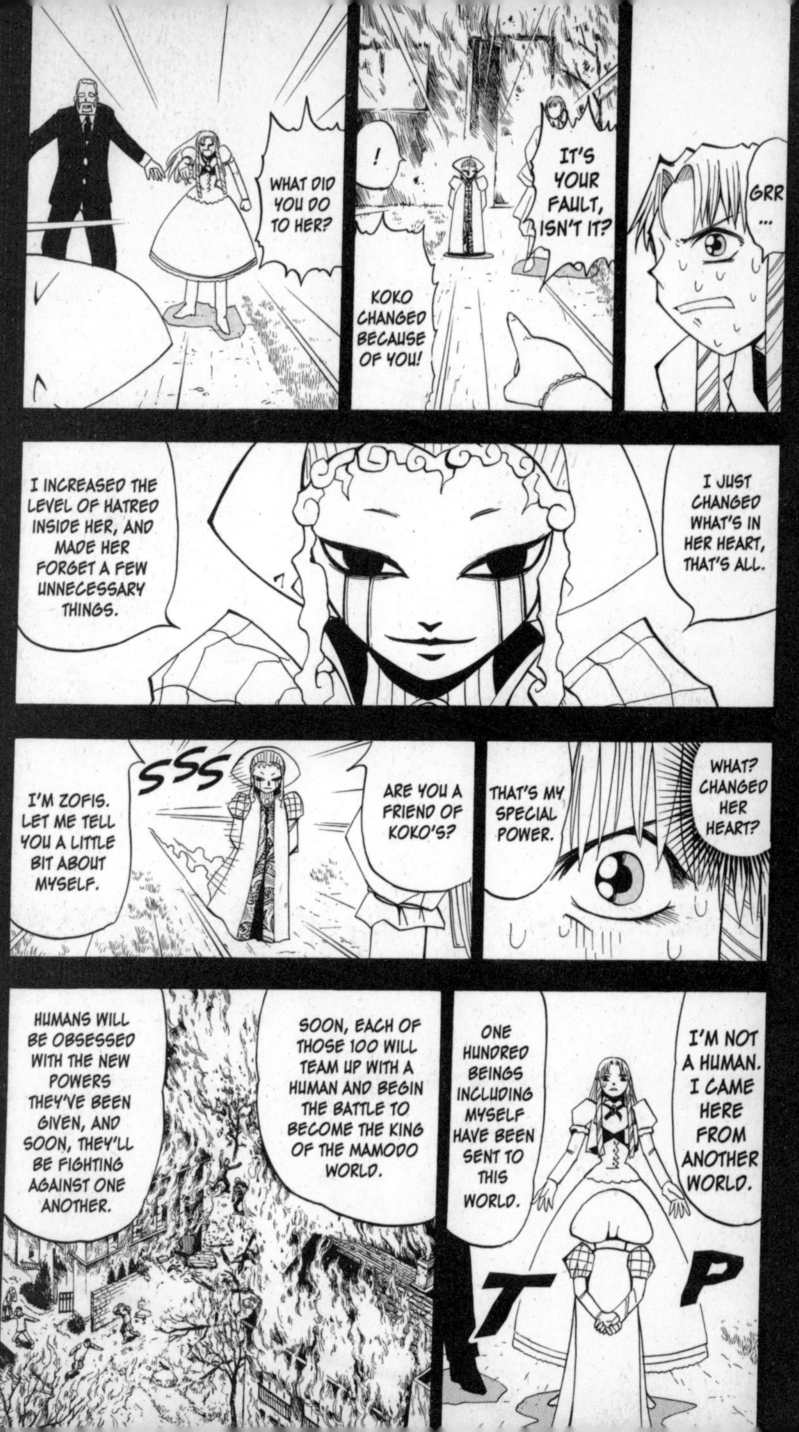
GRR ...
!
IT'S YOUR FAULT, ISN'T IT?
KOKO CHANGED BECAUSE OF YOU!
WHAT DID YOU DO TO HER?
I JUST CHANGED WHAT'S IN HER HEART, THAT'S ALL.
I INCREASED THE LEVEL OF HATRED INSIDE HER, AND MADE HER FORGET A FEW UNNECESSARY THINGS.
WHAT? CHANGED HER HEART?
THAT'S MY SPECIAL POWER.
ARE YOU A FRIEND OF KOKO'S?
SSS
I'M ZOFIS. LET ME TELL YOU A LITTLE BIT ABOUT MYSELF.
I'M NOT A HUMAN. I CAME HERE FROM ANOTHER WORLD.
TP
ONE HUNDRED BEINGS INCLUDING MYSELF HAVE BEEN SENT TO THIS WORLD.
SOON, EACH OF THOSE 100 WILL TEAM UP WITH A HUMAN AND BEGIN THE BATTLE TO BECOME THE KING OF THE MAMODO WORLD.
HUMANS WILL BE OBSESSED WITH THE NEW POWERS THEY'VE BEEN GIVEN, AND SOON, THEY'LL BE FIGHTING AGAINST ONE ANOTHER.

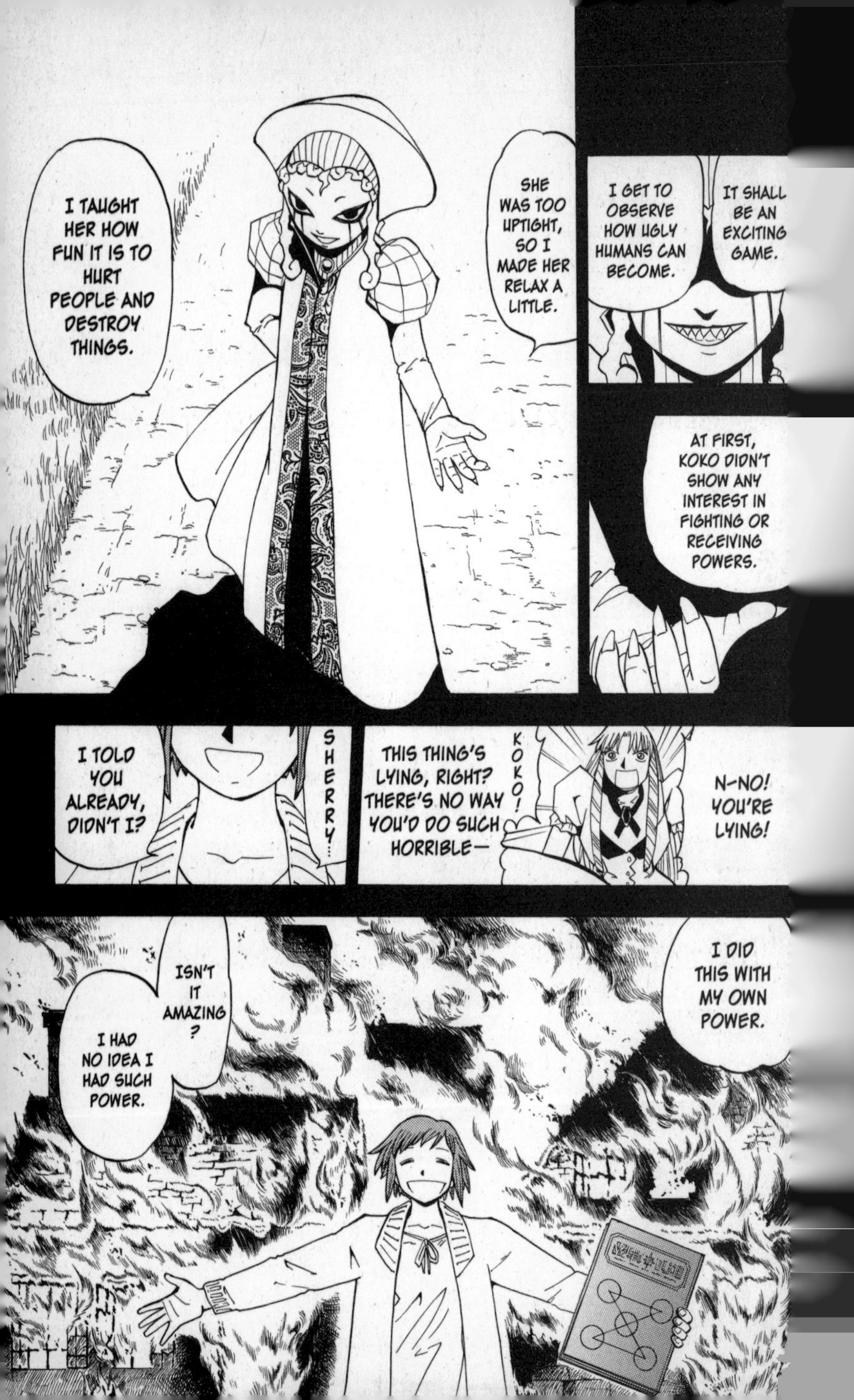
IT SHALL BE AN EXCITING GAME.
I GET TO OBSERVE HOW UGLY HUMANS CAN BECOME.
AT FIRST, KOKO DIDN'T SHOW ANY INTEREST IN FIGHTING OR RECEIVING POWERS.
SHE WAS TOO UPTIGHT, SO I MADE HER RELAX A LITTLE.
I TAUGHT HER HOW FUN IT IS TO HURT PEOPLE AND DESTROY THINGS.
N-NO! YOU'RE LYING!
KOKO!
THIS THING'S LYING, RIGHT? THERE'S NO WAY YOU'D DO SUCH HORRIBLE—
SHERRY...
I TOLD YOU ALREADY, DIDN'T I?
I DID THIS WITH MY OWN POWER.
ISN'T IT AMAZING?
I HAD NO IDEA I HAD SUCH POWER.

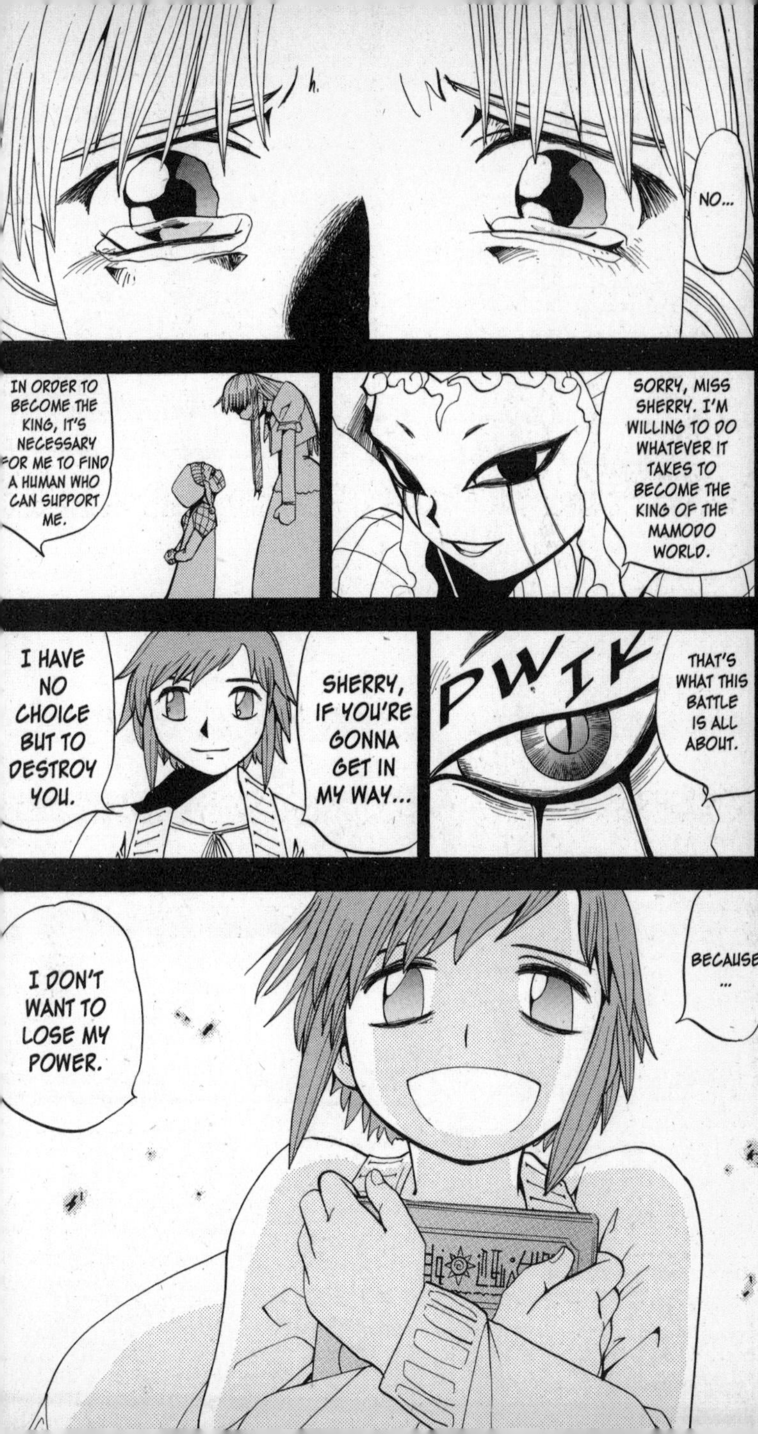
NO...
SORRY, MISS SHERRY. I'M WILLING TO DO WHATEVER IT TAKES TO BECOME THE KING OF THE MAMODO WORLD.
IN ORDER TO BECOME THE KING, IT'S NECESSARY FOR ME TO FIND A HUMAN WHO CAN SUPPORT ME.
PWIK
THAT'S WHAT THIS BATTLE IS ALL ABOUT.
SHERRY, IF YOU'RE GONNA GET IN MY WAY...
I HAVE NO CHOICE BUT TO DESTROY YOU.
BECAUSE ...
I DON'T WANT TO LOSE MY POWER.

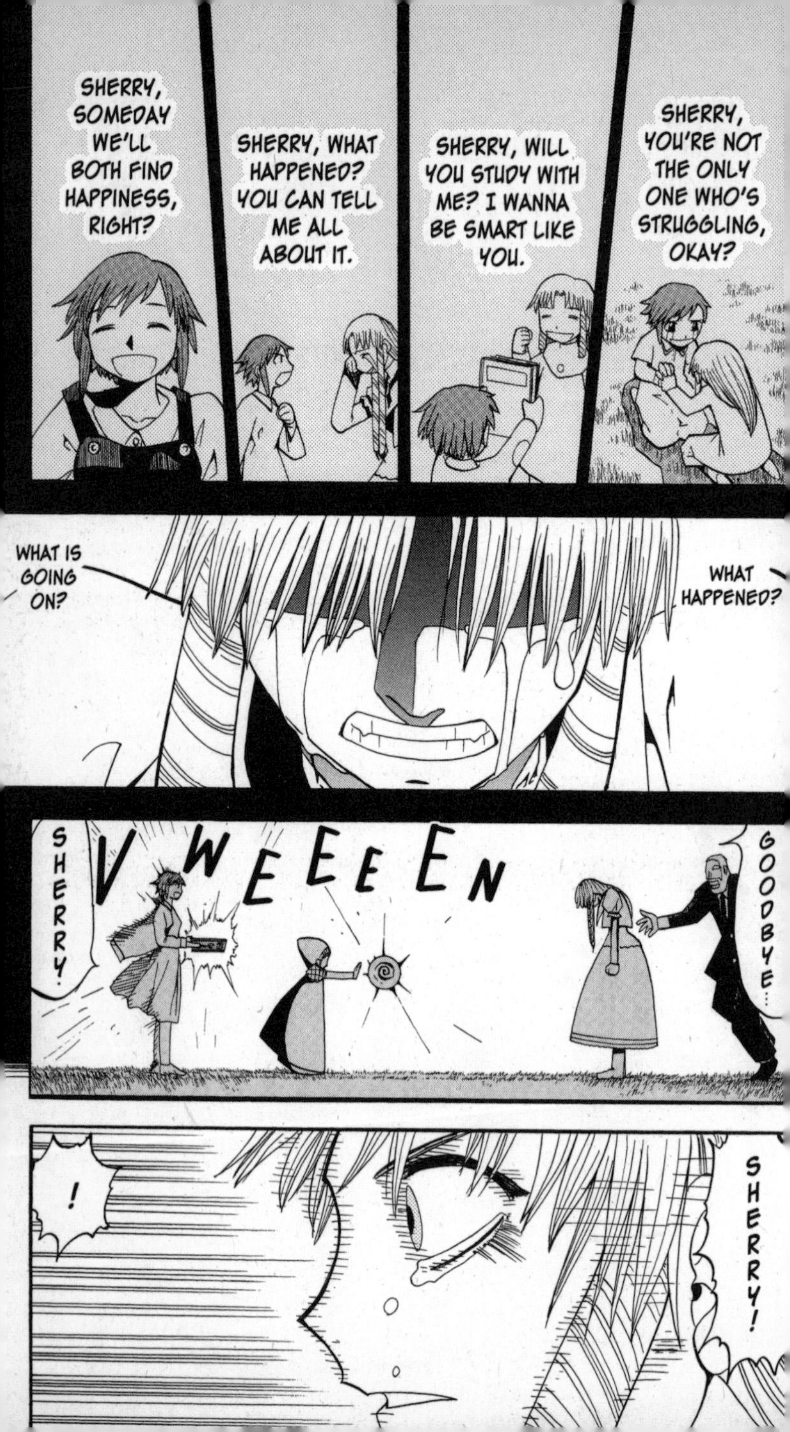

SHERRY, YOU'RE NOT THE ONLY ONE WHO'S STRUGGLING, OKAY?
SHERRY, WILL YOU STUDY WITH ME? I WANNA BE SMART LIKE YOU.
SHERRY, WHAT HAPPENED? YOU CAN TELL ME ALL ABOUT IT.
SHERRY, SOMEDAY WE'LL BOTH FIND HAPPINESS, RIGHT?
WHAT HAPPENED?
WHAT IS GOING ON?
GOODBYE...
VWEEEEN
SHERRY!
SHERRY!
!

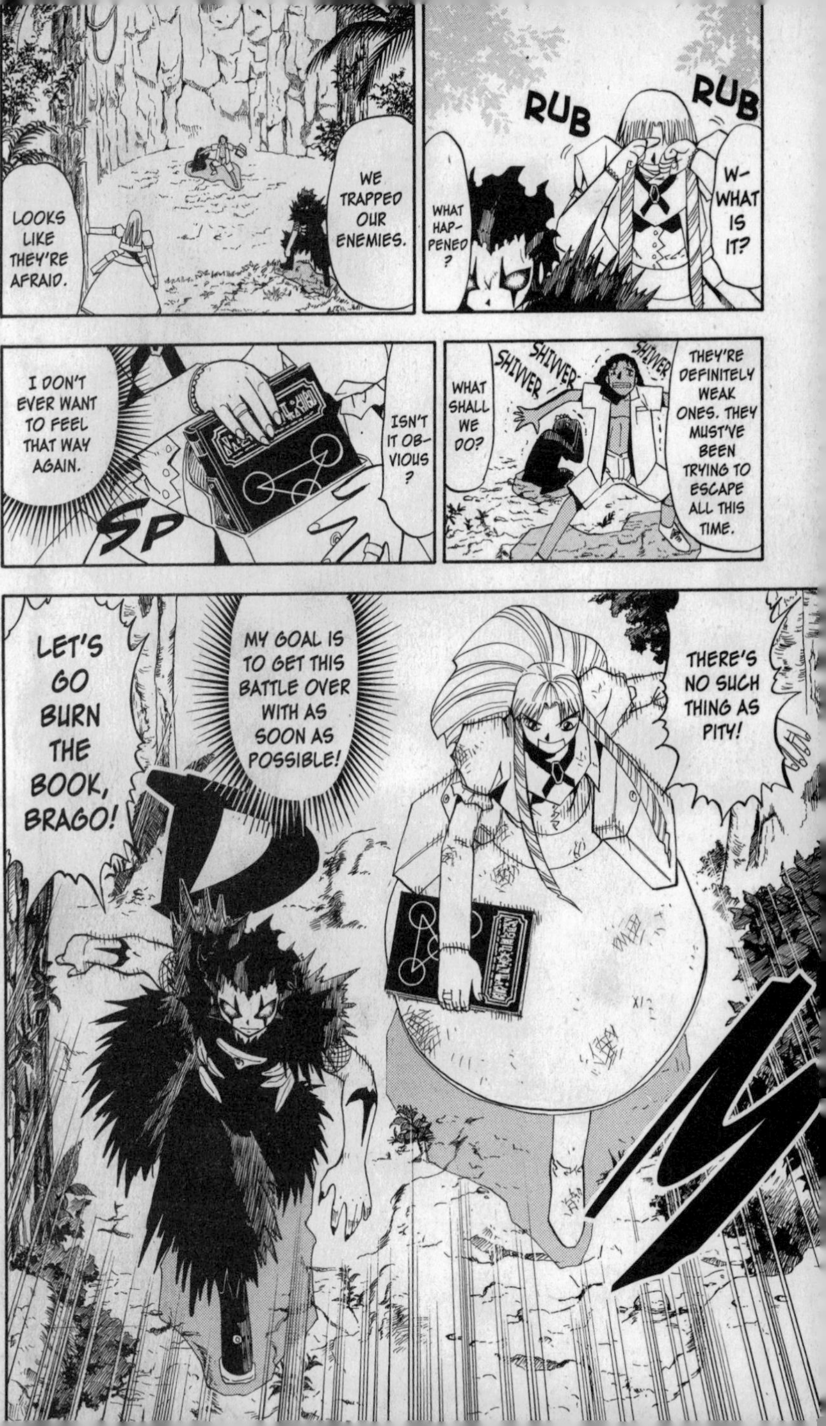
RUB
RUB
W-WHAT IS IT?
WHAT HAPPENED?
WE TRAPPED OUR ENEMIES.
LOOKS LIKE THEY'RE AFRAID.
THEY'RE DEFINITELY WEAK ONES. THEY MUST'VE BEEN TRYING TO ESCAPE ALL THIS TIME.
SHIVVER
SHIVVER
WHAT SHALL WE DO?
ISN'T IT OBVIOUS?
I DON'T EVER WANT TO FEEL THAT WAY AGAIN.
SP
THERE'S NO SUCH THING AS PITY!
MY GOAL IS TO GET THIS BATTLE OVER WITH AS SOON AS POSSIBLE!
LET'S GO BURN THE BOOK, BRAGO!

LEVEL 55: The Dark Tunnel

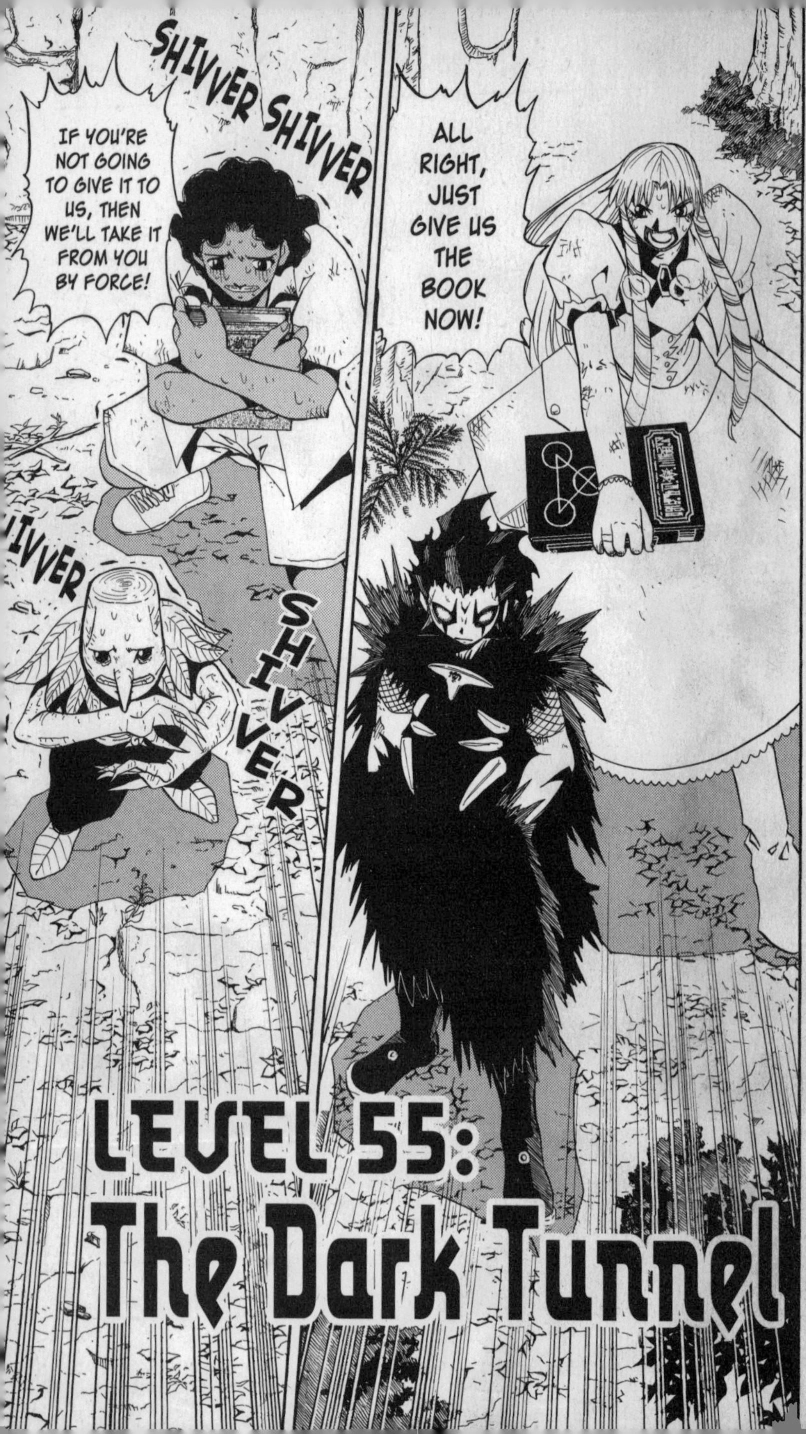
ALL RIGHT, JUST GIVE US THE BOOK NOW!
SHIVVER SHIVVER
IF YOU'RE NOT GOING TO GIVE IT TO US, THEN WE'LL TAKE IT FROM YOU BY FORCE!
SHIVVER

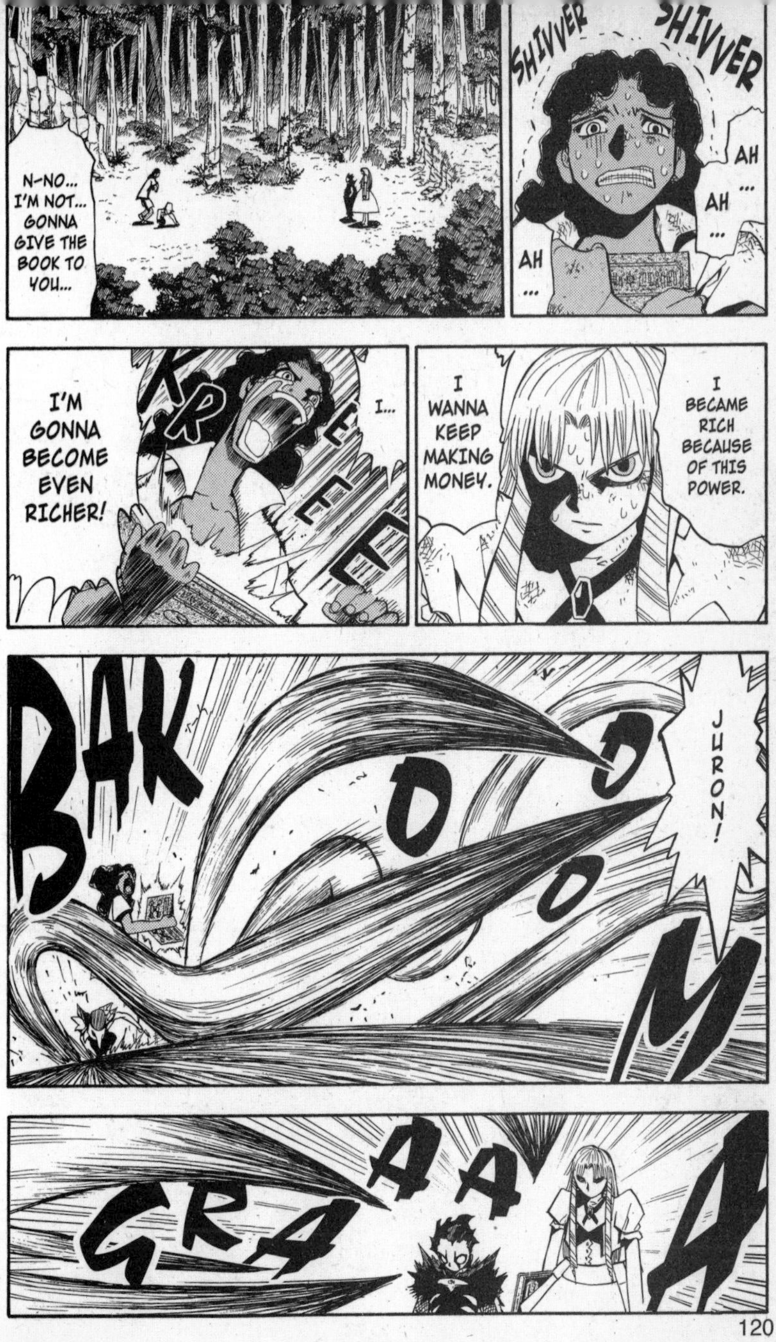
SHIVVER
SHIVVER
AH...
AH...
AH...
N-NO... I'M NOT... GONNA GIVE THE BOOK TO YOU...
I BECAME RICH BECAUSE OF THIS POWER.
I WANNA KEEP MAKING MONEY.
I...
I'M GONNA BECOME EVEN RICHER!
KREEEE
JURON!
BAKOOOM
GRAAAAA

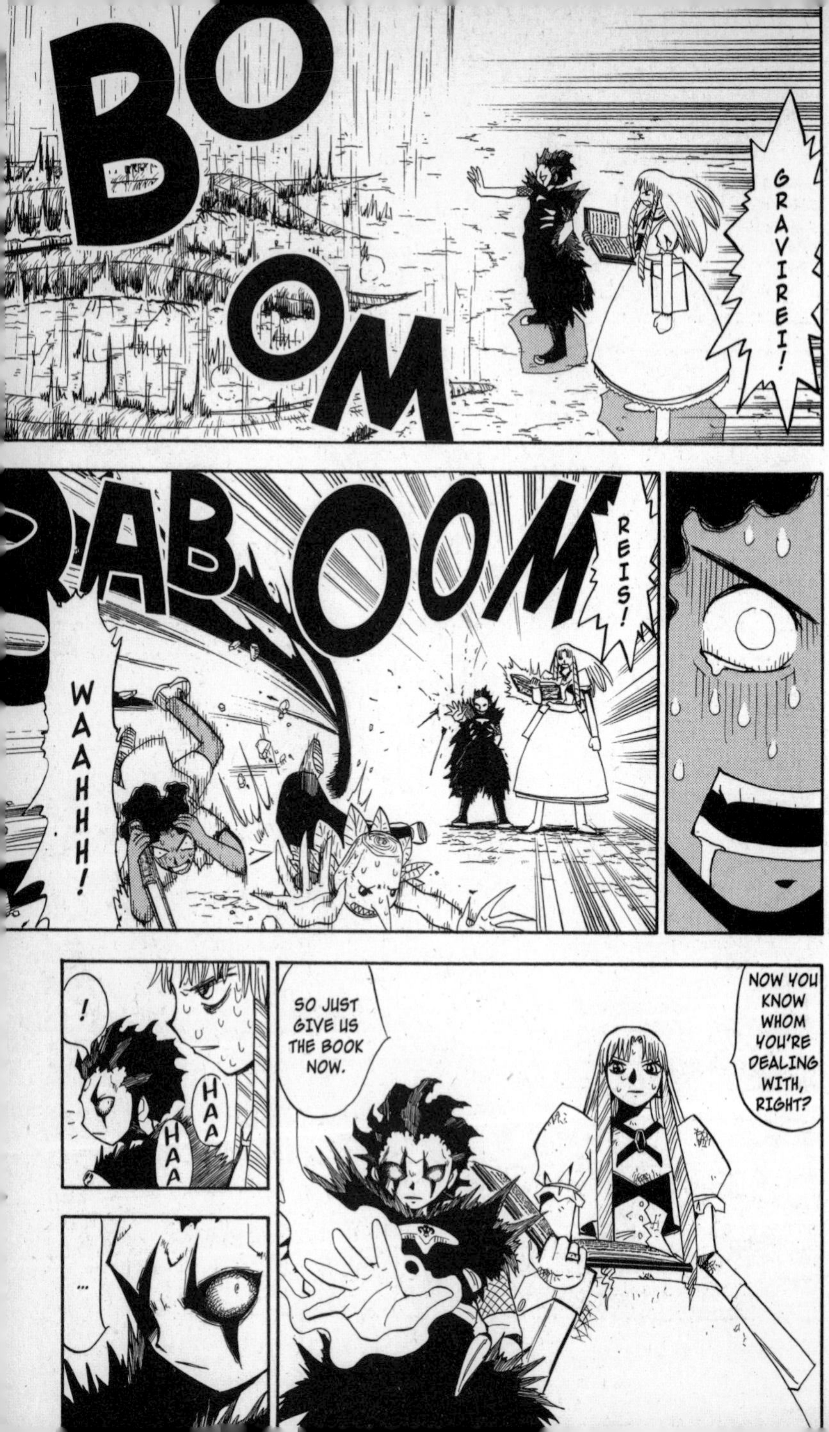
GRAVIREI!
BOOM
REIS!
RABOOM
WAAAHHHH!
NOW YOU KNOW WHOM YOU'RE DEALING WITH, RIGHT?
SO JUST GIVE US THE BOOK NOW.
!
HAA
HAA
HAA
...

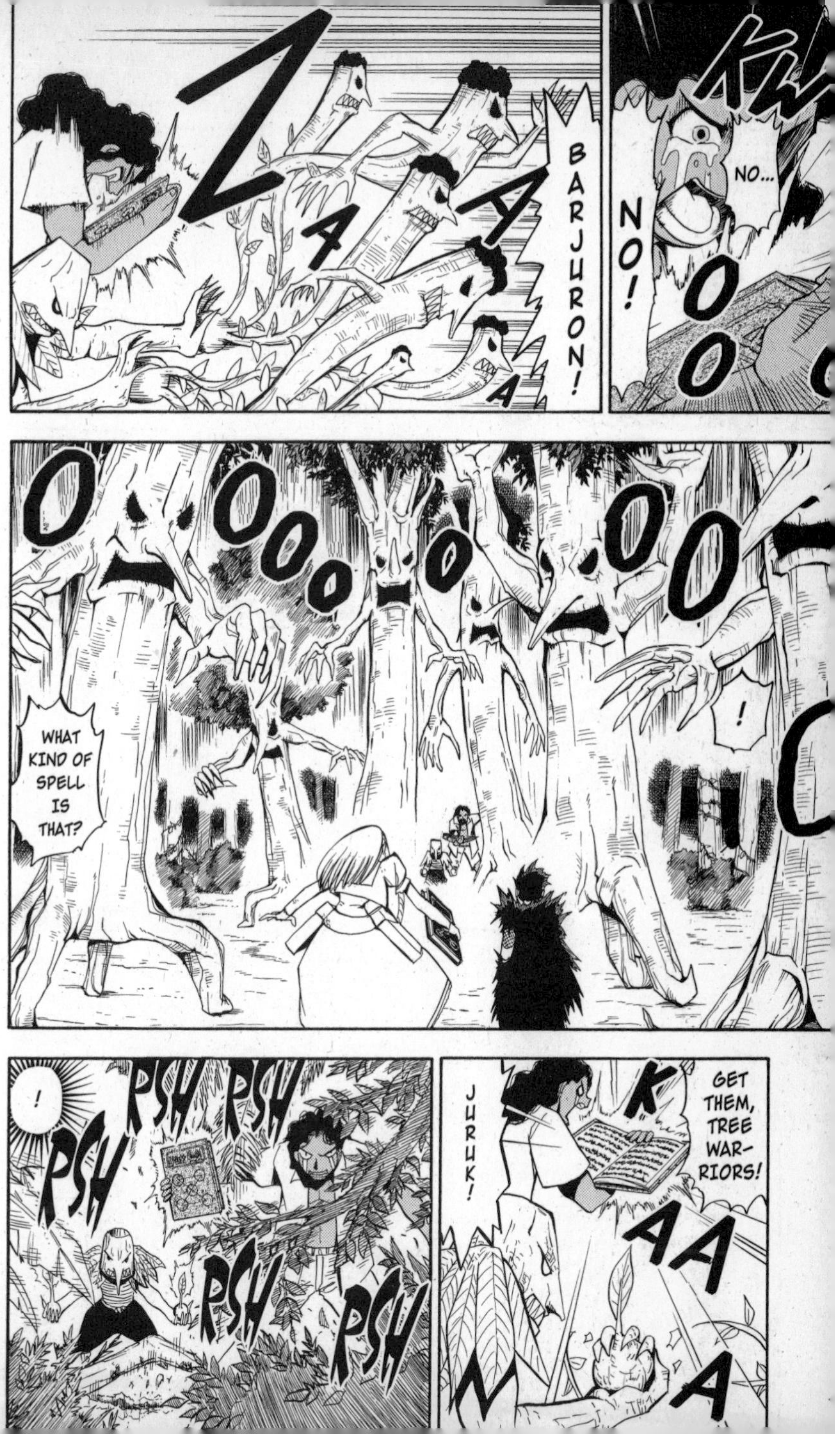

NO...
NO!
BARJURON!
WHAT KIND OF SPELL IS THAT?
!
GET THEM, TREE WARRIORS!
JURUK!
!
PSH PSH PSH PSH PSH PSH

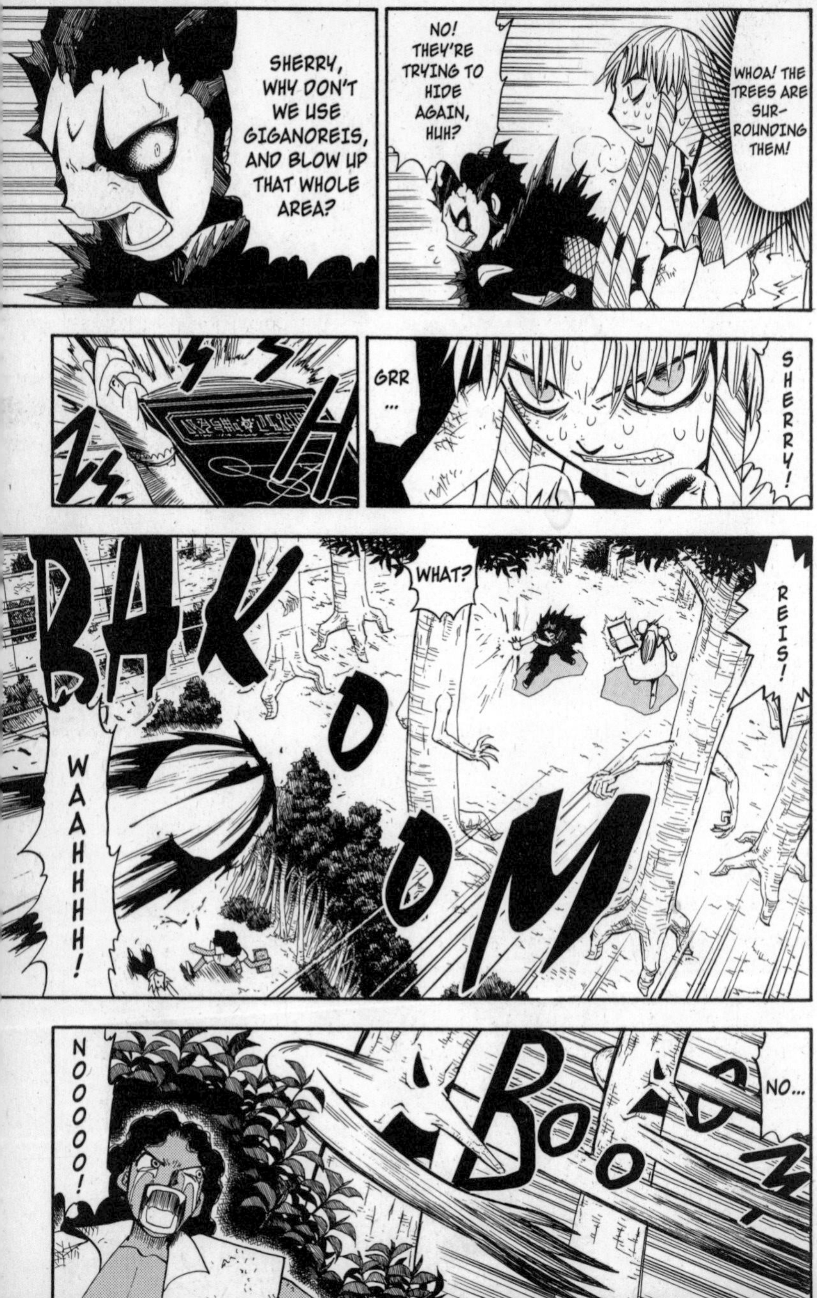
WHOA! THE TREES ARE SUR-ROUNDING THEM!
NO! THEY'RE TRYING TO HIDE AGAIN, HUH?
SHERRY, WHY DON'T WE USE GIGANOREIS, AND BLOW UP THAT WHOLE AREA?
SHERRY!
GRR ...
SHH
REIS!
WHAT?
BAKOOM
WAAHHHHH!
NO...
BOOOOM
NOOOOOO!

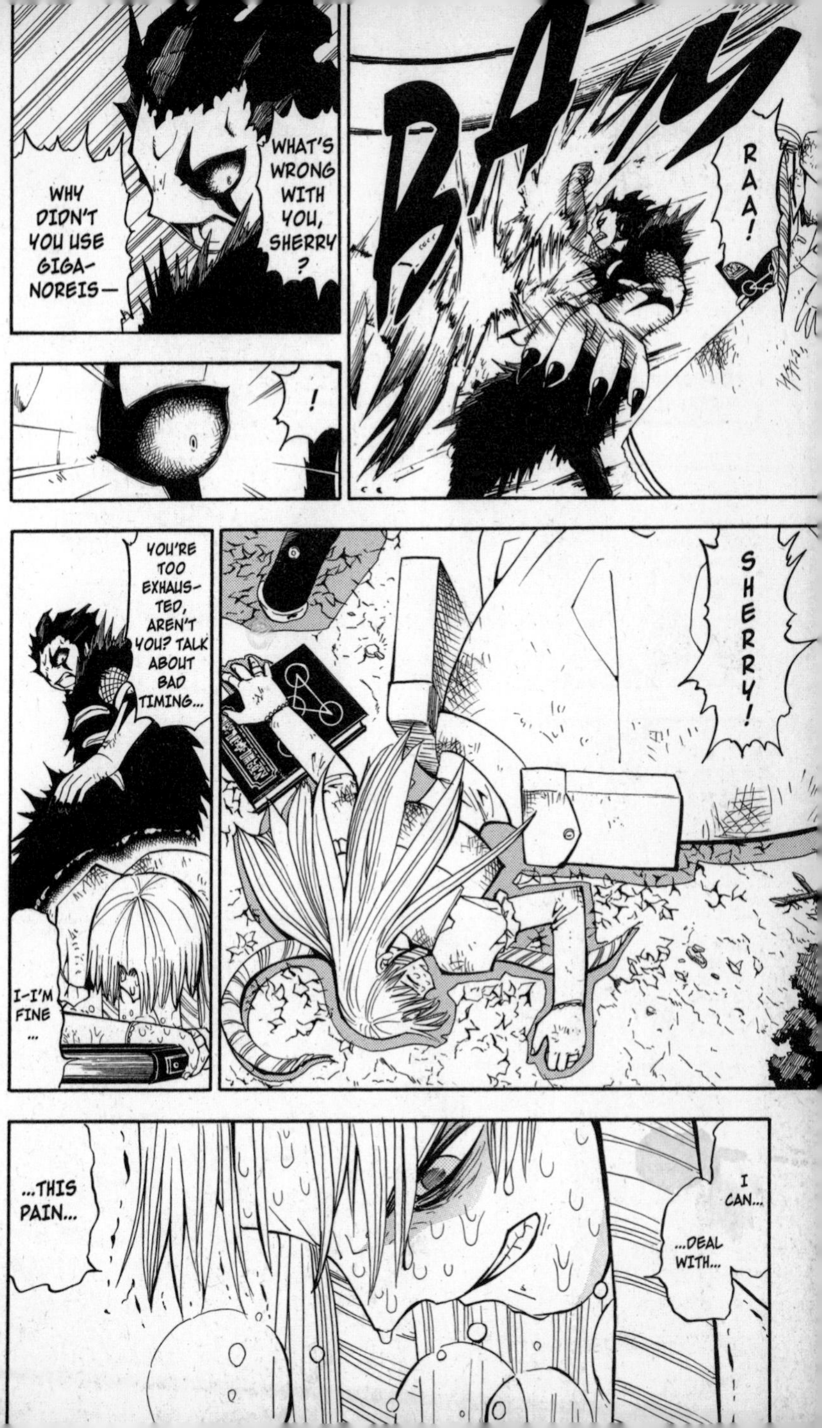
BAM
RAA!
WHAT'S WRONG WITH YOU, SHERRY?
WHY DIDN'T YOU USE GIGA-NOREIS—
!
SHERRY!
YOU'RE TOO EXHAUS-TED, AREN'T YOU? TALK ABOUT BAD TIMING...
I-I'M FINE...
I CAN...
...DEAL WITH...
...THIS PAIN...

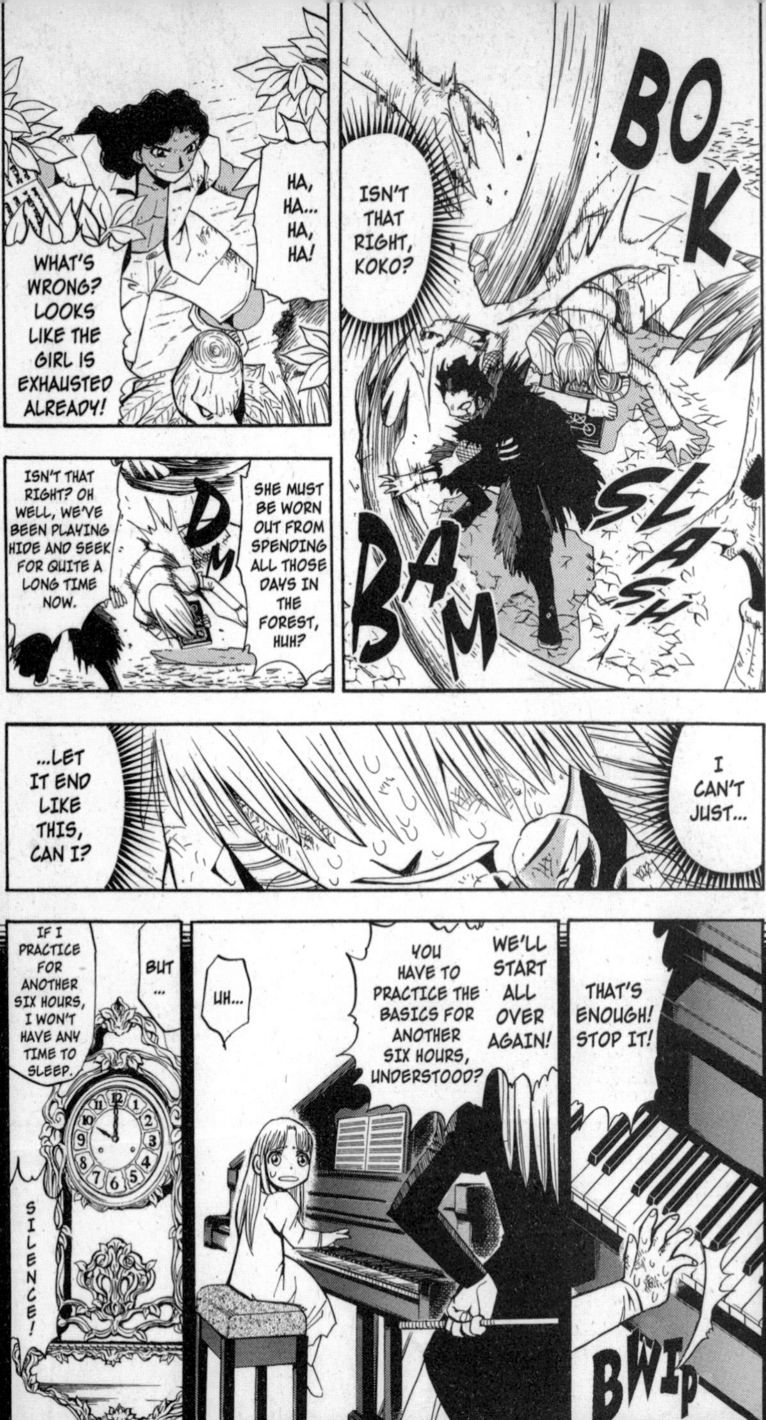
BOK
ISN'T THAT RIGHT, KOKO?
SLASH
BAM
HA, HA... HA, HA!
WHAT'S WRONG? LOOKS LIKE THE GIRL IS EXHAUSTED ALREADY!
SHE MUST BE WORN OUT FROM SPENDING ALL THOSE DAYS IN THE FOREST, HUH?
DM
ISN'T THAT RIGHT? OH WELL, WE'VE BEEN PLAYING HIDE AND SEEK FOR QUITE A LONG TIME NOW.
I CAN'T JUST...
...LET IT END LIKE THIS, CAN I?
THAT'S ENOUGH! STOP IT!
BWIP
WE'LL START ALL OVER AGAIN!
YOU HAVE TO PRACTICE THE BASICS FOR ANOTHER SIX HOURS, UNDERSTOOD?
UH...
BUT ...
IF I PRACTICE FOR ANOTHER SIX HOURS, I WON'T HAVE ANY TIME TO SLEEP.
SILENCE!

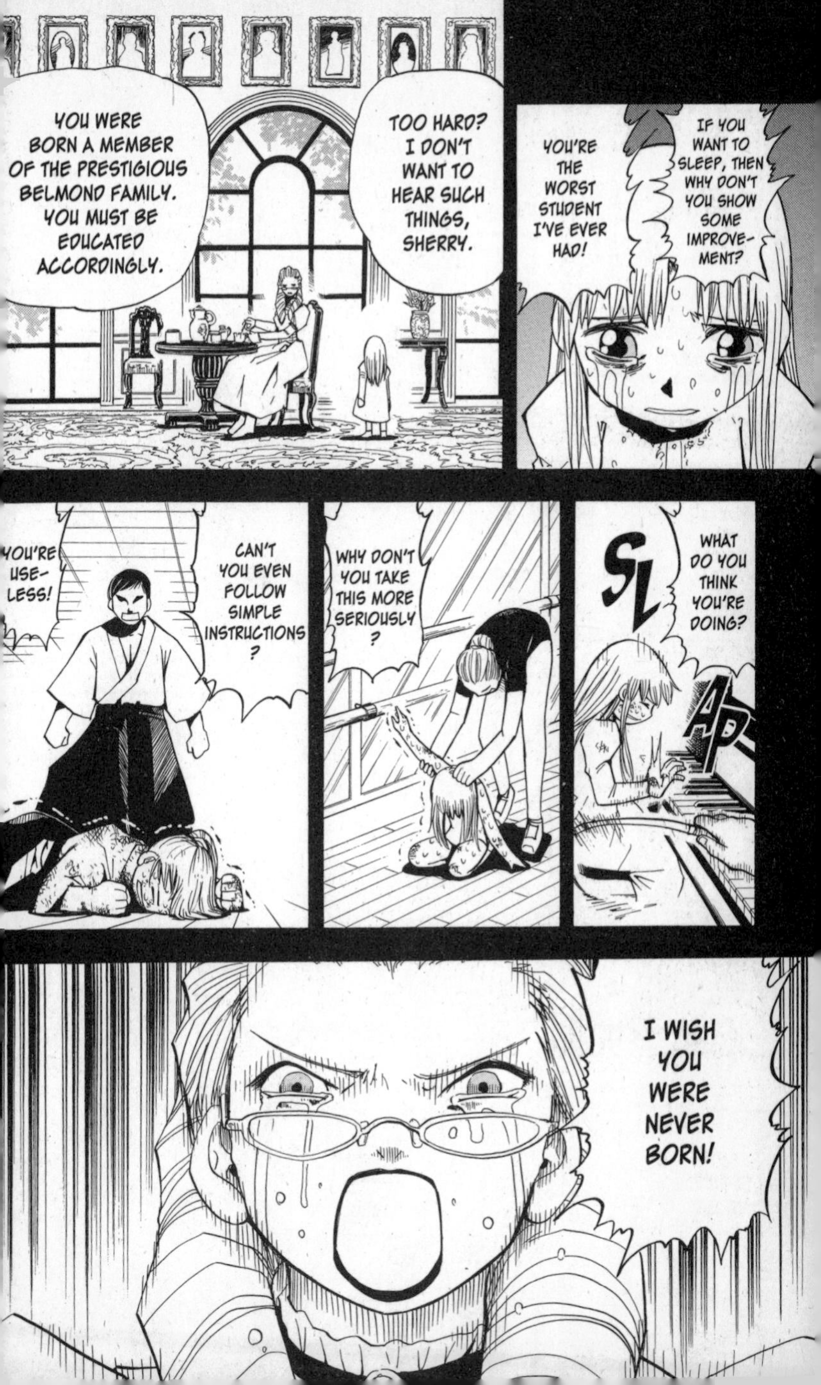
IF YOU WANT TO SLEEP, THEN WHY DON'T YOU SHOW SOME IMPROVEMENT?
YOU'RE THE WORST STUDENT I'VE EVER HAD!
TOO HARD? I DON'T WANT TO HEAR SUCH THINGS, SHERRY.
YOU WERE BORN A MEMBER OF THE PRESTIGIOUS BELMOND FAMILY. YOU MUST BE EDUCATED ACCORDINGLY.
WHAT DO YOU THINK YOU'RE DOING?
SL
AP
WHY DON'T YOU TAKE THIS MORE SERIOUSLY?
CAN'T YOU EVEN FOLLOW SIMPLE INSTRUCTIONS?
YOU'RE USELESS!
I WISH YOU WERE NEVER BORN!

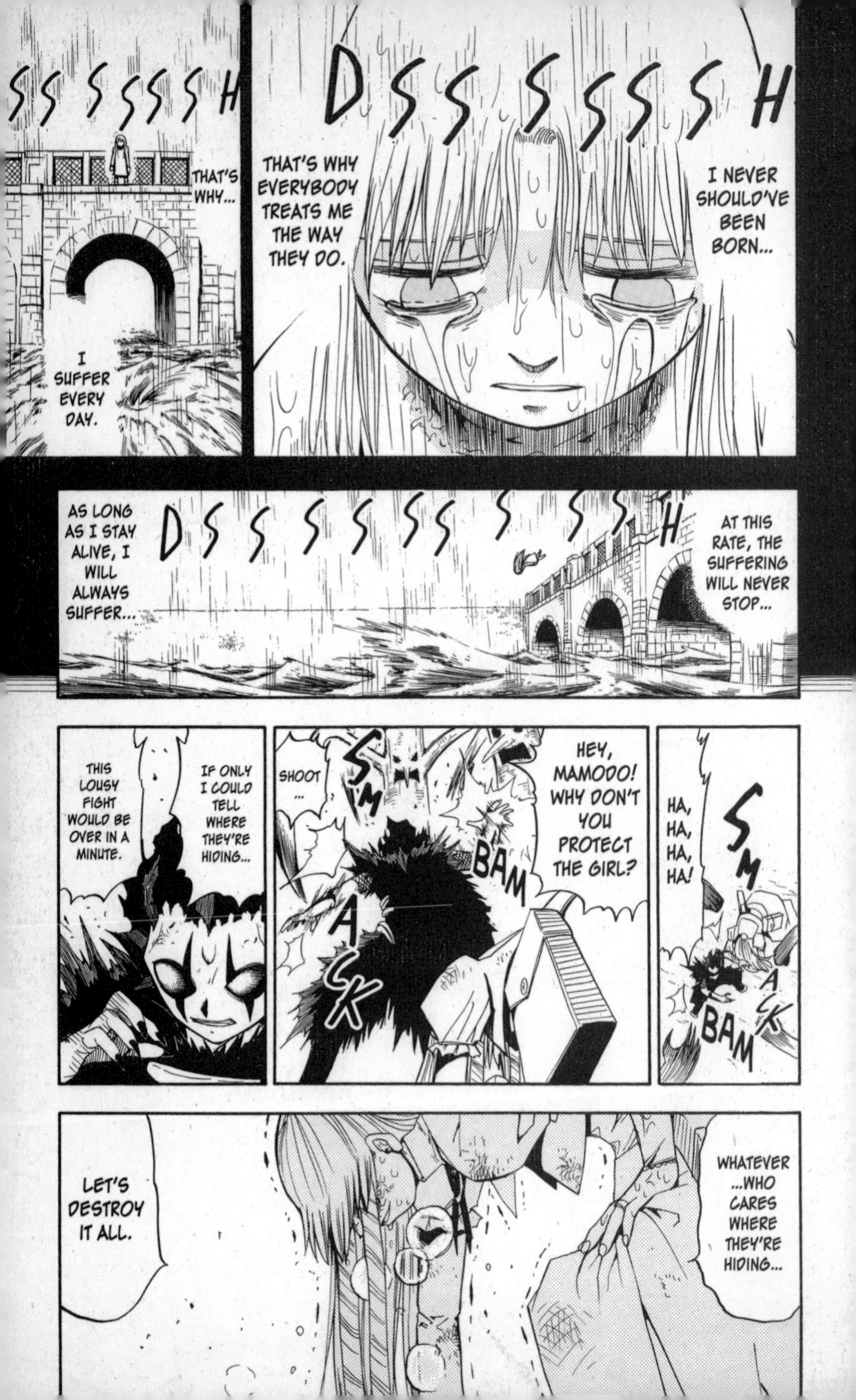
DSSSSSSH
I NEVER SHOULD'VE BEEN BORN...
THAT'S WHY EVERYBODY TREATS ME THE WAY THEY DO.
SSSSSSH
THAT'S WHY...
I SUFFER EVERY DAY.
AT THIS RATE, THE SUFFERING WILL NEVER STOP...
DSSSSSSSSH
AS LONG AS I STAY ALIVE, I WILL ALWAYS SUFFER...
HA, HA, HA, HA!
SMACK
BAM
HEY, MAMODO! WHY DON'T YOU PROTECT THE GIRL?
BAM
SMACK
SHOOT...
IF ONLY I COULD TELL WHERE THEY'RE HIDING...
THIS LOUSY FIGHT WOULD BE OVER IN A MINUTE.
WHATEVER ...WHO CARES WHERE THEY'RE HIDING...
LET'S DESTROY IT ALL.

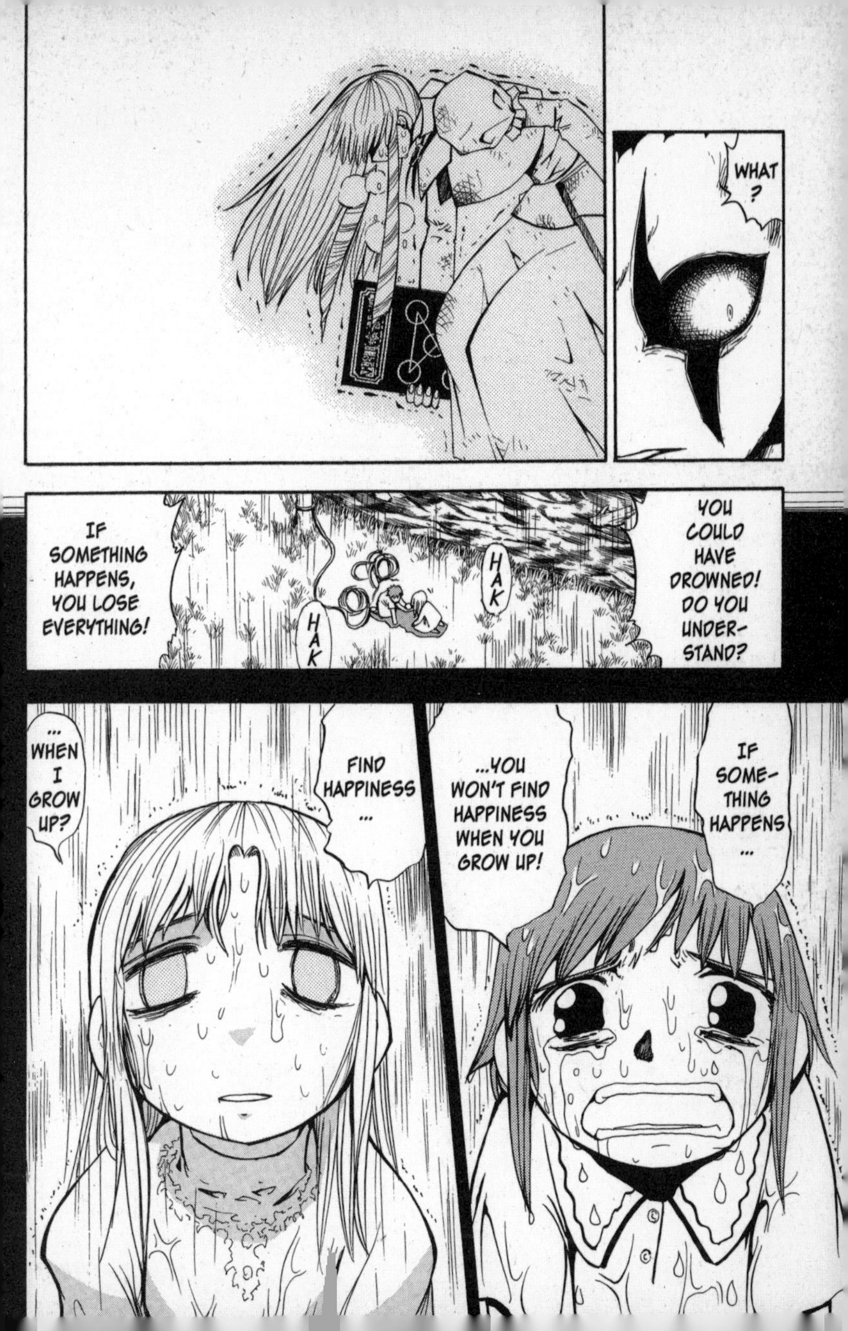
WHAT ?
YOU COULD HAVE DROWNED! DO YOU UNDERSTAND?
HAK
IF SOMETHING HAPPENS, YOU LOSE EVERYTHING!
HAK
IF SOMETHING HAPPENS ...
...YOU WON'T FIND HAPPINESS WHEN YOU GROW UP!
FIND HAPPINESS ...
... WHEN I GROW UP?

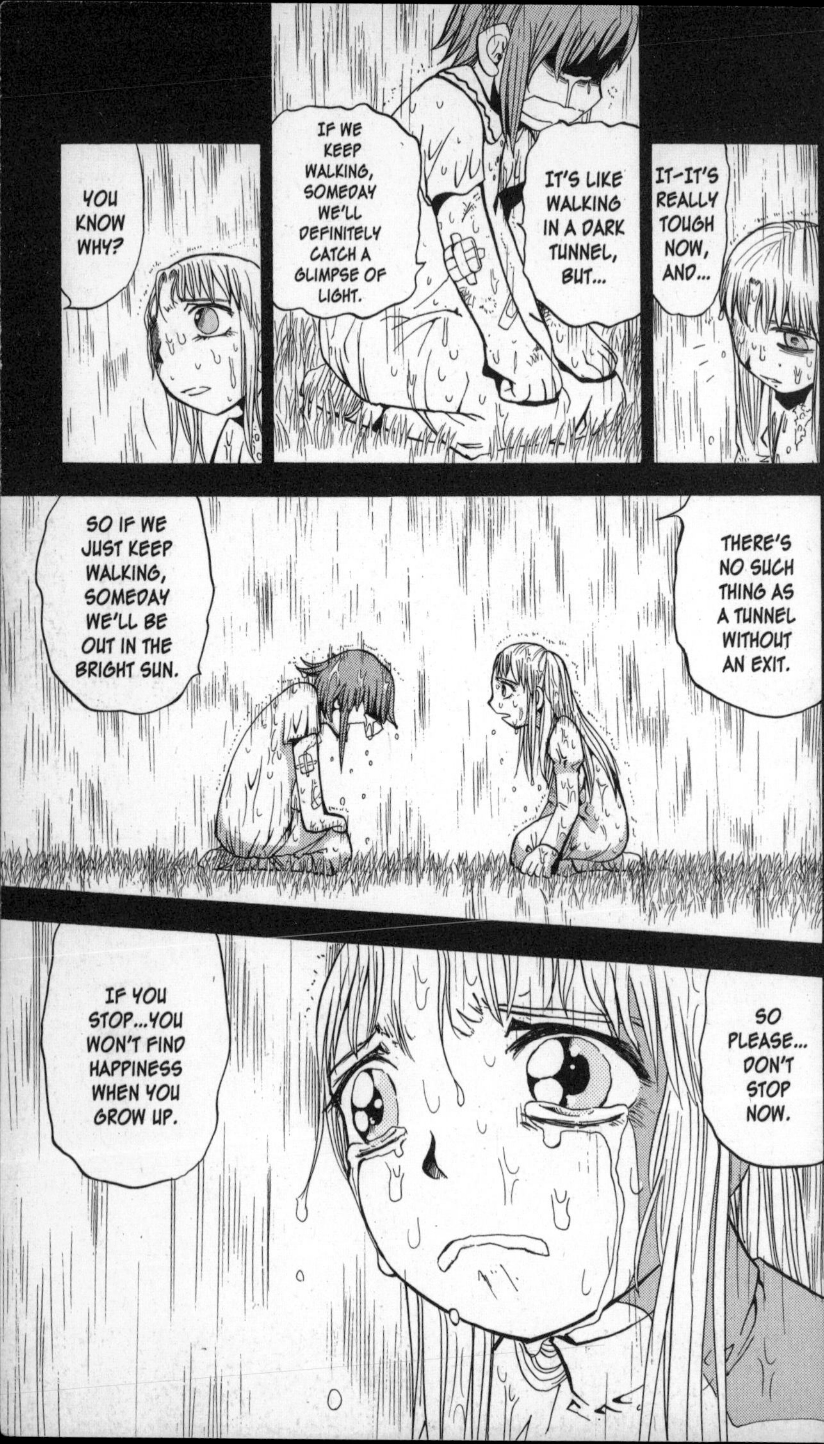
IT-IT'S REALLY TOUGH NOW, AND...
IT'S LIKE WALKING IN A DARK TUNNEL, BUT...
IF WE KEEP WALKING, SOMEDAY WE'LL DEFINITELY CATCH A GLIMPSE OF LIGHT.
YOU KNOW WHY?
THERE'S NO SUCH THING AS A TUNNEL WITHOUT AN EXIT.
SO IF WE JUST KEEP WALKING, SOMEDAY WE'LL BE OUT IN THE BRIGHT SUN.
SO PLEASE... DON'T STOP NOW.
IF YOU STOP...YOU WON'T FIND HAPPINESS WHEN YOU GROW UP.

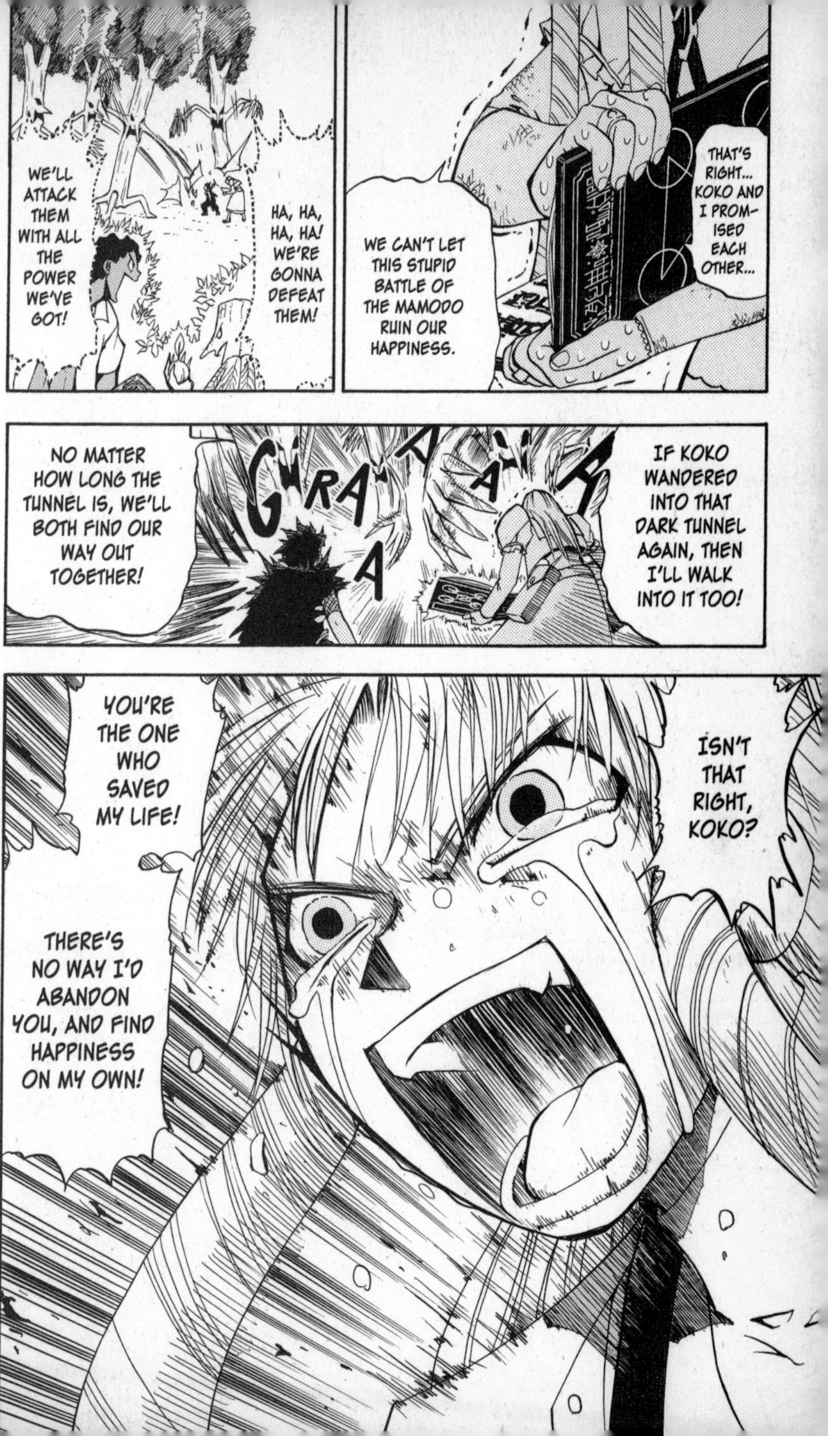
THAT'S RIGHT... KOKO AND I PROMISED EACH OTHER...
WE CAN'T LET THIS STUPID BATTLE OF THE MAMODO RUIN OUR HAPPINESS.
HA, HA, HA, HA! WE'RE GONNA DEFEAT THEM!
WE'LL ATTACK THEM WITH ALL THE POWER WE'VE GOT!
IF KOKO WANDERED INTO THAT DARK TUNNEL AGAIN, THEN I'LL WALK INTO IT TOO!
GRAAAAAAA
NO MATTER HOW LONG THE TUNNEL IS, WE'LL BOTH FIND OUR WAY OUT TOGETHER!
ISN'T THAT RIGHT, KOKO?
YOU'RE THE ONE WHO SAVED MY LIFE!
THERE'S NO WAY I'D ABANDON YOU, AND FIND HAPPINESS ON MY OWN!

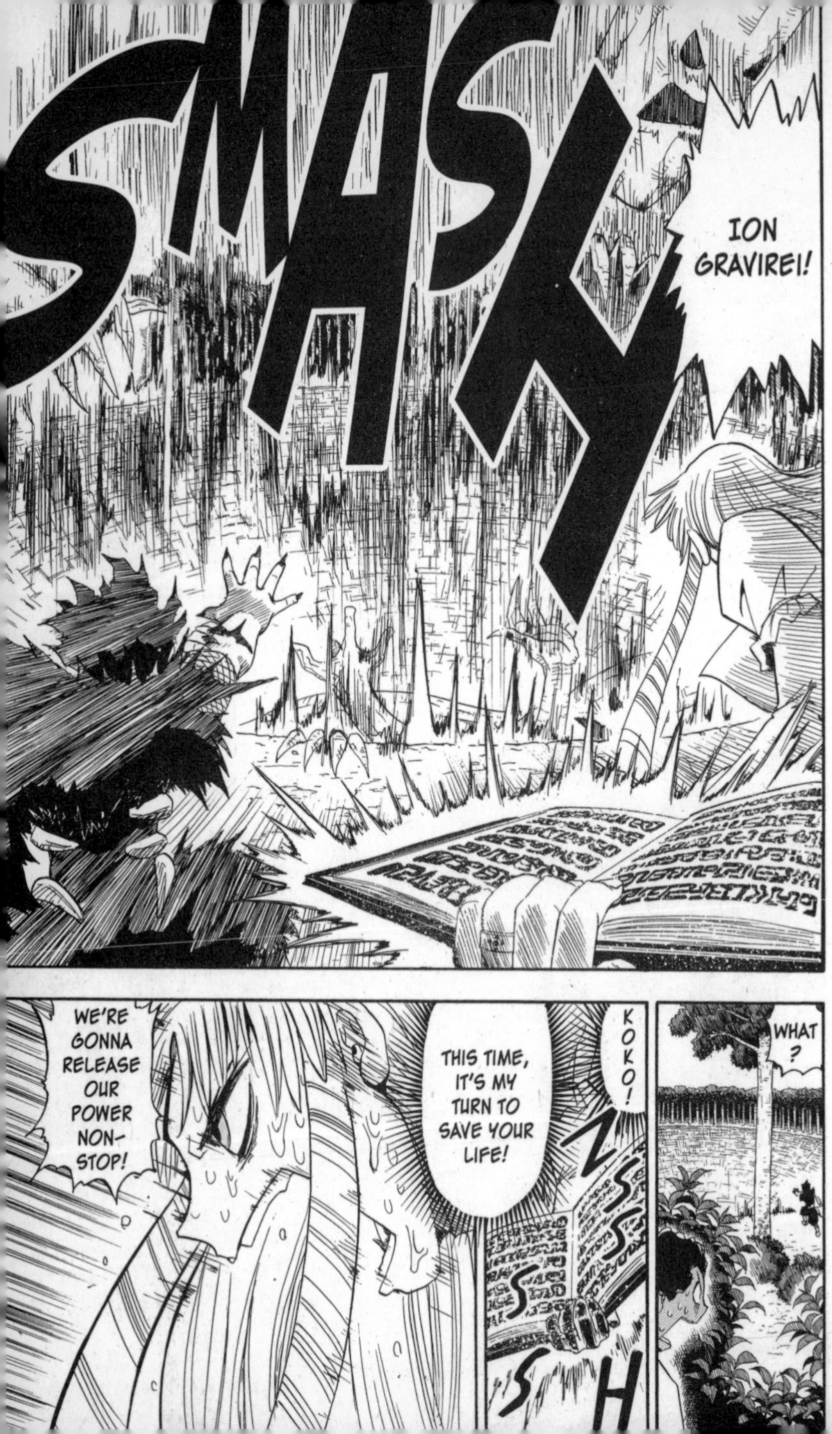
SMASH
ION GRAVIREI!
WHAT?
KOKO!
THIS TIME, IT'S MY TURN TO SAVE YOUR LIFE!
WE'RE GONNA RELEASE OUR POWER NON-STOP!

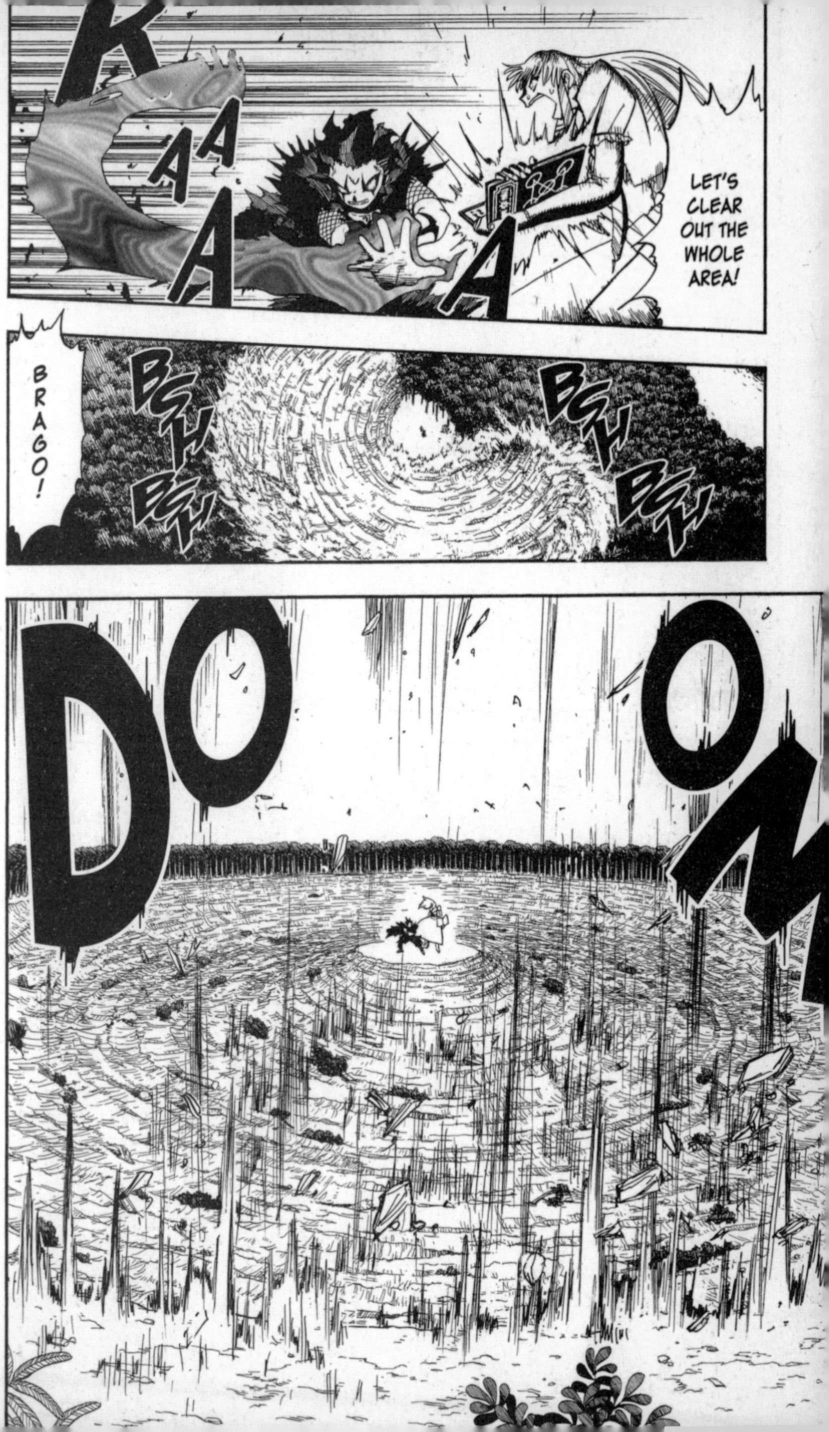
LET'S CLEAR OUT THE WHOLE AREA!
KAAAA
BSH BSH
BSH BSH
BRAGO!
DOOM

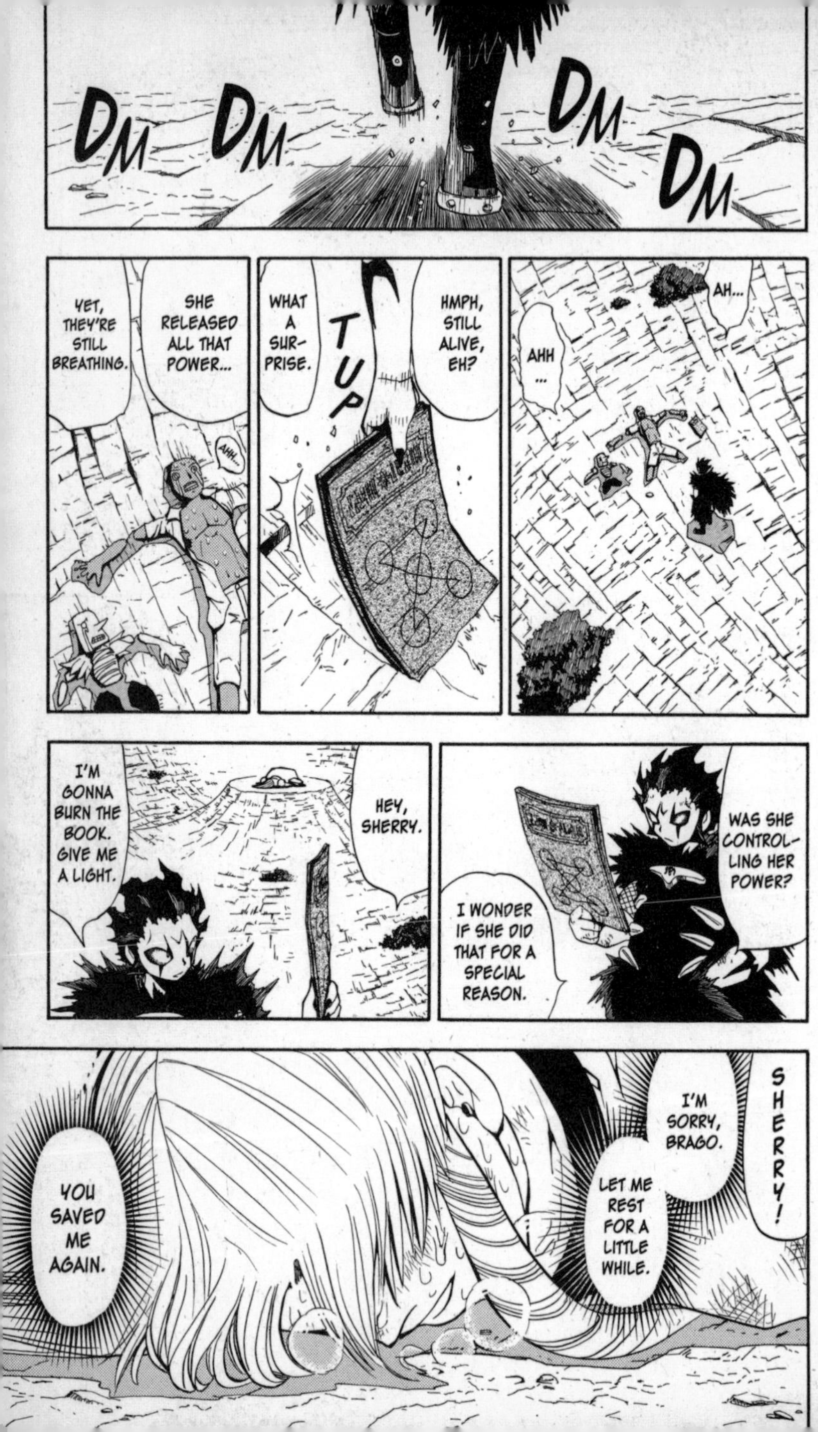
DM
DM
DM
DM
AH...
AHH ...
HMPH, STILL ALIVE, EH?
TUP
WHAT A SURPRISE.
SHE RELEASED ALL THAT POWER...
YET, THEY'RE STILL BREATHING.
AHH...
WAS SHE CONTROLLING HER POWER?
I WONDER IF SHE DID THAT FOR A SPECIAL REASON.
HEY, SHERRY.
I'M GONNA BURN THE BOOK. GIVE ME A LIGHT.
SHERRY!
I'M SORRY, BRAGO.
LET ME REST FOR A LITTLE WHILE.
YOU SAVED ME AGAIN.

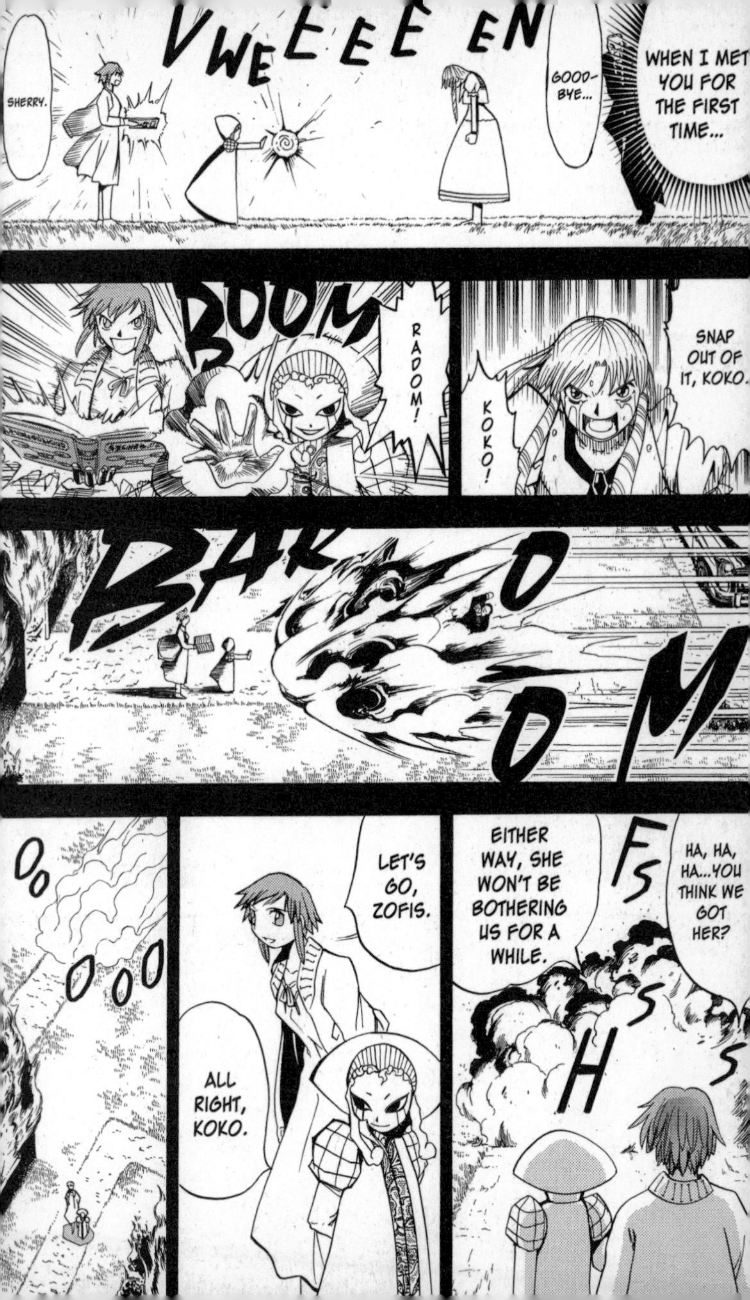
WHEN I MET YOU FOR THE FIRST TIME...
GOOD-BYE...
VWEEEEN
SHERRY.
SNAP OUT OF IT, KOKO.
KOKO!
RADOM!
BOOM
BAROOM
HA, HA, HA...YOU THINK WE GOT HER?
FSSHS
EITHER WAY, SHE WON'T BE BOTHERING US FOR A WHILE.
LET'S GO, ZOFIS.
ALL RIGHT, KOKO.
OOOOO

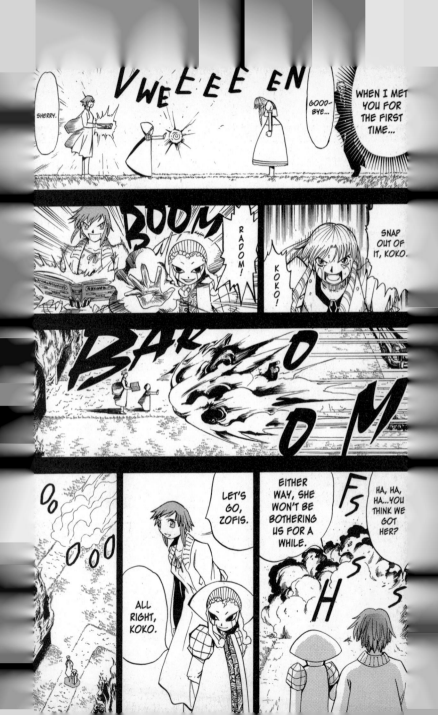

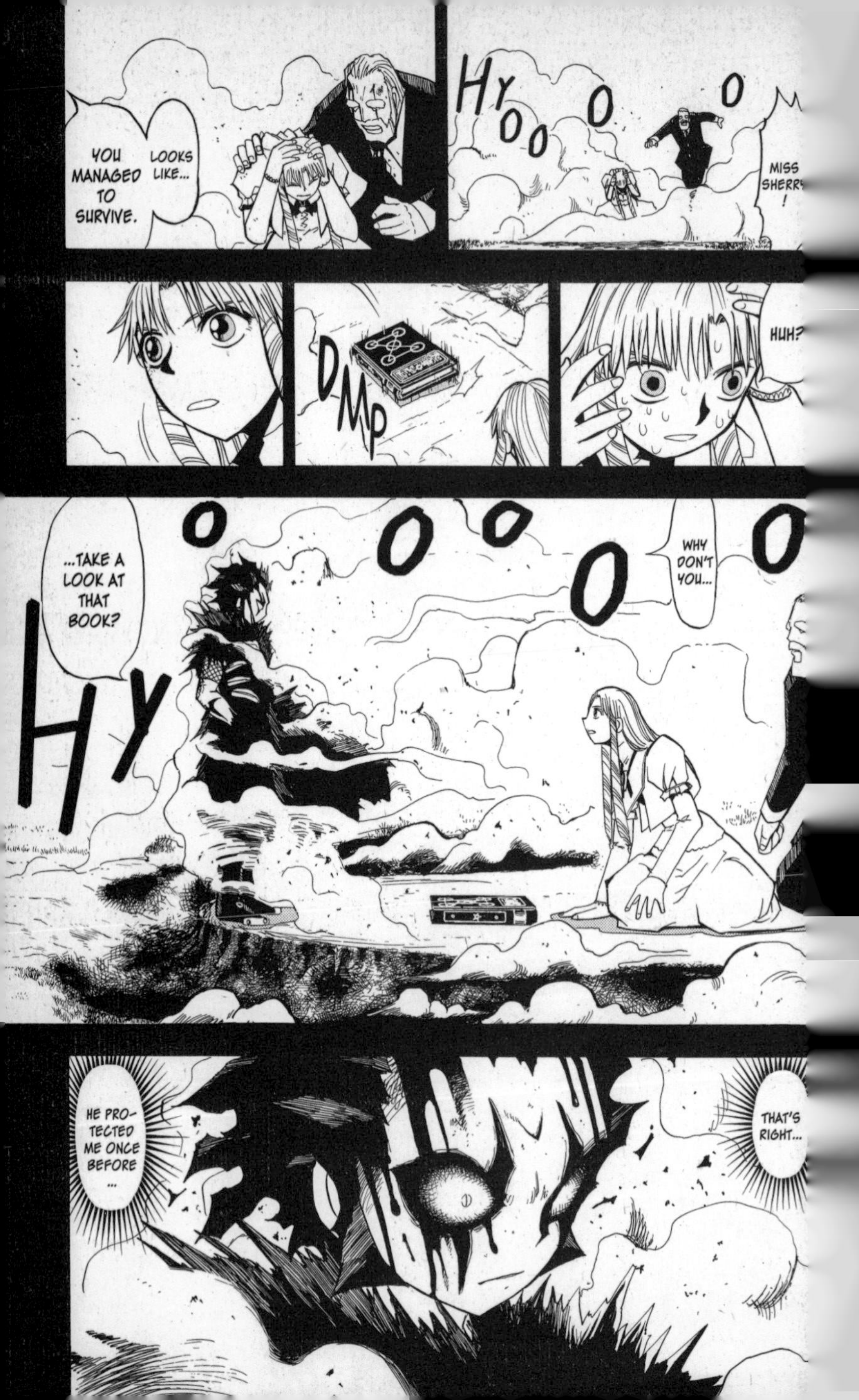
HYOOOOO
MISS SHERRY!
LOOKS LIKE...
YOU MANAGED TO SURVIVE.
HUH?
DMP
WHY DON'T YOU...
...TAKE A LOOK AT THAT BOOK?
HYOOOOOO
THAT'S RIGHT...
HE PROTECTED ME ONCE BEFORE...

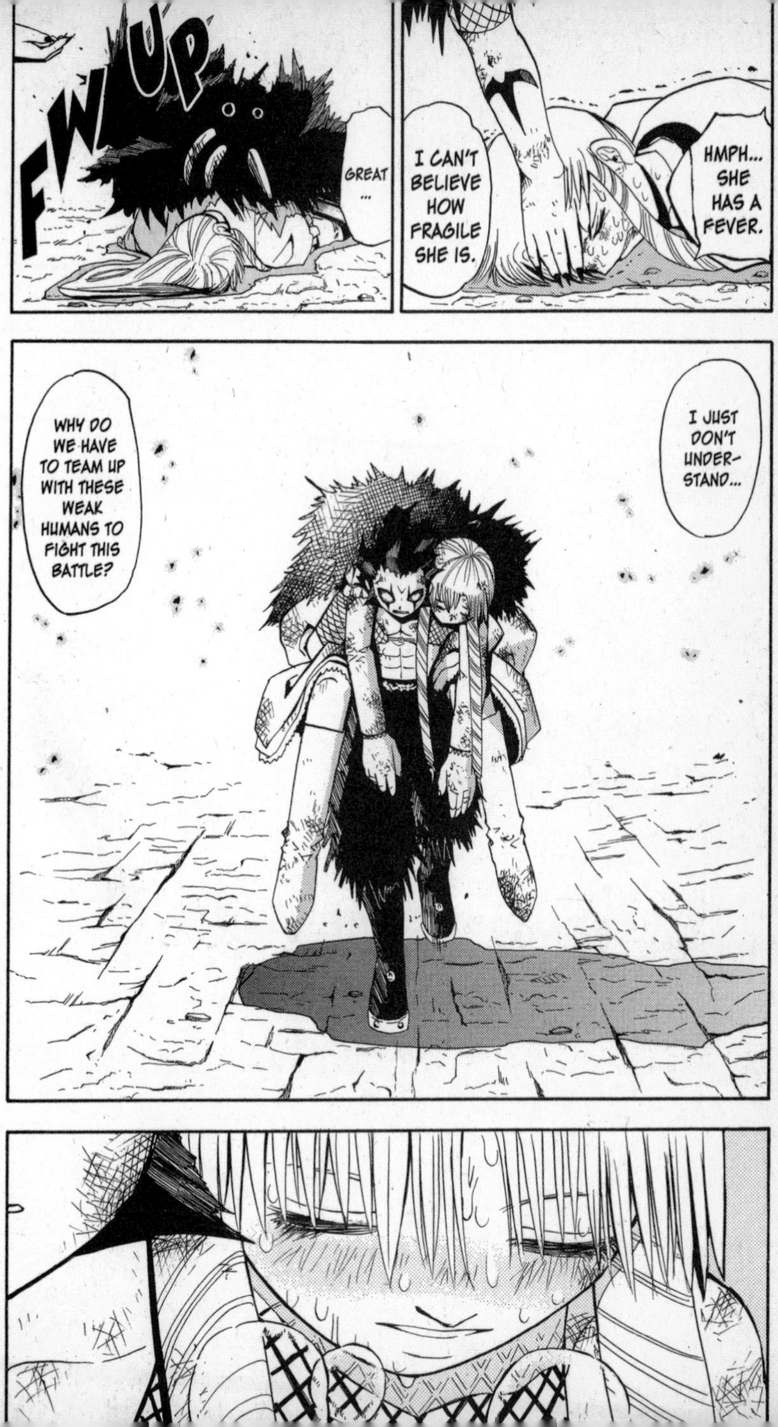
HMPH... SHE HAS A FEVER.
I CAN'T BELIEVE HOW FRAGILE SHE IS.
FWUP
GREAT...
I JUST DON'T UNDER-STAND...
WHY DO WE HAVE TO TEAM UP WITH THESE WEAK HUMANS TO FIGHT THIS BATTLE?

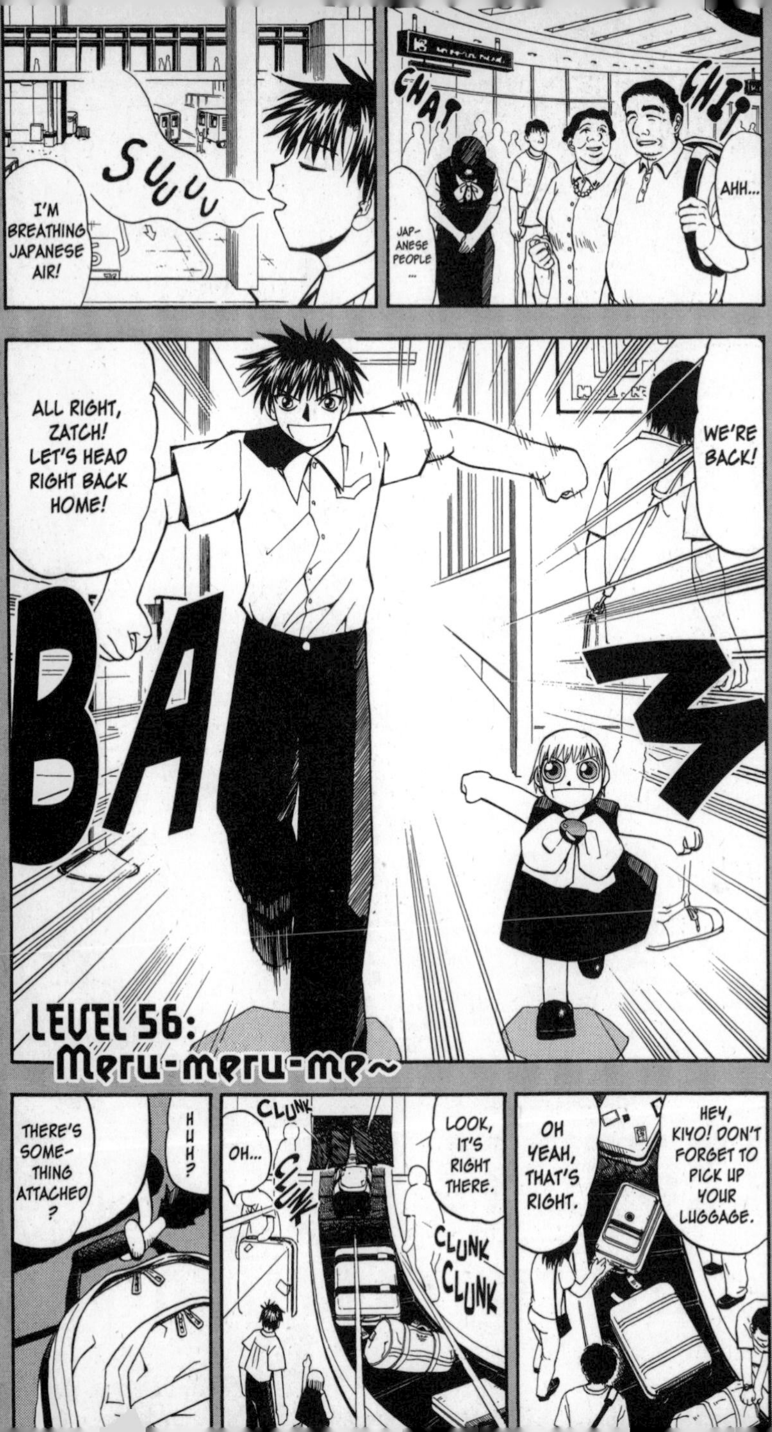
CHAT
AHH...
CHAT
JAPANESE PEOPLE...
SUUUU
I'M BREATHING JAPANESE AIR!
WE'RE BACK!
ALL RIGHT, ZATCH! LET'S HEAD RIGHT BACK HOME!
BAM
LEVEL 56: Meru-meru-me~
HEY, KIYO! DON'T FORGET TO PICK UP YOUR LUGGAGE.
OH YEAH, THAT'S RIGHT.
LOOK, IT'S RIGHT THERE.
CLUNK CLUNK
CLUNK
CLUNK
OH...
HUH?
THERE'S SOMETHING ATTACHED?

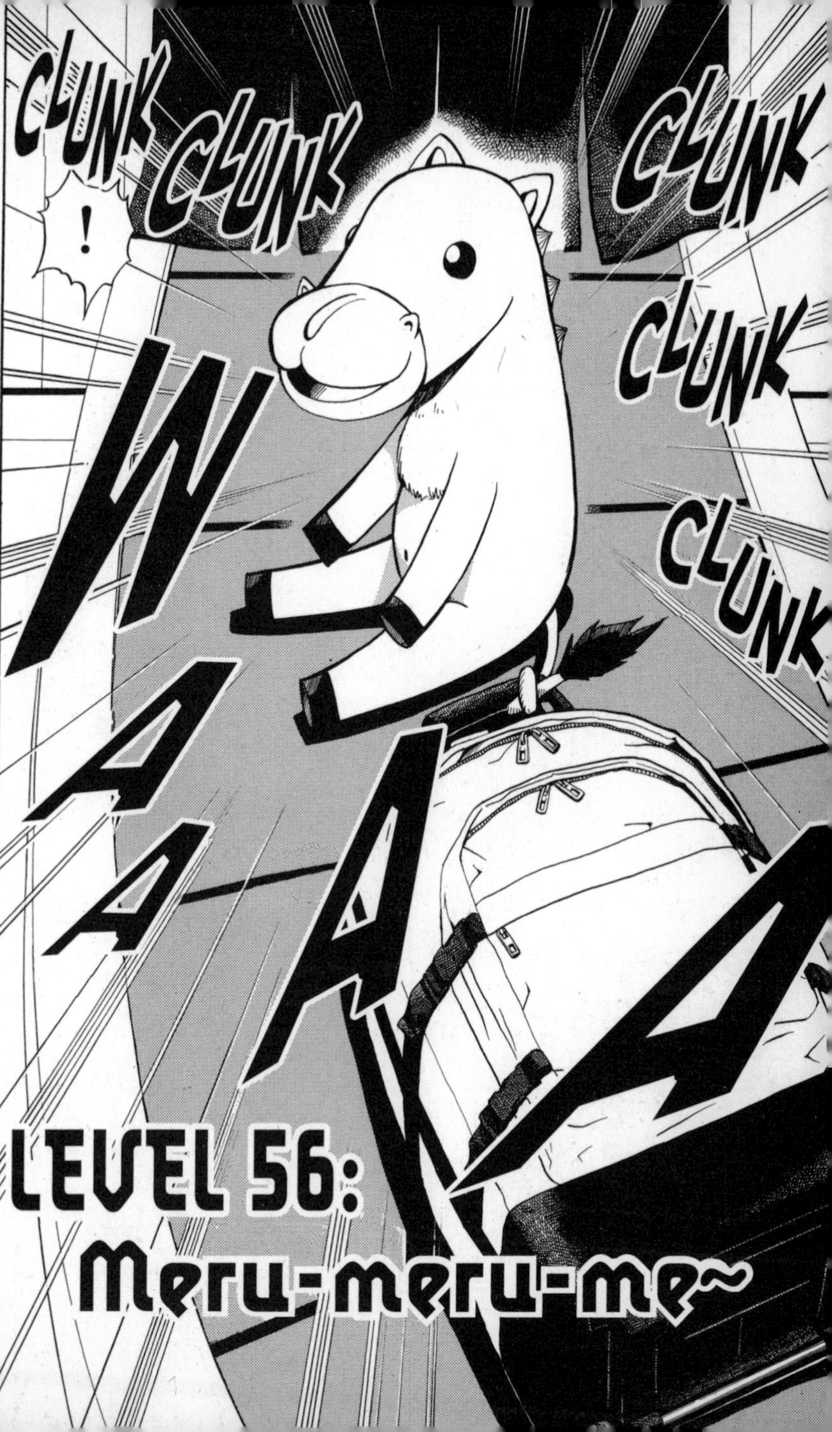
CLUNK
CLUNK
CLUNK
CLUNK
CLUNK
!
WAAAA
LEVEL 56:
Meru-meru-me~

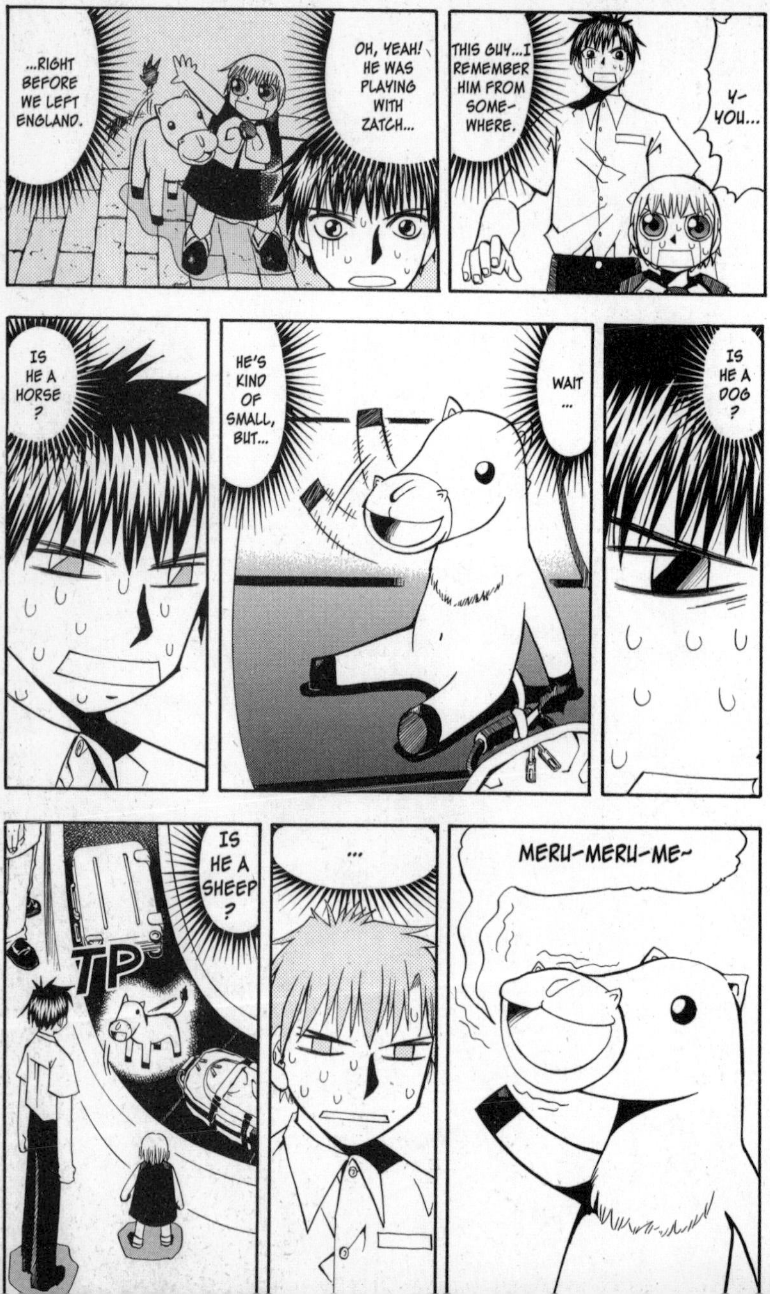
Y-YOU...
THIS GUY...I REMEMBER HIM FROM SOME-WHERE.
OH, YEAH! HE WAS PLAYING WITH ZATCH...
...RIGHT BEFORE WE LEFT ENGLAND.
IS HE A DOG?
WAIT...
HE'S KIND OF SMALL, BUT...
IS HE A HORSE?
MERU-MERU-ME~
...
IS HE A SHEEP?
TP

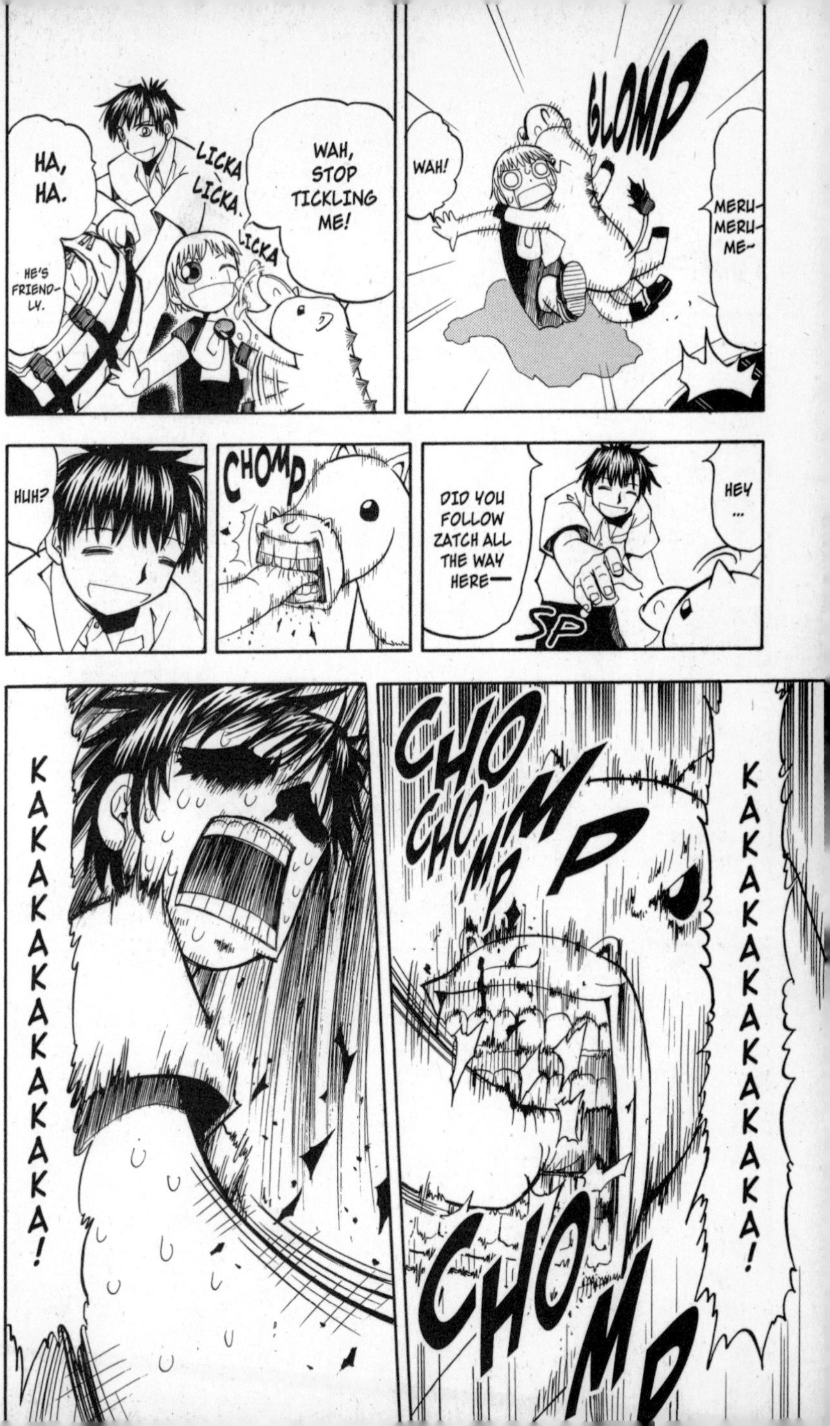
GLOMP
MERU-MERU-ME~
WAH!
WAH, STOP TICKLING ME!
LICKA LICKA
HA, HA.
LICKA
HE'S FRIEND-LY.
HEY ...
DID YOU FOLLOW ZATCH ALL THE WAY HERE—
SP
CHOMP
HUH?
KAKAKAKAKAKAKAKAKA!
CHOMP CHOMP
CHOMP
KAKAKAKAKAKAKAKAKA!

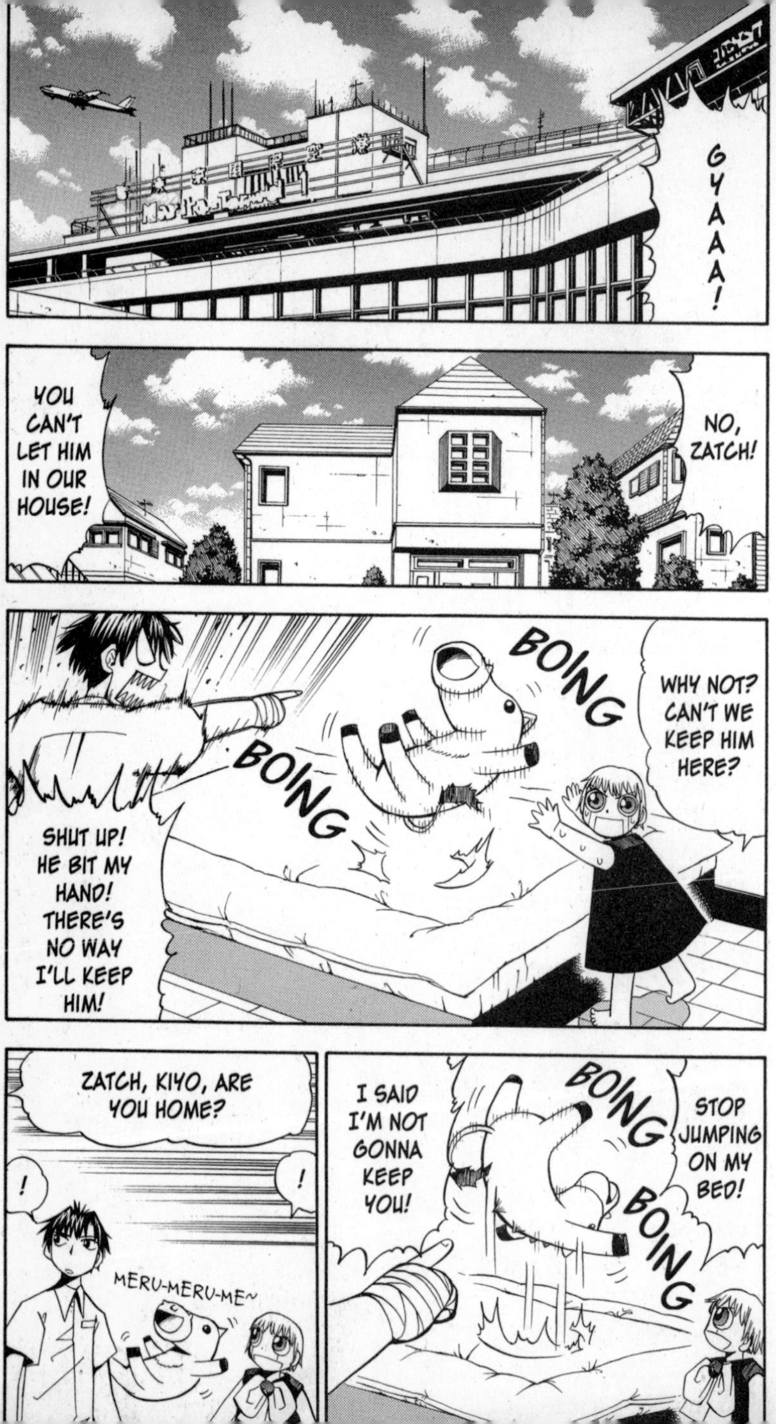
GYAAAA!
NO, ZATCH!
YOU CAN'T LET HIM IN OUR HOUSE!
WHY NOT? CAN'T WE KEEP HIM HERE?
BOING
BOING
SHUT UP! HE BIT MY HAND! THERE'S NO WAY I'LL KEEP HIM!
STOP JUMPING ON MY BED!
BOING
BOING
BOING
BOING
I SAID I'M NOT GONNA KEEP YOU!
ZATCH, KIYO, ARE YOU HOME?
!
!
MERU-MERU-ME~

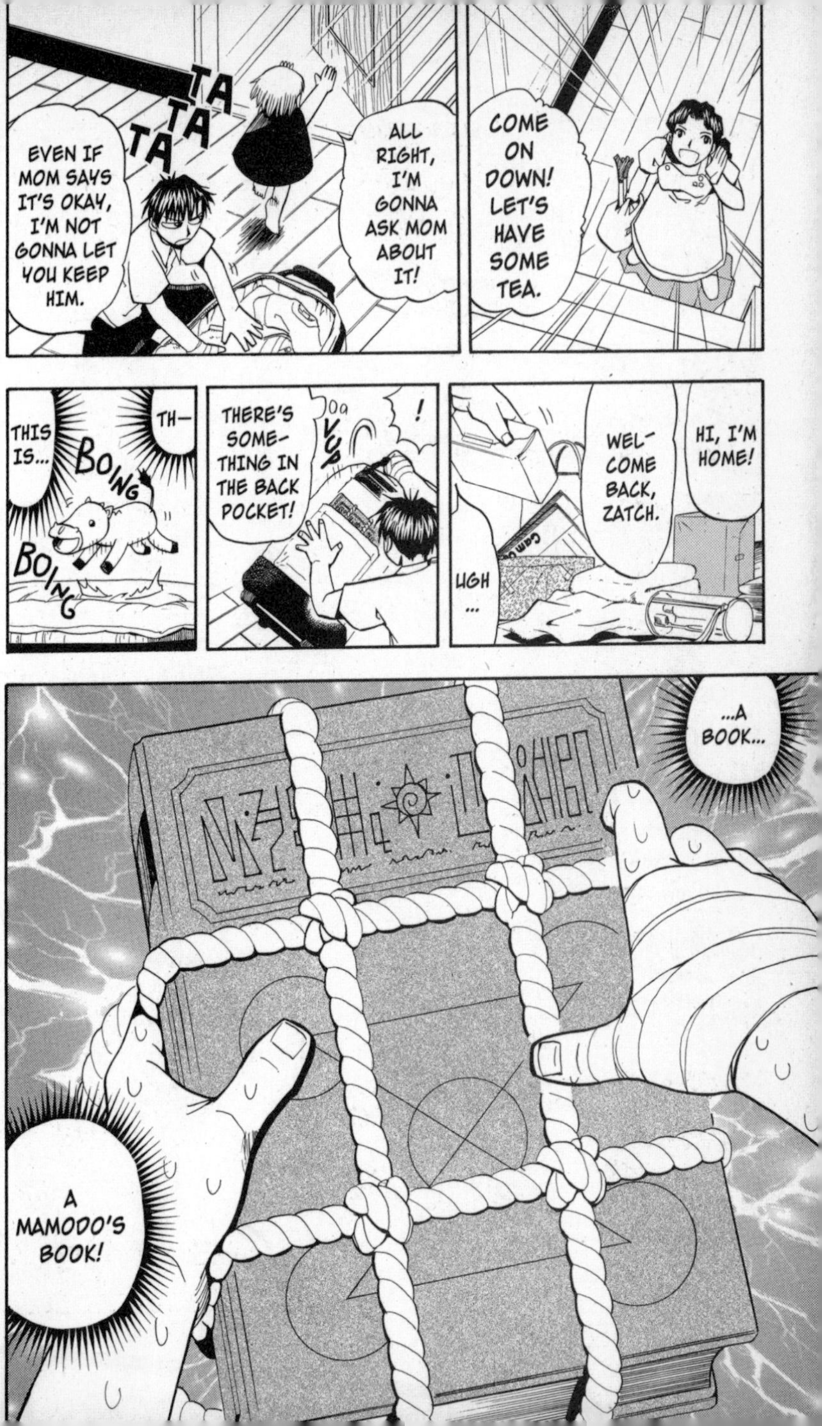
COME ON DOWN! LET'S HAVE SOME TEA.
ALL RIGHT, I'M GONNA ASK MOM ABOUT IT!
TA TA TA
EVEN IF MOM SAYS IT'S OKAY, I'M NOT GONNA LET YOU KEEP HIM.
HI, I'M HOME!
WELCOME BACK, ZATCH.
UGH...
!
VUP
THERE'S SOMETHING IN THE BACK POCKET!
TH—
THIS IS...
BOING
BOING
...A BOOK...
A MAMODO'S BOOK!

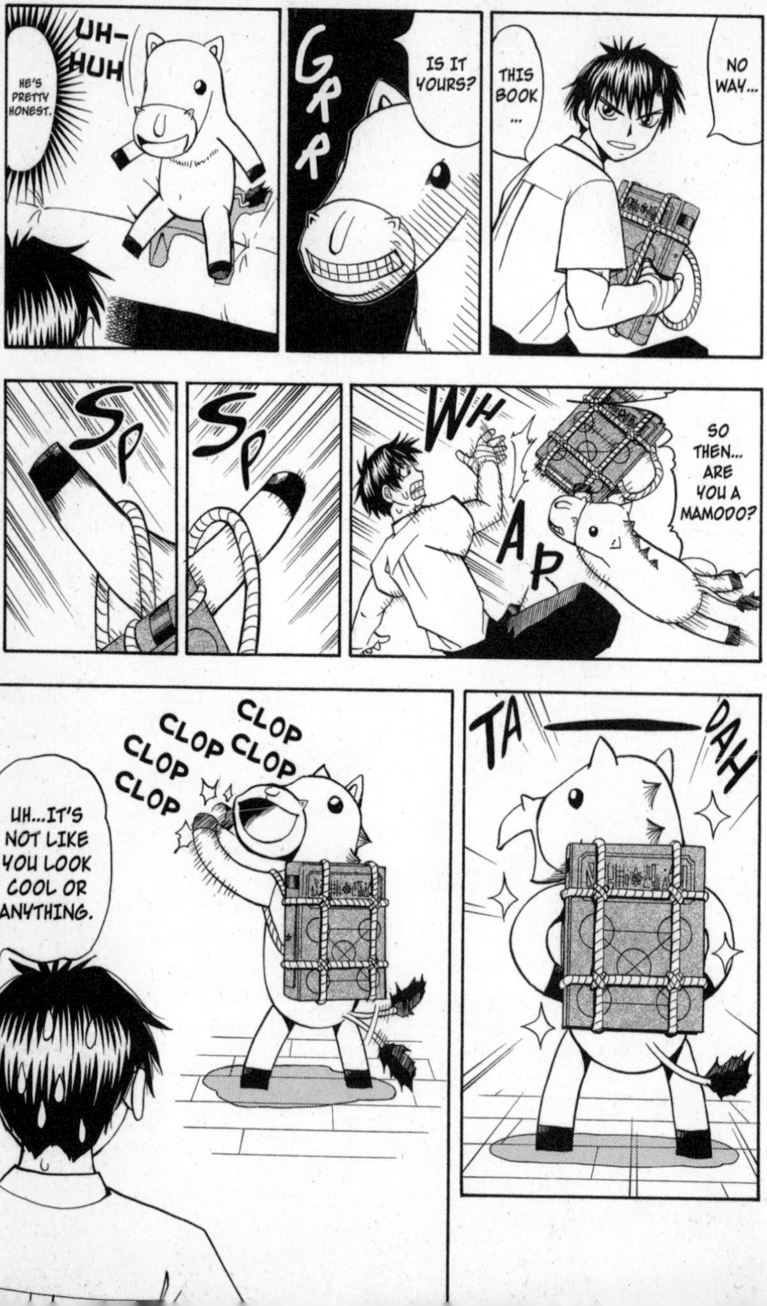
NO WAY...
THIS BOOK ...
IS IT YOURS?
GRR
UH-HUH
HE'S PRETTY HONEST.
SO THEN... ARE YOU A MAMODO?
WHAP
SP
SP
TA—DAH
CLOP CLOP
CLOP
CLOP
CLOP
UH...IT'S NOT LIKE YOU LOOK COOL OR ANYTHING.

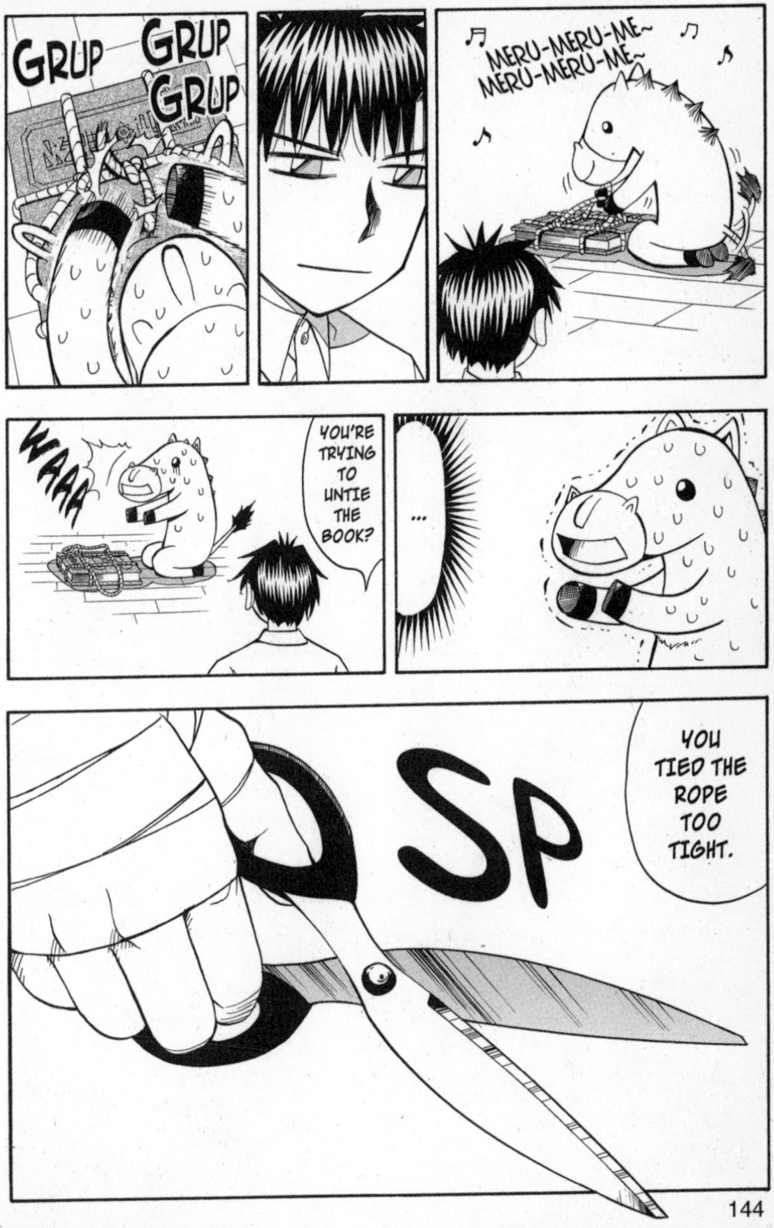
MERU-MERU-ME~
MERU-MERU-ME~
GRUP GRUP GRUP
...
YOU'RE TRYING TO UNTIE THE BOOK?
WAAA
YOU TIED THE ROPE TOO TIGHT.
SP

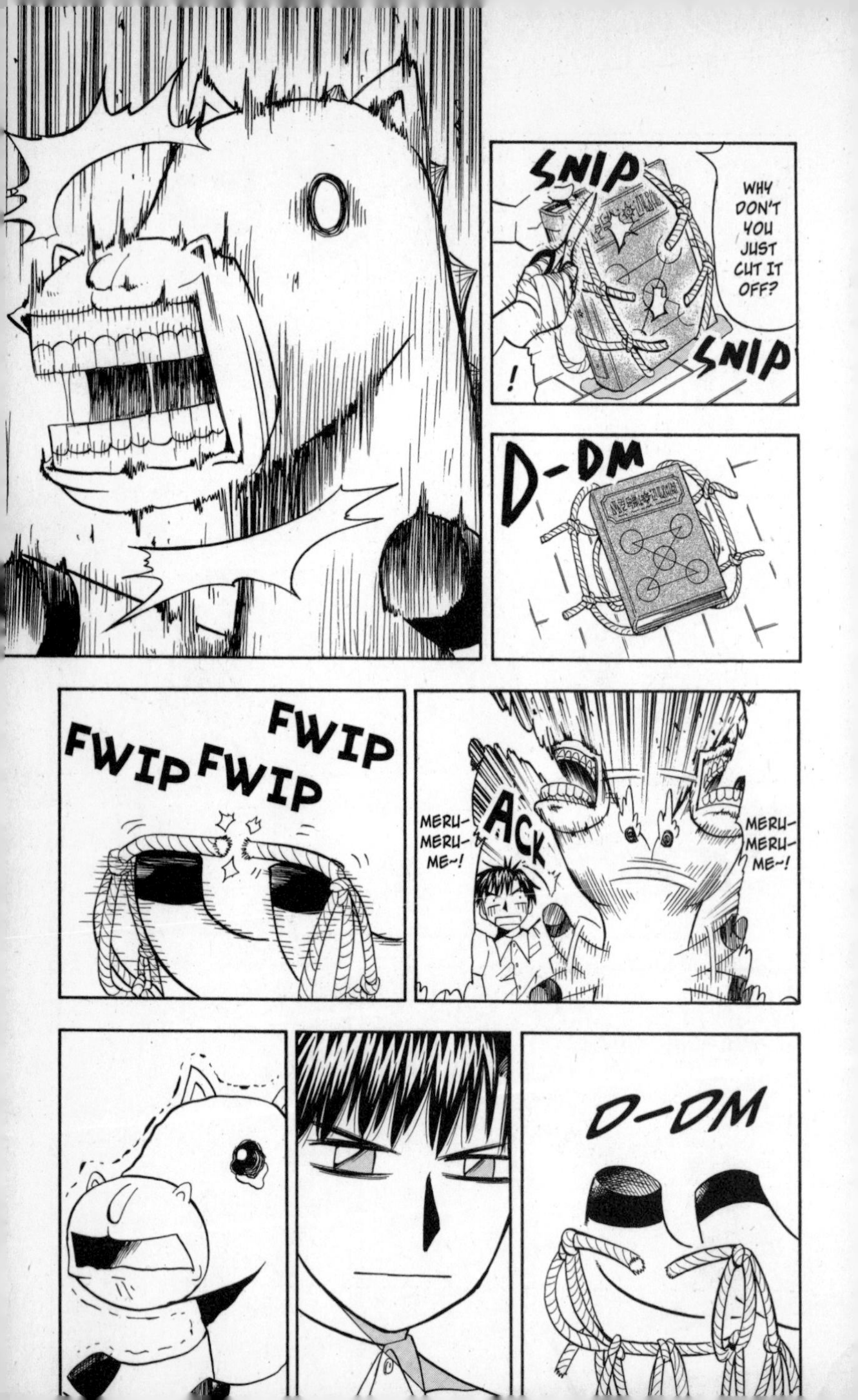
WHY DON'T YOU JUST CUT IT OFF?
SNIP
SNIP
!
D-DM
MERU-MERU-ME~!
ACK
MERU-MERU-ME~!
FWIP
FWIP FWIP
D-DM

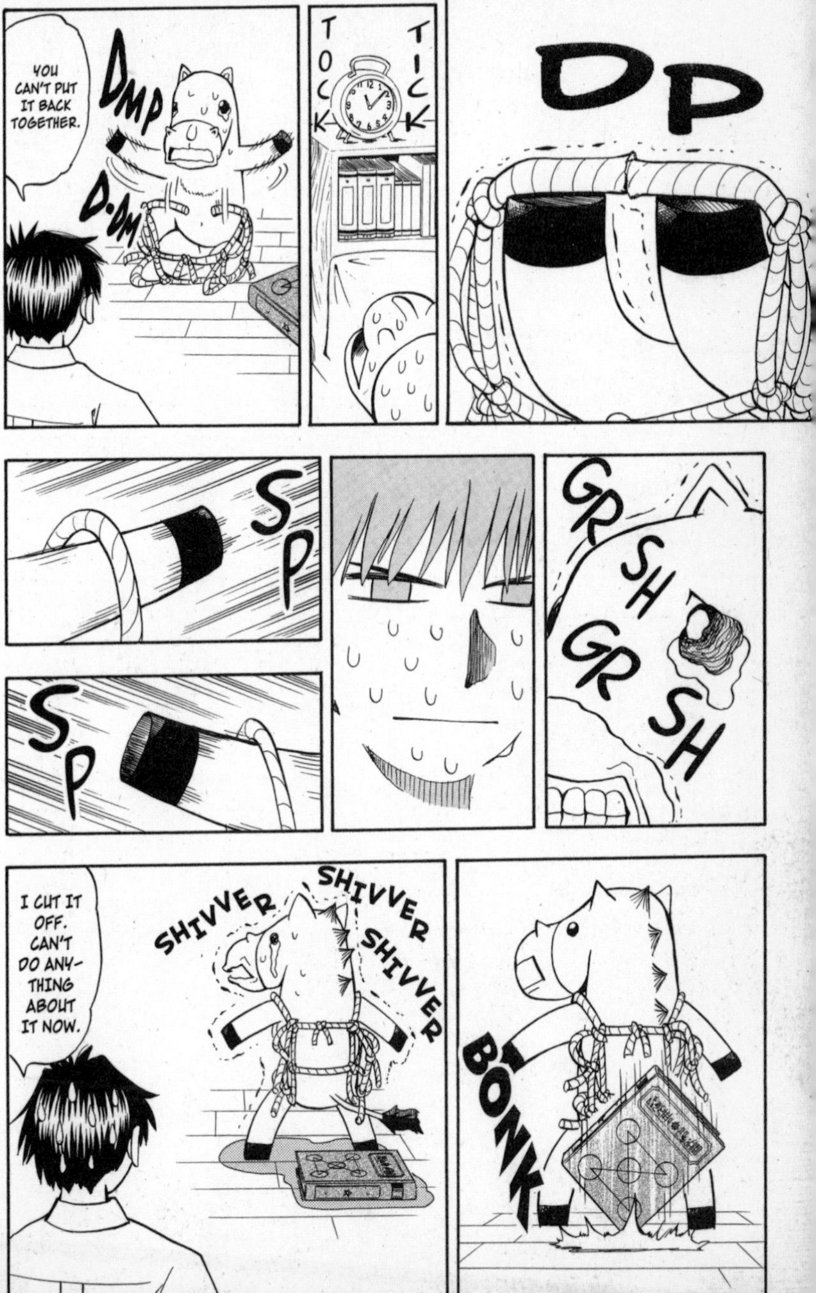
DP
TICK
TOCK
YOU CAN'T PUT IT BACK TOGETHER.
DMP
D-DM
GR
SH
GR
SH
SP
SP
BONK
I CUT IT OFF. CAN'T DO ANY-THING ABOUT IT NOW.
SHIVVER
SHIVVER
SHIVVER
SHIVVER

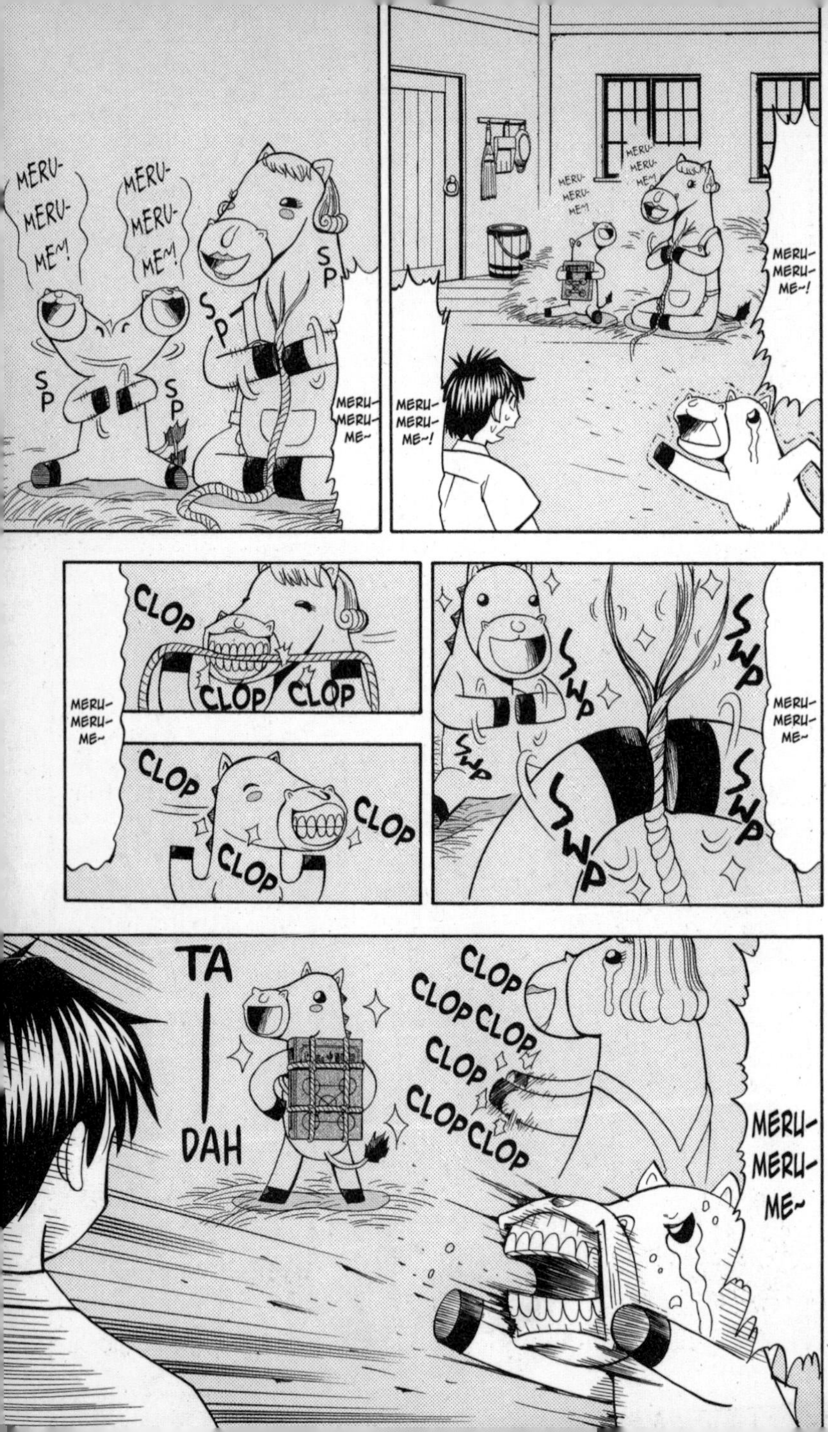

MERU-MERU-ME~
MERU-MERU-ME~
MERU-MERU-ME~!
MERU-MERU-ME~!
MERU-MERU-ME~!
MERU-MERU-ME~!
SP
SP
SP
SP
MERU-MERU-ME~
MERU-MERU-ME~
SWP
SWP
SWP
SWP
SWP
MERU-MERU-ME~
CLOP
CLOP
CLOP
CLOP
CLOP
CLOP
MERU-MERU-ME~
CLOP
CLOP CLOP
CLOP
CLOP CLOP
TA-DAH

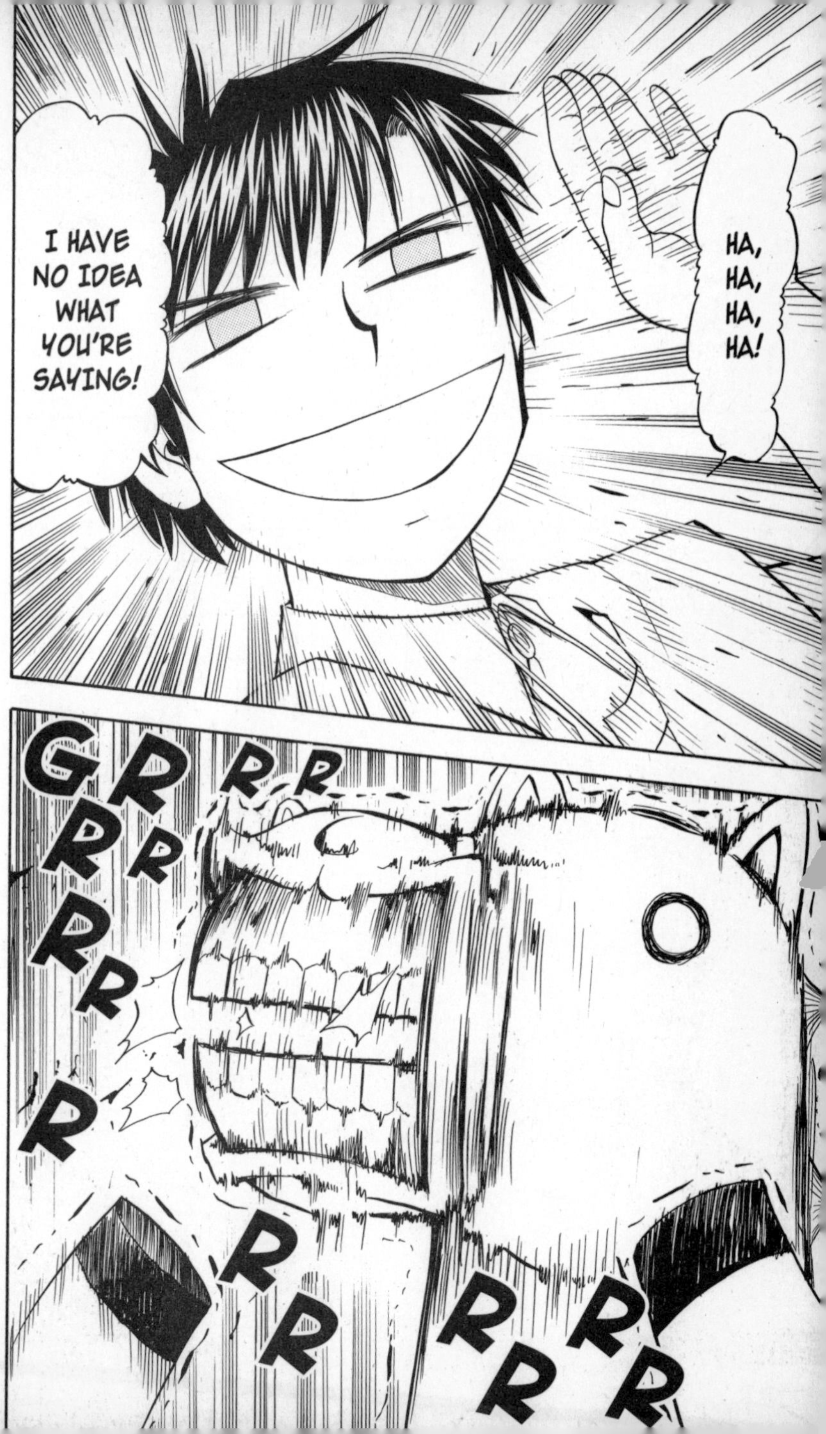
HA, HA, HA, HA!
I HAVE NO IDEA WHAT YOU'RE SAYING!
GRRRRRRRRRRRRRRR

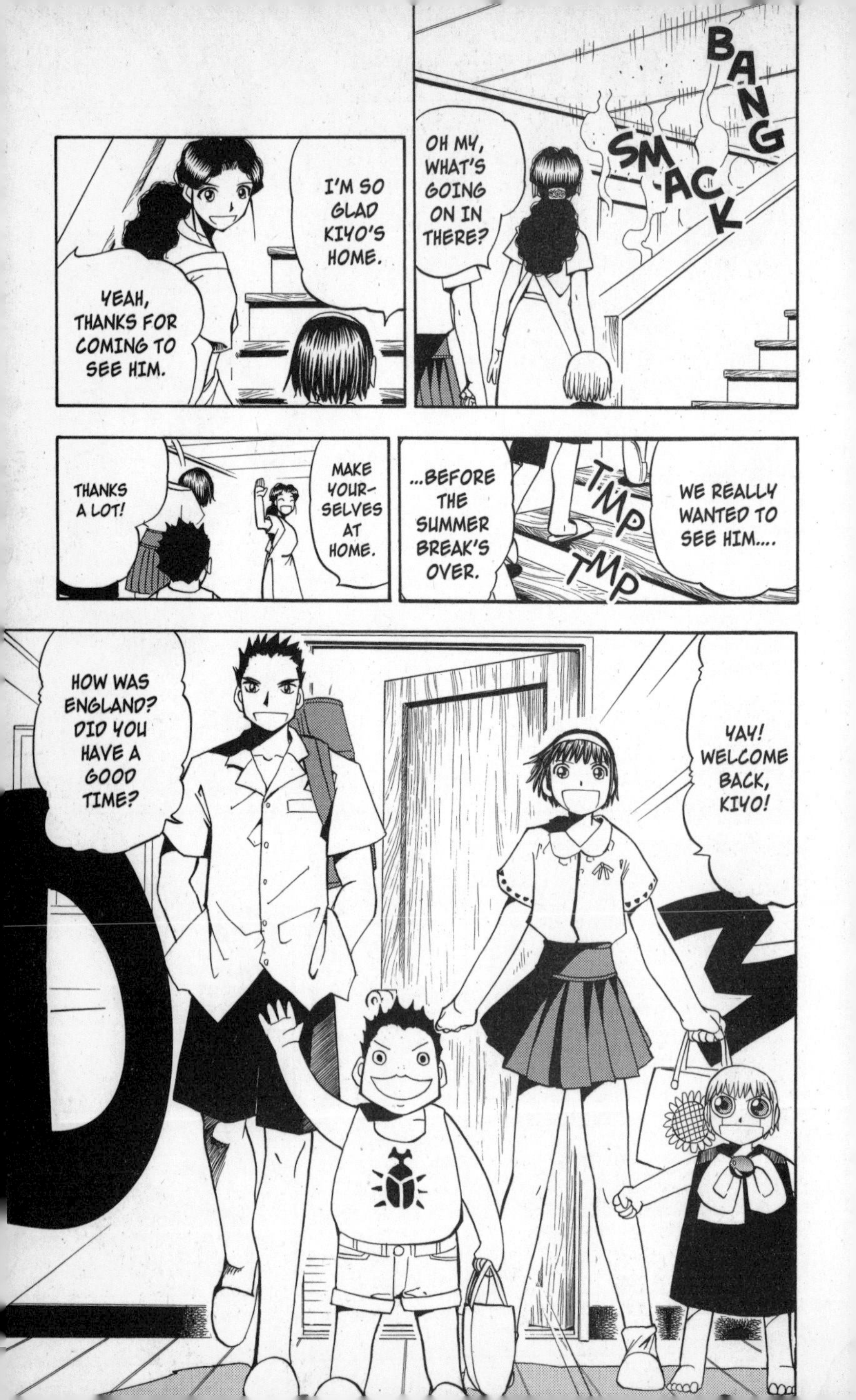
BANG
SMACK
OH MY, WHAT'S GOING ON IN THERE?
I'M SO GLAD KIYO'S HOME.
YEAH, THANKS FOR COMING TO SEE HIM.
WE REALLY WANTED TO SEE HIM....
TMP TMP
...BEFORE THE SUMMER BREAK'S OVER.
MAKE YOUR-SELVES AT HOME.
THANKS A LOT!
YAY! WELCOME BACK, KIYO!
HOW WAS ENGLAND? DID YOU HAVE A GOOD TIME?

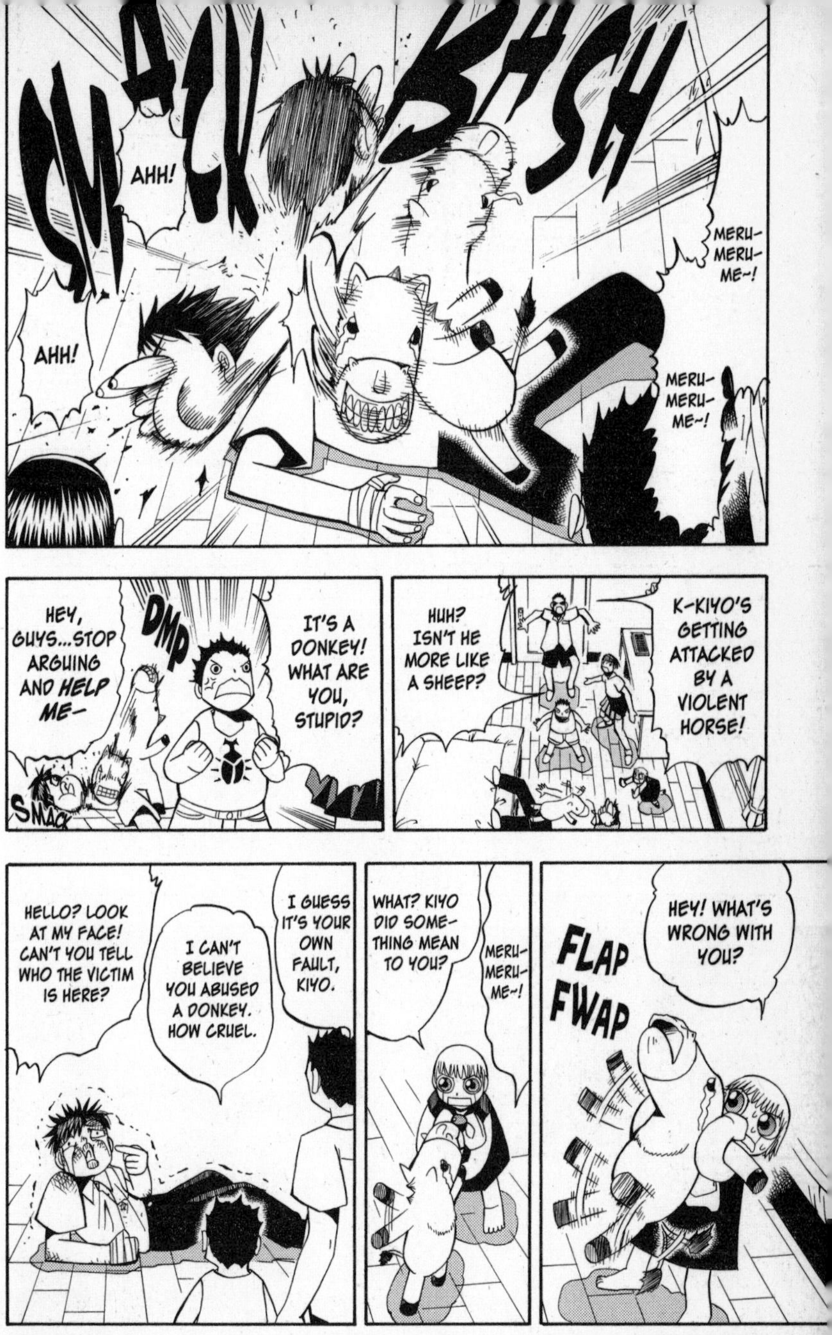
BASH
SMACK
MERU-MERU-ME~!
AHH!
MERU-MERU-ME~!
AHH!
K-KIYO'S GETTING ATTACKED BY A VIOLENT HORSE!
HUH? ISN'T HE MORE LIKE A SHEEP?
IT'S A DONKEY! WHAT ARE YOU, STUPID?
DMP
HEY, GUYS...STOP ARGUING AND *HELP ME*-
SMACK
HEY! WHAT'S WRONG WITH YOU?
FLAP
FWAP
MERU-MERU-ME~!
WHAT? KIYO DID SOMETHING MEAN TO YOU?
I GUESS IT'S YOUR OWN FAULT, KIYO.
I CAN'T BELIEVE YOU ABUSED A DONKEY. HOW CRUEL.
HELLO? LOOK AT MY FACE! CAN'T YOU TELL WHO THE VICTIM IS HERE?

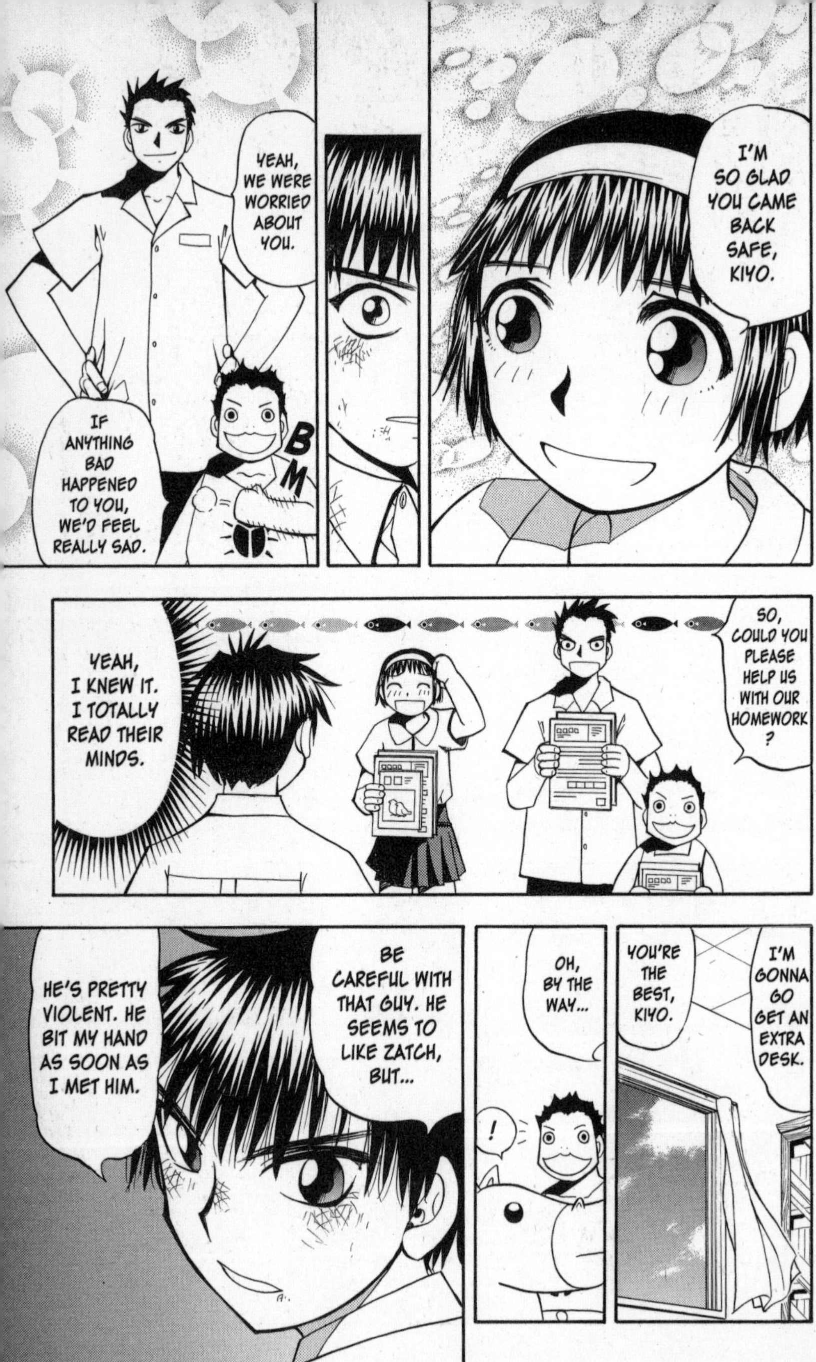
I'M SO GLAD YOU CAME BACK SAFE, KIYO.
YEAH, WE WERE WORRIED ABOUT YOU.
IF ANYTHING BAD HAPPENED TO YOU, WE'D FEEL REALLY SAD.
BM
SO, COULD YOU PLEASE HELP US WITH OUR HOMEWORK?
YEAH, I KNEW IT. I TOTALLY READ THEIR MINDS.
I'M GONNA GO GET AN EXTRA DESK.
YOU'RE THE BEST, KIYO.
OH, BY THE WAY...
!
BE CAREFUL WITH THAT GUY. HE SEEMS TO LIKE ZATCH, BUT...
HE'S PRETTY VIOLENT. HE BIT MY HAND AS SOON AS I MET HIM.

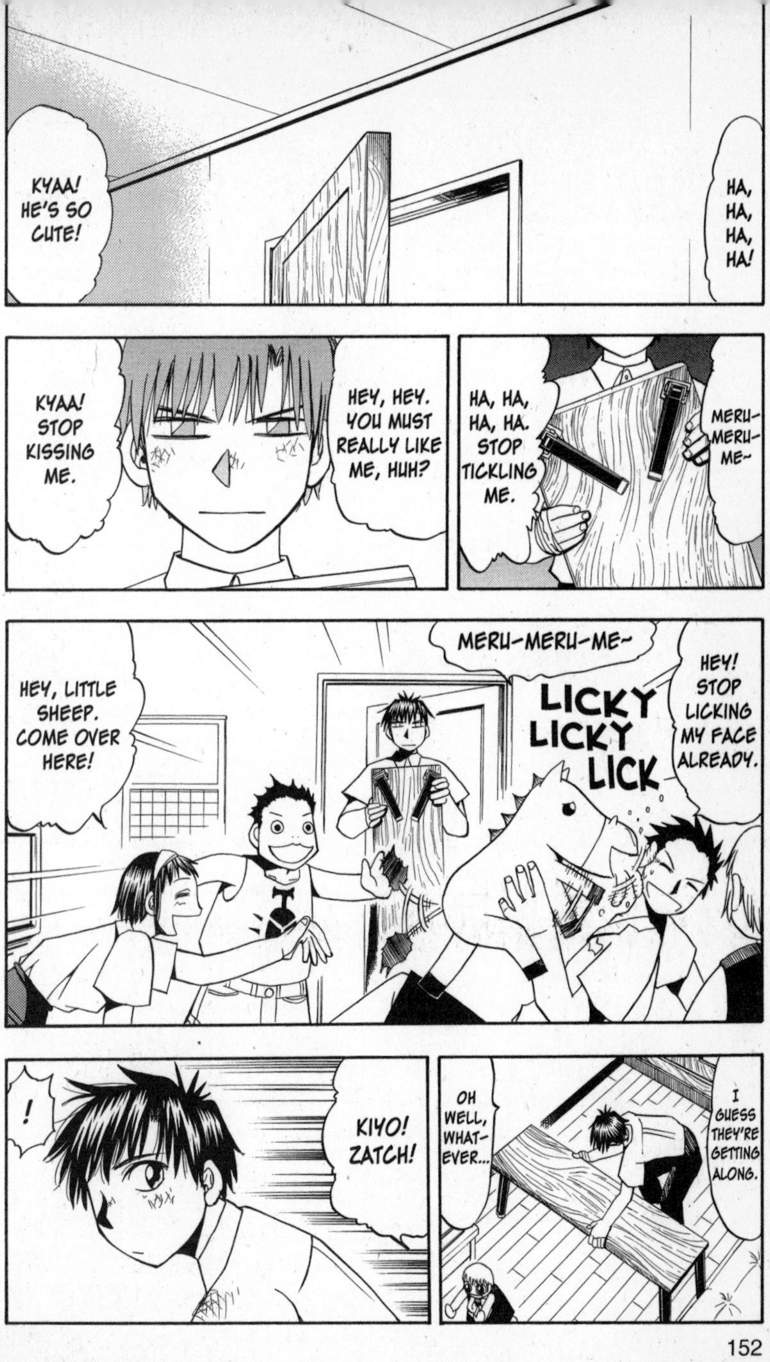
HA, HA, HA, HA!
KYAA! HE'S SO CUTE!
MERU-MERU-ME~
HA, HA, HA, HA. STOP TICKLING ME.
HEY, HEY. YOU MUST REALLY LIKE ME, HUH?
KYAA! STOP KISSING ME.
HEY! STOP LICKING MY FACE ALREADY.
MERU-MERU-ME~
LICKY LICKY LICK
HEY, LITTLE SHEEP. COME OVER HERE!
I GUESS THEY'RE GETTING ALONG.
OH WELL, WHATEVER...
KIYO! ZATCH!
!

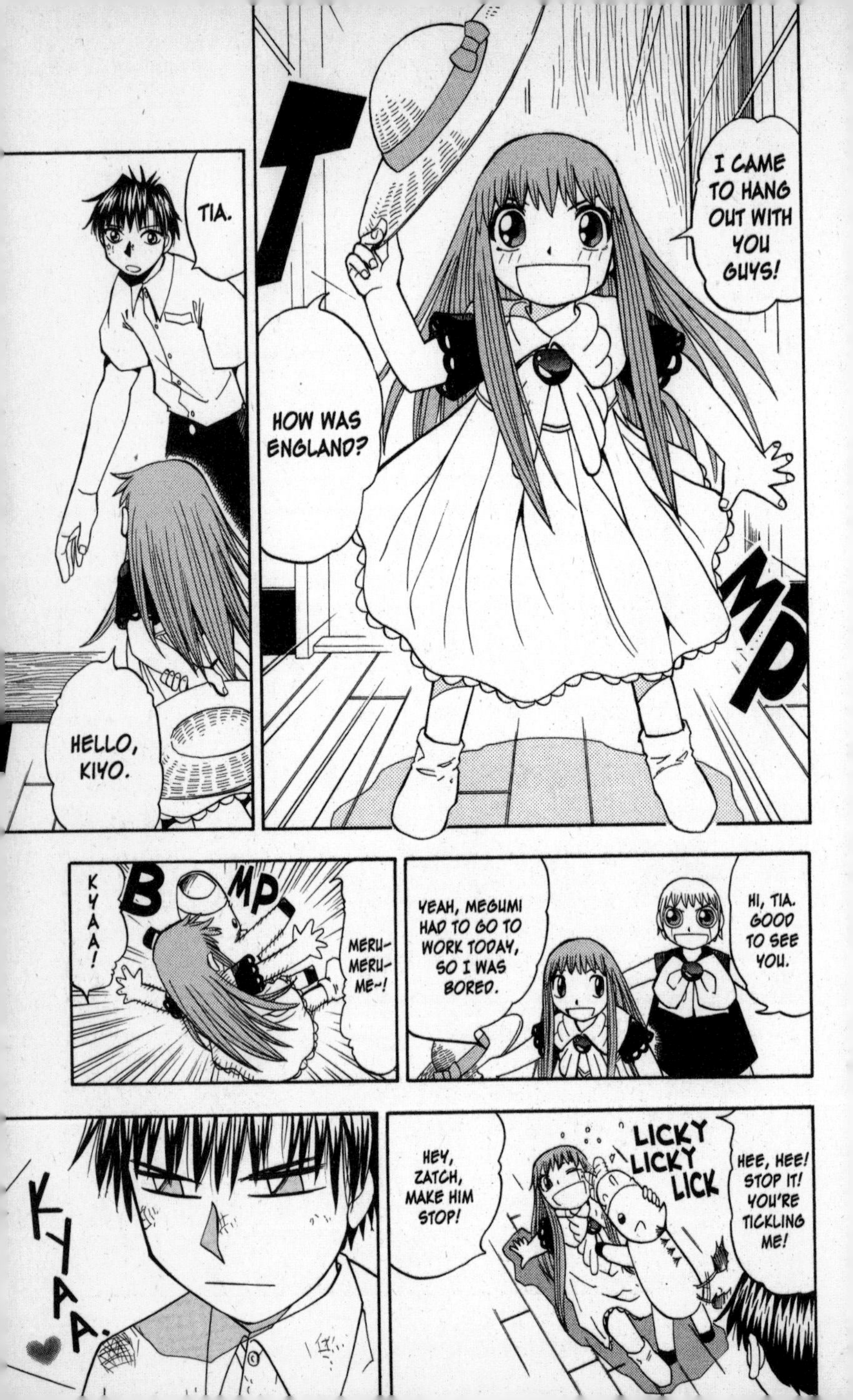
I CAME TO HANG OUT WITH YOU GUYS!
T
MP
HOW WAS ENGLAND?
TIA.
HELLO, KIYO.
HI, TIA. GOOD TO SEE YOU.
YEAH, MEGUMI HAD TO GO TO WORK TODAY, SO I WAS BORED.
MERU-MERU-ME~!
B MP
KYAAA!
HEE, HEE! STOP IT! YOU'RE TICKLING ME!
LICKY LICKY LICK
HEY, ZATCH, MAKE HIM STOP!
KYAA.

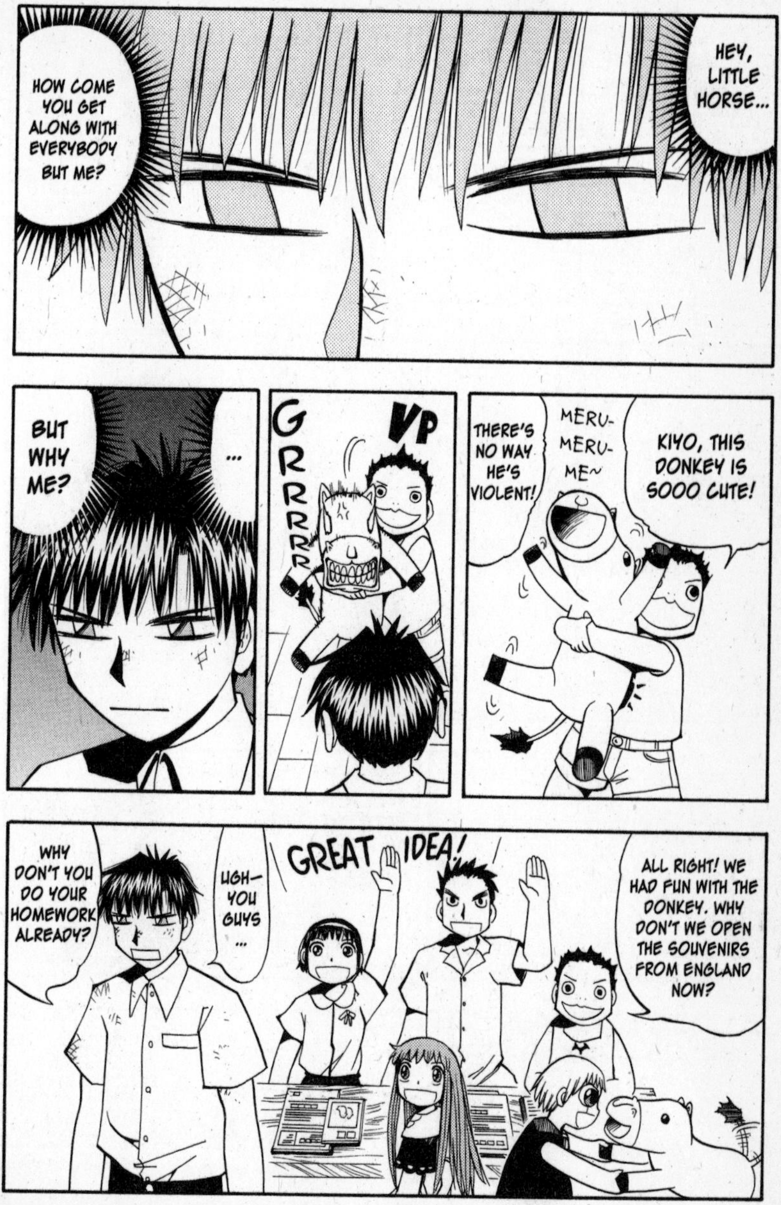
HEY, LITTLE HORSE...
HOW COME YOU GET ALONG WITH EVERYBODY BUT ME?
KIYO, THIS DONKEY IS SOOO CUTE!
MERU-MERU-ME~
THERE'S NO WAY HE'S VIOLENT!
VP
GRRRRR
...
BUT WHY ME?
ALL RIGHT! WE HAD FUN WITH THE DONKEY. WHY DON'T WE OPEN THE SOUVENIRS FROM ENGLAND NOW?
GREAT IDEA!
UGH— YOU GUYS ...
WHY DON'T YOU DO YOUR HOMEWORK ALREADY?

LEVEL 57: Until Then

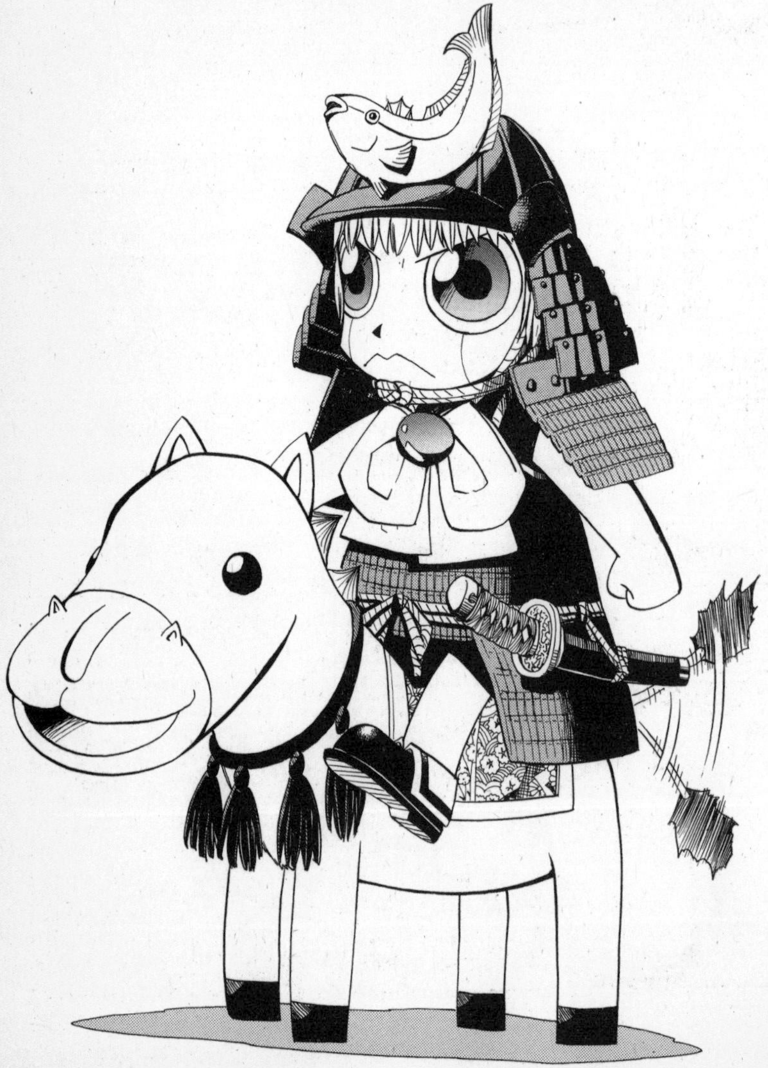

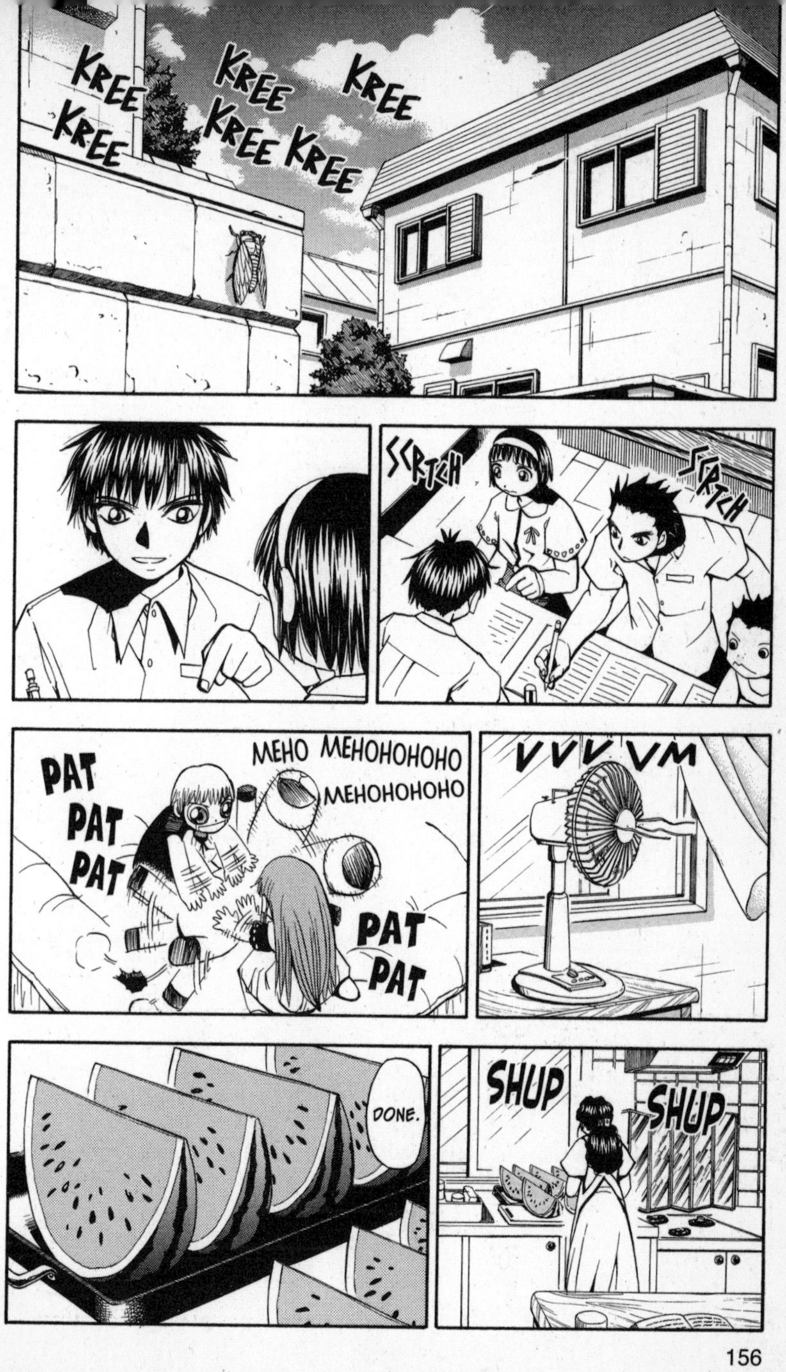
KREE
KREE KREE
KREE
KREE KREE
KREE
SCRTCH
SCRTCH
VVVVM
MEHO MEHOHOHOHO
MEHOHOHOHO
PAT
PAT
PAT
PAT
PAT
SHUP
SHUP
DONE.

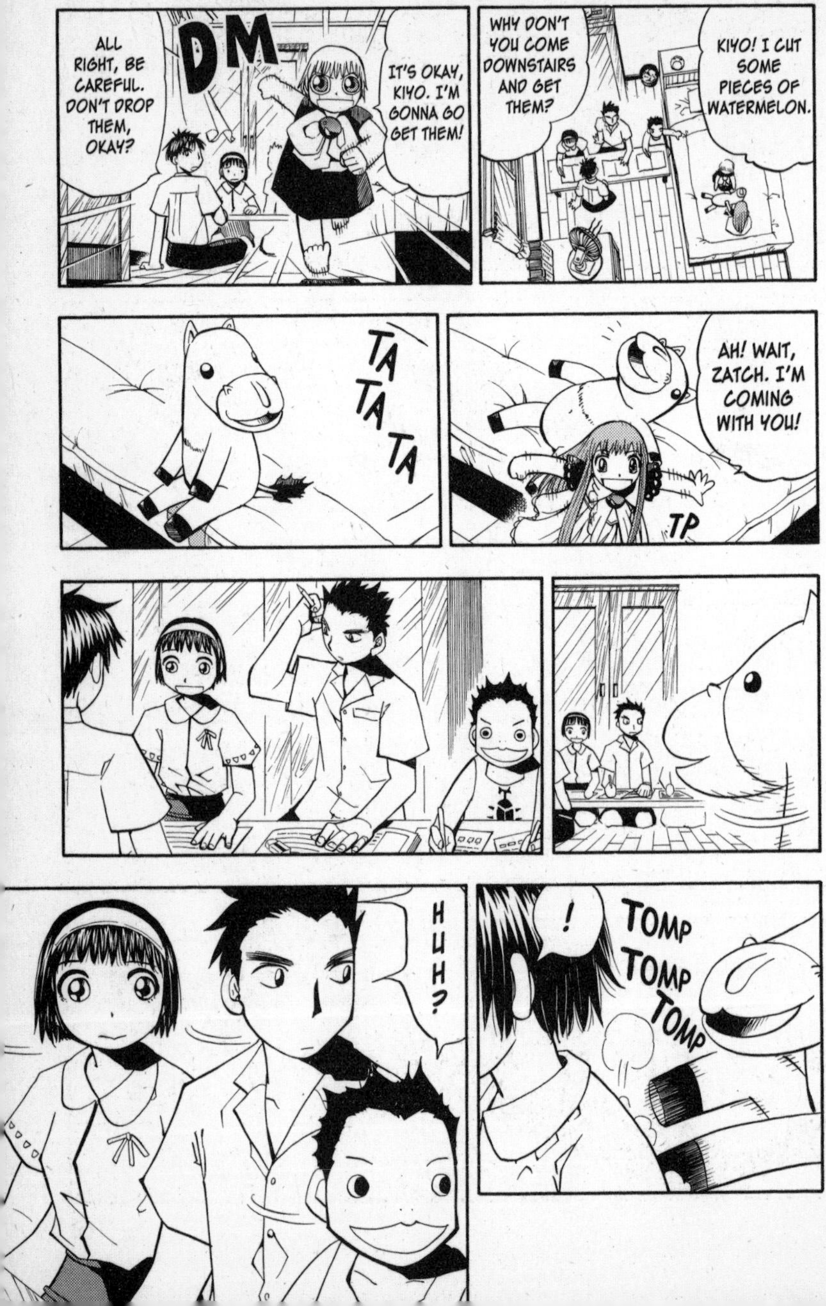
KIYO! I CUT SOME PIECES OF WATERMELON.
WHY DON'T YOU COME DOWNSTAIRS AND GET THEM?
IT'S OKAY, KIYO. I'M GONNA GO GET THEM!
DM
ALL RIGHT, BE CAREFUL. DON'T DROP THEM, OKAY?
AH! WAIT, ZATCH. I'M COMING WITH YOU!
TP
TA TA TA
!
TOMP TOMP TOMP
HUH?

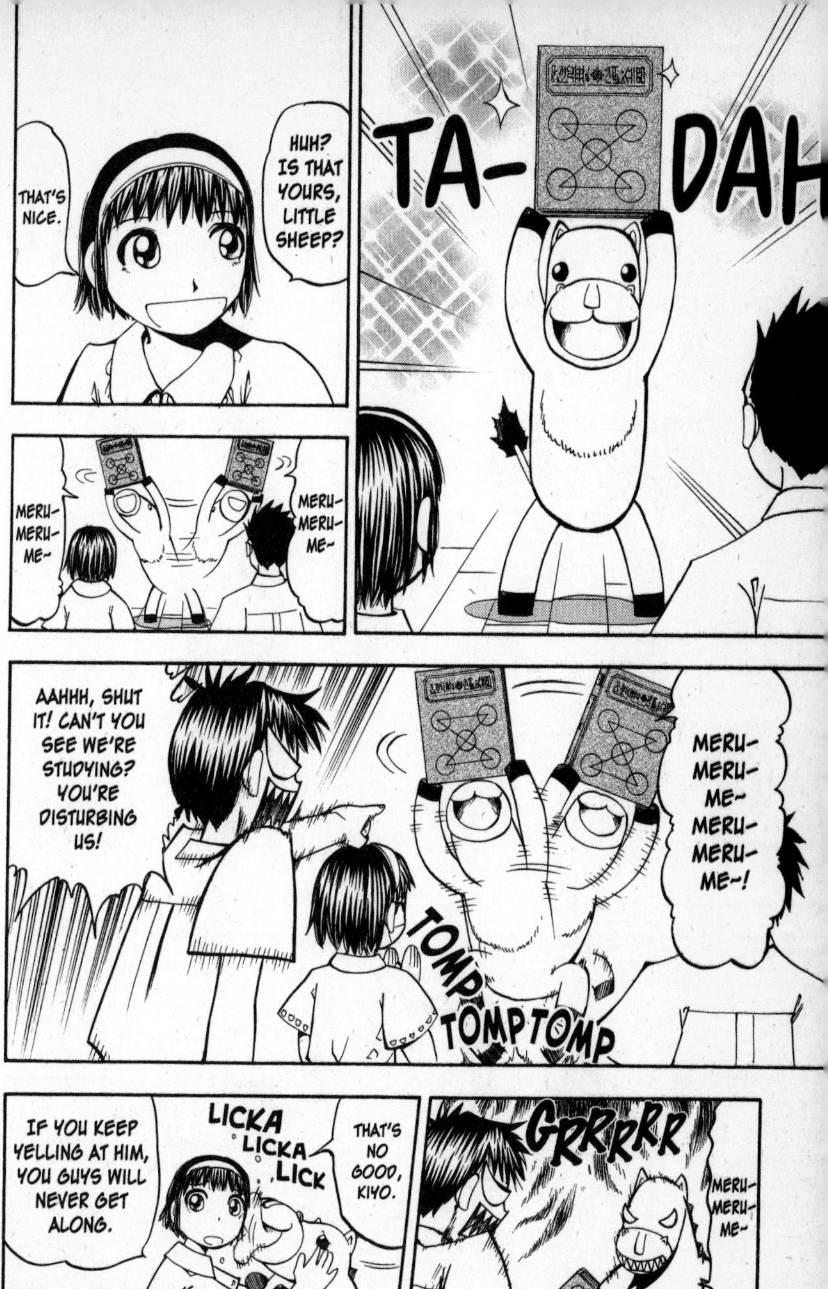

TA-DAH
HUH? IS THAT YOURS, LITTLE SHEEP?
THAT'S NICE.
MERU-MERU-ME~
MERU-MERU-ME~
MERU-MERU-ME~ MERU-MERU-ME~!
AAHHH, SHUT IT! CAN'T YOU SEE WE'RE STUDYING? YOU'RE DISTURBING US!
TOMP TOMP TOMP
GRRRRR
MERU-MERU-ME~
THAT'S NO GOOD, KIYO.
LICKA LICKA LICK
IF YOU KEEP YELLING AT HIM, YOU GUYS WILL NEVER GET ALONG.

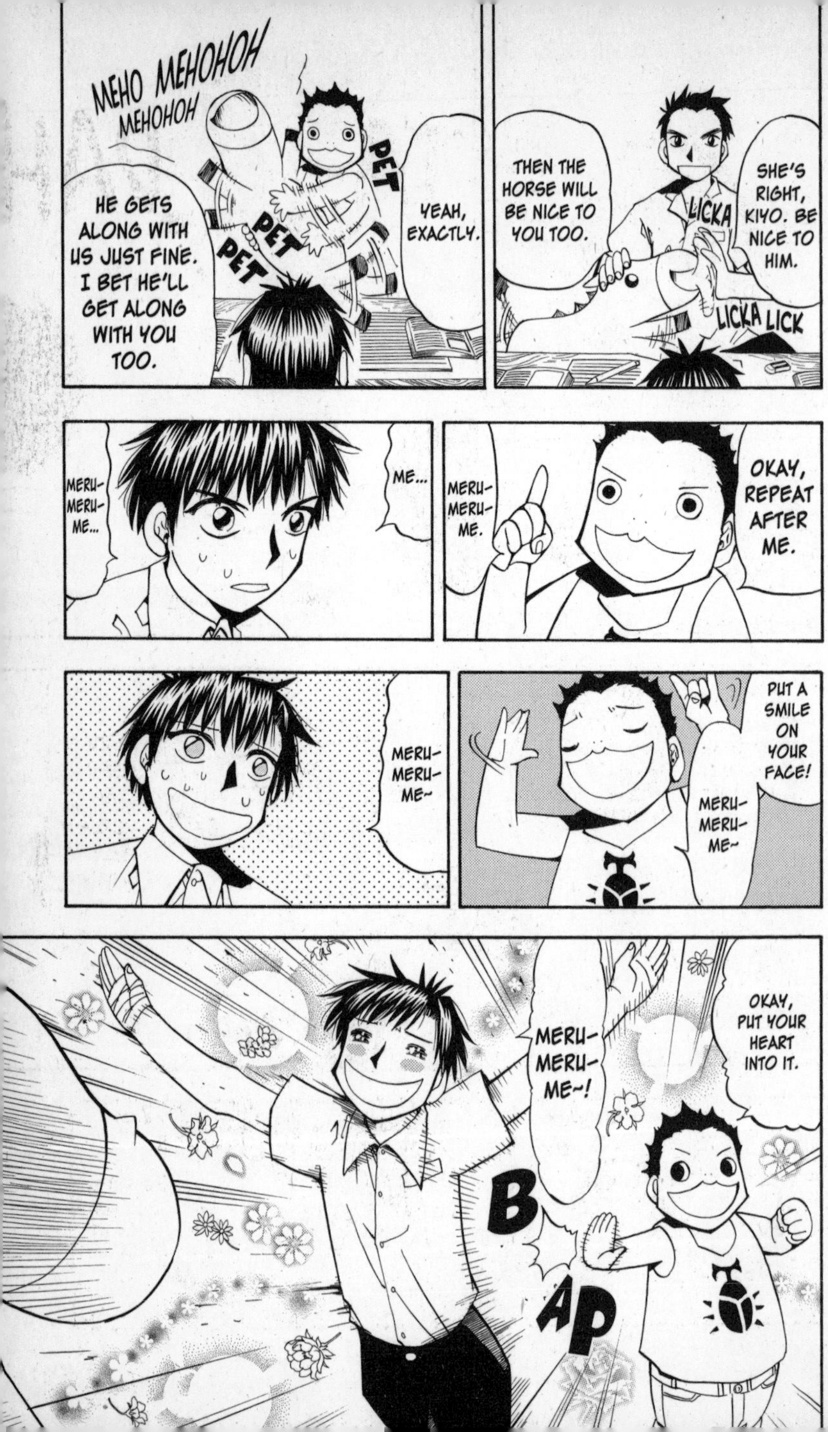

SHE'S RIGHT, KIYO. BE NICE TO HIM.
LICKA
LICKA LICK
THEN THE HORSE WILL BE NICE TO YOU TOO.
YEAH, EXACTLY.
PET
PET
PET
MEHO MEHOHOH MEHOHOH
HE GETS ALONG WITH US JUST FINE. I BET HE'LL GET ALONG WITH YOU TOO.
OKAY, REPEAT AFTER ME.
MERU-MERU-ME.
ME...
MERU-MERU-ME...
PUT A SMILE ON YOUR FACE!
MERU-MERU-ME~
MERU-MERU-ME~
OKAY, PUT YOUR HEART INTO IT.
MERU-MERU-ME~!
BAP

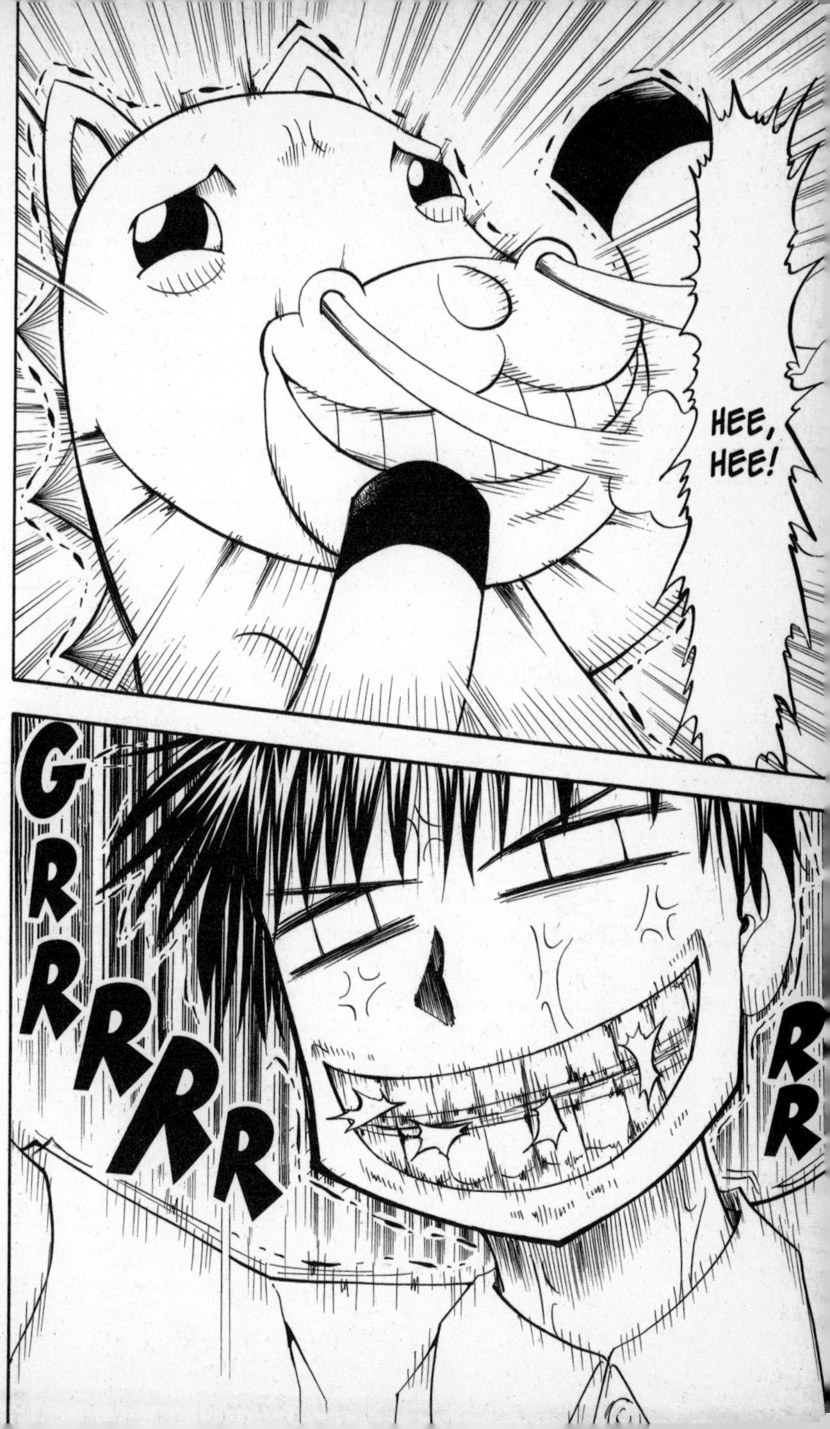
HEE, HEE!
GRRRRR
RR

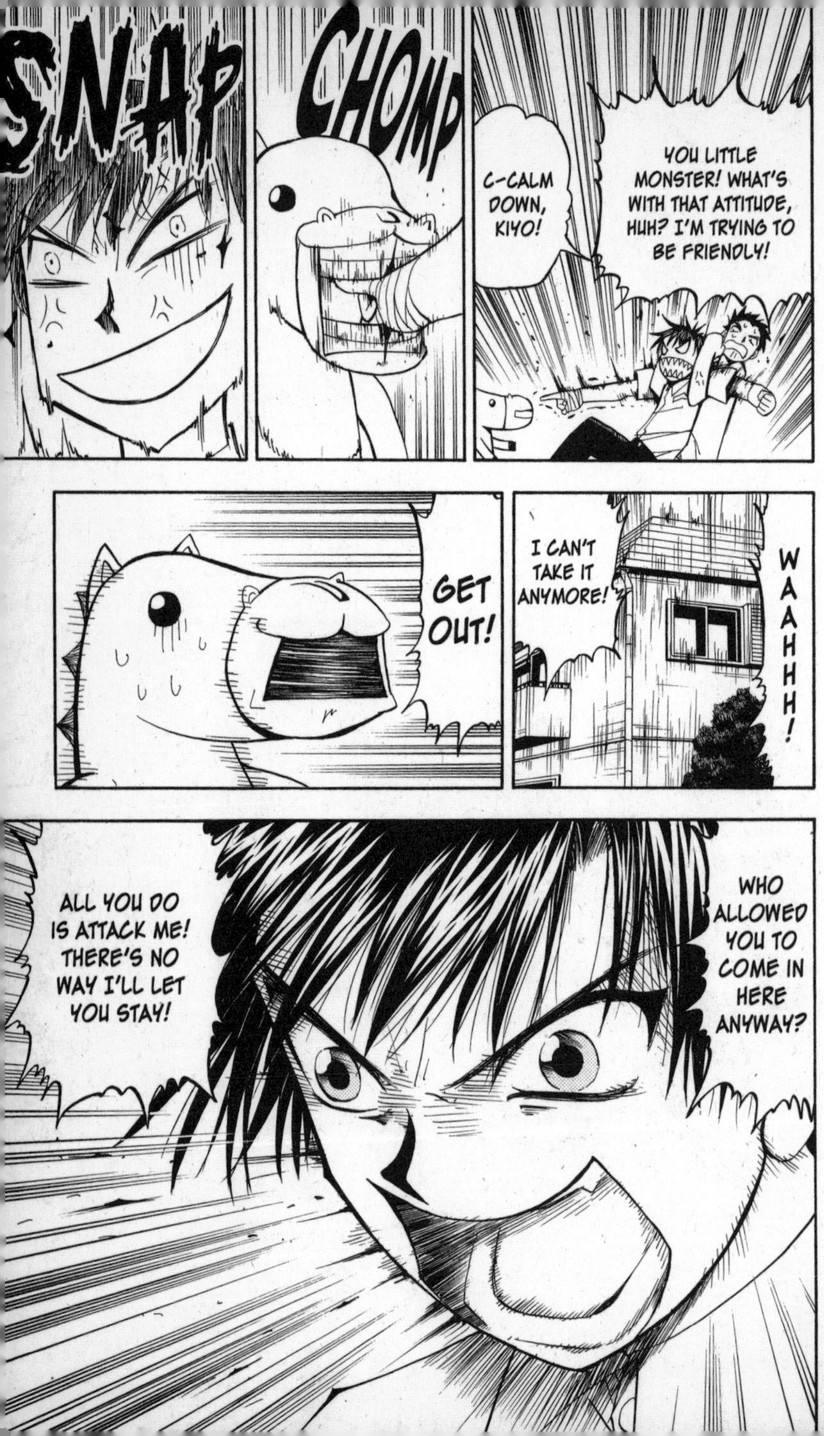
YOU LITTLE MONSTER! WHAT'S WITH THAT ATTITUDE, HUH? I'M TRYING TO BE FRIENDLY!
C-CALM DOWN, KIYO!
CHOMP
SNAP
WAAHHHH!
I CAN'T TAKE IT ANYMORE!
GET OUT!
WHO ALLOWED YOU TO COME IN HERE ANYWAY?
ALL YOU DO IS ATTACK ME! THERE'S NO WAY I'LL LET YOU STAY!

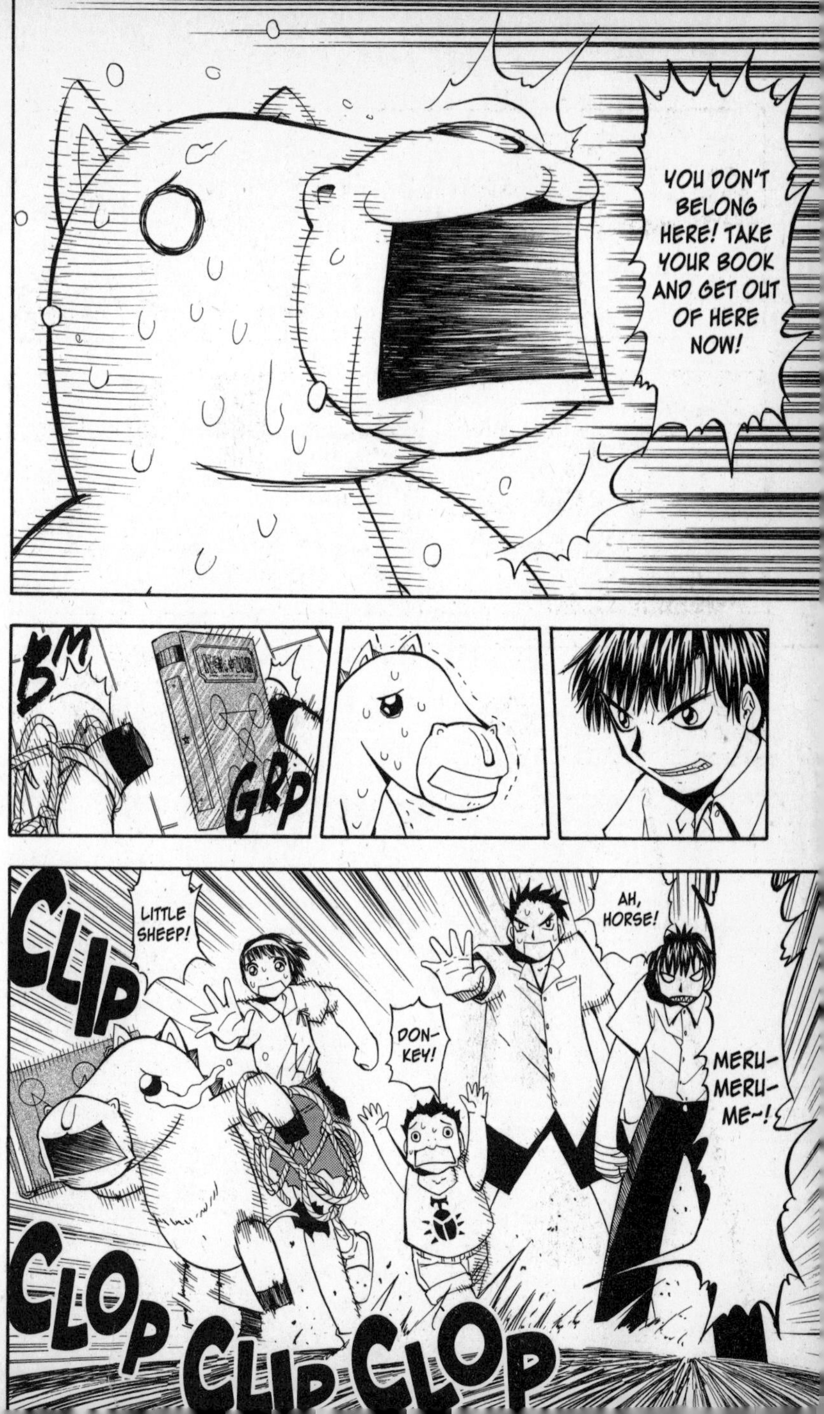
YOU DON'T BELONG HERE! TAKE YOUR BOOK AND GET OUT OF HERE NOW!
BM
GRP
MERU-MERU-ME~!
AH, HORSE!
DON-KEY!
LITTLE SHEEP!
CLIP
CLOP CLIP CLOP

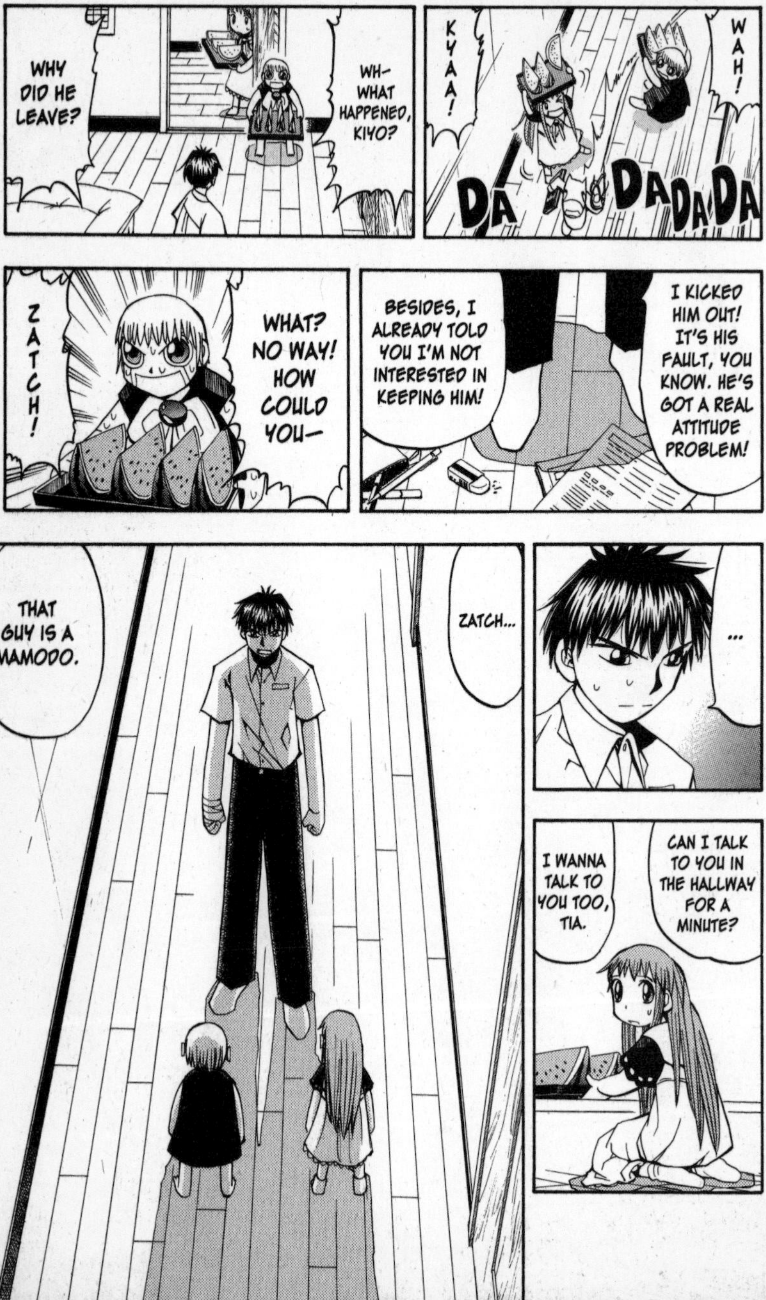
WAH!
KYAA!
DA DADADA
WH- WHAT HAPPENED, KIYO?
WHY DID HE LEAVE?
I KICKED HIM OUT! IT'S HIS FAULT, YOU KNOW. HE'S GOT A REAL ATTITUDE PROBLEM!
BESIDES, I ALREADY TOLD YOU I'M NOT INTERESTED IN KEEPING HIM!
WHAT? NO WAY! HOW COULD YOU—
ZATCH!
...
ZATCH...
CAN I TALK TO YOU IN THE HALLWAY FOR A MINUTE?
I WANNA TALK TO YOU TOO, TIA.
THAT GUY IS A MAMODO.

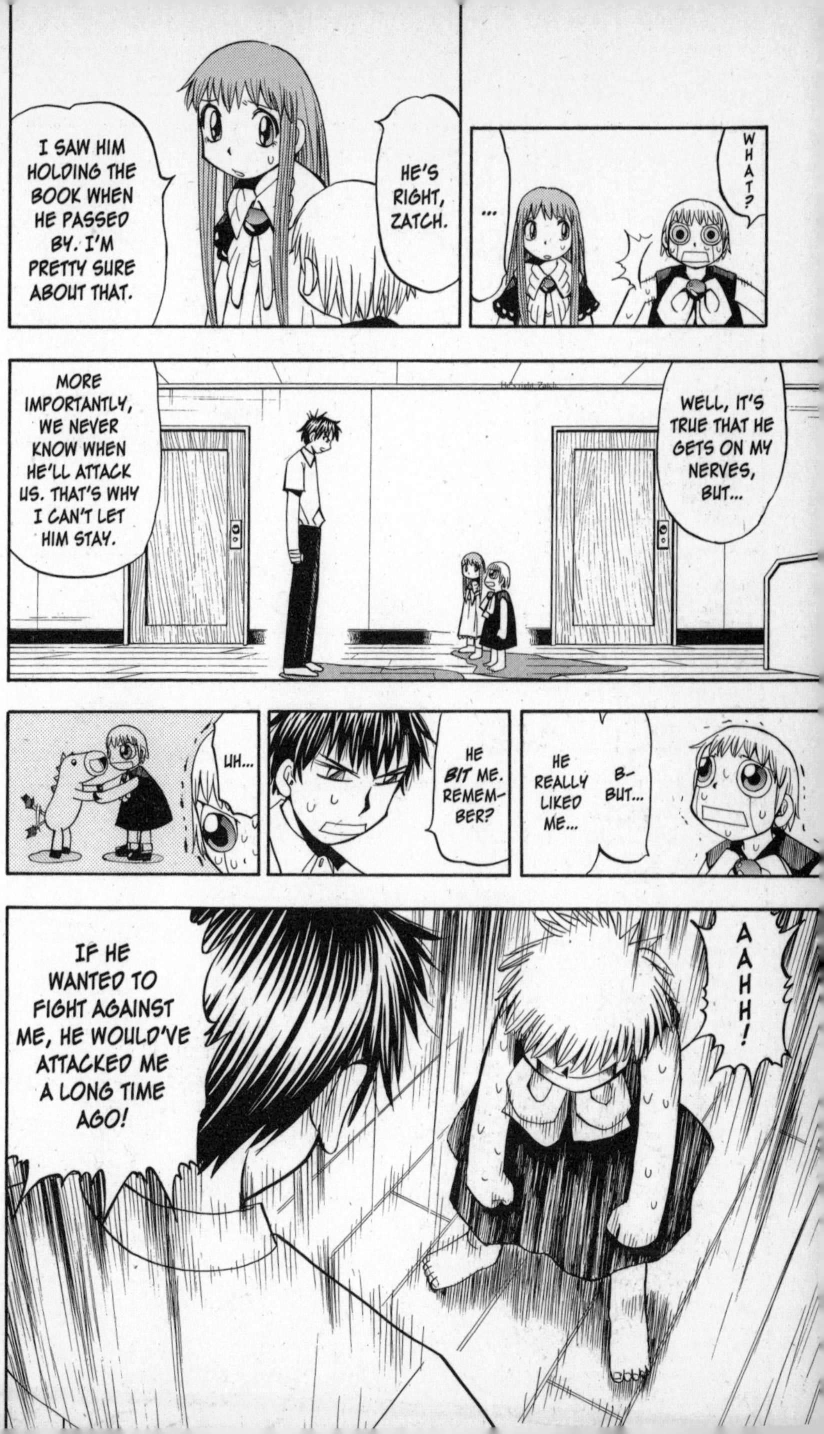
WHAT?
...
HE'S RIGHT, ZATCH.
I SAW HIM HOLDING THE BOOK WHEN HE PASSED BY. I'M PRETTY SURE ABOUT THAT.
WELL, IT'S TRUE THAT HE GETS ON MY NERVES, BUT...
MORE IMPORTANTLY, WE NEVER KNOW WHEN HE'LL ATTACK US. THAT'S WHY I CAN'T LET HIM STAY.
B-BUT...
HE REALLY LIKED ME...
HE BIT ME. REMEMBER?
UH...
AAHH!
IF HE WANTED TO FIGHT AGAINST ME, HE WOULD'VE ATTACKED ME A LONG TIME AGO!

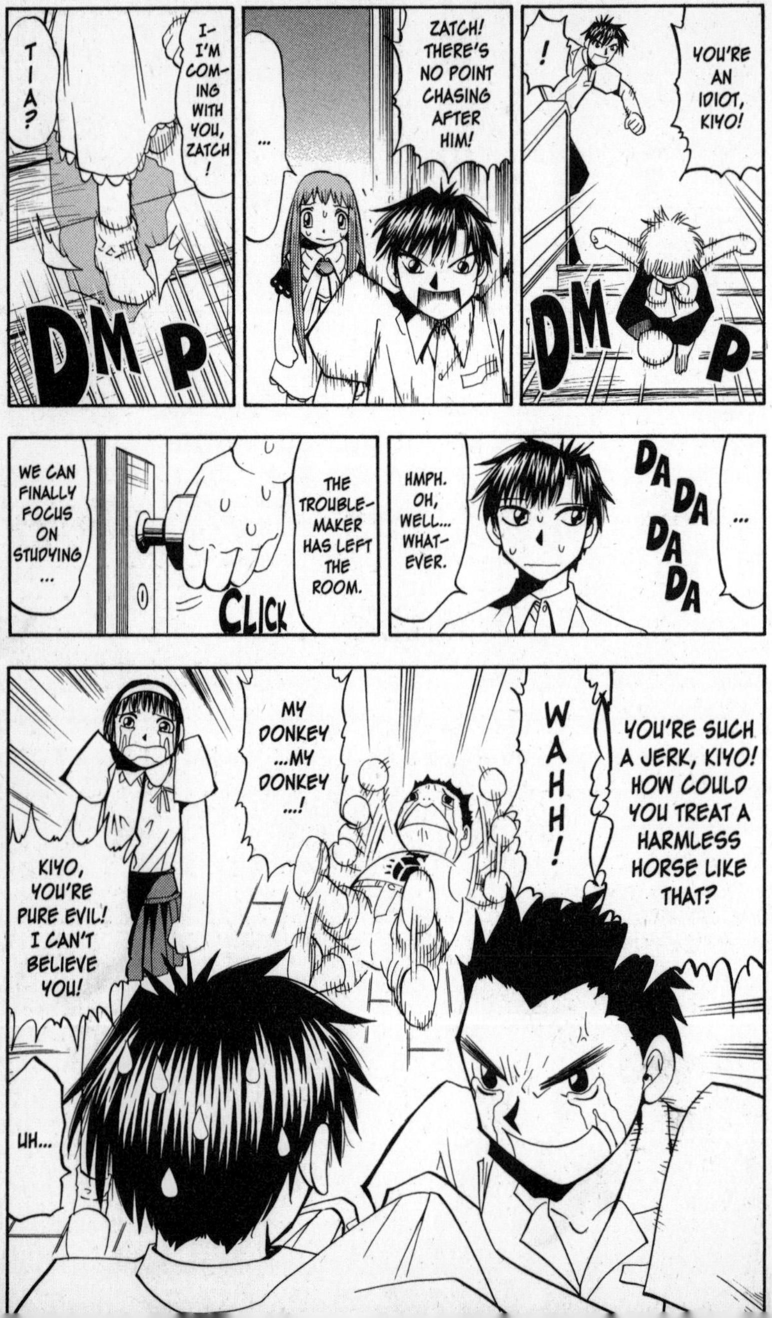
YOU'RE AN IDIOT, KIYO!
!
DMP
ZATCH! THERE'S NO POINT CHASING AFTER HIM!
...
TIA?
I- I'M COMING WITH YOU, ZATCH!
DMP
...
DA DA DA DA DA DA
HMPH. OH, WELL... WHATEVER.
THE TROUBLE-MAKER HAS LEFT THE ROOM.
CLICK
WE CAN FINALLY FOCUS ON STUDYING...
YOU'RE SUCH A JERK, KIYO! HOW COULD YOU TREAT A HARMLESS HORSE LIKE THAT?
WAHH!
MY DONKEY ...MY DONKEY ...!
KIYO, YOU'RE PURE EVIL! I CAN'T BELIEVE YOU!
UH...

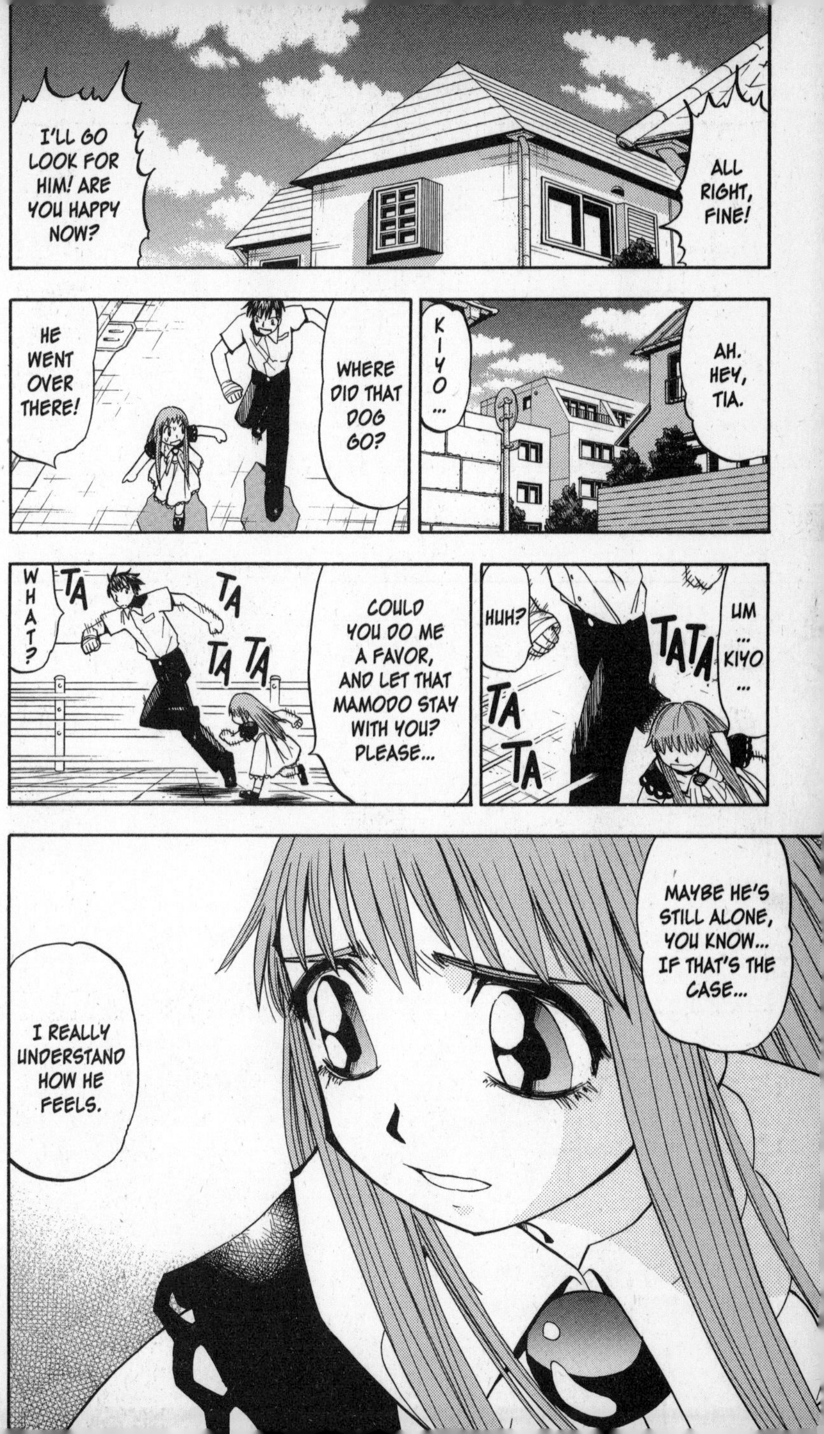
ALL RIGHT, FINE!
I'LL GO LOOK FOR HIM! ARE YOU HAPPY NOW?
AH. HEY, TIA.
KIYO ...
WHERE DID THAT DOG GO?
HE WENT OVER THERE!
UM ... KIYO ...
TATA
HUH?
TA TA
COULD YOU DO ME A FAVOR, AND LET THAT MAMODO STAY WITH YOU? PLEASE...
TA TA TA TA
WHAT?
MAYBE HE'S STILL ALONE, YOU KNOW... IF THAT'S THE CASE...
I REALLY UNDERSTAND HOW HE FEELS.

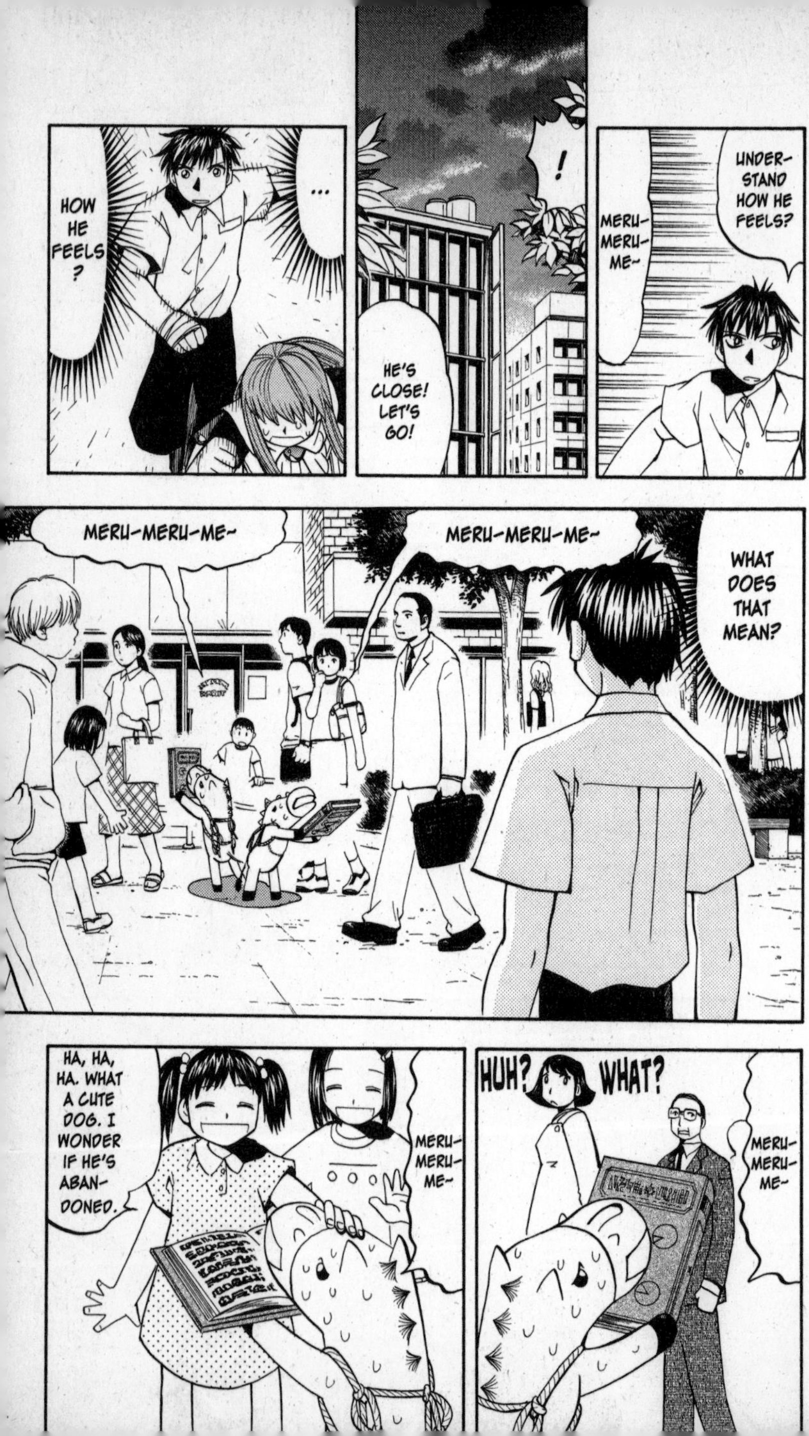
UNDER-STAND HOW HE FEELS?
MERU-MERU-ME~
!
HE'S CLOSE! LET'S GO!
...
HOW HE FEELS?
WHAT DOES THAT MEAN?
MERU-MERU-ME~
MERU-MERU-ME~
MERU-MERU-ME~
WHAT?
HUH?
MERU-MERU-ME~
HA, HA, HA. WHAT A CUTE DOG. I WONDER IF HE'S ABAN-DONED.

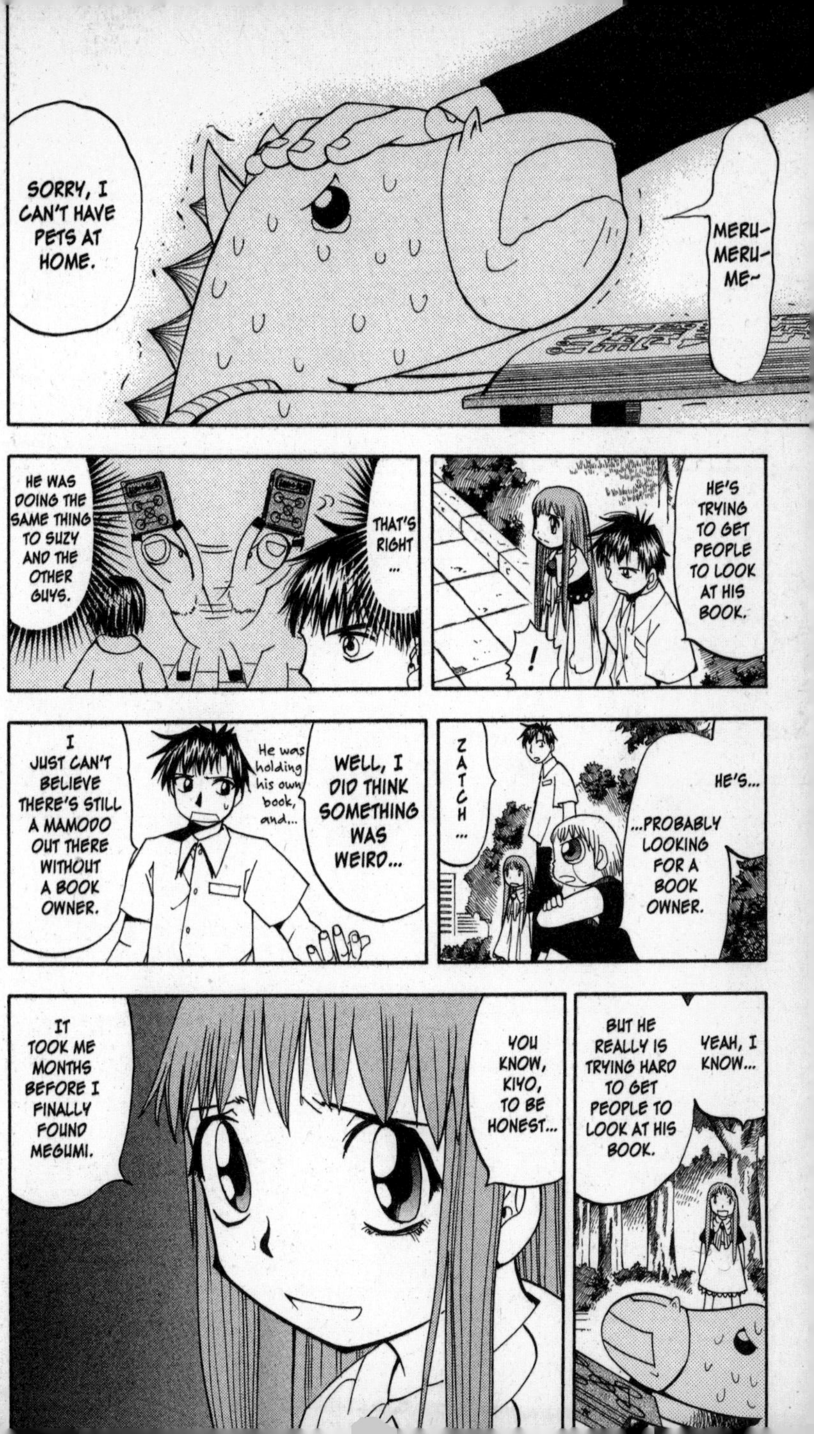
MERU-MERU-ME~
SORRY, I CAN'T HAVE PETS AT HOME.
HE'S TRYING TO GET PEOPLE TO LOOK AT HIS BOOK.
!
THAT'S RIGHT...
HE WAS DOING THE SAME THING TO SUZY AND THE OTHER GUYS.
HE'S...
...PROBABLY LOOKING FOR A BOOK OWNER.
ZATCH...
WELL, I DID THINK SOMETHING WAS WEIRD...
He was holding his own book, and...
I JUST CAN'T BELIEVE THERE'S STILL A MAMODO OUT THERE WITHOUT A BOOK OWNER.
YEAH, I KNOW...
BUT HE REALLY IS TRYING HARD TO GET PEOPLE TO LOOK AT HIS BOOK.
YOU KNOW, KIYO, TO BE HONEST...
IT TOOK ME MONTHS BEFORE I FINALLY FOUND MEGUMI.

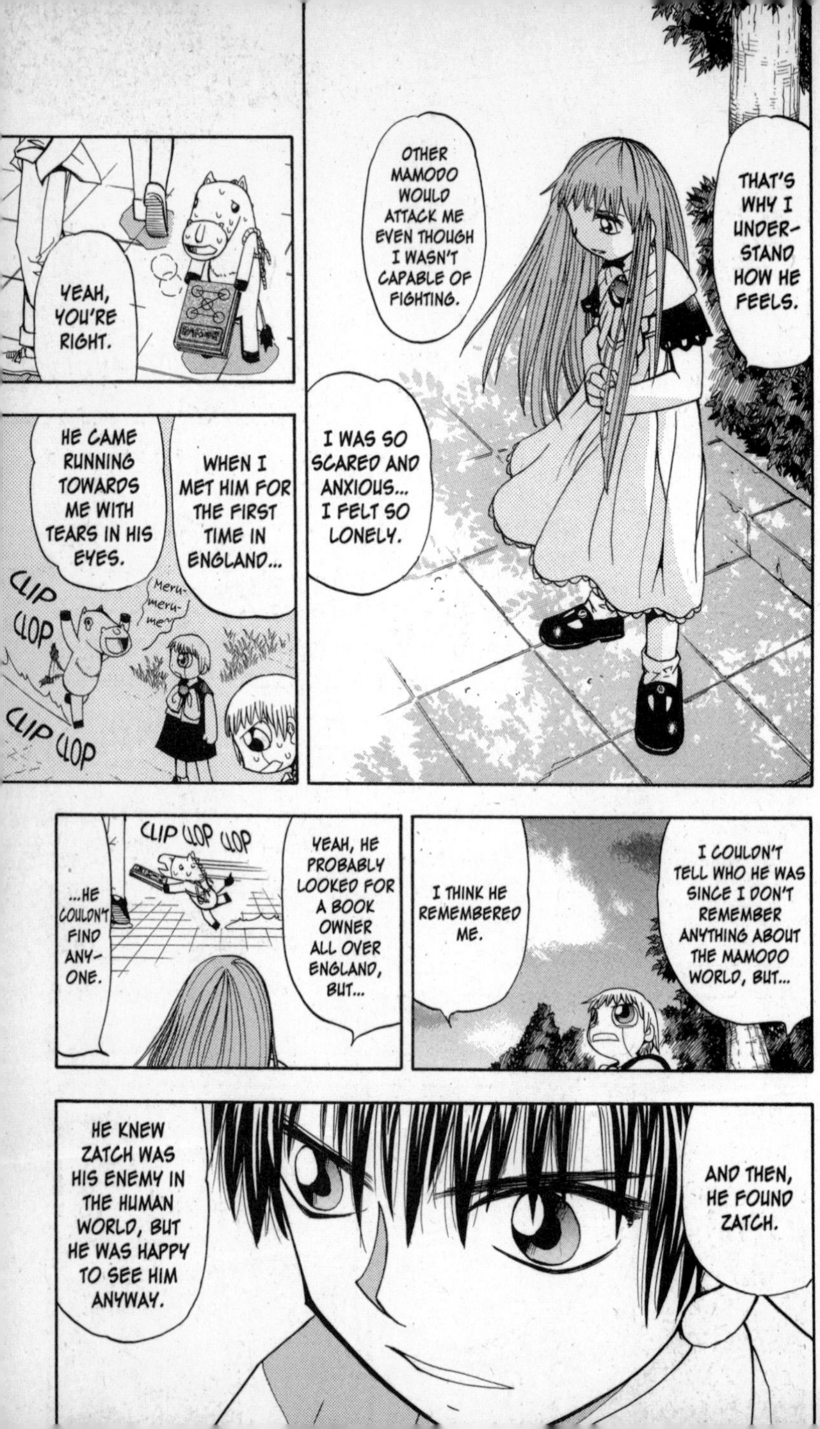
THAT'S WHY I UNDERSTAND HOW HE FEELS.
OTHER MAMODO WOULD ATTACK ME EVEN THOUGH I WASN'T CAPABLE OF FIGHTING.
I WAS SO SCARED AND ANXIOUS... I FELT SO LONELY.
YEAH, YOU'RE RIGHT.
WHEN I MET HIM FOR THE FIRST TIME IN ENGLAND...
HE CAME RUNNING TOWARDS ME WITH TEARS IN HIS EYES.
Meru-meru-me~
CLIP CLOP
CLIP CLOP
I COULDN'T TELL WHO HE WAS SINCE I DON'T REMEMBER ANYTHING ABOUT THE MAMODO WORLD, BUT...
I THINK HE REMEMBERED ME.
YEAH, HE PROBABLY LOOKED FOR A BOOK OWNER ALL OVER ENGLAND, BUT...
CLIP CLOP CLOP
...HE COULDN'T FIND ANYONE.
AND THEN, HE FOUND ZATCH.
HE KNEW ZATCH WAS HIS ENEMY IN THE HUMAN WORLD, BUT HE WAS HAPPY TO SEE HIM ANYWAY.

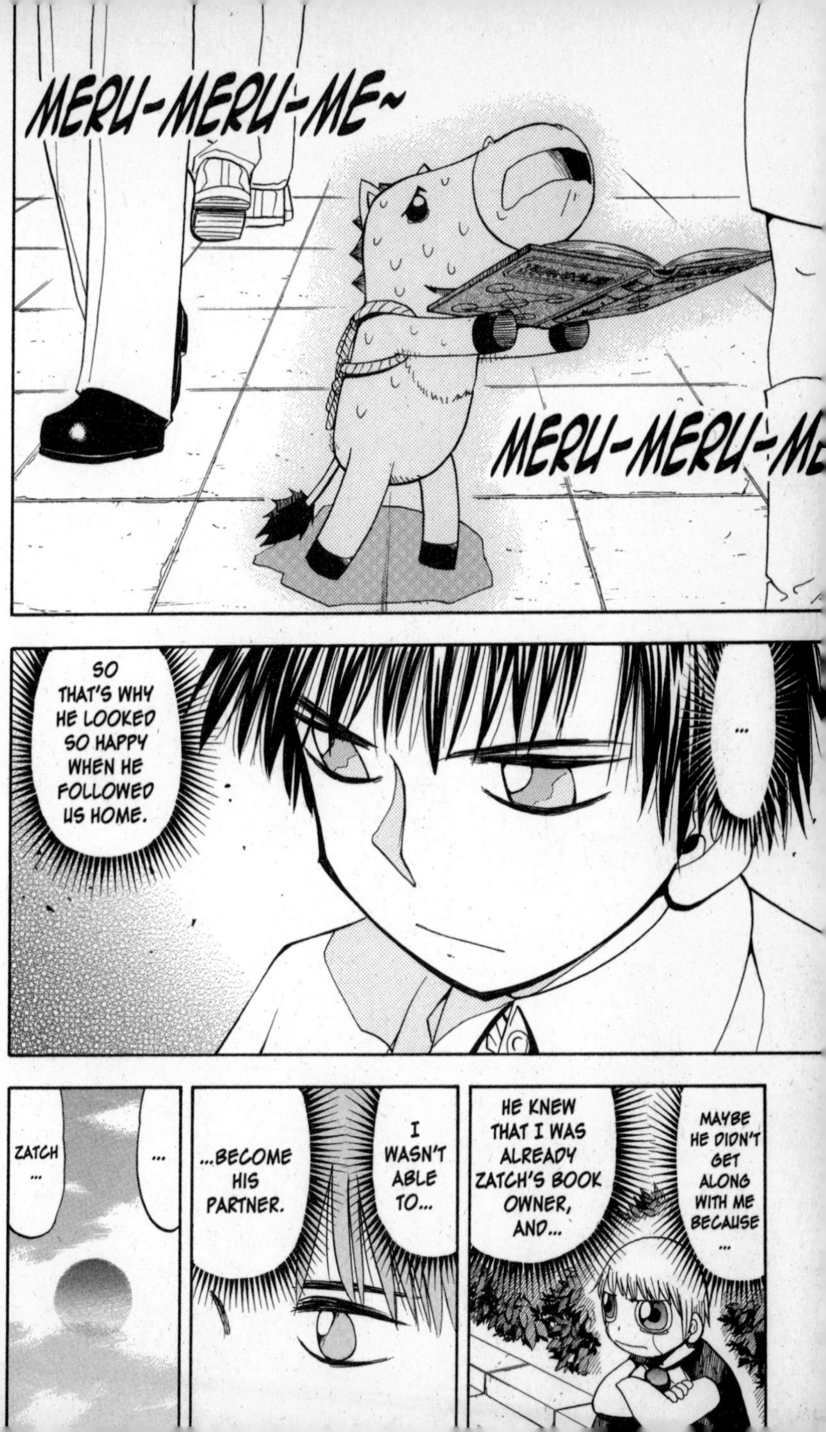
MERU-MERU-ME
MERU-MERU-ME~
...
SO THAT'S WHY HE LOOKED SO HAPPY WHEN HE FOLLOWED US HOME.
MAYBE HE DIDN'T GET ALONG WITH ME BECAUSE ...
HE KNEW THAT I WAS ALREADY ZATCH'S BOOK OWNER, AND...
I WASN'T ABLE TO...
...BECOME HIS PARTNER.
...
ZATCH ...

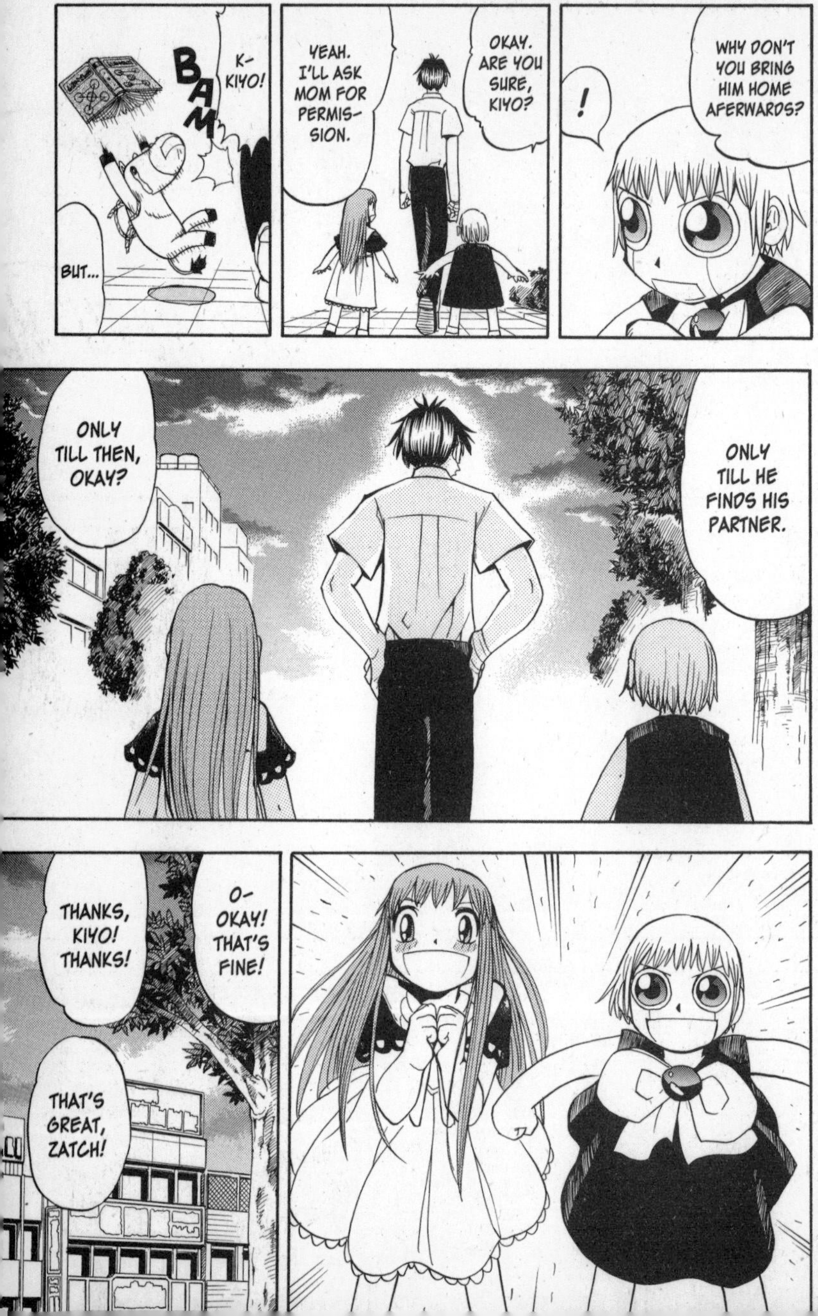
WHY DON'T YOU BRING HIM HOME AFERWARDS?
!
OKAY. ARE YOU SURE, KIYO?
YEAH. I'LL ASK MOM FOR PERMIS-SION.
K-KIYO!
BAM
BUT...
ONLY TILL HE FINDS HIS PARTNER.
ONLY TILL THEN, OKAY?
O-OKAY! THAT'S FINE!
THANKS, KIYO! THANKS!
THAT'S GREAT, ZATCH!

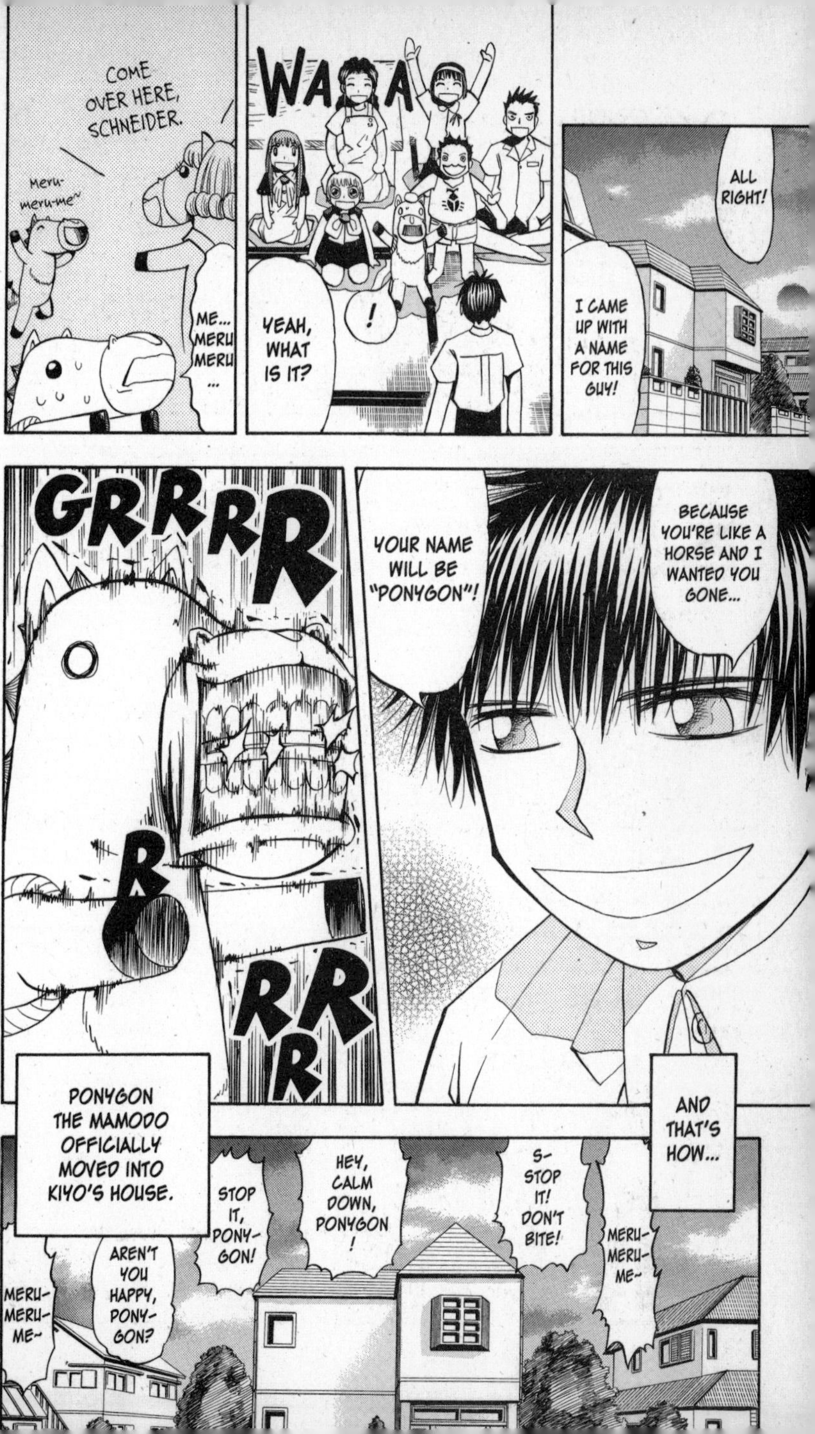
ALL RIGHT!
I CAME UP WITH A NAME FOR THIS GUY!
WAAA
!
YEAH, WHAT IS IT?
COME OVER HERE, SCHNEIDER.
Meru-meru-me~
ME... MERU MERU ...
BECAUSE YOU'RE LIKE A HORSE AND I WANTED YOU GONE...
YOUR NAME WILL BE "PONYGON"!
GRRRR
R
RRR
AND THAT'S HOW...
PONYGON THE MAMODO OFFICIALLY MOVED INTO KIYO'S HOUSE.
MERU-MERU-ME~
S-STOP IT! DON'T BITE!
HEY, CALM DOWN, PONYGON!
STOP IT, PONY-GON!
AREN'T YOU HAPPY, PONY-GON?
MERU-MERU-ME~

TO BE CONTINUED!!

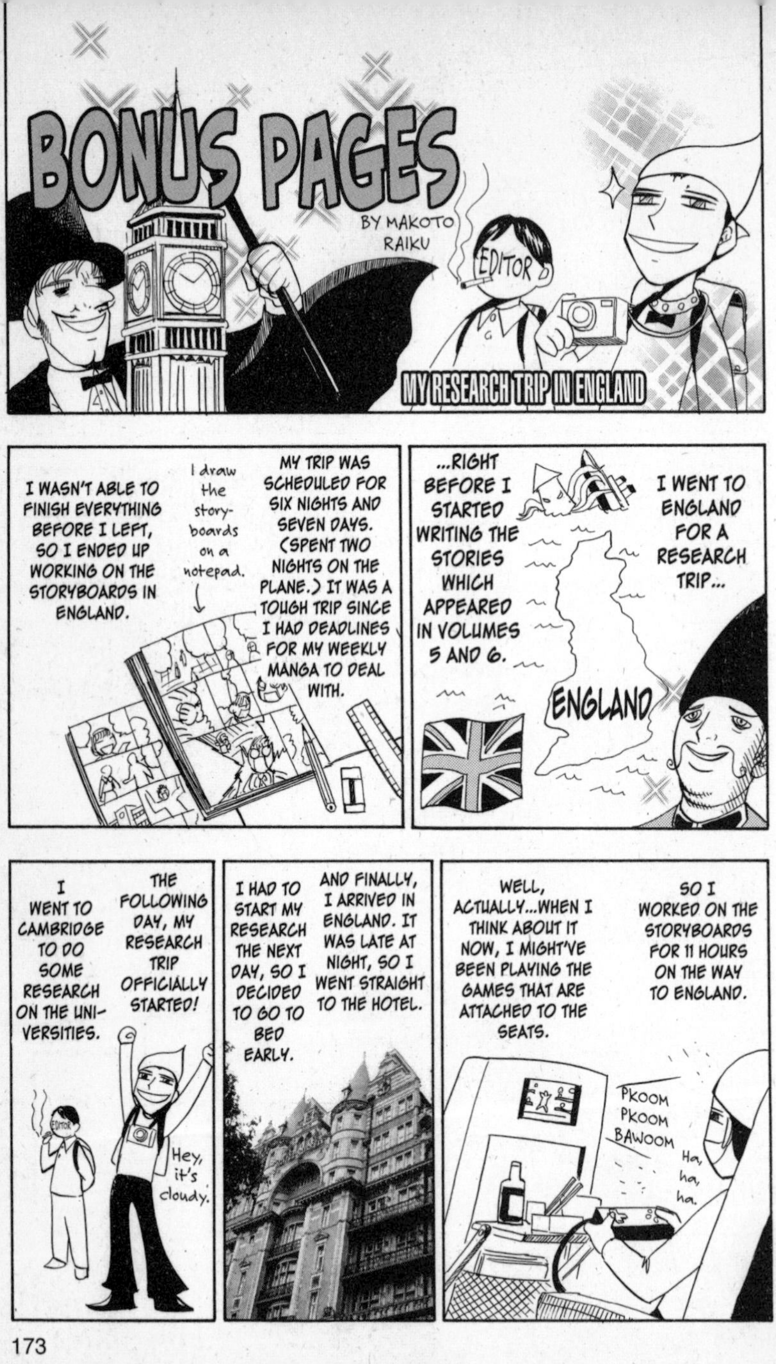
BONUS PAGES
BY MAKOTO RAIKU
EDITOR
MY RESEARCH TRIP IN ENGLAND
I WENT TO ENGLAND FOR A RESEARCH TRIP...
...RIGHT BEFORE I STARTED WRITING THE STORIES WHICH APPEARED IN VOLUMES 5 AND 6.
ENGLAND
MY TRIP WAS SCHEDULED FOR SIX NIGHTS AND SEVEN DAYS. (SPENT TWO NIGHTS ON THE PLANE.) IT WAS A TOUGH TRIP SINCE I HAD DEADLINES FOR MY WEEKLY MANGA TO DEAL WITH.
I draw the story-boards on a notepad.
I WASN'T ABLE TO FINISH EVERYTHING BEFORE I LEFT, SO I ENDED UP WORKING ON THE STORYBOARDS IN ENGLAND.
SO I WORKED ON THE STORYBOARDS FOR 11 HOURS ON THE WAY TO ENGLAND.
WELL, ACTUALLY...WHEN I THINK ABOUT IT NOW, I MIGHT'VE BEEN PLAYING THE GAMES THAT ARE ATTACHED TO THE SEATS.
PKOOM PKOOM BAWOOM
Ha, ha, ha.
AND FINALLY, I ARRIVED IN ENGLAND. IT WAS LATE AT NIGHT, SO I WENT STRAIGHT TO THE HOTEL.
I HAD TO START MY RESEARCH THE NEXT DAY, SO I DECIDED TO GO TO BED EARLY.
THE FOLLOWING DAY, MY RESEARCH TRIP OFFICIALLY STARTED!
I WENT TO CAMBRIDGE TO DO SOME RESEARCH ON THE UNI-VERSITIES.
EDITOR
Hey, it's cloudy.

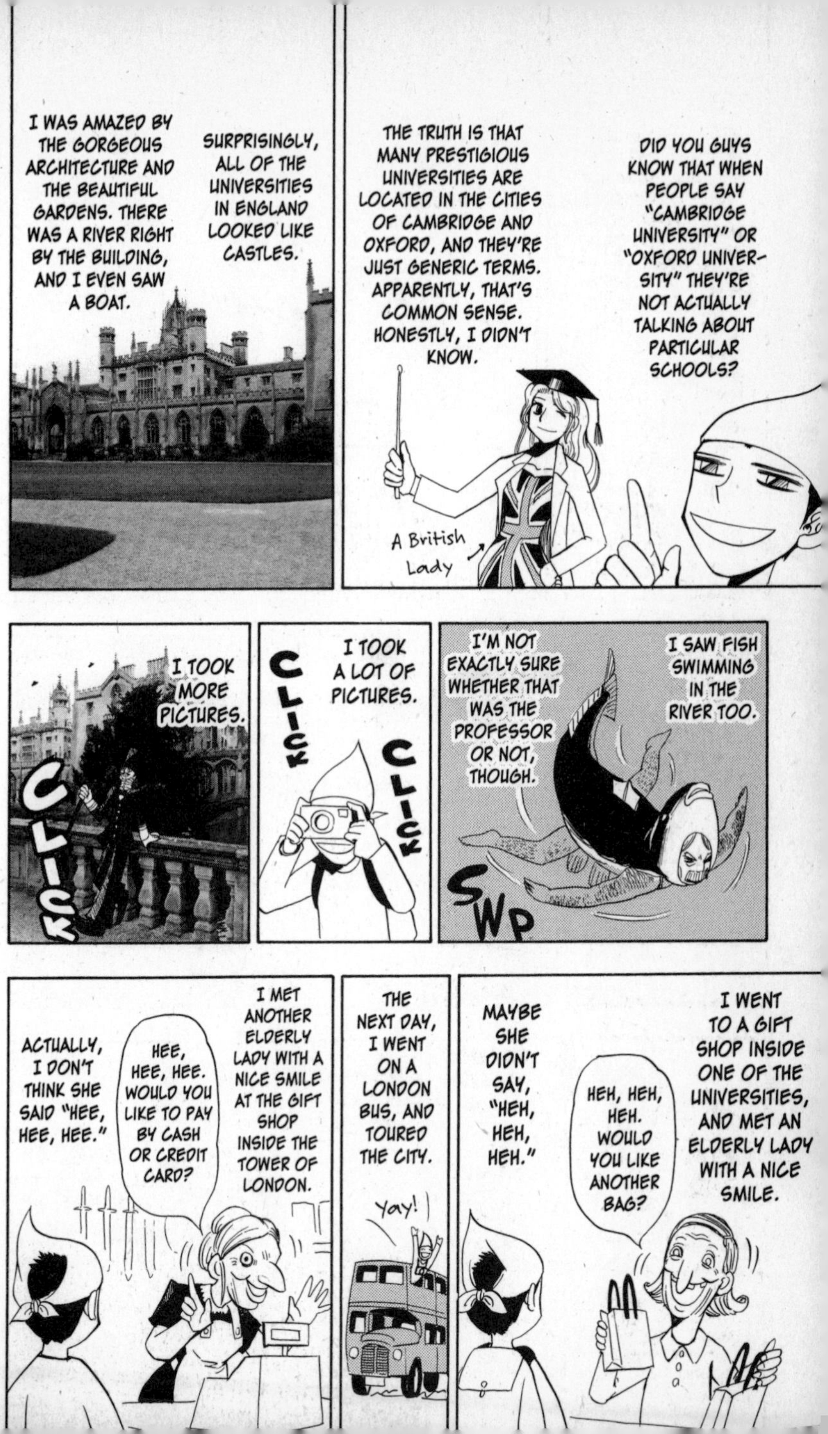
DID YOU GUYS KNOW THAT WHEN PEOPLE SAY "CAMBRIDGE UNIVERSITY" OR "OXFORD UNIVERSITY" THEY'RE NOT ACTUALLY TALKING ABOUT PARTICULAR SCHOOLS?
THE TRUTH IS THAT MANY PRESTIGIOUS UNIVERSITIES ARE LOCATED IN THE CITIES OF CAMBRIDGE AND OXFORD, AND THEY'RE JUST GENERIC TERMS. APPARENTLY, THAT'S COMMON SENSE. HONESTLY, I DIDN'T KNOW.
A British Lady
SURPRISINGLY, ALL OF THE UNIVERSITIES IN ENGLAND LOOKED LIKE CASTLES.
I WAS AMAZED BY THE GORGEOUS ARCHITECTURE AND THE BEAUTIFUL GARDENS. THERE WAS A RIVER RIGHT BY THE BUILDING, AND I EVEN SAW A BOAT.
I SAW FISH SWIMMING IN THE RIVER TOO.
I'M NOT EXACTLY SURE WHETHER THAT WAS THE PROFESSOR OR NOT, THOUGH.
SWP
I TOOK A LOT OF PICTURES.
CLICK
CLICK
I TOOK MORE PICTURES.
CLICK
I WENT TO A GIFT SHOP INSIDE ONE OF THE UNIVERSITIES, AND MET AN ELDERLY LADY WITH A NICE SMILE.
HEH, HEH, HEH. WOULD YOU LIKE ANOTHER BAG?
MAYBE SHE DIDN'T SAY, "HEH, HEH, HEH."
THE NEXT DAY, I WENT ON A LONDON BUS, AND TOURED THE CITY.
Yay!
I MET ANOTHER ELDERLY LADY WITH A NICE SMILE AT THE GIFT SHOP INSIDE THE TOWER OF LONDON.
HEE, HEE, HEE. WOULD YOU LIKE TO PAY BY CASH OR CREDIT CARD?
ACTUALLY, I DON'T THINK SHE SAID "HEE, HEE, HEE."

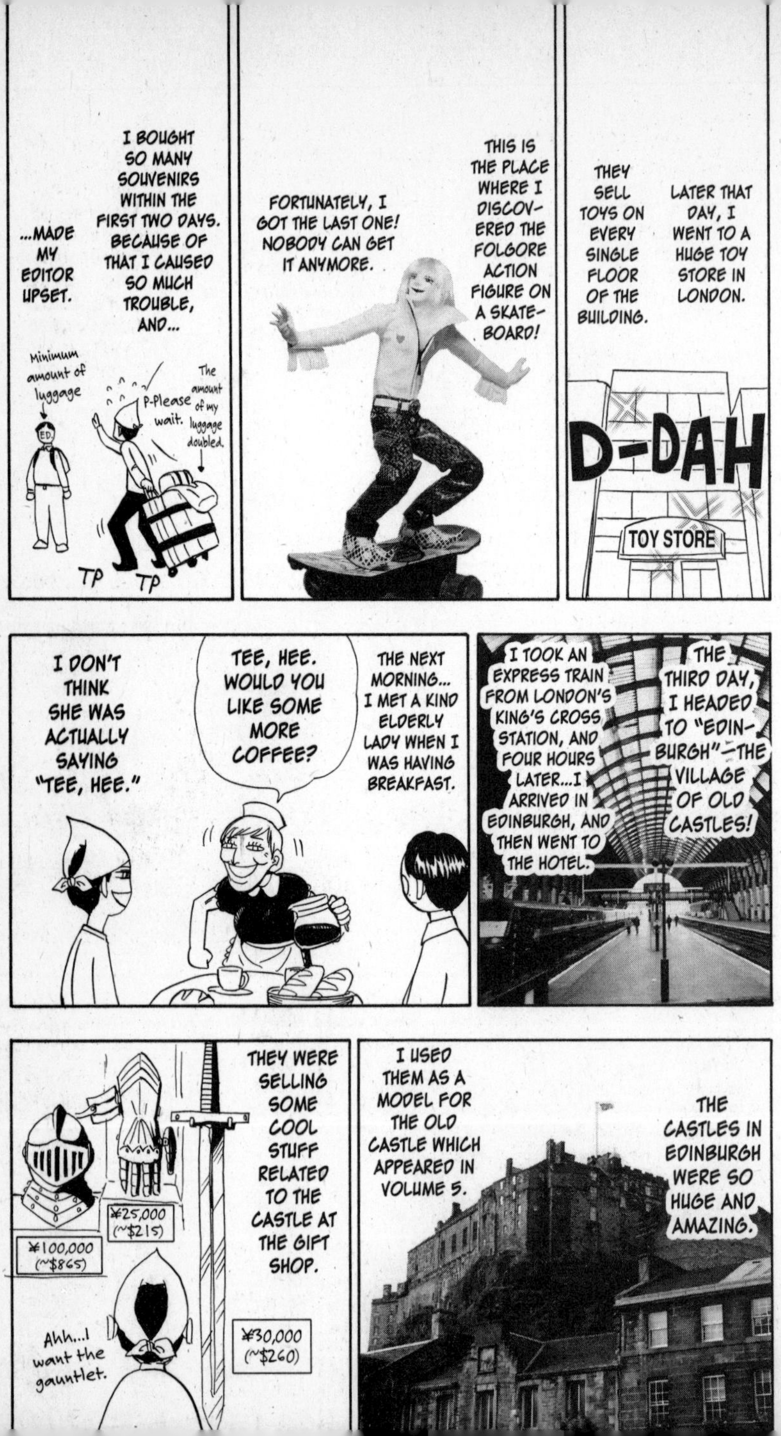
LATER THAT DAY, I WENT TO A HUGE TOY STORE IN LONDON.
THEY SELL TOYS ON EVERY SINGLE FLOOR OF THE BUILDING.
D-DAH
TOY STORE
THIS IS THE PLACE WHERE I DISCOVERED THE FOLGORE ACTION FIGURE ON A SKATEBOARD!
FORTUNATELY, I GOT THE LAST ONE! NOBODY CAN GET IT ANYMORE.
I BOUGHT SO MANY SOUVENIRS WITHIN THE FIRST TWO DAYS. BECAUSE OF THAT I CAUSED SO MUCH TROUBLE, AND...
...MADE MY EDITOR UPSET.
Minimum amount of luggage
ED.
P-Please wait.
The amount of my luggage doubled.
TP TP
THE THIRD DAY, I HEADED TO "EDINBURGH"—THE VILLAGE OF OLD CASTLES!
I TOOK AN EXPRESS TRAIN FROM LONDON'S KING'S CROSS STATION, AND FOUR HOURS LATER...I ARRIVED IN EDINBURGH, AND THEN WENT TO THE HOTEL.
THE NEXT MORNING... I MET A KIND ELDERLY LADY WHEN I WAS HAVING BREAKFAST.
TEE, HEE. WOULD YOU LIKE SOME MORE COFFEE?
I DON'T THINK SHE WAS ACTUALLY SAYING "TEE, HEE."
THE CASTLES IN EDINBURGH WERE SO HUGE AND AMAZING.
I USED THEM AS A MODEL FOR THE OLD CASTLE WHICH APPEARED IN VOLUME 5.
THEY WERE SELLING SOME COOL STUFF RELATED TO THE CASTLE AT THE GIFT SHOP.
¥25,000 (~$215)
¥100,000 (~$865)
¥30,000 (~$260)
Ahh...I want the gauntlet.

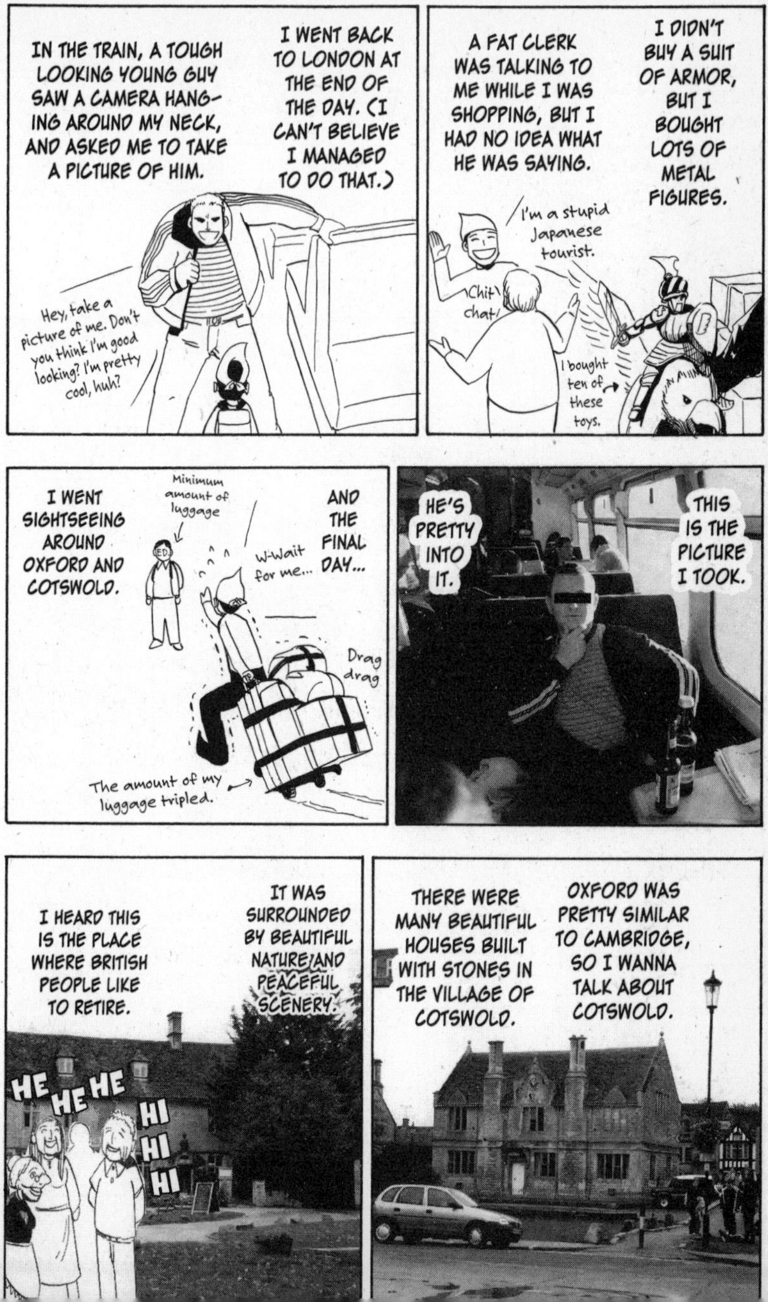
I DIDN'T BUY A SUIT OF ARMOR, BUT I BOUGHT LOTS OF METAL FIGURES.
A FAT CLERK WAS TALKING TO ME WHILE I WAS SHOPPING, BUT I HAD NO IDEA WHAT HE WAS SAYING.
I'm a stupid Japanese tourist.
Chit chat
I bought ten of these toys.
I WENT BACK TO LONDON AT THE END OF THE DAY. (I CAN'T BELIEVE I MANAGED TO DO THAT.)
IN THE TRAIN, A TOUGH LOOKING YOUNG GUY SAW A CAMERA HANGING AROUND MY NECK, AND ASKED ME TO TAKE A PICTURE OF HIM.
Hey, take a picture of me. Don't you think I'm good looking? I'm pretty cool, huh?
THIS IS THE PICTURE I TOOK.
HE'S PRETTY INTO IT.
AND THE FINAL DAY...
I WENT SIGHTSEEING AROUND OXFORD AND COTSWOLD.
Minimum amount of luggage
W-Wait for me...
Drag drag
The amount of my luggage tripled.
OXFORD WAS PRETTY SIMILAR TO CAMBRIDGE, SO I WANNA TALK ABOUT COTSWOLD.
THERE WERE MANY BEAUTIFUL HOUSES BUILT WITH STONES IN THE VILLAGE OF COTSWOLD.
IT WAS SURROUNDED BY BEAUTIFUL NATURE AND PEACEFUL SCENERY.
I HEARD THIS IS THE PLACE WHERE BRITISH PEOPLE LIKE TO RETIRE.
HE HE HE
HI HI HI

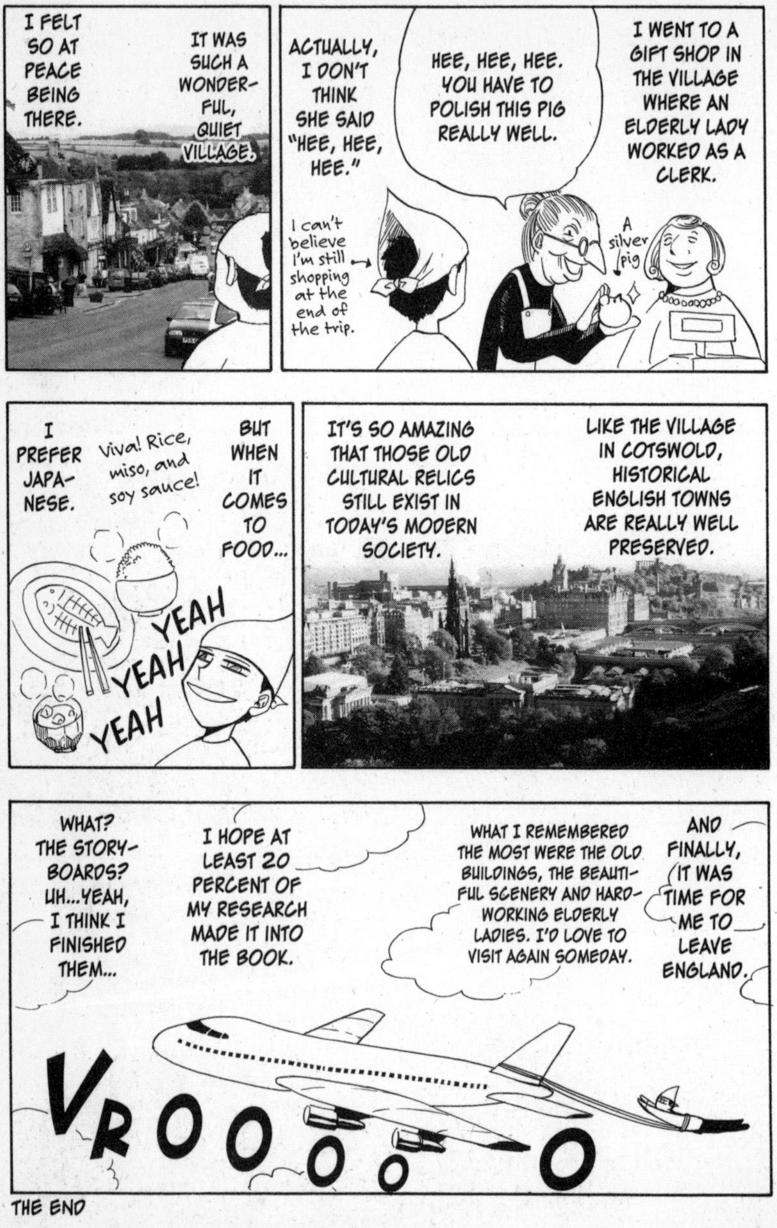
I WENT TO A GIFT SHOP IN THE VILLAGE WHERE AN ELDERLY LADY WORKED AS A CLERK.
HEE, HEE, HEE. YOU HAVE TO POLISH THIS PIG REALLY WELL.
A silver pig
ACTUALLY, I DON'T THINK SHE SAID "HEE, HEE, HEE."
I can't believe I'm still shopping at the end of the trip.
IT WAS SUCH A WONDERFUL, QUIET VILLAGE.
I FELT SO AT PEACE BEING THERE.
LIKE THE VILLAGE IN COTSWOLD, HISTORICAL ENGLISH TOWNS ARE REALLY WELL PRESERVED.
IT'S SO AMAZING THAT THOSE OLD CULTURAL RELICS STILL EXIST IN TODAY'S MODERN SOCIETY.
BUT WHEN IT COMES TO FOOD...
I PREFER JAPANESE.
Viva! Rice, miso, and soy sauce!
YEAH
YEAH
YEAH
AND FINALLY, IT WAS TIME FOR ME TO LEAVE ENGLAND.
WHAT I REMEMBERED THE MOST WERE THE OLD BUILDINGS, THE BEAUTIFUL SCENERY AND HARD-WORKING ELDERLY LADIES. I'D LOVE TO VISIT AGAIN SOMEDAY.
I HOPE AT LEAST 20 PERCENT OF MY RESEARCH MADE IT INTO THE BOOK.
WHAT? THE STORYBOARDS? UH...YEAH, I THINK I FINISHED THEM...
VROOOOO

THE END

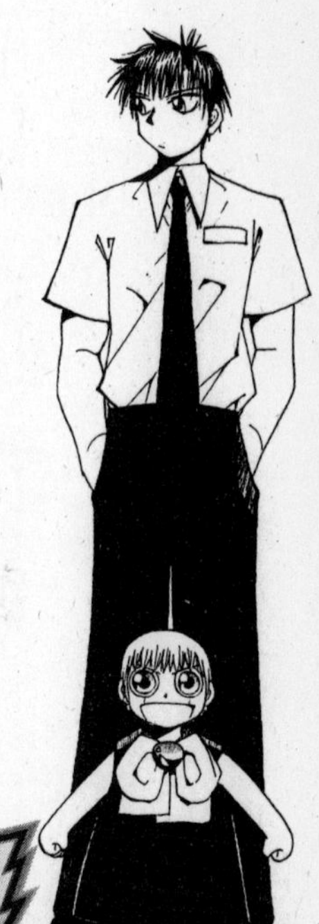

ZATCH BELL!

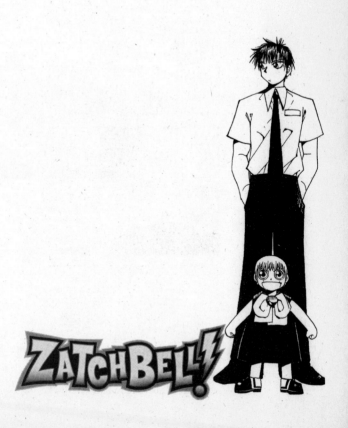

ZATCH & SUZY

BY MAKOTO RAIKU

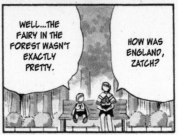

HOW WAS ENGLAND, ZATCH?
WELL...THE FAIRY IN THE FOREST WASN'T EXACTLY PRETTY.
REALLY? WELL, HOW WERE THE GENTLEMEN IN ENGLAND?
YOU KNOW, THOSE COOL ONES THAT ARE DRESSED IN BLACK SUITS AND A HAT WITH A CANE!
B-BMP
B-BMP
I THINK YOU'VE GOT THE TOTALLY WRONG IDEA ABOUT ENGLAND, SUZY...
WHAT?

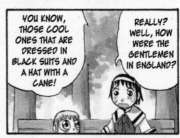

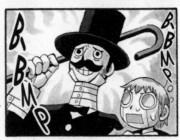

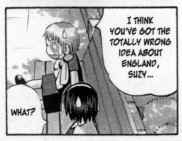

MAKOTO RAIKU

I bought this at a toy store in England.

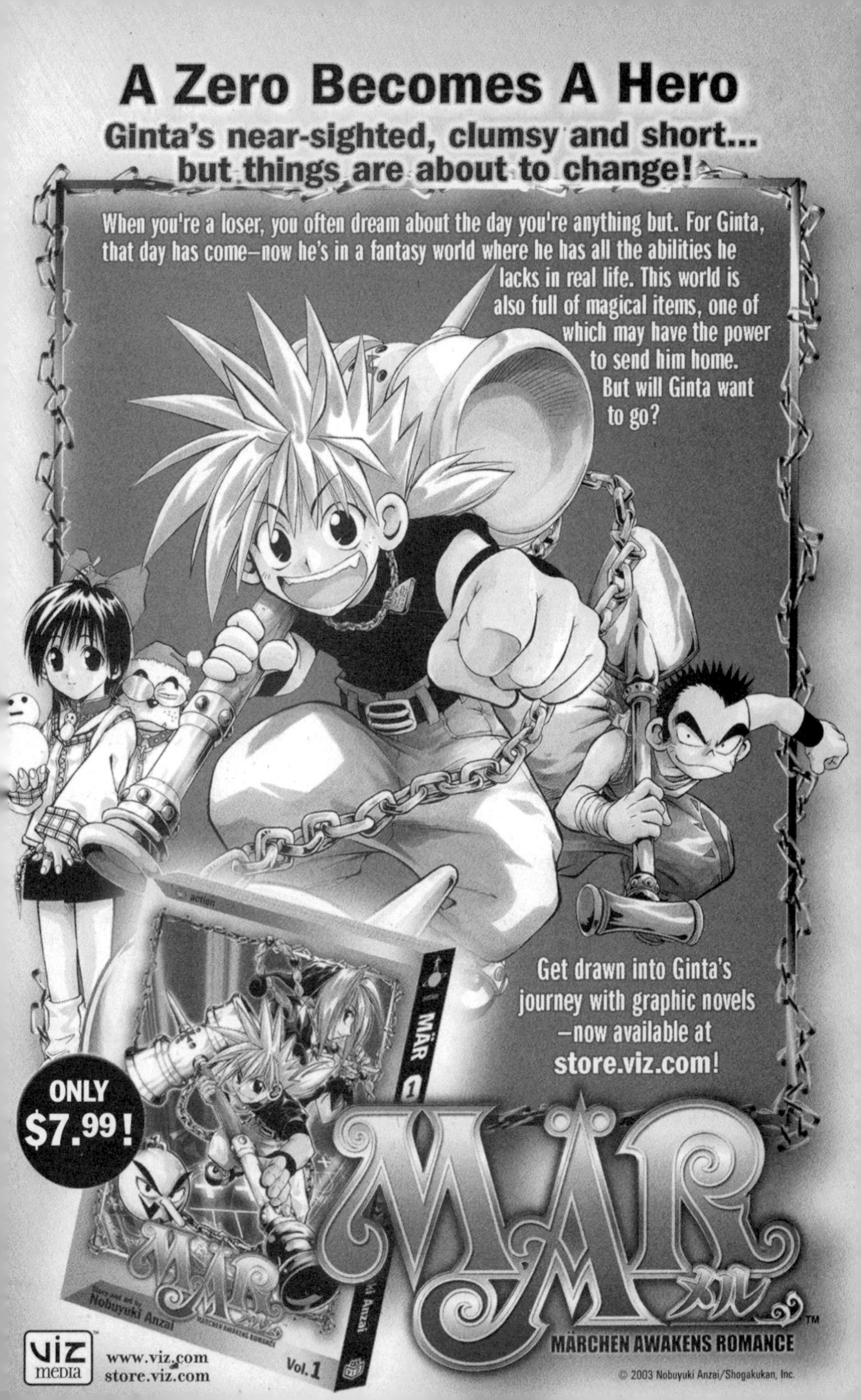

A Zero Becomes A Hero
Ginta's near-sighted, clumsy and short... but things are about to change!
When you're a loser, you often dream about the day you're anything but. For Ginta, that day has come—now he's in a fantasy world where he has all the abilities he lacks in real life. This world is also full of magical items, one of which may have the power to send him home. But will Ginta want to go?
Get drawn into Ginta's journey with graphic novels —now available at store.viz.com!
ONLY $7.99!
MÄR
MÄRCHEN AWAKENS ROMANCE
Story and art by Nobuyuki Anzai
Vol. 1
viz media
www.viz.com
store.viz.com
© 2003 Nobuyuki Anzai/Shogakukan, Inc.

LOVE MANGA?   LET US KNOW!

☐ Please do NOT send me information about VIZ Media products, news and events, special offers, or other information.

☐ Please do NOT send me information from VIZ Media's trusted business partners.

Name: _____

Address: _____

City: _____ **State:** _____ **Zip:** _____

E-mail: _____

☐ **Male** ☐ **Female** **Date of Birth** (mm/dd/yyyy): ___ / ___ / ___ (Under 13? Parental consent required)

What race/ethnicity do you consider yourself? (check all that apply)

☐ White/Caucasian ☐ Black/African American ☐ Hispanic/Latino

☐ Asian/Pacific Islander ☐ Native American/Alaskan Native ☐ Other: _____

What VIZ Media title(s) did you purchase? (indicate title(s) purchased) _____

_____

What other VIZ Media titles do you own? _____

_____

Reason for purchase: (check all that apply)

☐ Special offer ☐ Favorite title / author / artist / genre

☐ Gift ☐ Recommendation ☐ Collection

☐ Read excerpt in VIZ Media manga sampler ☐ Other _____

Where did you make your purchase? (please check one)

☐ Comic store ☐ Bookstore ☐ Grocery Store

☐ Convention ☐ Newsstand ☐ Video Game Store

☐ Online (site: _____) ☐ Other _____

How many manga titles have you p … titles?
(please check one from each column)

MANGA

- [ ] None
- [ ] 1 – 4
- [ ] 5 – 10
- [ ] 11+

- [ ] 1 – 4
- [ ] 5 – 10
- [ ] 11+

How much influence do special promotions and gifts-with-purchase have on the titles you buy?
(please circle, with 5 being great influence and 1 being none)

1 2 3 4 5

Do you purchase every volume of your favorite series?

- [ ] Yes! Gotta have 'em as my own
- [ ] No. Please explain: ______________________

What kind of manga storylines do you most enjoy? (check all that apply)

- [ ] Action / Adventure
- [ ] Comedy
- [ ] Fighting
- [ ] Artistic / Alternative
- [ ] Science Fiction
- [ ] Romance (shojo)
- [ ] Sports
- [ ] Other ______________________
- [ ] Horror
- [ ] Fantasy (shojo)
- [ ] Historical

If you watch the anime or play a video or TCG game from a series, how likely are you to buy the manga? (please circle, with 5 being very likely and 1 being unlikely)

1 2 3 4 5

If unlikely, please explain: ______________________

Who are your favorite authors / artists? ______________________

____

What titles would like you translated and sold in English? ______________________

____

THANK YOU! Please send the completed form to:

NJW Research
42 Catharine Street
Poughkeepsie, NY 12601

Your privacy is very important to us. All information provided will be used for internal purposes only and will not be sold or otherwise divulged.